Time for Reparations

PENNSYLVANIA STUDIES IN HUMAN RIGHTS

Bert B. Lockwood, Series Editor

A complete list of books in the series
is available from the publisher.

Time for Reparations

A Global Perspective

Edited by

Jacqueline Bhabha, Margareta Matache, and Caroline Elkins

PENN

UNIVERSITY OF PENNSYLVANIA PRESS

PHILADELPHIA

Published by
University of Pennsylvania Press
Philadelphia, Pennsylvania 19104-4112
www.upenn.edu/pennpress

Printed in the United States of America on acid-free paper
10 9 8 7 6 5 4 3 2 1

A catalogue record for this book is available from the
Library of Congress.

ISBN 978-0-8122-5330-6

To those enslaved, colonized, and exterminated,
our ancestors and others,
who never lived to see justice done

CONTENTS

Albie Sachs

It's not only the pain, it's the injustice of the pain. And it's not only the injustice of the pain, it's the fact that it continues to this day; transmitted from generation to generation. The continuity of inhuman pain is the binding theme of this poignant and powerful book. To what extent should states today be held liable for varied forms of extreme hardship and injustice imposed by their predecessors on diverse communities? The remedies for these harms, which are most often systematized through racism and patriarchy, range from reparations for colonization (Indonesia, Jamaica), for slavery (Romani people, Black Americans), for famine, genocide, and other crimes. Sadly, these claims span centuries and include all the continents of the world.

In contemporary terms, we associate reparations with the claims of surviving victims or their descendants seeking amends. As a result of West Germany accepting state responsibility and paying compensation to individual Jews who had survived the Holocaust, we have come to associate reparations with the seeking of amends by *victims* of inhuman treatment.

Yet historically, the term "reparations" was used to legitimize material plunder by *victorious* nations of countries they had defeated in war. Reparations were seen in physical, material terms—amends paid by *defeated* states to their victors. International law used the theory of reparations to justify victorious nations seizing and transporting everything from horses and cattle to whole factories to make up for the damage caused to themselves in the course of the war. In addition, the losers would be compelled to pay off financial installments to their conquerors.

The seizure of the spoils of war by the victors is one thing. Demanding recompense on behalf of subjugated and violated communities and sections of society who have been rendered powerless is quite another. Their continuing pain is derived precisely from the fact that they remain relatively powerless. They are not themselves in the position of authority that would enable them to enforce their will. Nor do they control the international institutions of the world that would facilitate the enforcement on their behalf of their compelling moral claims.

This collection of thoughtful, carefully researched, evidence-based as well as personal narratives constitutes a significant step toward correcting this imbalance of power. We cannot rewind history. But we can recast the historical narrative. We can give strong and authentic voice to the claims of the powerless. Therein lies this book's strength and therein lies its dilemma. Seizure of the spoils of war was legitimized both by conquest and by the victors controlling the rules of international law made by the power elites of the world. The dilemma of the claims of the subjugated is how to convert overwhelmingly powerful moral claims into instruments of meaningful repair in systems of international and national law still dominated by the powerful.

If this book does nothing more than shake up the consciousness and consciences of all those who claim to respect human dignity, it will have served a great purpose. It marks a step in the process of re-imagining and developing the law as an instrument to truly promote emancipation and affirm human dignity.

In the course of this process of humanizing international law, it would, in my view, be important not to limit the theme of reparations to seeking monetary compensation. My own personal experience has been relevant in this regard. When I was about to return to South Africa in 1990 after twenty-four years of exile, an attorney friend of mine, looking at my shortened right arm, said: "Great, Albie–we'll sue the bastards for damages for the bomb they put in your car." I actually felt quite shocked by the suggestion that somehow a monetary payment by the state would be fitting. The idea of juridicizing and commercializing the loss of my arm was quite distressing.

Yet, in certain circumstances, court proceedings could play a vital role in righting gross wrongs. In South Africa, class actions on behalf of miners suffering from silicosis had a spectacular effect. Not only did they result in material support for people still alive and still suffering from the dire effects of inhaling silica-laden dust, they signified an acknowledgment by the mine owners of their past culpability and represented a strong warning to them, and all employers, to take appropriate measures to protect the health and safety of workers. On the other hand, in a libel case in which I sat as a justice of the Constitutional Court in South Africa, a colleague and I strongly criticized the use of money awards as the main mechanism for salvaging the dignity and honor of the traduced person. Our contention, later adopted by the court as a whole, was that apology and suitable restorative justice amends would be far more meaningful than payment of a lump sum that would still leave the parties as enemies.

Money can often be quite the wrong moral currency, the wrong register. It abstracts pain from the human heart and puts it in the marketplace. In *The Soft Vengeance of a Freedom Fighter,* the book I wrote shortly after the bomb attack on me, I said that if we got freedom, democracy, and rights for all in South Africa that would be my soft vengeance; roses and lilies would grow out of my arm. Some years later, the operative who had been responsible for placing the bomb in my car asked if he could meet with me before going to the Truth Commission. We met twice. It was complicated and emotional, but I was glad that we had to a certain degree managed to humanize what had once literally been a lethal relationship. In my view, restorative justice can be far more enduring, far more meaningful than punitive or compensatory justice, though it can contain elements both of punishment and material recompense.

The key to reparations lies in active acknowledgment of past and continuing injustice and taking appropriate corrective responsibility for it. The widely divergent histories, contexts, approaches, and reflections gathered together in this volume reverberate strongly. They provoke many questions. Readers are given rich and pungent material for tussling with the ethics and evolving modes of reparations. Finding the right register in each case is critical when it comes to shaping contemporary state, societal, or intergovernmental responses to collective historical injustices. This book is hard, it is powerful, and it is important.

INTRODUCTION

Jacqueline Bhabha

Preventing injustice is always preferable to remedying it, but prevention is only an option for the present and the future. This is why the 1948 UN Genocide Convention requires state parties to commit to both prevention and punishment.[1] And it is why those concerned with injustice, particularly injustice on a massive scale, need to be concerned with both intervention strategies. For past atrocities, prevention is obviously not a possibility: the alternatives are remediation (including punishment) or acquiescence. This choice is not value neutral. Acquiescence, even when motivated (as it has been on occasion) by the overarching goal of building a new collective peace with the past firmly left behind, can be interpreted as exoneration. Not everyone, however, shares this view. Javier Marías, the famous Spanish novelist, in writing about the *pacto del olvido*, or "pact of forgetting," that enveloped post-Franco Spain, said: "The promise of living in a normal country was far more alluring than the old quest for an apology or the desire for reparation."[2] His argument was that silence about past atrocities could be a sign of courage at a particular historical juncture because one could not be sure what "the future of the past" would turn out to be. But the moral trade-offs linked to the culture of silence have an afterlife. They transmit an inaccurate historical record, deny survivors or their heirs their due, and can vitiate present and future efforts to prevent injustice. Remediation, by contrast, whether or not effective in imposing punishment or allocating reparatory measures, stimulates public attention to past injustice and by so doing can enhance

present and future prevention efforts. At the same time, it can prolong the
sense of insecurity and apprehension tied to the past.

These simple observations highlight the urgency of the reparation agenda.
It is not only a matter of righting past wrongs for the public record—"peer[ing]
into [one's] history," as a dismissive former British minister of state recently
told his Jamaican audience—or for the posthumous respect of those injured,
important though both those objectives are.[3] It is a matter of preventing ongoing and future injustice, or at least strengthening efforts to do so. As lives
continue to be lived under the shadows of past injustice, time does not stand
still. For the legacy of unremediated past injustice endures—the wounds remain unhealed—on the bodies and in the minds and souls of survivors, their
descendants, their communities, their polities.[4]

Remediation has the capacity to reduce the impact of the legacy of harm
and suffering. "Now I can die. You know the truth," a survivor of the Darfur
mass atrocities in Sudan giving evidence about the murder and rape of his
entire nuclear family told an investigative team from the International Criminal Court.[5] The very act of having one's testimony elicited and attended to
can alleviate mental agony. And yet, the topic of reparations remains deeply
controversial, and the claims for reparation continue to be highly contested.
For both principled and pragmatic reasons, across the political spectrum opposition to reparation claims is widespread. The main principled arguments
against reparations have tended to be legal in nature. They include the un-
availability of accurate evidence because of the passage of time (or the lapse
of limitation periods), either because of the death or advanced age of perpetrators or because of the loss or destruction of documentary traces. Several
chapters in this volume refer to these arguments.[6] Principled opposition to
reparations also invokes the lack of responsibility of surviving populations
or successor governments for atrocities committed by their predecessors and
the corresponding lack of entitlement to reparation of heirs of victims, arguments that imply a lack of continuity in the legacy of past harm on the
infliction of contemporary injustice.[7] Governments that are successors to
imperial regimes bear no responsibility, it is suggested, for wealth or land dis-
tributions that predate their terms of office; individuals whose ancestors
were beneficiaries of past atrocities cannot equitably be held liable or be deprived of assets that are now protected by the rule of law. Conversely, descendants of abused populations have no sufficiently proximal connection to the
abuse to justify reparation, particularly when the issue is material compensation.[8] Yet another principled argument centers on a core tenet of natural

justice: that reparations in many cases—the Nuremberg post-Holocaust trials being the most evident exemplar—involve the abuse of victors' justice to create new criminal liability and impose retroactive culpability on vanquished populations unable to effectively resist these measures. Injustice at the service of justice, it is argued, is not justice.[9]

These arguments are complemented by, and often merge with, pragmatic considerations. Thus, as several chapters in this volume show, protection of the status quo is a major reason for the opposition to reparations advanced by self-serving beneficiaries with entrenched vested interests. A clear case in point is the failure—whether deliberate or negligent—to make publicly available documentary evidence pertinent to proof of past harm. Colonial archives continue to be a contested front in this battle. Destruction, concealment, and denial of access to contemporaneous official documents continue to be strategies deployed by former oppressors and their successors.[10]

Opposition to reparations extends beyond the nondisclosure of pertinent documentary evidence. The legal and administrative framework responsible for promoting the infliction of harm may have been superseded, as in the case of slavery or colonialism. But the ideology's material legacy of preferential economic and political status reflected in patterns of land ownership, financial wealth, and social capital accumulation endures. This legacy is generally fortified by legal provisions that make successful challenge elusive. Indeed, legal strategies, despite some dramatic examples of success, are typically fraught with difficulty as a means for delivering reparations. This has been the experience of reparations advocates across continents and categories of harm: as chapters in this book explain, colonized populations in Guadeloupe and enslaved populations in the U.S. South, among others, have all seen their court-based struggles for effective repair of past atrocities defeated.[11] Armenians and Cambodians have also been disappointed by the outcomes of litigation to secure some form of reparation.[12] This should not be a surprise. As Mutua notes in Chapter 1 in this volume: "By its nature, the law is a conservative tool when deployed in the struggle for social change, and courts are naturally cautious and skeptical of property claims by the poor and marginalized, especially where such claims have the potential to upset legal precedent and reorder society." This is the challenging terrain with which this book seeks to engage.

Our main argument throughout this volume is that the traces carved by unrepaired past injustice endure in the political, social, and economic arrangements bequeathed to the present and future: the systems for transmission of property, wealth, status, authority, power. No clearer evidence for this proposition exists than the enduring disparities between white and Black Americans. Despite the abolition of slavery and over half a century of civil rights legislation, the median white household in the United States is *ten times* wealthier than the median Black one.[13] Clearly legal changes have not erased the traces of slavery, any more than they have erased the accumulated disparities built on a never-leveled playing field.

The same point can be made about political changes. Without a panoply of associated measures, such changes alone do not erase the infrastructure generated by past injustice, any more than they erase the divergent political and human capital accrued by differentially positioned social actors. Emancipation from slavery without attendant land reform and restitution of the stolen wealth generated by centuries of slave labor did not put formerly enslaved populations in a position to resist exploitative labor contracts post emancipation. Similarly, European Union citizenship without attendant social and economic investment has not increased the European Romani population's protection from stigmatization, discrimination, and violence. Nor has it corrected their pre-existing lesser social and material status, disparities that have affected their relative success in securing reparations, by comparison with more powerful survivor constituencies.[14] As several chapters in this volume argue, only a holistic set of interventions to repair past harm and foster comprehensive implementation of rights is likely to yield enduring progress on these manifold fronts.

Repairing past injustice is still a repair, not a substitution for a pre-harm status quo ante. And repair without due process, without guarantees of fairness, can precipitate adverse social and political responses. But, and this is our strong if contested claim, repair is a necessary condition for enhancing prevention of injustice moving forward, for laying the foundation for a more just future. The enduring legacies of slavery, of genocide, of colonialism, in their different manifestations—political, economic, psychological, and cultural—attest to this. Fiscal concerns about the magnitude of potential financial obligations derived from reparation claims have to contend with countervailing claims about the magnitude of ongoing and multiplying harms. While pragmatic considerations may justifiably influence outcomes, as a matter of principle and logic they do not trump the validity of the claim for reparative justice.

Morality has no monopoly on the validity of one set of reparative strategies as opposed to others. Survivor repugnance toward blood money—"the wrong moral currency" as Albie Sachs argues in his Preface to this volume—is as legitimate a perspective, in our view, as its opposite, the robust demand for financial compensation. The same is true about the competing claims of truth telling and criminal prosecution. The highly differentiated historical terrain on which reparation claims are advanced requires multiple philosophical and strategic approaches. Painstaking evidence, presented in the following pages, attests to the continuing impact of past injustice, both the harms it wreaks on survivors and their descendants and the unfair advantages it showers on beneficiaries and their successors. These impacts take multiple, often intersecting, forms. They manifest themselves in the unequal burden of disease between different communities, the disparate economic circumstances of racial groups, the educational differentials between different social and ethnic constituencies. Conversely, reparation efforts have both restorative and preventative potential, and cumulative beneficial spin-offs that merit the social and political investment they require. Our hope is that the chapters in this volume make both sides of this complex case with clarity, cogency, and empirical rigor.

We suggest, in the pages that follow, that the time for reparations is now. Regrettably, this remains a minority view, one, incidentally, that was not supported by former U.S. president Barack Obama. The demand for reparation for past injustice is often seen as divisive, a claim that privileges sectional advancement over collective well-being, that pits one community against another, that enshrines backward-looking retributive reasoning over forward-looking programmatic innovation. Inherited property traceable to the legacy of past injustice, whether in the form of land holding or business enterprise, is attributed to the diligence and competence of ancestors rather than to the cumulative impact of inequity and exploitation. The 2001 UN World Conference against Racism, Racial Discrimination, Xenophobia and Related Intolerance in Durban, a global convening that provided an opportunity for a collective statement on the topic, demonstrated instead the extent of opposition to reparation claims. Opinions have not changed dramatically since then. According to a 2016 Marist poll, 68 percent of American adults opposed reparations to the descendants of enslaved Africans, while only 15 percent were in favor. A 2014 YouGov poll found that, according to a majority of white respondents (but only 14 percent of

Black respondents), the legacy of slavery was "not a factor at all" in the wealth gap between whites and Blacks.[15]

But the tide seems to be turning, at least in part. The only concerted American political effort to highlight the imperative of reparations for slavery, H.R. 40, a bill presented to Congress every year since 1989 by Rep. John Conyers, never even made it to a vote. Rep. Conyers retired in 2017 and passed away in 2019. As of this writing, by contrast, eight out of twenty Democratic candidates for the U.S. presidency in 2020 had included a demand related to reparations in their political agendas, an unprecedented situation. A common approach is to support establishment of a commission to examine the issue of reparations fully, presumably as a prelude to further action. A brilliant article by the journalist-turned-public intellectual Ta-Nehisi Coates published in *The Atlantic* in 2014 provided a compelling argument and meticulous documentation on the enduring legacy of slavery in the United States. As the editor of *The New Yorker* commented, with justified hyperbole, in June 2019, "It's not often that an article comes along that changes the world, but that's exactly what happened" with Coates's article.[16] It provoked thought, discussion, and organizing where little had existed for decades. Political activism spearheaded by the Black Lives Matter movement, built on this groundswell, catalyzing forces of resistance to reparations denial that had long been dormant. At the same time, resurgent white supremacy unleashed during the 2016 presidential elections and subsequently catalyzed by a sympathetic White House demonstrated for all to see the enduring ideological legacy of racism.[17] These currents do not mean that the call for reparations is a widely supported political issue yet. But, to quote Coates, "people have stopped laughing" when the topic is raised.[18] Complementary to these initiatives, as we demonstrate in the following pages, the insistence on reparations as a key element in the quest for accountability for past state wrongs has mobilized a newly energized and coordinated global public. Across a diverse range of political, geographic, and ethnic constituencies, and for disparate reasons, significant civil society movements unused to collaborating across identity-defined silos now invoke reparations for harms suffered as a key component of their common advocacy toolkit. In so doing, they raise important questions about state accountability and responsibility, and about the mechanisms needed to translate claim making into concrete and tangible redistributive gains.

Is it realistic to expect governments responsible for devastating historic or ongoing injustice to initiate processes that lead to formal acknowledgment of past wrong-doing and to material reparations, whether individual or collective? Are intergovernmental or civil society–led organizations the key to establishment of processes for reparations for slavery, genocide, or other massive past atrocities? How should the addressees of reparations claims be defined? What are commonalities that link different groups with comparable histories of injustice? *Time for Reparations* addresses these questions. The volume bridges individual cases, discrete histories, and different regions to generate a multinational and multidisciplinary engagement with questions of reparations. Inevitably, practical constraints have limited the number of cases covered in this volume, a limitation over which we had no control but which we deeply regret. Some particularly egregious exemplars of state harm that we have not been able to address include those perpetrated against aboriginal populations in Australia, against vast numbers of Cambodian citizens by the Khmer Rouge, and against Haitian peasants by the French colonial government. We would also like to have added a chapter on U.S. government responsibility to the two chapters on aspects of reparations for slavery in the United States that are included. The legacy of each of these unrepaired crimes lives on, diminishing the rights and harming the prospects of survivor generations. If, despite these omissions, the volume adds comparative heft and new perspectives to the reparations literature and to related movements in different corners of the world, it will have fulfilled our aspirations.

Moving from general points to more specific recent developments, it is clear that a very diverse set of players, some defined by race, others by nationality, religion, gender, social class, or caste, have fueled the rekindled interest in reparations. For example, despite decades of pressure from postcolonial African states, policy makers across Europe have only recently started discussing in earnest the imperative of returning African artifacts taken by colonizers and held in Western museums or other collections. In a highly significant move, French president Emmanuel Macron established a commission in 2018 to investigate the vast African art holdings in France and make recommendations about their return. Given that between 90 and 95 percent of sub-Saharan cultural artifacts are still held outside Africa, the urgency of these reparative moves seems evident.[19] In April 2018, Belgium finally issued an apology to communities affected by the racist and eugenic population policies in force during its colonial rule of Burundi, Congo, and Rwanda. Interracial marriage in Catholic churches was banned and interracial relationships were frowned upon. The policies in question led to "the kidnapping, segregation, deportation, and forced adoption" of an estimated ten to twenty thousand so-called métis children born to mixed-race couples during the eighty years of Belgian colonization. Thousands of children were removed from their parents and handed to orphanages or foster care institutions. As late as the 1960s, when Belgian colonization finally came to an end, thousands of these children, many still alive today, were adopted by white families or placed in Belgian boarding schools. As the Belgian premier said, belatedly: "In the name of the federal government, I present our apologies to the métis stemming from the Belgian colonial era and to their families for the injustices and the suffering inflicted upon them."[20]

Other reparation strategies are also coming to fruition after decades of unsuccessful pressure. Less than a year after Coates's hard-hitting article, during a 2015 Oxford Union debate, Shashi Taroor, former UN undersecretary general for communications and public information and an Indian state minister, argued that Great Britain should establish reparations for India in a speech that went viral.[21] In 2013, Caribbean heads of state as well as National Committees on Reparations called for comprehensive reparations. Sir Hilary Beckles has argued that this would amount to "payment of reparations by the former colonial European countries to the nations and people of the Caribbean Community, for Native genocide, the transatlantic slave trade and a racialized system of chattel slavery." As he noted, these claims are predicated on the idea that "this is not about retribution and anger, it's about atonement; it's about the building of bridges across lines of moral justice."[22] This framework has grounded the formal establishment of the CARICOM Reparations Committee and the National Committees on Reparations, deliberative bodies for "establishing the moral, ethical, and legal case for the payment of Reparations by the Governments of all the former colonial powers and the relevant institutions of those countries."[23]

Pressure from Beckles and others eventually led the University of the West Indies (UWI) and Glasgow University to formally allocate £20 million to support a development research fund based at UWI. The amount selected matches the "compensation" paid to British enslavers following the abolition of slavery.[24] Similar calls have been made to establish reparations for France's centuries-old immiseration of Haiti, and for Romanian enslavement of its Roma population. Marian Mandache, director of the Roma Center for Social Intervention and Romani Studies (Romani CRISS), has noted, with the Roma case in mind, that reparations are "about past and prevailing moral injustice. There should be no statute of limitations on resolving human suffering."[25]

This growing momentum sets the scene for our volume. It generates prospects for advancing a more comprehensive and far-reaching historical and ethical exploration of the legitimacy of redress for past wrongs than has been the case to date. It also presents an opportunity for strengthening a joint advocacy movement on reparations claims across historical and geographical spheres. Across the many jurisdictions where claims are being advanced, reparations remain, as they are in the United States, a highly controversial topic. But other reparations claims, for example, for starvation crimes discussed in the chapter by de Waal and Conley, are new—raising issues never consistently addressed to date.

A range of reparatory measures have been explored, generating fascinating variation within the potential reparations political agenda. Some countries, including Britain's former colonies, have emphasized the importance of individual compensation and redress, modeling themselves on Germany's response to Holocaust victims and survivors. Advocates at the 2001 UN World Conference against Racism in Durban pressed governments for substantial social and economic public investment in programs targeting grievously harmed communities still afflicted by poverty and stigma. As already noted, these views have met with little success so far. Yet others, including advocates interested in Roma slavery, have prioritized memorialization through symbolic remedies, including public monuments, apologies, commemorative days, or the rewriting of national histories.[26] Advocates increasingly acknowledge the need to integrate a range of reparative strategies, from legal processes that invoke long-standing normative principles to socioeconomic transformations that reflect emerging demands for political accountability.

The book is divided into four parts. The first, "Addressing the Legacy of Slavery," takes on the most egregious contemporary reparations challenge: the ongoing legacy and moral breaches of past state-sponsored slavery. This section explores the consequences of slavery comparatively—across historic and geographic regions as well as through the lens of different academic disciplines. Makau Mutua opens the section with a framing chapter that reviews the diverse history of reparative claims, some successful, some much less so, that have followed periods of extensive injustice. Drawing lessons from the past, he makes the case for a multipronged strategy to address reparations for people of African descent. Constitutional reform and related legal strategies have limited impacts, he argues, because law tends to protect powerful vested interests. In the absence of a coordinated movement that includes effective grassroots political mobilization in tandem with legal and structural reforms, reparative measures remain partial solutions at best. A case in point is contemporary South Africa, where, Mutua argues, apartheid has been frozen in place, with economic power largely unchanged.

This chapter is followed by two U.S. case studies on reparative intervention. Chapter 2 describes the effort by Georgetown University to respond to the demands of a large community of direct descendants of the university's former enslaved persons and make amends for its egregious history of slave ownership and sale. In painstaking detail, Adam Rothman documents the series of measures, building on careful historical research about the university, that have been undertaken to remediate the atrocious crimes of the past: investigation, documentation, apology, memorialization, creation of a digital archive, financial compensation, and targeted interventions in university admissions policy. The second case study, in Chapter 3, describes the complex and intriguing case of slave-holding by the Cherokee nation in Oklahoma. With deft subtlety and analytic acuity, Tiya Miles probes the "tension between differently racialized peoples who share a violently and at times valiantly intimate history" and asks what it means to consider oneself "sovereign" in a racialized and colorized postcolonial context. Again, space constraints have prevented us from including other important contemporary work on this topic.

Three other chapters, centered on the Caribbean, continue the discussion of slavery's legacy. In Chapter 4 Bert S. Samuels explores the enduring impact of slavery in Jamaica, vividly illustrating the continuing pain—both material and psychic—that colonial planters left in their wake. Raising an issue made by other contributors to this volume, he shows how emancipation was followed by population-wide unemployment accompanied by antivagrancy laws, which forced the formerly enslaved to work for their previous owners. What is more, the perverse logic of the emancipatory program generated compensatory payments to the former enslavers but no reparatory measures at all for the enslaved people. Samuels's essay is followed by another examination of the impact of the history of slavery on Caribbean society. In a trenchant examination in Chapter 5, Sir Hilary Beckles describes the far-reaching links between universities in the Caribbean and slavery, both in terms of the ideological underpinnings of both institutions and in terms of the financial dependence of the former on the latter: "As enslavers, college principals and professors built the colonial and national higher education agenda on the legal platform of property rights in enslaved Africans." Conceptually, Beckles shows, seventeenth-century British thought, epitomized by the work of John Locke, promoted the notion that human liberty was compatible with investment in human property in the form of enslaved people. Materially, the vast profits accumulated from slavery provided the economic bedrock on which the slave-owning classes and their institutions depended. Beckles's long-standing scholarship and advocacy have recently been vindicated by dramatic success. As already noted, in August 2019, a trend-setting agreement between a British university and a Caribbean university—Glasgow and UWI—resulted in an unprecedented award of slavery-related wealth to the Caribbean university to seed relevant anticolonial research. The final chapter in this first section takes the discussion of slavery's enduring legacy to another Caribbean site, the French dominion of Guadeloupe. In Chapter 6, Mireille Fanon Mendez, a human rights advocate engaged in litigating cases on behalf of the descendants of enslaved Guadeloupe agricultural workers, provides a searing description of French colonial crimes against humanity on the island. Focusing on the land issue, and on the enduring property theft perpetrated by slavery and bolstered by ensuing legal measures, she too highlights the paradoxical consequences of emancipation for human rights— the colonizers' self-declared appropriation of local land, the payment of reparations to former enslavers as compensation for their human property "loss," and these same owners' insistence on share-cropping arrangements postemancipation that ensured their ability to continue extracting crops from those formerly enslaved.

The book's second part, "Reparations: Precedents and Lessons Learned," covers a diverse set of recent reparation experiences, each of them a rich case study in coalition building. Caroline Elkins, in Chapter 7, describes the landmark work she spearheaded, initially as an intrepid and visionary graduate student, documenting the brutal abuses perpetrated by British rulers on Kenyan Mau Mau detainees held in colonial detention camps following their uprising against British domination in the 1950s. Drawing on her original archival and ethnographic work spanning years, she demonstrates how careful historical research can yield significant social justice gains, particularly when allied to well-organized civil society mobilization and expert legal intervention. Elkins tells the dramatic story of reparations litigation on behalf of 5,228 elderly Mau Mau defendants, some of whom traveled from rural Kenya to the High Court in London to present their case against a tenacious British establishment. The second chapter in this section covers another landmark case—the unprecedented scope of the reparations program established following Colombia's protracted and devastating civil war. Kathryn Sikkink, Doug Johnson, Phuong Pham, and Patrick Vinck succinctly outline in Chapter 8 the wide-ranging measures—the most ambitious ever—launched by the Colombian government to address the multifaceted devastation caused by years of brutal violence, during which paramilitary and guerilla forces inflicted extensive damage on the population. With more than 15 percent of the Colombian population now included in the victims' registry, the scope of reparatory measures projected is both unprecedented and daunting.

A different Latin American precedent-setting reparations story is set out in Chapter 9, about Guatemala. Here too, for thirty-six years during the mid-twentieth century, a brutal civil war decimated the country's peasant population, with landowning elites taking the place of Spanish colonials in meting out violence and exploitation on indigenous peoples . A UN-sponsored truth commission found the Guatemalan state guilty of crimes against humanity and accountable for the genocide of 200,000 people, mostly Mayan indigenous populations. Yet, as has been the case in another UN-sponsored reparations effort on the other side of the globe, in Cambodia, prosecutions have been limited. What the UN truth commission did not focus on but has since become a target of civil society advocacy is the atrocious history of gender-based violence running through Guatemalan history. Irma Velásquez Nimatuj here documents this brutalization of indigenous Guatemalan women, an endemic aspect, she argues, of the relentless persecution of Guatemala's indigenous population at the hands of colonial and then postcolonial rulers. And she describes the reparative process that eventually led the courts to convict senior members of the Guatemalan military of crimes against humanity related to this pervasive sexual violence.

The final chapter in this section shifts the scene from the Americas to Asia, to postcolonial Indonesia still battling with the legacy of Dutch colonization and brutality. In Chapter 10, Nicole Immler draws on the colonial archive and on more contemporary evidence to paint a nuanced picture of the complex process of reparatory justice and compensation forged by the heirs of executed Indonesian freedom fighters. In all the cases analyzed in Part 2, the tension between individual reparatory measures and collective justice permeates the narrative, demonstrating that, for all their impressive achievements, the process of reparations remains a fraught tool for building social healing.

The third part of the book moves the analytical focus from reparative outcome to enduring injustice. Rashid Khalidi opens the section with an account of the "unhealed wounds" from World War I. In Chapter 11, he shows how unrepaired injustice from decades past continues to permeate contemporary social and political arrangements, perpetuating displacement, loss, and oppression for affected communities. He carefully illustrates that Armenians, Kurds, and Palestinians, in their different but comparable ways, are forced to experience the enduring impact of historical defeat, expropriation, and injustice; all three communities continue to contend with the present-day consequences of property theft, atrocity denial, enforced exile, and, in the case of the Kurds and Palestinians, suppression of their long-standing claims to full autonomy and self-determination.

Chapter 12 focuses in more detail on the ongoing and unremediated injustice against Palestinians. Michael Fischbach charts the complex history of the Palestinian people during and following the Nakba, or "catastrophe," that left three-quarters of a million Palestinians as refugees after their defeat by Israel in the 1947–48 war. He shows how Israeli Nakba denial has combined with the appropriation of Palestinian land and an enduring refusal to agree to reparations for Palestinian refugees. International measures, including many brokered by the United Nations, have singularly failed to temper this oppressive situation, leading to a de facto occupation that persists to this day.

The contested terrain of colonial archives, their scope, their ownership, their location, their control, is taken up again in Chapter 13—as it was in Chapters 7 and 10, by, respectively, Elkins and Immler—in Susan Slyomovics's inquiry into the enduring battle over the archive of French Algeria. Slyomovics makes the compelling argument that the ongoing contestation over control of the archive—in the case of Algeria, still largely in French hands and on French soil—is in part a proxy for a broader set of reparation claims relating to colonization, including not only the right to know but also the right to document, and receive reparations for, past atrocities. Just as enslaved people in America and Guadeloupe received no reparative payments following emancipation for the theft of their land, their labor, and their families, while their oppressors were compensated for the loss of their human property, so too in Algeria following independence the colonizers returning to France were generously compensated and comfortably housed, while the colonized in Algeria suffered further injustice after 132 years of colonization—no compensation for exploitation and violence, but instead their historical records stolen, moved from their land to France.

The most celebrated and extensive enactment of restitution measures is the German program establishing wide-ranging reparation payments

following the Holocaust. It has provided a precedent followed by many—
Armenians, Guatemalans, Kenyans, and Jamaicans, among others.[27] As
Susan Neiman notes in her inspiring book *Learning from the Germans*, there
is much to learn from the hard work of repair that postwar Germany has done
to address its atrocious past extermination and persecution of Jews.[28] There
is, however, a much-less-celebrated post-Holocaust story. Only one of the two
peoples singled out for extermination by the Nazis received German restitution. The other is still pressing their claim. In Chapter 14, Ian Hancock presents this largely unknown story in compelling detail. He describes the
situation of the Romani people, a community of approximately 11 million
people, long settled in Europe but relentlessly targeted by racism and exploitative stigmatization. Like the Jews, the Roma were picked for elimination by
Nazi genocidaires, classified as an inferior people not worthy of life. According to Hancock, 70 percent of Europe's Roma population was exterminated
by the Nazis in the course of the Holocaust, or Porrajmos, to use the Romani
term. Unlike the Jews, however, the Romani population, long enslaved in
Eastern Europe before the rise of National Socialism, lacked social or economic capital, and they also had no national state, or powerful political allies linked to that state, to advocate on their behalf. Their leverage in pressing
claims for reparation was thus considerably weaker than that of Jewish Holocaust victims. What is more, and this is the disturbing story that Hancock
develops, prominent Jewish advocates militated against inclusion of Romani
claims in the reparations process, in order to preserve the allegedly unique
claims of Jews.

The fourth and final part of the book turns from the past to the future, to
ask what might lie ahead in the quest for reparative justice for the many unrepaired harms still in evidence. It draws together many themes developed
earlier in the volume, from the limitations of one- dimensional remedial
strategies such as litigation or memorialization, to the imperative of syn-
cretic thinking to learn from productive strategies wherever deployed.
These final chapters also stress the centrality of building political alliances
across different domains as a key tool for repairing past atrocities. Chapter 15, by Margareta Matache and Jacqueline Bhabha, integrates a substantial body of historical and legal material to advance a specific yet holistic
case for reparative justice for the Romani people. It sets out the egregious
history, from slavery to present-day institutional discrimination, that continues to brutalize the lives of the largest European minority community, in
the most advanced rights-respecting region on earth. The chapter reviews

the many domains—political, social, economic, and educational—where Roma continue to experience discrimination; but it also reviews the broad range of reparatory strategies that Romani advocates are using to build the case for reparations.

Other chapters follow a similar pattern of forward-thinking and constructive strategizing. But they also develop more broad-ranging conceptual arguments for how reparations claims can be rethought and applied to new domains. An example of this broad-ranging rethinking is in Chapter 16, by Alex De Waal and Bridget Conley, on starvation crimes. The authors advance the compelling, but previously uncharted, case that victims of famine deserve reparations just as victims of other forms of brutal abuse of political power do. They argue that famine is a political consequence of abusive governance that merits reparative justice. Moreover, consistent with other chapters in the volume, the authors argue that a range of conceptual frameworks—from human rights norms to international humanitarian law, from feminist theorizing about structural inequality and its social and political spillovers to international criminal law—can and should be invoked to structure reparative justice appropriately for victims of starvation crimes. The authors move from historical examples, including German colonial deployment of starvation in the service of the genocide of the Herero people of South Western Africa and the Bengal famine in British India to contemporary starvation crimes in Darfur and Yemen, to make the case that this state strategy for inflicting massive harm must be included in the reparations canon. In the final chapter, Chapter 17, Luis Moreno Ocampo draws on his years of experience as the first prosecutor of the International Criminal Court. In 2006, the UN General Assembly adopted principles and guidelines about reparations, which the chapter discusses.[29] But though the international community recognized the right of individuals to remedies for egregious forms of state injustice, it did not create obligations to enforce or achieve those remedies. This remains the situation today. Reparative measures, Ocampo argues, are essential, but court-based strategies that draw on international legal norms will continue to have only limited impact unless they are allied to political forces that complement those efforts with national heft. This sobering conclusion is both a realistic assessment of current realities and a call to action.

We hope that at this juncture, when reparations are more prominently on the collective mind than they have been in a long while, the insights and arguments advanced in this volume will contribute to long overdue justice for victims of past, and all-too-often enduring, state-sponsored atrocities.

PART I

Addressing the Legacy of Slavery

CHAPTER 1

Reparations for Slavery: A Productive Strategy?

Makau Mutua

Introduction

Slavery negates individual autonomy and equality—both in the abstract and in substance—when a person or institution holds another human being as chattel or property.[1] Slavery is a system in which society, or a fraction thereof, applies the rules of commerce, the market, and property to human beings. It is a legal regime in which people and institutions can buy and sell human beings. In this sense, the term "slave" itself is a misnomer because it implies a certain normalcy of the condition. It shifts responsibility for slavery from the trader—the trafficker—in human beings, or the owner of the enslaved person, to the enslaved. This is an important distinction because it argues that a human being cannot be a slave per se. The fact of enslavement does not turn one into a slave. This central but fine distinction to some—in the academy and in public discourse—lies at the heart of the question of whether human beings can normatively become chattel or property.

Scholars and commentators in public discourse in the United States often use the term "slave" when referring to enslaved Africans or African Americans before the Emancipation Proclamation and the passage of the Thirteenth Amendment.[2] The argument here is that the law can rob people of their freedom through enslavement, but it cannot vacate their inherent and innate dignity as humans.

A person cannot be a slave as such. As an empirical matter, a person can be enslaved, but that does not vacate or nullify their inherent human dignity as a normative question. To argue otherwise is to ratify an immorality and a normative impossibility. Even those born into slavery are not intrinsically slaves but enslaved human beings. This argument sits at the core of the justification for reparations for slavery. Enslavement of human beings is a wrong that transcends all known morality. It cannot be justified as a matter of history, law, morality, or culture. That is why absolutist demands for reparations for slavery should be unarguable.

Reparations for slavery fall within a large genre of claims for compensatory and social justice for historical injustices.[3] There are several famous cases in recent history of reparations for historical injustices. The first is that of persons of Japanese heritage, most of them Japanese Americans, who the United States interned during World War II on false claims of disloyalty, espionage, and sabotage on behalf of the Japanese government.[4] The other is the compensation to Jewish victims of the Nazi-perpetrated Holocaust.[5] A third, which is more recent and involves colonial abuses, is the British compensation for atrocities against the Mau Mau freedom fighters in Kenya (see Chapter 7, by Elkins, in this volume).[6] In 2013, the British government expressed regret for the actions of its colonial administration in Kenya and agreed to pay £19.9 (US$30.8) million as compensation to 5,228 Kenyan claimants as "full and final settlement" for the court action.[7] British foreign secretary William Hague told the House of Commons that "We [British] understand the pain and grief felt by those who were involved in the events of emergency in Kenya. The British government recognizes that Kenyans were subjected to torture and other forms of ill-treatment at the hands of the colonial administration."[8] Hague added that: "The British Government sincerely regrets that these abuses took place and that they marred Kenya's progress to independence. Torture and ill-treatment are abhorrent violations of human dignity which we unreservedly condemn."[9]

The language employed by Hague appeared calculated to avoid legal liability. While he does not deny the commission of torture and other atrocities, he nevertheless only "sincerely regrets" those abominations but does not "sincerely apologize" for them. The British government appeared to have been concerned that an "apology"—as opposed to an expression of "regret"—could be an admission of legal liability actionable in a court of law. It is unclear as a matter of legal interpretation whether a court of law would find such a distinction in a legal opinion. Even so, Hague vowed that the Kenyan settlement did not set a precedent and that the British government would defend claims from other British colonies.

It is notable that the British government only settled the Mau Mau claims in a suit that the Kenya Human Rights Commission and the Mau Mau War Veterans Association brought in the United Kingdom. A British court rejected the government's arguments that the statute of limitations barred the claims and that there would be "irredeemable difficulties" in obtaining evidence and availing witnesses.[10] The court also dismissed the British government's attempt to shift the burden for any compensation to the government of Kenya by arguing that any responsibility for colonial atrocities had passed to the government of independent Kenya in 1963.[11] At a public ceremony on September 12, 2015, at Uhuru Park in Nairobi, the British high commissioner, Christian Turner, spoke at the unveiling of the British-funded monument to the Mau Mau and other freedom fighters.[12] The Kenyan case represents the first time that a colonial power has compensated victims of colonial atrocities. More cases against other colonial powers are sure to follow. In January 2017, the Herero and Nama peoples of Namibia sued Germany through a court in New York over the 1904 genocide.[13]

There are other important reparations programs in history—some going as far back as 1872, when France paid Germany reparations after the Franco-Prussian War.[14] However, the more recent cases of reparations for historical injustices include U.S. payments of monies to Native Americans and reparations for Japanese internment.[15] Elsewhere, there were reparations in the form of property restitution after the Cold War to individuals from whom Soviet bloc states in Eastern and Central Europe took property.[16] Beyond these cases, there have been heated and complex debates about whom should be compensated—or seek reparations—for historical injustices, and why, how, and in what form.[17] This is particularly the case where positive law is lacking, or difficult to establish. But one thing seems to be clear: there is a political economy to a successful claim for compensation or reparations. Claimant groups with social capital, economic clout, and backing from powerful actors and states have met with more success. Victims of the Nazi-perpetrated Holocaust had powerful allies in Israel and the United States. Since 2017, the Me Too movement (#MeToo)—an international uprising against sexual harassment and assault—is the latest demonstration of the power of the confluence of social capital and political awakening to create accountability beyond the strictures of positive law.[18] This is why accountability for past injustices need not be negated by statutes of limitation or the absence of clear positive law.

This chapter interrogates the politics, claims, and strategies for reparations for slavery for Africans, African Americans, and the larger African Diaspora. With the hindsight benefit of both the strategic successes and shortcomings that other groups deployed for reparations, the chapter explores the approaches that advocates of reparations for persons of African descent have adopted. It examines legal, political, and moral strategies as entry points for reparations. It looks at why some groups have succeeded in their quest for reparations and not others. The chapter explores legal fictions used to punt, deny, and belittle claims for reparations for persons of African descent, as well as the deficit of political will in Africa, the West, and the Arab world to come to terms with the staggering cost of the enslavement of Africans and their descendants. Finally, the chapter closes by making a case for multi-pronged strategies and approaches employing all levers of advocacy to seek reparations for people of African descent.

The Quandary of Historical Injustices

There can be little doubt that the idea of justice is historically contextual in the sense that as a civilizational value it is contingent on time and place. Whether a particular norm of justice is transcendent is a question of debate.[19] Is a particular norm of justice applicable only nationally, or does it have international, or universal, purchase beyond its geographic place of origin? At what point does a narrow culturally tailored social norm become universal? Particular societies at specific historical moments construct social, moral, and legal norms. Should such a limitation matter in a question of accountability at a future date for historical injustices? How should society today address harms that did not carry social, moral, and legal liability at the time they were committed? The historical text suggests a shifting standard of accountability for past abuses and justices. Global hegemons can make new rules and apply them retroactively, even if such ex post facto rules violate long-standing legal precedents or norms. In the legal realm, the Allied powers' legal responses to the vanquished Axis powers after World War II provide a most telling example of the creation of new norms and their retroactive application.

The 1945–46 trial at Nuremberg of major war criminals—predominantly Nazi Party leaders and military officials—not only launched the modern human rights movement but fashioned laws out of new cloth. The charter that the victors of World War II—the United States, Britain, France, and the USSR—annexed to the London Agreement established the International Military Tribunal at Nuremberg to try war criminals.[20] Among the innovations of the charter were the expansion of crimes and sanctions applicable to offenders for actions that did not constitute crimes at the time of their commission.[21] For example, crimes against peace, or *jus ad bellum*, as opposed to war crimes, or *jus in bello*, were an innovation. The concept of crimes against humanity was another innovation.[22] So was the application of individual criminal responsibility for a number of international crimes. There have been divergent views on these stark developments at the dawn of modern international criminal law. Some jurists, most notably U.S. Supreme Court chief justice Harlan Fiske Stone, were scathing in their disagreement with these innovations. Stone called the Nuremberg trial "an attempt to justify the application of the power of the victor over the vanquished" by dressing it "with a false façade of legality." He called the trial a "high-grade lynching party" and a "sanctimonious fraud."[23]

The Nuremberg trials demonstrate that the international community—as represented by the hegemonic powers of the day—can rewrite existing rules to reach backward and punish a wrong. Nuremberg was easy to accept because of the gravity of the Holocaust and the atrocities of the Axis powers (although the Allied powers exempted their own grave brutalities such as the massive bombing of cities with high civilian casualties and the nuclear destruction of Hiroshima and Nagasaki). The trial's defects and contradictions are more palatable because of its launch of the human rights movement. One can see why the Holocaust pushed the Allied powers to bend legal precedents. For one, it was an opportunity for the Anglo-Saxon tradition of the rule of law to demonstrate its superiority over Nazi barbarities at the dawn of a new international legal and political order under the leadership of the United States. For another, the punished atrocities had taken place in the heart of Europe against the Jews (and although less acknowledged and repaired, against other groups too, including the Romani people, see Chapter 14 by Ian Hancock), an influential, though long-persecuted community that had been the target of many pogroms. It is highly doubtful, as history bears out, that the West would have marshaled a similar response for atrocities against Africans. Unlike Jews, Africans did not have influential organizations such as the World Zionist Organization, or its internationally dominant leader Chaim Weizmann, who served as the first president of Israel. Weizmann convinced the United States to recognize the newly created state of Israel.[24]

Nuremberg did something else that is helpful to those seeking reparations for people of African descent. It gave unarguable status to war crimes, crimes against humanity, and crimes against peace as the most abominable universal offenses known to man.[25] Genocide made it on this ignominious list soon thereafter.[26] The existence of positive law ex ante is not necessary for accountability for these heinous crimes and other historical abuses. As the Nuremberg trial clearly showed, global powers can will accountability ex post facto for gross abuses even where no extant law prohibited such actions. Nuremberg is a great example of a constitutional moment in which society realizes that certain abuses, though not criminalized, are so inimical to morality and decency that leaving them unpunished sets an untenable precedent. In such a situation, dispensing with the general prohibition against retroactive laws is the more plausible option. The most exceptional circumstances may dictate an expedient waiver of this particular legal formality—or an aversion to retroactivity—as was the case in Nuremberg. Actions that shock the human conscience, such as slavery, should follow suit.

There is a further question of statutes of limitations. Does the passage of time bar what can reasonably be sanctioned? In common and civil law, there are statutes of limitation or statutes of prescription to ensure the fair and effective administration of justice. Traditionally, statutes of limitation served three purposes: to ensure that a claimant or plaintiff with a valid cause of action would pursue it with diligence; to ensure that evidence did not get lost, or the defendant was still alive; and finally, to ensure that a long-dormant claim does not deny a defendant justice.[27] In most jurisdictions, however, the statute of limitations is inapplicable to the most heinous crimes, such as murder. The 1970 Convention on the Non-Applicability of Statutory Limitations to War Crimes and Crimes Against Humanity disallows limitations on war crimes, genocide, and crimes against humanity, including gross offenses related to apartheid.[28] The 1998 Rome Statute of the International Criminal Court—ratified by 127 states—provides that genocide, crimes against humanity, and war crimes "shall not be subject to any statute of limitations."[29] This is a legal recognition that accountability for heinous crimes cannot be excused in spite of the passage of time, however long.

In the more recent past, there is growing recognition that particular historical injustices—colonialism, apartheid, and slavery—were so egregious that they cry out for justice. The United Nations repeatedly and annually condemned apartheid—which formally lasted in South Africa from 1948 to 1990—as a crime against humanity; and, in 1966, it declared apartheid a crime against humanity.[30] In 1984, the UN Security Council affirmed apartheid a crime against humanity.[31] Previously, in 1973, the UN had adopted the Convention on the Suppression and Punishment of the Crime of Apartheid.[32] It is notable that only four countries—the United States, United Kingdom, Portugal, and South Africa—voted against this convention, while ninety-one countries voted in favor.[33] The Apartheid Convention declared that apartheid is a crime against humanity and further provided that "inhuman acts resulting from the policies and practices of apartheid and similar policies and practices of racial segregation and discrimination" are international crimes.[34] The use of the term "international crimes" is significant because it elevates them over mere, or common, crimes and gives all states and relevant international tribunals the permission to prosecute them.

Unlike the case of apartheid, there is no similar international consensus on the legal status of colonialism and slavery. There is little doubt that colonial powers committed barbaric acts that amount to crimes against humanity. However, there has been a reluctance to declare colonialism itself a crime against humanity. In 2001, the Declaration of the World Conference against Racism (WCAR) in Durban, South Africa, employed clever rhetoric to defuse tension on the question of whether colonialism and slavery were crimes against humanity for which reparations must be due. The declaration's language on colonialism is woefully inadequate. It condemned colonialism as morally outrageous in the strongest terms but fell short of calling it a crime against humanity for which descendants or successors of the colonizers should pay reparations.[35] The declaration was a little stronger on slavery. It explicitly termed slavery and the slave trade crimes against humanity. It acknowledged, in part, "We recognize that slavery and the slave trade, including the transatlantic slave trade, were appalling tragedies in the history of humanity not only because of their barbarism, but also in terms of their magnitude, organized nature and especially their negation of the essence of the victims, _and further acknowledge that slavery and the slave trade are a crime against humanity and should always have been so, especially the transatlantic slave trade_" (emphasis added).[36]

The failure of the declaration to recognize slavery, the slave trade, and colonialism as crimes against humanity, with explicit repercussions for the former colonizers and the states that engaged in slavery and the slave trade, disappointed many observers. Kenya's Amina Mohamed, the spokesperson for the Africa group, lamented the lack of an explicit apology for slavery and the absence of any commitment for reparations. She called the declaration "terribly imperfect" but said it "provides a basis to build on."[37] Nkosazana Dlamini Zuma, then South Africa's foreign minister, said, "Something historic happened here." She added, "We have agreed that the depredation of the systems of slavery and colonialism had a degrading and debilitating impact on those who are black, broadly defined."[38] The United States, which had sent low-level representatives to the conference, and Israel, withdrew from the conference, citing objections to the draft of the declaration.[39]

At least one important Western leader—France's Emmanuel Macron— has called colonialism a crime against humanity. He said French actions in the 132-year colonization of Algeria involved "crimes and acts of barbarism" that would today be termed "crimes against humanity."[40] The question then remains: Where does the international community go from here?

The Legitimation of Reparations for Slavery

In the last several decades, the idea of reparations for slavery has gained momentum even though it remains out of the political mainstream. A succession of events has raised the profile of the reparations debate. The reparations movement, if it can be called that, spans the entire globe, wherever people of African descent are domiciled. In the United States, several antecedent events have inched the debate forward. Not since Reconstruction—when the United States attempted to appropriate and confiscate land in the American South and give African Americans who had been freed from slavery "forty acres and a mule"—have there been more calls for reparations.[41] In the face of southern states' fierce opposition, President Andrew Johnson rescinded "forty acres and a mule."[42] He ordered the eviction of Africans Americans and the return of the land to those who had enslaved them. Thus, the United States has not made reparations for slavery.

Even so, several entities have paid reparations and issued apologies for a number of related historical injustices and brutalities. In 1995, the Florida legislature approved reparations for the victims and descendants of the 1923 Rosewood Massacre.[43] In a frenzy of racist violence, whites descended on Rosewood, where they murdered blacks, and pillaged, ransacked, and destroyed the town. Survivors and victims received sums ranging from $375 to $150,000.[44] In 1997, the United States paid monetary compensation and gave an apology to African American victims of the Tuskegee syphilis experiments.[45] The reparations for the internment of Japanese Americans and the apology—without reparations—for the illegal overthrow of the sovereign Hawaiian Nation in 1893 and the subsequent mismanagement of the Hawaiian trust lands, have boosted claims for reparations for the enslavement of African Americans.[46] A 1946 settlement for claims by Native American tribes for lands taken forcibly or by deception is a powerful precedent for African Americans.[47] So, too, is the 1971 payment by the United States of $1 billion and the return of 40 million acres as reparations to Native Alaskans.[48] Nevertheless, Public Law 103-150, or the so-called Apology Resolution, explicitly rejected claims for slavery reparations by providing in the disclaimer: "Nothing in this Joint Resolution is intended to serve as a settlement of any claims against the United States."[49]

The United States is not the only jurisdiction where claims for reparations have found both traction and resistance. Africa, the Caribbean, and Europe have been a major part of the debate to legitimize claims for reparations for slavery. In Africa, there have long been demands for reparations for both the transatlantic slave trade and the Arab slave trade.[50] In the so-called Indian Ocean slave trade, Arabs captured millions of Africans and sold them into slavery in the Middle East and European colonies in Asia.[51] Historians and scholars estimate that up to eighty thousand Africans, whom Arabs had captured in East and Central Africa, died each year even before reaching the slave markets in Zanzibar.[52] Ali A. Mazrui, one of Africa's pre-eminent global intellectuals, captured well the impact of the Arab slave trade in black Africa.[53] However, it is the transatlantic slave trade, not the Indian Ocean one, that has received more attention from scholars and policy makers. Claims for reparations against Arab countries have either been muted or nonexistent. The prominence of the Africa Diaspora in the political, academic, civic, and economic spheres in the West has led to a more heightened public discourse of historical injustices, including slavery. Conversely, the concomitant invisibility of the African Diaspora in the milieu of the Middle East and Asia has suppressed any public clamor for reparations. In 2010, Muammar Gaddafi became the first and only Arab leader to apologize for the Arab enslavement of Black Africans. He said, "I regret the behavior of the Arabs. . . . They brought African children to North Africa, they made them slaves, they sold them like animals, and they took them as slaves and traded them in a shameful way."[54]

In Africa, there has been the occasional robust debate on reparations for slavery. In 1992, Chief Mashood Abiola, the late Nigerian billionaire politician, prevailed on the Organization of African Unity (OAU) to establish the

Group of Eminent Persons for Reparations.[55] The group committed the OAU to press for reparations for slavery. In 1999, the African World Reparations and Repatriation Truth Commission issued the Accra Declaration, in which it called for the West to pay US$777 trillion in reparations for slavery to Africa within five years.[56] However, these claims have not received any traction or advanced beyond the rhetorical stage. In 2001, the World Conference against Racism in South Africa recognized the enslavement of Africans as a historical evil but fell short of calling for reparations for fear that this would tear the conference apart. Abdoulaye Wade, then president of Senegal, was a lone oppositional voice breaking the consensus of the African group at WCAR in its call for reparations.[57] Predictably, Western states—many of them culprits of the transatlantic slave trade—were opposed to reparations at the WCAR.[58] In the Caribbean, there have been spirited, state-led, regional claims for reparations for slavery against the West. It is significant that Caribbean states themselves are pushing for reparations at the risk of alienating powerful Western states. Jamaica, Guyana, and Antigua and Barbuda are among the Caribbean states to press for reparations. In 2014, fourteen Caribbean states vowed to sue European states if negotiations failed to produce a settlement for reparations.[59] Most significantly, the Caribbean Community (CARICOM)—the official regional body for Caribbean nations and dependencies—formed the Caribbean Reparations Commission in 2013.[60] The commission's "Ten Point Action Plan" calls for a full apology and reparations from the West in a number of social, economic, and cultural sectors.[61]

There have been movements for reparations for slavery in two of the most important Western states: the United States and the United Kingdom. These two states were major players in slavery and the slave trade in Africans. It is worth noting that the two countries have large African diasporic populations and, together, have to play important roles in the reparation movement's success. In both the United States and the United Kingdom, advocates for reparations have employed a number of strategies, including lawsuits, legislative and other political actions, and public advocacy. While the reparations movement has witnessed ebbs and flows in the United States, it has not gained widespread acceptance among the populance, nor the elite classes. Former president Barack Obama opposed the calls for reparations for slavery.[62] As president, he instead advocated for incremental and remedial investments in health, education, and other social sectors for African Americans.[63] In fact, he opposed reparations as a candidate for U.S. president.[64] Obama persisted in his opposition in spite of strong cases made by leading African American scholars, especially Ta-Nehisi Coates.[65] One thing is clear—the clamor for reparations for slavery in the United States will not go away in spite of divisions on the issue among African Americans and outright rejection by many white Americans. Significantly, the United Nations Working Group on People of African Descent termed slavery a crime against humanity and recommended reparations for slavery by the United States.[66] The UN Working Group was unequivocal in its comprehensive list of recommendations for reparations for slavery and related historical injustices visited by the United States on African Americans.[67] As advocates' strategies amply demonstrate, reparations for the redress of slavery will not go away and cannot be forgotten, or swept under the rug.[68]

Legal Strategies

One of the enduring paradoxes of the law is its proclivity to render injustice instead of justice. Much as the rule of law is one of the most important issues that stand between the tyranny of the state and the citizen, it is a double-edged sword. It was not for nothing that Charles Dickens in *Oliver Twist* popularized the English expression the "law is an ass—an idiot."[69] The law's rigidity as well as paradoxically its malleability can cut both ways. That is why the law's application does not always result in a just or fair outcome. The tradition of legal positivism—the most enduring judicial philosophy—clads the law with a veil that often hides and protects the interests of the wealthy and powerful in society. Can the law excavate and reduce deeply embedded social and economic inequities, or is it a handmaiden for hegemonic interests? Can the law stand at the intersection of the powerful and the powerless and become an effective lever for the latter? In other words, can the law and legal discourse—especially in a democracy—be tools for transformative liberation? What is the law's liberatory potential? What role can the courts play as agents of deep social change?

The law's career as a tool of liberation is at worst disappointing, and at best mixed. The one poignant example in recent history is Nelson Mandela's attempt, in postapartheid South Africa, to uproot the previous regime's crimes largely by resorting to legal discourses. That experiment has been disappointing, as the lot of Black South Africans—the country's overwhelming majority—has stubbornly refused to improve.[70] South Africa's new constitutional rights framework, while uplifting and a cause célèbre around the world, seemed to freeze the hierarchies of apartheid in place and thus preserve the apartheid status quo. As law scholar Ibrahim Gassama observes:

> Disenchantment echoes the critique of the rights discourse's double-edged quality: rights can be deployed to protect the powerful and the status quo just as easily as they can be wielded to advance the interests of the weak and the excluded. The power of this observation should be increasingly apparent to rights activists in South Africa. It is not altogether surprising that even as the attainment of political participation rights by blacks in South Africa is celebrated, rights-rhetoric is being successfully deployed to protect the economic status quo—the private property rights—of the white minority in the country.[71]

Karl Klare, the legal academic, underscores this point, stating "rights discourse does not and probably cannot provide us with the criteria for deciding between conflicting claims of right."[72] Critiques of the use of law to transform society abound, and most leading scholars agree on the law's limitations to do substantive justice.[73] The poor and the marginalized can use the rights idiom to improve their plight at the margins—and even to capture state power as happened in South Africa—but there is ample evidence to suggest that those victories are partial, at best. Economic power does not always follow political power, as the history of postcolonial states demonstrates.[74] This reality tempers enthusiasm for the use of rights language and legal forums to vindicate socially and economically difficult problems. We must resort to other discourses for a fuller agenda of liberation. That is why the use of the law as a pathway to reparations for slavery—whether in the United States or elsewhere—is fraught with difficulty. By its nature, the law is a conservative tool when deployed in the struggle for social change, and courts are naturally cautious and skeptical of the property claims of the poor and marginalized, especially where such claims have the potential to upset legal precedent and reorder society.

The limitations imposed by rights language and the courts have not deterred advocates of reparations for slavery. Advocates have filed a number of lawsuits in the United States and Europe in pursuit of reparations. Caribbean states have threatened a lawsuit for reparations at the International Court of Justice at The Hague.[75] In 2004, a number of African Americans brought a class action lawsuit in Britain against Lloyds of London, the corporate insurance marketplace, claiming that it was culpable for genocide for insuring and financing slave ships.[76] The courts dismissed the case and rejected all appeals.[77] While there have been several actual and threatened lawsuits in other jurisdictions, the most sustained use of the courts for reparations for slavery has been in the United States. This partly reflects African Americans' progressive and persistent efforts and the perception that vindication and redress for slavery are possible within the American legal system. At various points in history, U.S. courts have made landmark rulings in the struggle for racial equality. In spite of many horrendous decisions, such as *Plessy v. Ferguson* (1896), several rulings of the U.S. Supreme Court, among them *Brown v. Board of Education* (1954) and *Grutter v. Bollinger* (2003),[78] buoy the narrative that U.S. courts can be one of the many useful sites in the struggle for racial justice. However, in spite of their reputed openness and accessibility, American courts have not looked at claims for reparations for slavery with favor.

Opponents of claims for reparations in general—and within the courts in particular—raise a number of objections. Since *Korematsu v. United States*, the 1944 case challenging the constitutionality of the executive order on the internment of Japanese Americans,[79] the courts have been an unreliable forum for the adjudication of race-based claims. In *Korematsu*, the court denied any legal claim for compensation. However, in the 1980s, the courts breathed new life into the reparations movement through *Korematsu* and *Hirabayashi v United States* in a writ of *coram nobis*.[80] A review of the original cases showed that the government had destroyed and suppressed key evidence that would have altered the outcome. Although the original Supreme Court *Korematsu* ruling has never been explicitly overturned, these latter cases established the validity of the legal claims for reparations and gave advocates more material for battle. This, together with the *Report of the Congressional Commission on Wartime Relocation and Internment of Civilians: Personal Justice Denied*, made possible the realization of reparations for Japanese Americans.[81] In other words, establishing a clear legal claim within the strictures of law, with living victims, and using the political process through a congressional commission was instrumental to the successful claims of Japanese Americans. The African American reparations movement no doubt looked to the Japanese American cases as precedent.

Framing reparations claims in legal jargon is fraught with peril. Opponents of reparations for African Americans for slavery try to use the law to defeat the claims. One argument is that civil rights and affirmative laws are sufficient to address social and racial inequities and provide African Americans equal opportunities to change their fortunes. Legal scholar Eric Yamamoto has captured well the narrow legal objections that opponents of reparations use: "They [opponents of reparations] argue the criminal law defense of lack of bad intent on the part of the wrongdoers; they assert the procedural bar of standing by claimants (the difficulty of identifying specific perpetrators and victims); they cite the lack of legal causation (specific acts causing specific injuries); and they cite the impossibility of calculating damages (or compensation)."[82]

Implicitly jettisoning white American responsibility for the enslavement of African Americans, these narrow traditional legal objections are supposed to be a complete bar to reparations. They reject collective responsibility by a demographic that has benefitted from the legacy of slavery.[83] No one captures these objections better than Eric A. Posner and Adrian Vermuele.[84] They reject collective moral taint and guilt for the evil of slavery.[85] They make these arguments in the face of overwhelming evidence that African Americans continue to suffer from the legacy of slavery, and that remedial measures such as affirmative action have failed to redress the institution's wrongs.[86] These common law paradigms and arguments are ill-suited to respond to deep historical social and economic injustices and inequities.[87] Others argue that reparations conceived as tangible racial restitution are simply an impossibility—because of the lack of specificity of the claims and claimants and the absence of political legitimacy.[88] The courts—like the scholars who object to legal redress for reparations—have been unyielding in their myopic application of the law and understanding of claims for reparations for slavery.

The few cases in U.S. courts have come up empty. In 2002, descendants of enslaved blacks filed several lawsuits in the United States. The lawsuits sought reparations from various U.S. corporations. The plaintiffs argued that the corporations (financial, textile, tobacco, insurance, and railroad) had either directly, or indirectly through their predecessors, enriched themselves unjustly through slavery and the transatlantic slave trade.[89] The courts consolidated the suits into one action. The district court dismissed the suit on the grounds that it raised a "political question" that the judiciary could not adjudicate, that the claimants lacked standing, and that the statute of limitations barred the claims.[90] In 2006, the U.S. Court of Appeals for the Seventh Circuit affirmed the lower court's ruling but reversed the dismissal of the plaintiffs' fraud claims; that is, whether the companies defrauded the plaintiffs by failing to disclose their collaboration with slavery.[91] The court dismissed the balance of the claims. In 2007, the U.S. Supreme Court ended the lawsuit when it declined to hear the case on appeal. Advocates have not mounted other major legal challenges for reparations in U.S. courts.

Apologies and Political Strategies

While courts have proven to be an unproductive forum for pressing reparations claims, the political arena seems to hold some limited promise. Advocates for reparations have been able to extract "apologies" or "expressions of regret" from some European countries and the United States. France recognized slavery as a crime against humanity in 2001 and has established the Slavery Remembrance Foundation.[92] In 2007, UK prime minister Tony Blair issued an official statement of apology for slavery.[93] In 2008, the U.S. House of Representatives passed a resolution apologizing for slavery and discriminatory laws.[94] The Senate followed suit in 2009.[95] However, these resolutions make no mention of reparations for slavery. In fact, both congressional resolutions explicitly reject in a disclaimer any authorization, support, or the idea of a settlement for reparations for slavery against the United States. It is empty rhetoric. The U.S. Congress has only considered one major bill on reparations for slavery. Rep. John Conyers introduced the "Commission to Study Reparation Proposals for African Americans Act" each year from 1989 until he retired in 2017.[96] The bill sought to establish a commission to study the impact of slavery and recommend reparations. His departure from Congress may put an end to further initiatives for reparations through legislation.

Conclusion

The West and the Arab world's enslavement and trade in Africans is one of the most egregious historical acts of inhumanity. People of African descent—in Africa and the African Diaspora—continue to suffer from the legacy of slavery and the associated abomination of colonialism. It is heartening that these two gross chapters of human history are being recognized, albeit slowly, for the brutalities they were. The abolition of chattel slavery, although pockets of it remain in the modern world, was a great advance. So is recognizing slavery as a crime against humanity and offering an apology for it. However, recognition of the evil and an apology are not enough. The world must address the legacy of slavery and colonialism directly. It will not suffice to employ cynical legalese to blunt the issue. Admittedly, it is a complicated and politically explosive question. Several things are clear: neither avoiding the issue nor putting up rhetorical roadblocks to reparations will work; the argument that slavery and the slave trade were legal when they took place will not hold water.

Advocates for reparations need to use all the available tools for advocacy. They need to bring their claims in multiple forums in several jurisdictions. They need to employ many strategies, including those that are legal, political, and educational.[97] They need a social movement drawn from all the continents where large numbers of people of African descent live. They need a unity of purpose. It is imperative that they agitate and organize in every facet of national and global life. The Kenyan Mau Mau case, in which the British provided restitution for their colonial atrocities, is a great study in coordination, persistence, and advocacy in the courts of law and the courts of public opinion. It was a tribute to the organizational abilities of Kenyan civil society and the mobilization of shame and public rage over the atrocities against the Mau Mau. The Kenyan case utilized academics to great effect. The works of leading scholars—in particular, Elkins's path-breaking *Imperial Reckoning*—were key to the advocacy by lawyers and civil society groups. More coordinated collaboration among advocacy groups, lawyers, and academics is necessary if the reparations movement is to gain wider acceptance. The settlement of the Mau Mau case and Britain's "expression of regret" set an important precedent. Reparations for slavery are a much more difficult challenge. However, the states against whom the claims are being made are the wealthiest and the most prosperous in the world. There is no defensible reason they cannot address this blight of history.

CHAPTER 2

Slavery, Universities, and Reparations

Adam Rothman

A remarkable gathering took place at Georgetown University in Washington, DC, on April 18, 2017. Leaders of the university and the Society of Jesus, along with descendants of people whom the Maryland Jesuits had owned and sold in the nineteenth century, joined together for a "Liturgy of Remembrance, Contrition, and Hope." Speaking to the hundreds assembled in Gaston Hall and many more watching remotely, Georgetown's president, John J. DeGioia, expressed "solemn contrition for our participation in slavery, and the benefit our institution received."[1] Father Tim Kesicki, SJ, the president of the Jesuit Conference of Canada and the United States, offered a heartfelt apology for the Jesuits' participation in the American slave economy. "We have greatly sinned," he declared.[2] Sandra Green Thomas, a member of the descendant community and president of the GU272 Descendants Association, spoke as well: "We the descendants return to our ancestors' homeplace, acknowledging contrition, offering forgiveness, hoping for penance, but more importantly, seeking justice for them and for ourselves."[3]

Recent investigations into the history of slavery at Georgetown and other universities have raised the question of the relationship between history and justice in a new and important way. Historians have been studying the history of slavery for a long time, but it is only fairly recently that we have trained our research on our own institutions, the places where we work and that pay our salaries.[4] This situation places a premium on not just academic freedom but also the active willingness of universities to support assiduous research into their own histories no matter where it leads. This introspection inevitably exposes deeply troubling occurrences, but much more troubling would be these institutions' refusal to recognize their history and confront its legacies.[5] Moreover, paying closer attention to our own universities' histories of slavery presents great opportunities for teaching and learning. This history is too important to be left to historians alone; it must be taken up by philosophers and theologians, economists and political scientists, and poets and dancers.

Since September 2015, I have been deeply involved in Georgetown's reckoning with its history of slavery. This essay reflects my personal experience, and I wish to make clear that I do not speak for or write on behalf of the university. Among all the universities that have examined their histories of slavery, Georgetown stands out because of the coalescence of a sizable descendant community that has made claims for reparations based on the historical harm that was done to ancestors to whom they can prove genealogical connections. It is a particularly vivid and instructive case, therefore, for thinking in concrete terms about the relationship between history and justice. Why reparations? Who should receive them? What form should they take?

Georgetown's President DeGioia launched a Working Group for Slavery, Memory, and Reconciliation at Georgetown at the start of the 2015–16 academic year and asked the Working Group to advise him "on how best to acknowledge and recognize Georgetown's historical relationship with the institution of slavery; examine and interpret the history of certain sites on our campus, to include Mulledy Hall; and convene events and opportunities for dialogue."[6] The immediate reason for the formation of the Working Group was the reopening of newly renovated Mulledy Hall. Rev. Thomas Mulledy, SJ, was a Jesuit priest who served as president of Georgetown in the 1830s and was the chief architect of the sale in 1838 of nearly three hundred people owned by the Maryland Jesuits. Some of the proceeds of that sale went to pull Georgetown College out of a crushing debt. President DeGioia knew this history already, and in the shadow of the shooting of Michael Brown in Ferguson, Missouri, in August 2014, the massacre in South Carolina at Charleston's Emanuel AME Church in June 2015, and spreading Black Lives Matter protests, a process of thoughtful reflection on Georgetown's own history of slavery and racism must have seemed to him like a good idea.

The Working Group was composed of sixteen people from across the university, including faculty, staff, and students. Several historians (including me) were members of the Working Group. The chair of the Working Group, David Collins, is both a historian and a Jesuit. There were two other Jesuit faculty members on the Working Group as well. One of the faculty members of the Working Group, the historian Marcia Chatelain, had been a graduate student at Brown University when its president, Ruth Simmons, initiated that school's pioneering Steering Committee on Slavery and Justice, which has been the model for so many other universities. Throughout the 2015–16 academic year, the Working Group conducted research and held events on campus to educate the university community about our history. Despite the fact that Georgetown's history of slavery had been studied by scholars for decades, written into the school's bicentennial history published in the 1990s, and even woven into the American Studies curriculum, few people on campus or elsewhere knew anything about it. Even members of the Working Group were surprised to learn the full extent of Georgetown's and the Jesuits' complicity in slavery. In short, Georgetown exemplifies all the ways that slavery shaped higher education in early America. Its history is closely tied to the growth of Catholicism in the colonial Chesapeake and the early United States. A basic understanding of this multifaceted history is the necessary starting point for grasping the significance of contemporary efforts to come to grips with its legacies.

Georgetown was founded by a Catholic elite in Maryland whose wealth was based on the labor of the enslaved people who worked their tobacco fields. The Society of Jesus had been in Maryland, a haven for English Catholics, since the founding of the colony in the 1630s. The Jesuits amassed thousands of acres of land and established several tobacco plantations to fund their activities. The earliest records of Jesuit slaveholding in Maryland date back to the 1710s, when Chesapeake planters famously switched from European indentured servants to captive Africans as the basis of their workforce, but the Jesuits were no strangers to slave labor. The Jesuits had been dealing in slaves across the Atlantic world since the 1500s, a practice they justified on the grounds that slavery was an instrument for the Christianization of heathen people.[7] By the 1830s, nearly three hundred enslaved people worked on several Jesuit-managed plantations in southern Maryland whose profits were supposed to subsidize the education of white boys and men. It didn't quite work out that way, since the Jesuit plantations were never very profitable. Their most profitable activity was probably the selling of people whose labor they no longer needed. After a long debate spanning two decades, the Jesuits decided to get out of the business of running plantations with slave labor. In 1838, Rev. Mulledy (who was then the leader of the Maryland Province) sold nearly the entire Maryland Jesuit slave community to two Louisiana planters, Henry Johnson and Jesse Batey, for $115,000. Depending on how one counts, that sum is the equivalent of somewhere between $3.2 million and $1.5 billion in today's money.[8]

Enslaved people also worked on Georgetown's campus from the time it opened in 1789 until emancipation in Washington, DC, in 1862. One of the first enslaved workers was a woman named Sukey.[9] The last was Aaron Edmonson; the twelve dollars he earned each month went to his owner, Ann Green, who also was paid $109.50 by the federal government when Edmonson was freed.[10] The government compensated Washington, DC, owners for the loss of their human property, but nobody repaid the former slaves for the robbery of the fruits of their labor. The presence of enslaved people on campus was at times substantial. In 1814, for example, 12 slaves lived on campus out of 102 people—one in every ten people was enslaved.[11] They were owned by the Jesuits or rented from students' families or local owners in the neighborhood of Georgetown. They worked as carpenters, valets, maids, and cooks. Billy the Blacksmith was buried in the Old College Ground in 1817.[12] His bones and those of hundreds of others have probably turned to dust deep under Georgetown's Reiss Science Building, built in the 1950s.

Faculty and students at Georgetown gave moral legitimacy to the slave economy by accepting it in their daily routine and, what's more, actively endorsing it. The college's Philodemic Society held several debates about slavery in the antebellum era, usually (though not always) supporting the proslavery side.[13] In this, they followed the lead of Father James Ryder, SJ, the founder of the Philodemic, who publicly condemned abolitionism in an 1835 speech in Richmond, Virginia. "God is a God of order," he declared.[14] Georgetown tilted sharply toward the Confederacy during the U.S. Civil War, with a strong majority of students and alumni who fought in the war doing so on the Confederate side. The original ethos of Georgetown, the Jesuits, and the Catholic Church in the antebellum United States was, in a word, proslavery. Georgetown's school colors, blue and gray, were adopted in 1876 as an emblem of sectional reconciliation after the war. Whether students today know it or not, the gray represents the Confederacy.[15] The layers of irony are thick, because the school colors were adopted at a time when the school's president, Rev. Patrick Healy, SJ, was a man who had been born into slavery in Georgia, risen up through the ranks of the Jesuit order, and "passed" as white. There were no black undergraduates at Georgetown until 1950, when the School of Foreign Service admitted Samuel Halsey Jr.[16]

Georgetown was built on the backs of enslaved people. The school is not alone in this regard. As Craig Wilder has shown, and other scholars continue to elaborate, most other American schools that date back to the colonial era, including the Ivy League as well as southern schools, are implicated one way or another in the transatlantic slave economy and regimes of racist knowledge that it spawned. Nor is Georgetown alone in reckoning with its history. As is well known, many other schools, beginning with Brown University more than a decade ago, are engaged in similar efforts to wrestle with their histories of slavery. The Universities Studying Slavery consortium, initiated by the University of Virginia, now has more than fifty member institutions, including schools in Canada, Ireland, and the United Kingdom—most recently as I write this, the University of Glasgow.[17] What is behind this international movement? These efforts, it seems to me, arise out of the demands by black students for recognition of the legitimacy of their place in their universities and deeper understanding of the roots and persistence of racism in the bastions of higher education. Confronting the history of slavery and its legacies is not merely or even mostly about the past; it's about the present and future.[18]

The "dialogue" that President DeGioia launched at Georgetown took off in unexpected directions in the 2015–16 academic year. Student protests in the fall forced a renaming of the buildings named after the Jesuit priests who orchestrated the slave community sale, Thomas Mulledy and William McSherry.[19] The Georgetown Memory Project, an independent nonprofit organization founded by Georgetown alumnus Richard Cellini, began to identify and track down descendants of the Maryland Jesuit slave community, commonly known as the GU272 (a term that originated as a social media hashtag during the student protests in the fall). And the *New York Times* took an interest in what was going on, publishing a major story in April 2016 with the headline: "272 Slaves Were Sold to Save Georgetown. What Does It Owe Their Descendants?" Written by Rachel Swarns, the article was one of the *Times*'s most-read articles of 2016. It elevated Georgetown's reckoning with the history of slavery to national significance and raised the controversial issue of reparations. The genealogical research of the Georgetown Memory Project, combined with the intense interest spurred by the *New York Times*'s story, created a new constituency in the living descendants of the GU272.[20]

The Working Group submitted its report to President DeGioia in May 2016, and after visiting members of the GU272 descendant community over the summer, President DeGioia released it to the university community in

September at a public gathering in Gaston Hall in which he pledged to carry out many of its recommendations.[21] At the conclusion of that event, several representatives from the descendant community rose from the audience to read aloud a declaration announcing their intent to pursue reconciliation while insisting upon having a seat at the table. "Nothing about us without us," said Joseph Stewart.[22] Stewart's idea of reconciliation took shape over the next few days as he and other descendants outlined a vision for a $1 billion foundation whose goals would be worked out in collaboration with Georgetown, the Jesuits, and other academic and philanthropic institutions.[23]

Although a $1 billion foundation has not yet materialized, Georgetown has taken steps to acknowledge its history of slavery through symbolic gestures of apology and memorialization. The university renamed Mulledy Hall after Isaac Hawkins, the first enslaved person listed in the 1838 articles of agreement between Thomas Mulledy and the buyers from Louisiana. Isaac Hawkins was the patriarch of the large and multigenerational Hawkins family, which lived at the Jesuit plantation of White Marsh in what is today Bowie, Maryland. It appears that Isaac Hawkins himself, who was in his sixties, remained behind at White Marsh while his family made the long voyage to Louisiana.[24] McSherry Hall was renamed after Anne Marie Becraft, a free woman of color who opened a school for black girls in the neighborhood of Georgetown in the early nineteenth century, and went on to become a nun.[25] Nevertheless, the demarcation of historical sites connected to slavery on campus remains incomplete. There are signs identifying Isaac Hawkins Hall and Anne Marie Becraft Hall but no physical markers that explain who they were or why they are significant. The location of the old college burial ground, where many free and enslaved people of color were once buried, remains unmarked. And few are aware that Georgetown's first student, William Gaston, for whom Gaston Hall is named, was himself a slave owner who wrote important opinions having to do with slavery and the rights of free people of color when he was a justice on North Carolina's supreme court.[26]

Georgetown has devoted resources to research and teaching about its history of slavery. I now teach a class in the American Studies Program called "Facing Georgetown's History." Colleagues in fields as diverse as art history, film studies, government, performing arts, and theology have taken up Georgetown's history of slavery in their own classes in exciting ways. For example, students in a class on African American art and culture came up with a proposal for a permanent campus memorial to the GU272.[27] The university supports the online Georgetown Slavery Archive (https://slaveryarchive.george town.edu/), a digital repository of archival materials relating to slavery, Georgetown, and the Maryland Jesuits. This ongoing project, which I direct, involves undergraduate and graduate students and postdoctoral researchers in making archival material accessible to the public. My own hope is that the Georgetown Slavery Archive will be useful not just to scholars, teachers, and students, but also to people researching their own family histories back to the Maryland Jesuit slave community in the eighteenth and nineteenth centuries. Writing in *The American Archivist*, the journal of the Society of American Archivists, Anne Robinson-Sweet argues that "the creation of the digital archives itself serves as a reparative mechanism by making the full history of one of the United States' most prestigious universities widely available and known."[28]

The emergence of the GU272 descendant community has been the most striking aspect of Georgetown's reckoning with its history of slavery. In the last two years, hundreds of living descendants of the GU272 have learned of their family trees dating back to the Maryland Jesuit slave community and the 1838 sale. The Georgetown Memory Project identified hundreds of living people as descendants, while many others have arrived at this self-knowledge through their own genealogical research and curiosity. The descendants' family stories are a microcosm of the whole African American experience. These families—the Hawkinses, Butlers, Scotts, Queens, and many others—formed over generations in the tobacco fields of Maryland. Some of the Maryland Jesuits' slaves sued for their freedom in the late 1790s and early 1800s in Maryland and Washington, DC, courts and won.[29] Others would remain behind in Maryland as their kinfolk were shipped to the cane and cotton fields of Louisiana in 1838. Those banished to the Deep South managed to endure. Family, faith, land, and education kept them together. In the late nineteenth century, members of the GU272 community donated their own land to the Catholic Church in Louisiana to create a school for black children.[30] Even today, there is a little town about thirty minutes outside of Baton Rouge called Maringouin, where several hundred GU272 descendants remain. Some of them still own the land that their forebears once worked in bondage. Others migrated from central Louisiana throughout the twentieth century and are now dispersed across the United States.

An unusually rich archival record documents the history of the Mary- land Jesuit slave community and their descendants. Few African Americans have access to the kind of documentation of their family histories dating back to the era of slavery that is available to the descendants of the GU272. Some who have come to Georgetown's campus have had the bittersweet experience of seeing in person the old, fragile baptismal registers and bills of sale in which their ancestors' names are scrawled. These records, along with additional archival materials scattered across Maryland and Louisiana, enable people to trace their family trees across the rupture of the domestic slave trade, overcoming what the sociologist Orlando Patterson has called the "natal alienation" that characterizes slavery.[31] Yet the documentation is incomplete, and many people fall through its cracks. Genetic testing has helped to identify possible family ties where archival documentation is lacking, and today members of the GU272 descendant community continue to discover new "cousins" using the tools of the digital age, including Ancestry.com and Facebook, along with traditions such as community gatherings and family reunions. A community that was divided in 1838 is being reunited.[32]

While these reunions take place, the descendants are also forging a new relationship with Georgetown and the Society of Jesus. The events of April 18, 2017, were an early milestone, not a finish line. The university has granted "legacy status" to descendants, which places them on the same footing as the children of faculty, staff, and alumni for the purpose of undergraduate admission. The first GU272 descendants have now matriculated at Georgetown, and more will surely come in the years ahead. (I had the pleasure of teaching two of them during the 2017–18 academic year, including Mélisande Short-Colomb, who, at sixty-three, is the oldest first-year student in Georgetown's history.[33]) While meaningful to those who benefit from it, legacy status is a very modest gesture and one that tacitly accepts a system of privilege that normally disfavors African Americans. A "need-blind/full-need" school, Georgetown provides financial aid for needy students that descendants who matriculate can benefit from, as well as good programs to help poor and first-generation students thrive at the school, but advocates of material reparations argue that these policies and programs are insufficient. The vast majority of living descendants will never attend Georgetown, and legacy status does not help them.[34]

What would? Members of the GU272 descendant community have offered specific ideas that go far beyond what Georgetown's Working Group proposed. Joseph Stewart has not given up on the idea of a billion-dollar foundation. Some have called for a separate scholarship fund for descendants who attend Georgetown that would help them pay not just for college but also for graduate school. A broader demand is that Georgetown and the Society of Jesus do more to expand educational opportunities for descendants who do not want to attend Georgetown or who may not have the educational credentials to qualify for admission. Georgetown and the Jesuits could offer tutoring and college-prep programs to descendants; provide scholarships for descendants who want to attend college or graduate school at other Jesuit and Catholic schools or Historically Black Colleges and Universities (HBCUs); and support adult literacy and lifelong learning programs for older descendants.[35]

While it may seem apt for a school that benefited from slavery to repay its debts in the coin of educational opportunity, other descendants argue that what they are owed is not educational opportunity but money in their pockets. For example, a lawyer for one descendant organization, the 272 Legacy of Isaac Hawkins, proposed that the university create "a reasonable fund for the unpaid labor of their enslaved ancestors, the restoration of a lost inheritance."[36] There does not appear to be any consensus within the descendant community about what form reparations should take, or even if descendants should be seeking material reparations for themselves at all. Speaking to journalist Noel King of NPR's *Planet Money* in 2017, GU272 descendant and Louisianian Debra Tilson suggested that seeking reparations from Georgetown could set a precedent that might upset things in Maringouin, where GU272 descendants live next door to the descendants of the people who bought and owned their ancestors. If Georgetown paid reparations, Tilson asks, "So now do I go over and I ask them—say, hey, look, Georgetown paid me off for them selling me, but what about you owning me?"[37] As I write this, representatives of the GU272 descendant community and the leadership of Georgetown University and the Society of Jesus have been participating in meetings facilitated by the Kellogg Foundation in the hope of finding common ground.[38]

In the meantime, Georgetown students have taken matters into their own hands. Frustrated by the university administration's hesitation to fulfill many of the recommendations of the Working Group's report, a group of students (including GU272 descendants now attending the school) committed to the idea of material reparations for slavery formed a Students for GU272 advocacy group on campus and launched an ambitious campaign. Working through Georgetown's established student government, the Students for GU272 successfully lobbied for a referendum that would allow all Georgetown undergraduates to vote for or against a new student activity fee or "Reconciliation Contribution" of $27.20 per semester to create a fund administered by a board of students and GU272 descendants to support programs that would directly benefit the descendants of people owned by the Maryland Jesuits. After a frenzied few weeks of organizing and debate, the referendum passed on April 11, 2019. A record 57.9 percent of students voted, and two-thirds voted in favor of the referendum. It was a landmark victory for reparations. Still, the ultimate outcome remains uncertain. The vote does not establish a university policy, and the Board of Directors must approve of the fee for it to be implemented. Our story ends, for now, on a cliffhanger.[39]

As with the rest of Georgetown and the Maryland Jesuits' history of slavery, the debate over reparations on campus is a microcosm of something broader. The campus debate featured classic arguments on both sides. Supporters of the referendum argued that Georgetown students enjoy the benefit of their school having been saved by the sale of human beings, which imposes a moral responsibility to acknowledge the fact and provide redress to the descendants of those who were harmed by the act and who continue to suffer from the persistent legacies of slavery.[40] Although many of the opponents of the referendum acknowledged that the university and the Society of Jesus have a responsibility to atone for the sins of the past, they argued that students should not be compelled to bear the burden, especially at a time when tuition is already astronomically high.[41] At a student-organized town hall that I attended before the vote, the main point of contention was whether students on financial aid would have to pay the fee. Opponents argued that imposing a mandatory fee was unfair to students who were already struggling to afford college, while supporters argued that students on financial aid would either not have to pay or might be willing to do so. Some international students and black students also wondered why they should have to pay—the former because slavery is not their history, and the latter because it is. After the vote, one perceptive undergraduate told me that the referendum won because of effective organizers who convinced their fellow Georgetown students to come down on the "right side of history."

The case of Georgetown, the Jesuits, and the GU272 discussed here differs from some of the other cases in this volume because Georgetown and the Jesuits are not state actors. Here it is particular institutions of civil society—a school and a religious order—that are being called to account for historical wrongs that their predecessors committed. Yet the state was not absent. Slavery was legal at the time when Rev. Mulledy sold the Jesuits' slaves from Maryland to Louisiana, and the complex machinery of local, state, and national government was essential to the transaction. Public documents (tax, customs, notarial, and court records) comprise an archival paper trail that sheds light on the history of the GU272 and reveals how the government authorized, facilitated, regulated, and recorded the commercial transactions of a slave society.[42] Thus, while it is important to recognize the history of particular private agents in the U.S. slave economy and to hold them accountable, it is equally important to recognize the public dimensions of their activities. Slavery was a national wrong with countless local manifestations. Will Georgetown and the Jesuits become a scapegoat for this vast history? Or will they craft an agenda of reparations and reconciliation in tandem with the GU272 descendant community that provides a model for others and the country as a whole? After all, whether African American citizens of the United States receive reparations for slavery (or postslavery forms of racism) should not be based on their ability to trace their genealogy back to a particular enslaver.

It is not difficult to understand the appeal of campaigns for local or microreparations at a time when seeking reparations at the level of national politics appears quixotic. (Indeed, one conclusion that may be drawn from historian Ana Lucia Araujo's recent study of reparations over the long haul is that such a politics has always failed to deliver tangible results.[43]) It may seem easier to call upon Georgetown and the Jesuits, or other schools, churches, and corporations, to provide reparations for their well-documented complicity in slavery than to beat one's head against the brick wall of American politics. For nearly three decades, until his resignation in 2017, Rep. John Conyers repeatedly introduced H.R. 40, a bill to create a commission to study reparations, to no avail.[44] Student activism, national media attention, and effective advocacy from the descendants might compel a private school with a progressive self-image like Georgetown to take steps toward a more robust program of material reparations. On the other hand, a glance at the profile of Georgetown's Board of Directors suggests that the odds of this actually happening are low. Are the business leaders who oversee the university likely to accede to grand visions of material reparations, or even a small student fee approved by a large majority of the students in a democratic vote?

Whether or not the students' and descendants' efforts to secure greater reparations from Georgetown and the Jesuits succeeds, some real good has already come out of the effort to research and publicize this history and wrestle with its implications today. It has drawn attention to the importance of slavery in the history of American education and religion. It has changed the

landscape of historical memory at Georgetown and other Catholic and Jesuit schools and inspired other similar research projects.[45] These efforts have
enriched historical memory rather than erasing it. Hundreds of African
Americans now have a deeper understanding of their family histories than
they ever imagined was possible, and the discoveries of the GU272 have in
turn inspired other people to look into their own genealogies. As GU272 descendant and former high school principal Cheryllyn Branche has written,
this can be a "painful process of discovery" but also a meaningful one.[46] It
has provided a real-world example of the possibilities and tensions of reconciliation over and reparation for slavery. The students' vote on the GU272 referendum has garnered national and international media attention at a
moment when the issue of reparations has re-entered U.S. politics.[47] One
important lesson of this history is to show how economic self-interest has de-
formed the moral sense in the past. Georgetown's President DeGioia, who is
a moral philosopher by training, has argued for using this history to expand
our "moral imagination" beyond that of our predecessors and achieve progress.[48] One can always hope.

CHAPTER 3

"Free Citizens of This Nation": Cherokee Slavery, Descendants of Freedpeople, and Possibilities for Repair

Tiya Miles

Captain Shoe Boots was a man famed for boldness and braggadocio in the early nineteenth-century world of the Cherokee Nation. He was known as a war hero, a social carouser, and a colorful dresser who favored a British military coat and the tasseled boots that inspired one of his many names. After bringing glory to himself in the fierce U.S. battle against Creek "rebels" in 1813–14 during which Cherokee elites fought alongside Andrew Jackson as allies to quash resistance to American influence in Creek territory, Shoe Boots also became known as "Crowing Cock." While his fellow Cherokee farmers and warriors, as well as statesmen who orchestrated governmental affairs in the tribe, admired Shoe Boots for his brash bravery and flamboyant personal style of dress, they distinctly disapproved of an unusual action the captain had taken prior to the Redstick War. Near the turn of the nineteenth century, on his riverside farm located on land that now falls within the state boundaries of Georgia, Shoe Boots had begun a sexual relationship with an enslaved Black adolescent girl. Shoe Boots owned this young woman, whose name was Doll (also spelled Daull). He had acquired her through trade, and, over time, as his mid-sized farm prospered on the fertile, riverine soil, he would come to own several Black people: women, men, and children. Five of these individuals were Shoe Boots's own children, born to and mothered by Doll, who was never freed by Shoe Boots and would grow into old age held as property within the post–Indian Removal borders of the Cherokee Nation in present-day eastern Oklahoma.[1]

Shoe Boots's ownership of Black slaves was not the cause for concern among his high-status circle of warriors, planters, and statesmen. Small numbers of the growing Cherokee political and economic elite had begun to take up the practice of racial slavery in the late 1700s and would intensify their commitment to holding people as property in the coming decades. Shoe Boots's intimate relationship with a woman he claimed as his property was also a matter that, while not encouraged, might have been quietly overlooked by his peers. Rather, it was Shoe Boots's formal request to have his children become "free citizens of this nation" that stirred anxiety among his fellows and caused swift social recriminations as well as a legal backlash. With the aid of a Protestant missionary to whom he dictated his words, Shoe Boots submitted a petition to the Cherokee Chiefs in Council in the autumn of 1824. The emotional appeal revealed Shoe Boots's predicament. He explained with a tone of shame and urgency:

> Being in possession of a few Black People and being crost in my affections, I debased myself and took one of my Black women by the name of Daull, by her I have had these children named as follows, the oldest Elizabeth about the age of Seventeen, the next the name of John about the age of Eleven, the next the name of Polly about the age of Seven years. These is the only Children I have as Citizens of this Nation, and as the time I may be called on to die is uncertain, My desire is to have them as free citizens of this nation. Knowing what property I may have, is to be divided amongst the Best of my friends, how can I think of them having bone of my bone and flesh of my flesh to be called their property, and this by my imprudent conduct, and for them and their offspring to suffer for generations yet unborn, is a thought of too great a magnitude for me to remain silent any longer. I therefore humbly petition your honors that you may pass a resolution . . . to carry into execution my desires.[2]

In response to this uncomfortable appeal, the male members of the Cherokee governing body, most of them slaveholders, granted Shoe Boots's wish for the freedom and tribal belonging of his daughters and son while admonishing the petitioner to "cease begetting any more Children with his said slave *woman*." Three weeks later, the Cherokee legislators passed a law making intermarriage with Blacks illegal and punishable by fifty-nine lashes in the case of male offenders and twenty-five lashes in the case of female offenders. The chiefs granted Shoe Boots a pass for his indiscretions, but did not wish to see further examples of Cherokee Indian citizens pressing for slave emancipations and rights.[3]

Shoe Boots's petition and the Cherokee government's panicked reaction to it illustrate that Black presence and Black-red interracial sexual relations were not necessarily viewed as threats by Cherokee leaders, unless such occurrences led to demands for social visibility and political inclusion for Afro-Cherokees. *Citizenship* was the rub as well as the crux in this case. In Shoe Boots's expressed understanding, citizenship status had to be conferred along with freedom in order to guarantee his children's future security in Cherokee society. Shoe Boots was Cherokee, he saw his children as Cherokee, and he wanted them to be defined and viewed fully as such by other members of the Cherokee Nation. Shoe Boots's sisters, Peggy and Tekasteskee, also viewed Shoe Boots's children with Doll as Cherokee people, as did many neighbors in their local community. The couple's daughters, Elizabeth and Polly, married into Cherokee families and were integrated into Indigenous households. The couple's eldest son, John, suffered a more precarious fate. He was captured and sold during the tumultuous Georgia gold rush of 1829 and later escaped to California. Following Shoe Boots's death, the couple's youngest sons, William and Lewis, twins conceived after the 1824 emancipation decision, never received freedom or Cherokee citizenship despite their paternal aunts' impassioned plea before the Cherokee Council. William Shoeboots settled into an African American community in Kansas following the Civil War, while Lewis was lost to slavery and the historical record. When William returned to Indian Territory in the 1880s in order to apply for Cherokee citizenship, he was rejected because Shoe Boots, his father, had died before the creation of the Dawes Allotment Roll, the base census used for determining enrollment in the Cherokee Nation. Although this rejection was not explicitly tied to race, it stemmed from the family's hazardous historical position that had been characterized by enslavement rooted in racial categorization and compulsory mobility.[4]

Slavery and growing anti-Black prejudice fractured the fragile family unit created through the coercive intimacies of Shoe Boots and Doll. Shoe Boots's petition and its outcome: a begrudgingly bestowed freedom attached to social shaming and legal prohibition, captures the marginal situation of many people of African-Native descent defined as slaves or former slaves of

Cherokees. As the decades turned, Cherokee freedpeople, some of mixed-race Cherokee ancestry, all of bicultural Cherokee and African-descended heritage, would come to occupy a precarious place within the Cherokee nation-state.

The meaning of civic belonging for Blacks in the United States has been muddied and contested over the last century and a half. The long shadow of slavery, the legal and social imprint of Jim Crow segregation, and the stains of racial bias and violence have guaranteed such contestation. Within the Cherokee Nation, where approximately 1,600 people of African descent were possessed as slaves in 1835, and 4,000 were held in 1860 just prior to the U.S. Civil War, the contest over citizenship is even more vexed due to overlapping histories of settler colonialism and slavery. In the U.S. Supreme Court decision *Cherokee Nation v. Georgia* (1831), Chief Justice John Marshall defined the Cherokee Nation as a "domestic dependent nation" with a relationship to the United States resembling that of a "ward to his guardian."[5] Located within the jurisdiction of the self-proclaimed ruling colonial power that was the U.S. federal government, the Cherokee Nation would have to push against the confines of its assigned "dependency" in order to express political autonomy. Through this judicial ruling, which composed part of the famous "Marshall Trilogy" of cases underpinning much of federal Indian law, the Cherokee Nation was made subject to the United States. Like the United States, its imperial overlord, the Cherokee Nation had legalized Black slavery. Enslaved people *within* the Cherokee Nation were therefore subject to their Cherokee owners, the Cherokee Nation, and the U.S. federal government. This violently enmeshed relationship meant that, after the United States and the Cherokee Nation each abolished slavery as a result of the American Civil War, Black people in the Cherokee Nation would be located in a liminal legal as well as social space, and trapped in the morass of Cherokee and American arguments about the scope and limits of tribal sovereignty in a "post"-colonial era. And as recent and new scholarship is continuing to unveil, this vexed situation has parallels among all of the southern native nations that adopted racial slavery: the Creeks, Choctaws, Chickasaws, and Seminoles.[6]

Officials of the Cherokee Nation responded to the newly freed Black population with both formal acceptance and felt resentment. Following the Civil War, in which the Cherokee Nation had eventually sided with the Confederacy after at first attempting to maintain neutrality, the Cherokee Nation entered into a peace agreement with the United States known as the

Treaty of 1866. This was in essence a document of surrender for the Cherokee Nation, which repudiated a previous treaty with the Confederate states
and conceded to U.S. federal power in particular domains. In Article 9, The
Treaty of 1866 dictated the abolition of slavery (already effectively ended by
the Cherokee Emancipation Acts of 1863) and the inclusion of formerly enslaved people in the citizenry. Upon pressure from the U.S. treaty negotiators, Cherokee representatives agreed to adopt people of African descent
whom they had formerly enslaved, bestowing upon this group designated
"freedmen" as well as their "descendants": "all the rights of native Cherokees."[7] Though Cherokee acceptance of this stipulation in the Treaty of 1866
was not enthusiastically granted, it should be noted that other governing bodies among the five slaveholding tribes did not adhere to this requirement
quickly or at all.[8] The Cherokee Nation set aside two residential districts for
their former bondspeople, who were granted land but at the same time relegated to racially segregated communities. In addition to access to common
lands, freedpeople in the Cherokee Nation also had immediate political representation in the Cherokee Council since representatives were elected by district. And as the economic historian Melinda Miller found through a
comparison of Cherokee freedpeople and American former slaves in the
U.S. South, Cherokee freedmen and women did better economically during Reconstruction and after in large part due to landed resources.[9] After
the passage of the Dawes Allotment Act in 1887 and the Curtis Act in 1898,
when the U.S. government compelled Cherokees to divide communal lands
into separate lots attached to individual households, African-descended freedpeople received allotments as well. As one descendant, journalist Kenneth
Cooper explained, "Our great-grandmother Florence Rogers . . . is listed
as a Cherokee Freedman on that census, the Dawes Roll. . . . Like every en-
rollee, she received 160 acres. . . . Her oldest children got land too."[10] The predicament of formerly enslaved people in Cherokee society was arguably both
better and worse than that of Blacks in the United States: Cherokee freedmen and women had greater economic opportunity; they enjoyed political
representation longer than formerly enslaved African Americans (whose
political opportunities plummeted after the conclusion of Congressional Reconstruction); and they were less subject to vigilante racial violence. At the
same time, freedpeople in the Cherokee Nation existed in a double marginal
zone, and hence occupied an extremely vulnerable position as a racially
marked minority population within a colonized "domestic dependent" Indigenous nation.

Over time, as the Cherokee government's commitment to freedpeoples' already tenuous inclusion diminished, especially regarding federal disbursements tied to the sale of a large parcel of land known as the Cherokee Outlet, freedmen and women found themselves left behind by both the Cherokee and U.S. governments, neither of which saw Black Cherokee travails as political priorities. As historians Celia Naylor, Daniel F. Littlefield, and Fay Yarbrough have shown, Cherokee freedpeople by necessity began organizing for political inclusion and a share of federal disbursements promised to other Cherokee citizens during the decades following the Civil War. They launched what has become a transgenerational struggle to retain, exercise, and then regain citizenship rights carried out now by active members of a descendant population estimated at nearly three thousand people.[11]

More than a century after the conclusion of the Civil War, descendants of Cherokee freedpeople, often called "Black Indians" in popular parlance, faced a blatant rebuke to their national belonging. In 1983, freedmen and women descendants who attempted to vote in a tribal election and were turned away from the polls discovered that Cherokee government officials had made an adjustment to the Cherokee National Code that undercut Article 9 of the Treaty of 1866. Because these individuals did not fall under the racialized category of "Cherokee by blood," a new stipulation for citizenship added in the 1970s, freedmen and women descendants no longer had the rights of suffrage. Following this rude awakening, a series of heated political and legal battles have been waged at the Cherokee local and national and U.S. national levels over the citizenship status of these descendants of people owned as slaves in the Cherokee Nation of Oklahoma. Descendants and their allies launched a series of law suits in U.S. and Cherokee courts pressing for a reassessment of their exclusion. Legal challenges to the revocation of freedpeople descendants' citizenship status surged in 1997 and 2004 with membership appeals brought to the Cherokee courts by Bernice Rogers Riggs and Lucy Allen, both women with documented Cherokee ancestry. Although Riggs's case that was based on proving her blood relationship to Cherokees did not succeed (because her Cherokee ancestors appeared on documents other than the Dawes Roll, the only acceptable census for citizenship), Lucy Allen's case, which questioned the legality of the change to Cherokee enrollment procedures, did gain traction.[12]

Allen v. Cherokee Nation Tribal Council et al., filed by Cherokee citizen David Cornsilk on behalf of Lucy Allen, resulted in a 2006 Cherokee Supreme Court decision rendering the late twentieth-century "by blood" requirement unconstitutional.[13] Leaders on the Cherokee Council disagreed with the majority opinion of the court, written by Justice Stacy L. Leeds, and launched an effort to amend the Cherokee constitution of 1975 in order to legalize the "by blood" stipulation. In 2007, the contest over freedmen and women descendants' place in the nation reached a fevered pitch when then principal chief Chadwick Smith, a vocal opponent of inclusion, called for the voters to decide whether descendants should be deemed citizens. Chief Smith argued in a Cherokee Council meeting that land allotments during the Dawes era had constituted "slave reparations" for freedpeople, whose progeny should now be cut off from access to social services and electoral rights, the debt having been paid. As the anthropologist Circe Sturm has astutely pointed out, this argument was spurious. All enrolled Cherokee citizens received allotments. Formerly enslaved people and their children saw no special land benefits in recognition of their stolen labors and emotional sufferings. Nevertheless, Smith succeeded in his bid to circumvent the court ruling by way of a popular vote.[14]

The campaign leading up to the 2007 Cherokee Nation special election on the freedmen issue was contentious. While some citizens (defined as those with a lineal ancestor on the Dawes "Cherokee by blood" roll) supported the descendants' cause, others accepted the racial definition of Cherokeeness as blood derived and saw these claimants as non-Indians who should not be entitled to suffrage or services provided for tribal members. Biased and inflammatory commentary lowered the level of public debate, as past and present Cherokee Council members as well as private citizens insisted that freedmen and women descendants were merely "black" people aiming for economic gain (i.e., welfare hand-outs) and insinuated that the freedmen population posed a sexual threat to Cherokee women. The "by blood" supporters prevailed in public debate as well as the voting booth. The referendum resulted in a constitutional amendment ratifying the civic expulsion of approximately 2,800 freedmen and women descendants. Led by Marilyn Vann, a descendant of the extended family of one of the wealthiest Cherokee slaveholders, James Vann, and president of the Descendants of Freedmen of the Five Civilized Tribes Association, the expelled members responded by heightening their strategy of public protest and legal appeals.[15]

Representatives of the U.S. government responded swiftly to the Cherokee government's action. Officials of the Bureau of Indian Affairs of the Department of the Interior fired off a letter to Cherokee Nation leadership stating that federal approval was required for constitutional revisions and that the descendants' citizenship could not be unilaterally withdrawn. The Black Congressional Caucus defended the descendants' cause and devised financial means to pressure the Cherokee Nation. Rep. Diane Watson, a Democrat from California, introduced legislation to block $300 million in federal funds to the Cherokees, and Rep. Melvin Watts, a Democrat from North Carolina, submitted an amendment to the federal housing bill to withhold funding from the Indigenous nation. The Department of Housing and Urban Development then suspended disbursement of more than $37 million that would have been distributed to the Cherokee government.[16] The national political and cultural press followed the story, tending to cover the escalating conflict between the Cherokee government and the federal government in a tone critical of the Cherokee decision.[17]

In this fraught political and media environment, the heated arguments leveled for and against freedpeople descendants' inclusion in the Cherokee Nation became mired in a rhetorical battle framed as Black civil rights versus Native sovereign rights. Government officials in the Cherokee Nation, the National Congress of American Indians, and opinion writers and cartoonists in the American Indian press vociferously defended Cherokee sovereignty and lambasted what they saw as a revocation of the U.S. trust relationship with Native tribes and a diminishment of the Cherokee state's sovereign right to determine its own membership. Freedmen and women descendants insisted that their place in the Cherokee Nation is rooted in ancestral kinship ties, a shared cultural past, and especially the Treaty of 1866, which guaranteed them the rights of full membership. As the journalist and descendant Kenneth Cooper put it: "We do have blood Cherokee ancestry too, as my research has found in the tribe's own records. . . . I and my close relatives want our Cherokee citizenship. It is our birthright."[18]

Native American intellectuals and legal scholars of Native and non-Native ancestry entered this public disagreement carefully but conscientiously, seeking to burst the bubble of U.S. innocence in the affair, to expose the fiction of Cherokee racial homogeneity, to challenge the view that sovereignty should stand as an uninterrogated category, and to destabilize the notion that Cherokee and Cherokee freedmen and women's interests must be oppositional. Chickasaw literary theorist Jodi Byrd astutely and provocatively charges that the accusations of anti-Black racism leveled against Cherokees by the press and members of Congress in this public debate placed Cherokee people in a double (post)-colonial bind in which their historical acquiescence to demands for "civilization" (as demonstrated through owning slaves and building capital) morphs into evidence of their contemporary savagery. Writes Byrd: "In its projection of itself as civilized and civilizing, the United States propagates the fiction that the U.S. has already resolved these issues by sanctioning the Cherokees for their racism and participation in slavery. In the process, the Cherokee Nation, once civilized and now slaveholding, is rewritten back into the discourses of savagery as Congress chastises them for violating the rule of law."[19] Byrd argues that the brutal battle over race and belonging in Cherokee country had become a national spectacle allowing America's own unfinished business of granting equality and reparations for the descendants of enslaved Blacks to be projected onto Cherokees. The United States was itself a country that had encouraged Cherokee slaveholding historically and excluded African Americans for generations following the Civil War.

Ojibwe literary scholar Scott Richard Lyons published an op-ed in *Indian Country Today* that undercuts the merits of the Cherokee Nation's "by blood" requirement by highlighting the racial complexity of the Cherokee populace determined in part by the Cherokee Nation's own treaty-making decisions in the past. Lyons asserts: "For well over a century the Cherokee Nation has been a multiracial nation, one whose sovereignty rests largely upon treaty-based relationships with others," and he urges the Cherokee Nation to protect "its hard-won national identity" by upholding treaty agreements. Osage literary scholar Robert Allen Warrior focuses on ethics in an opinion piece in *News from Indian Country*, asserting that "the moral case against the Cherokees is straightforward" and urging "Native American writers, scholars and artists, not to mention elected leaders, presidents, and chiefs to stand up and be counted on the right side of this moral question." Legal scholar Lolita Buckner Inniss argues that racial categorization has been used as a tool in "the sovereign's exercise of power over populations." Just as the Cherokee Nation has been victim of this tool at the hands of the United States, Inniss suggests, as a sovereign state, the Cherokee Nation could abuse the tool as well. Anthropologist Circe Sturm significantly refines explanations of the way in which sovereignty and racialization co-exist, arguing that notions of American Indian sovereignty carry racial valences. Because settler colonialism was at heart a "racialized project" dependent on racial ideologies to assure land dispossession and labor extraction, the rhetoric of sovereignty that rose in response to colonialism is mired in that pre-existing dynamic. Calls for a sovereign imperative, Sturm suggests, can never be free of racial assumptions and implications, especially regarding Black Cherokees (and other descendants of slaveholding Native nations) for whom the protections of tribal sovereignty and civil rights are enmeshed. Sturm attempts to wed the values of sovereign self-determination and the tribal state's moral obligation to multifaceted communities. Building on Robert Warrior's language, Sturm endorses the "empower[ment]" of "tribes to act as moral sovereigns committed to protecting the civil rights of their own citizenry." The Louisiana Choctaw ethnic studies scholar Brian Klopotek has perhaps offered the most plain-spoken analysis of how historical ideologies and structures of power shape these ongoing tensions. He points the finger at "white supremacy," charging: "Such is the power of race that it leads us to disown our own kin, undermining the most basic human bond and principles of tribal people."[20]

As scholars weighed in about the historical and ideological underpinnings of the conflict, as well as the contemporary stakes, political and legal wheels continued to turn within and outside of the Cherokee Nation. Despite the outcome of the 2007 special election, freedpeople descendants were permitted to vote in the next election for principal chief due to a temporary agreement reached between the Bureau of Indian Affairs and the Cherokee Nation in federal court in September of 2011. The descendant vote most likely contributed to the selection of a new principal chief, Bill John Baker, who had indicated openness toward the notion of restoring their citizenship.[21] The Department of the Interior then sought a permanent settlement of the long-term dispute in the form of a "clear resolution" in federal court, a process that took several years. In 2014, hearings for the pivotal case, *Cherokee Nation v. Raymond Nash, et al., and Marilyn Vann, et al., and Ryan Zinke, Secretary of the Interior, and the United States Department of the Interior,* began in Washington, DC.[22] On August 30, 2017, U.S. District Court Judge Thomas F. Hogan rendered a thunderous decision, ruling against the Cherokee Nation, upholding the validity of the Treaty of 1866, and reaffirming freedmen and women descendants' citizenship rights.[23]

This long-awaited declaration of legal belonging was a triumph for the descendants of enslaved people in the Cherokee Nation and also for the civil rights of marginalized minority populations writ large. After the ruling, Marilyn Vann wrote in a Facebook message to supporters: "I want to thank so many that have helped the Cherokee freedmen tribal members win our case in DC. We first of all thank God for this great victory. We also thank the Honorable Judge Thomas Hogan for his air tight legal opinion which carefully considered all of the arguments." The attorney general for the Cherokee Nation, Todd Hembree, stated in response to the decision: "The Cherokee Nation respects the rule of law. . . . I do not intend to file an appeal."[24] While this federal court decision was momentous and may have sealed off the legal controversy at present, the question of slave reparations that Chief Chadwick Smith cynically raised to frame the 2007 referendum may not be fully settled. Resentment and suspicion remain on both sides of this conflict about what appears to be the Cherokee Nation's forced submission to federal authority. It is significant that Chief Baker, his Council, and the Cherokee Nation legal team fought to uphold the Nation's special election barring descendant citizenship even though the descendant vote enabled Baker's chieftaincy. The emotional turmoil and political division sown in slavery and its aftermath continues to shade legal, political, social, cultural, and psychological domains.

The vitriol surrounding the case of Cherokee freedpeople has been both sign and symptom of a distance between differently racialized peoples who share a violently and, at times, valiantly intimate history. This distance has been created and cemented, to a great extent, by practices and policies imposed on these groups by the U.S. government, rather than by internal cultural values that once elevated kinship over color and communalism over capitalistic gain. Indeed, the Cherokee Nation sanctioned slavery and recouped the proceeds of slave sales in large part because the U.S. government had pressed for Cherokees to exhibit the habits of "civilization"—meaning Euro-American racial, gendered, and pecuniary practices—for more than a century. The logic of race-based exclusion and hierarchy did not originate in Indigenous American or African diasporic populations. And yet, as Judge Thomas Hogan found in *Cherokee Nation v. Nash*, "the Cherokee Nation was complicit in legitimizing slavery within the Nation and securing the intended durability of the practice, as well as the disenfranchisement of people of African descent."[25] U.S. state-sponsored colonial coercion and violence, and Cherokee state-sponsored slavery and exclusion, are intimately interconnected. Responsibility for their parts must be borne by both nations.

So how might Cherokees "by blood" and Cherokee freedmen and women descendants (in many cases, groups with overlapping identity claims) move toward reparations—which I define broadly as emotional, spiritual, and relational repair? In her article "Tribes and Tribulations: Beyond Sovereign Immunity and Toward Reparation and Reconciliation for the Estelusti," Carla Pratt, a specialist in federal Indian law, outlines the complex histories of Black slavery in Native tribes and boldly argues that since slavery benefited these nations as well as individual citizens, a debt is owed.[26] Pratt calls for the U.S. government as well as tribal governments to extend "micro-reparations" to descendants of enslaved people. She focuses on strategies for remediation within the U.S. courts and supports the waiving of sovereign immunity for Native nations as a means of accomplishing a just end. I continue to hope for a multitribal or United Nations–arbitrated process that can be viewed by all sides of this struggle as fair, ethical, and, importantly, situated outside of a corrupted U.S. colonial context.[27] But beyond the bounds of any court, former slaveholding Native nations would, ideally, pursue this work of relational repair of their own volition. They might begin by critically examining their operational definition of what it means to be sovereign in a racialized, colorized (post)-colonial context and by adopting an approach that Inniss describes as "a human rights model of sovereignty." Another term for this human rights model might be "radical sovereignty," which Byrd defines as a political stance that would draw on the "kinship sovereignties that have so long been a part of our kinship structures."[28]

It is perhaps no accident that many of the Native scholars who publicly pushed for a Cherokee reckoning with histories of colonialism and racism work in the fields of literature and postcolonial theory. Visions for relational repair will likely be shaped through creative and collaborative projects engaged in by many actors: Cherokees "by blood," members of other tribal nations that once held slaves, freedpeople descendants, writers, artists, and activists in the Native social movement challenging tribal disenrollment practices. The Cherokee people and the descendants of those once enslaved in their territory share a potent story. It is a story of injustice, survival, and resilience that their ancestors shaped together, and from which they must heal through mutual acknowledgment in a long-term project of relational repair. Cherokee Nation principal chief Bill John Baker may have behaved in contradictory ways during this difficult time for his nation, but his words of yearning issued across a historical and emotional breach resonate nevertheless. After his election following a particularly ugly phase of the protracted freedmen descendants' rights battle, Baker reportedly expressed: "It's time for the healing to begin."[29]

CHAPTER 4

The Jamaican Case for Reparations Against the British Government for Slavery and Colonization

Bert S. Samuels

It can be said that the largest case of illicit human trafficking in recorded history involved the capture, transportation, and setting to work of more than 15 million enslaved Africans by several European nations, lasting more than three centuries. This number does not include those souls who died in their coffles before reaching the African coast. Were an indictment to be taken out against the parties involved, the particular offenses would include, but not be restricted to:

1. The forceful separation of millions of male and female enslaved from their families, leading to the destruction of family life on the continent of Africa. As Walter Rodney pointed out in *How Europe Underdeveloped Africa*, it also represents the theft of the working class of West Africa;[1]
2. The subhuman conditions under which the enslaved were transported; and
3. Genocide, for the failure to maintain, or care for the well-being of the newly captured being transported in inhumane conditions, resulting in the countless loss of lives at sea.

When enslaved Africans arrived in the Caribbean, conditions were just as brutal as on the galleys. As Caribbean historian C.L.R. James describes it:

"There was no ingenuity, that fear, or a depraved imagination could devise, which was not employed, to break the slaves' spirit and satisfy the lusts and resentment of their owners and guardians—irons on the hands and feet, the tin-plate mask designed to prevent the slaves eating sugar-cane, the iron collar."[2]

November 1781 brought the horror of the *Zong* massacre, in which 133 of the enslaved being transported were thrown overboard because there was not enough water for everyone on board. Once the vessel reached Jamaica, the ship owners immediately made claim for the value of the slaves they had insured. The same slaves they had murdered with impunity! The "loss" led to a claim by the *Zong*'s owners in which the English High Court, in the case of *Gregson v. Gilbert*, decided that, in some circumstances, the deliberate killing of slaves was legal and that insurers could be required to pay for the slaves' deaths![3]

Once the enslaved reached Jamaica's shores, they were further tortured by people like Thomas Thistlewood, overseer and eventual slave owner in the parish of Westmoreland. From his detailed diaries, life for the enslaved within reach of his whip was meticulously recorded, and eventually examined by modern day academics. "His willingness to subject his slaves to horrific punishments, which included savage whippings of up to 350 lashes and sadistic tortures of his own invention, such as Derby's dose, in which a slave defecated into the mouth of another slave whose mouth was then wired shut, reveal Thistlewood as a brutal sociopath."[4]

For most of us, any resurrection of this dark chapter of human history is painful enough to make us want to forget this more than three-hundred-year holocaust for Africa and the Americas, even if its reenactment is as short as recent films like *12 Years a Slave*.[5] This is why it is a historical fact that Middle Passage voyages and plantation slavery represent genocide at its worst in recent human history.

As horrific as the experience may be, however, we owe it to those who jumped or were thrown overboard, as much as to those who survived the journey, to ensure that they did not labor in vain, and it is our call to address the justice they could not claim but are, nonetheless, entitled to, as members of the human family. And for lawyers in particular, there is no escape. No matter how horrific the crime, or the disfigurement of the injured claimant, or the despicable negligence surrounding the deaths of multiple premature babies, for example, lawyers have sworn to protect, defend, and uphold the highest tenets of reparatory justice.

One of the obstacles for the reparation movement is the issue of computing the value of the lives of the enslaved, and the value of their work. In Jamaica, enslavers made sure that contracts in relation to the conveyance of their property, the enslaved people, were safely and copiously documented. I decided to take on this challenge by visiting the Island Records Office.

Section 19 of the Record Office Act enacted on February 1, 1879, forty-one years after the abolition of slavery and remaining on the law books in Jamaica today, provides for the transcribing of old records to ensure their continued preservation. This section allows the deputy keeper to transcribe, in summary form, "agreements or documents or parts of the same relating to slaves; assignments of personal property."[6]

Bearing in mind the rule of evidence that the claimant must not merely throw undocumented figures at the court to substantiate his losses, in 2016, I visited the Records Office to see whether I could locate details relating to the sale of any of my great-grandparents. My grandfather, Joshua, was born in 1865, the year of the Morant Bay massacre. His father, my great-grandfather, Edward, was a young slave boy on August 1, 1838, when our holocaust was formally terminated. On arrival at the Records Office, I told the staff of my mission and was taken to the section that housed those records—the Conveyance Department. Yes, I was reminded by the department's name of my own history, that the enslaved were deemed to be property at the time, inclusive of land, horses, and cattle, and were not, by any means, recognized as humans.

I began to examine these conveyance records, stored in huge bound volumes, and discovered from the first recorded transfer of humans I ever laid eyes on, that my search would be in vain. The first recorded "transfer" was from "old folio 47" and, whereas it referred to the transferor as Davis John and the transferee as George Reavis, the "property" had no surname; it simply referred to the subject matter of the sale as "one slave known as jack," with the rules relating to the naming of a person not being applied, as there was no uppercase "J" in the name "jack." My personal dilemma was that "property records" had no surname. We were not considered part of the human family, so there was no family name for the enslaved, hence the impossibility of my finding the sale price of any "Samuels" for the purpose of quantification. Isn't this fact of namelessness a part of the perpetuation of our pain, and for which we are entitled to compensation?

It speaks volumes that our enslaved ancestors were simply handed new, English, Christian names in place of the ones their loving parents chose.

Apparently, their souls would not be saved by their masters' Redeemer without first being re-identified, even if they were left without the benefit of a surname.

Though disappointing, the Records Office exercise certainly had its value. The sale of that "property" known as "jack" had a price for his head. He was sold on November 16, 1747, for forty-five pounds. I stumbled upon another conveyance of interest, "a love and affection transfer" by deed, dated January 24, 1757. That love and affection was, of course, not for the enslaved, but only meant that ownership changed without money changing hands. Heath Thomas transferred his slave "hannah" to Mary Baker as a gift. The point I wish to make is this—the trading of those enslaved people was recorded as commercial transactions, and money values for these transactions exist, which our reparatory actuaries can update for use in an assessment court.

Unprecedented circumstances require innovative ways to address those circumstances. Transatlantic slavery cannot be addressed by employing the settled norms of civil claims as we know them. That is why, for example, the state reserves the right to declare a state of emergency during which civil remedies, including the treasured right to habeas corpus and the right to property, are suspended.

During the state of emergency declared in Jamaica on May 23, 2010, clients of mine had to give up possession of their three-floor place of business, which was forcibly occupied by the army for several days. Reparations, I submit, must be accepted as akin to a "state of emergency," where certain rules of evidence are suspended to facilitate the overriding objective of justice for the voiceless. It is by no means a coincidence that the murder rate in Jamaica is the fourth highest globally. A marginalized male population with no recent history of strong family life—having historically been put to breed enslaved females to maintain slave stock—has become the norm in Jamaica, as reported by Edith Clarke in her sociological study *My Mother Who Fathered Me*.[7]

In 2015, entitlement to reparations from the British received unanimous bipartisan support in the Jamaican law-making arm of the state, the Parliament. The reparations movement has the support of Jamaican Justice Patrick Robinson, a judge of the International Court of Justice, who added his voice to the cause in an address at the 2015 University of the West Indies homecoming: "There is nothing novel about the claim for reparation, which is nothing more than a form of compensation or redress by a state for its wrong."[8]

The fact that the rights of an individual can accrue to his or her heirs and successors is settled law. The successors—the descendants of the enslaved—are now challenged to represent and press for their claim for reparatory justice. To allow those who alone benefitted from the forced labor of the claimants to continue to enjoy their unjust enrichment undisturbed represents complicity with the travesty of justice. The wealth gained through slavery passed between generations and so, too, should the responsibility. That is why Article 14 of the UN General Assembly's "Basic Principles and Guidelines on the Right to Remedy and Reparation" accepts that there must be "an adequate, effective, and prompt remedy for gross violations of international human rights."[9]

The Slavery Abolition Act passed on August 28, 1833, by the British Parliament declared that 179 years of enslavement of Africans in Jamaica would finally come to an end on August 1, 1834. The full title, which summarizes the content of the act, is reflective of the issues relevant, not to the enslaved, but rather to those who lost their free labor. It reads: "An Act for the Abolition of Slavery throughout the British Colonies; for promoting the Industry of the manumitted Slaves; and for *compensating* [my emphasis] the Persons hitherto entitled to the Services of such Slaves."[10]

In effect, though this new law was to give liberty to enslaved people, it guaranteed substantial material benefit to their owners. Reparations, called "compensation" in the act, were paid out to the planters in the Caribbean by a law that made them legally entitled to that compensation of £20 million. This concept, in my view, permits the idea of reparations to be considered as both economic and legal. In the Abolition Act, planters were deemed to be "entitled to the services of such slaves." We, in the reparations movement on behalf of the enslaved, are fortified in our position that they, too, are entitled to compensation for their forced services. Moral and legal justification for compensation for the enslaved is underpinned by the planters being paid by the British government for their losses, while the enslaved remained unpaid for their labor and suffering. In that sense, we now have a "wages and general damages" claim, which is assessable by a court of law. The British made sure to protect their already wealthy planter class citizens, and now we must look after descendants of the enslaved today. The evidence relating to the payout of the British Parliament to its planter class citizenry is well documented, and the University College of London even now hosts a project online detailing individual payouts to each owner of the enslaved. In short, the empirical evidence is available to form the possible bases of calculating compensation for the enslaved.

On August 1, 1838, among the African Jamaican population, there was 100 percent unemployment. The penniless, illiterate, and landless became the victims of vagrancy laws created to oppress and compel the newly freed to go back to work for the compensated planters. With not one square inch of property belonging to any of the formerly enslaved, land distribution occurred only within the planter class. Land that did not belong to planters belonged to the British Crown, what we shamefully retain today as "crown lands." Part of the call for reparations, therefore, is land reform; to determine how habitable crown lands can be fairly transferred to the landless. This would witness the government of Jamaica leading Britain by example. The day following emancipation, every piece of land walked upon by the freed enslaved belonged to others. They were all, in short, dispossessed, unrewarded trespassers. Let us not shy away from this reality; that "free" Jamaica's economy was left by the British to survive on 100 percent poverty among the Black population. That was the starting point from which nation building was to take place. Concomitantly in history, Britain was called the "Workshop of the World," which experienced an economic boom, kick-started by the earnings from slavery. That undeniably parasitic contrast is, in itself, sufficient to make the case for reparations.

The British have dared to defend their position in response to claims for reparations by referring to their "aid" programs. This drop-in-the-bucket is of marginal help. The abject poverty in the postemancipation period of Jamaica's history lends significant support to the case for reparations. Jamaica is in need of more than prisons. It needs for those who walked away compensated and who left the mess here to clean it up by funding health, education, and the justice system in a meaningful way, not as handouts, but as payback for the wealth that Jamaica, this jewel in the British crown, gave to their economy. May I remind Britain that her former colony, the United States of America, funded the establishment of the most prestigious Harvard Law School in 1817, with money gained from the labor of enslaved people owned by an American family named Royall![11]

The Law Reform (Miscellaneous Provisions) Act (June 6, 1955) was enacted to allow for all Jamaicans: "on the death of any person after the commencement of this act all causes of action subsisting against or vested in him shall *survive* [my emphasis] or, as the case may be, for the benefit of his estate."[12] This piece of legislation paves the way for us to step into the shoes of those who have passed, and make our claim for reparations on their behalf. It, therefore, allows us to surmount the hurdle of the enslaved not being here to make the claim themselves. Wealth survives even while individuals do not. In April 2019, Britain announced that it will compensate immigrants (mainly from Jamaica) collectively known as the Windrush Generation, or their surviving children, for hardships brought upon them when unable to prove their British citizenship. We, in the reparations movement, welcome this precedence-setting action, as it allows survivors to claim compensation on behalf of deceased relatives who had been previously unable to claim benefits or access services in the United Kingdom, and who may have even faced immigration action and deportation.[13]

There is a legal principle that courts cannot oppose awarding damages merely because the circumstances make it difficult to quantify the loss the claimant has suffered. Nonpecuniary damages can be arithmetically calculated into money. Yet, as determined by Lord Halsbury LC in the decided case of *The Mediana* "How is anybody to measure pain and suffering in moneys counted? Nobody can suggest that you can by arithmetical calculation establish what is the exact sum of money which would represent such a thing as the pain and suffering which a person has undergone."[14] Those of us concerned with the task of making the case for reparations start at the point of payout by the British taxpayers to the slave owners of compensation for their economic loss as a consequence of the loss of their property, their freed slaves.

The planters, unlike the enslaved people who were not recognized as humans in the year of payout—1834, lobbied and got their reparation. Losses suffered by the white planter class were assessed at £20 million for the entire Caribbean, one-third of that sum going to Jamaica. This payout by the British state in 1834 represented 40 percent of British public expenditure for that year!

If the loss suffered by the planters was the loss of their property—the enslaved people—and if the payout to them represented 40 percent of the UK's public expenditures, isn't there a valid case that descendants of the enslaved should be now paid a similar percentage? For the fiscal year 2019–20, the UK's public expenditures were estimated to be £842 billion.[15] The Centre for the Study of the Legacies of British Slave-ownership (UCL) has researched and published the precise amounts paid to individuals, corporations, and churches that held enslaved people. It must be an embarrassment to the British that a member of their recent Parliament—the former prime minister, David

Cameron—is related to a compensated owner of 202 slaves, but remains in denial regarding the legitimacy of Jamaicans' reparations claims.[16]

Such an approach to the assessment of the entitlement of the descendants of the enslaved would represent economic losses only. In addition, however, they, unlike the planters, suffered general damages and must be compensated in a larger sum, for their grave pain and suffering.

The British Parliament originally voted for slavery to be abolished in the year 1834. What the all-powerful planter class then did was to force Parliament to extend the original 1834 abolition year by four years, as an add-on to their already hefty compensation package.

The enslaved had an additional four years stolen from their lives—euphemistically called "apprenticeship"—working without pay for forty-eight additional months, which represents further compensation to be added to the £20 million voted on and paid to the planters. Professor Hilary Beckles, vice-chancellor of the University of the West Indies and chairman of the CARICOM Reparations Committee, has calculated that this additional four years of free labor was valued at £27 million,[17] bringing the total payout to £47 million. This is a 27 percent add-on to the 40 percent of GDP referred to previously. In short, enslaved people had to pay for their own freedom! In fact, during the debate surrounding the conditions under which the enslaved people were to be freed, there was a strong call from the planters to have the enslaved pay them for their own freedom before, using the ironic words of former British prime minister David Cameron, they would be permitted to "move on" to freedom bestowed by British benevolence.[18]

The idea that enslaved people should pay the planter class for, first, their freedom, and, second, their (the planters') losses, though a seemingly warped expectation, is not as far-fetched as it may seem. When the people of Haiti, a nation three hundred miles east of Jamaica, in a historic, successful slave revolt, gained their independence from France in 1804, they were forced to pay reparation to the French government for ending their enslavement. This payment was successfully extracted when France made it clear its warships were on the ready to invade, and also shamelessly enforced by the international community, which refused to recognize Haiti until it agreed to this arrangement. Beginning in 1825, the Haitian people paid 150 million francs to compensate former plantation owners who had lost their "property," which included the former enslaved Haitians themselves. Haiti eventually paid the modern equivalent of US$21 billion to France, with the last installment made in 1947.[19] This payment by way of extortion has left Haiti the poorest country in the Western Hemisphere, ironically, a fact used by some to justify the falsehood that freed African people are unable to successfully rule themselves.

The lie that the enslaved were freed by benevolence—and not by greed— is what made Cameron's boast on a visit to Jamaica in 2015, that Britain "led the way" among other European former slave-owning countries to give the enslaved freedom, particularly insulting. This is the same Cameron whose relative, General Sir James Duff, was compensated for his enslaved Jamaicans in 1833.

When Cameron visited Jamaica, he addressed the parliament about the issue of reparations. He recommended that the people of Jamaica should not remain preoccupied with such a claim but rather should "move on from this painful legacy and continue to build for the future." Then, in 2017, Lord Tariq Ahmad, British minister of state with responsibility for the Caribbean, Commonwealth, and the United Nations, on a visit to Jamaica again told Jamaicans that they should not "peer into their history," adding that the fight for reparations would be a mistake of "massive proportions."[20] Professor Verene Shepherd, co-chair of Jamaica's National Council on Reparation, strongly rebutted this veiled threat in a letter to the press: "The mistake would be for the UK to ignore the growing support in the Caribbean and other countries for the need for reparatory justice."[21]

Britain has long sought to use aid to its former colonies as sufficient redress for the state in which they left former plantation societies, when they paid their planters millions of pounds in compensation, leaving a newly freed population penniless, landless, and with no formal education to commence nation building. Ironically, in January 2016, a year after the former British prime minister made his insensitive remarks, he celebrated his country's intention to build a Holocaust memorial outside its parliament. He made the announcement as he marked Holocaust Memorial Day, stating that "the darkest hour of humanity" will never be forgotten. He urged survivors of Nazi atrocities to record their memories so that "powerful and moving" experiences would be captured for future generations.[22]

So, on the subject of payout, the enslaved are speaking from the grave through their heirs and successors to make their just claim, and make it now!

A recent example of the innovative approach I mentioned earlier, with respect to the British government's compensation pay out to Kenyan claimants in 2013, was a full five decades after the lapse of the three years imposed by the relevant statute of limitation. This was to facilitate the righting of wrongs—including the forcible castration of victims—committed against the Mau Mau freedom fighters of Kenya (see Chapter 7 by Elkins in this volume). Ironically, they got almost the same figure (£19.9 million) paid to Caribbean planters 180 years ago. The Kenyan payout took place fifty-plus years after the events of the case. The justice of that case superseded the imposition of technical man-made bars to reparatory redress.

Enslaved people were considered their owners' assets. When an enslaved person became very ill, an assessment was made, taking into consideration the extended cost of medical care versus the cost of a new enslaved person as replacement. Where the latter was less costly, the sick slave was left to die. When the enslaved became too old to work, and spending on their care viewed as uneconomic, they too, were left to fend for themselves.

In the case of *Bourhill v. Young* (1943), the jurist Lord Wright said, "The damage must be attributable to the breach by the defendant of some duty owing to the Plaintiff."[23] Applying this definition to our case first, in law, the owner of enslaved people, horses, and cattle, *ejusdem generis*, owed no duty of care to this class of property. They were his, he could work them at will, give no wages, and like his cattle, their offspring were his and he could slaughter (kill) them at will, as the definition of murder could not apply to nonhumans. Second, slavery was deemed not illegal in the colonies at the time. But the laws legitimizing slavery are unsustainable in international law. Consider the Jamaican Parliament making legal the enslavement of a racial minority. That law would be struck down as unconstitutional, unsustainable, and an affront to accepted international laws and values. How can a law premised on a biological falsehood—the dehumanization of the African race—be relied on to defeat a claim for reparations? Does the fact that these crimes are seventeenth- and eighteenth-century offenses make them no less culpable? Other forms of slavery, such as the enslavement of Europeans by other Europeans—except the case of the Romani peoples' enslavement in Romania (see Chapter 15 by Matache and Bhabha)—were not premised on the classification of the enslaved as subhuman, and so should not be compared with our chattel slave experience.

The British exported their laws to the colonies wholesale when it suited them. The laws of England were the laws of the colony for centuries. The reliance on the point that slavery was legal in Jamaica and that, as a result, there was no breach of the law to have owned those enslaved, is based on a falsehood that those the English enslaved were not humans. No law based on this untenable, unnatural, and unscientific position should be entertained, let alone recognized. Respectfully, we have not evolved into humans since August 1, 1838!

In the case of *Somerset v. Stewart*, Lord Mansfield determined in 1772 that Somerset, an enslaved man brought from the state of Virginia by a Mr. Stewart—who was detained on a ship on the River Thames in English territory and destined for Jamaica where Stewart intended to sell Somerset— was to be freed on the basis that slavery was not legal in England.[24] How can you be a human being in one part of the British Empire but subhuman in another?

If the basis on which a claim is to be entertained is that the enslavement of Africans was a crime against humanity, then the legal barrier relating to the notion that enslavement was "legal" at the time is easily removed. As part of any civilized system of justice, the persons who benefitted from a crime are not entitled to rely on legal fiction and/or niceties to avoid liability. That is why there is no statute of limitations in relation to crimes against humanity. Reparatory justice and the new approach in mediation for the settlement of disputes have not fettered themselves with the constraints of settled legal principles if those principles will prevent the just and equitable resolution of a legitimate claim. The Mau Mau claim was settled fifty-plus years after the crimes were committed. In fact, by way of example, there is now a principle in criminal law known as "historical child sexual abuse," where the victims of such abuse may bring to justice the perpetrators, decades following the crime. This is to make sure that victims have closure for their suffering, no matter how old the infractions may be.

In 1880, Lord Blackburn defined the measure of damages in the case of *Livingstone v. Rawyards Coal Co.* as: "that sum of money which will put the party who has been injured, or who has suffered, in the same position as he would have been in if he had not sustained the wrong for which he is now getting his compensation or reparation."[25] Goff and Jones, in *The Law of Restitution*, state the principle of unjust enrichment: "Most mature systems of Law found it necessary to provide, outside the fields of contract and civil wrongs, for the restoration of benefits on the ground of unjust enrichment. There are many circumstances in which a defendant may find himself in possession of a benefit which in justice, he should restore to the Plaintiff."[26] The writer cites an example of unjust enrichment as occurring when the "plaintiff conferred the benefit by compulsion."[27] This principle, which makes unpaid labor by compulsion illegal—and enslavement is a compulsion unmatched in human history—more than qualifies the claim for reparations for the enslaved as a fit and proper one for the unjust enrichment of the British planter class by way of reparation.

The names, British addresses, and amounts paid to each planter for the release of his or her property, the formerly enslaved, are now available online. That is why the connection to enslavers of David Cameron's lineage is a recorded fact. Their enrichment, being unequivocally unjust, inescapably leads to a proper case for that enrichment to revert to their descendants.

As the Trinidadian historian Eric Williams long ago demonstrated, corporate England had blood money fueling it in meaningful ways.[28] It is no secret that the Welsh slate industry, Manchester textile mills, and the Glaswegian, Bristol, and Liverpool banking, shipbuilding, and heavy engineering industries were all fueled by profits from the plantations. Slavery kick-started Britain's industrial revolution, which occurred in the late 1700s, continuing to the mid-1800s. Sugar earnings even ended up in the coffers of the Church of England. Compensation paid to planters was not pumped back into the Jamaican economy. It is a recorded fact that it was all injected into the British economy, and this led to an unprecedented nineteenth-century push-start for Britain. Postemancipation Jamaica was, at the same time in history, left to limp along, and starved of any capital base to lift it out of economic decline. The inevitable result was social and economic decay, leading to the Morant Bay revolt in 1865. The painful irony of Jamaica being referred to as a jewel in the British crown is that its wealth was reflected in Britain only, whose parasitic relationship with Jamaica continued beyond slavery, with the island serving as a mere producer of raw material and an importer of finished product, with all the attendant negative implications for economic growth.

The shame of compensating planters with the blood, unpaid work, and pain of African Jamaicans, with not a penny paid to them, should, itself, spark the need to apologize. To restrict the response to the enslaved's suffering to a *"regret simpliciter"* is an insult to them and a shame on the British. To boast that Britain led the way among other former slave-owning countries is to add insult to the injury enslavement left in its wake, not to mention its inaccuracy. The beginning of the end of slavery was in the actions of the enslaved: in the actions of the rebels at Morant Bay and Haiti, and everywhere else across the Atlantic. But even in comparison to the actions taken by other European nations, the actions taken by Great Britain to date stand out only for their pusillanimity. An apology is the first step in redressing a wrong. It is recognition that there is an act of misconduct from which a victim has been created.

The shameful British refusal to tender an unequivocal apology would be best guided by the example of the Church of England, which, on February 7, 2006, apologized to the descendants of victims of the "slave trade" when Rev. Simon Bessant described the church's involvement in the trade by conceding that "we were at the heart of it."[29] At the same General Synod event, Rowan Williams, the archbishop of Canterbury, said the apology was "necessary." He went on to apply the principles of the Christian faith, saying: "The body of Christ is not just a body that exists at any one time, it exists across history and we therefore share the shame and the sinfulness of our predecessors and part of what we can do, with them and for them in the body of Christ, is prayer for acknowledgement of the failure that is part of us not just of some distant 'them.'"[30]

The Church of England's act of contrition was 168 years late. The slave-owning church continued to worship for 168 years after the abolition of slavery before it finally converted to its current position. During an emotional meeting of the church's governing body in London, Rev. Bessant explained the involvement of the "Society for the Propagation of the Gospel in Foreign Parts" in the slave trade. This organization, a part of the Church of England, owned the Codrington Plantation in Barbados, where slaves had the initials "SPG" branded on their backs with a red-hot iron. He conceded that there was gross injustice when the emancipation of slaves took place in 1833 and compensation was paid, not to the slaves, but to their owners.[31]

He also reported that the bishop of Exeter and three colleagues were paid nearly £13,000 in compensation for 665 slaves. He confessed openly when he admitted that "we were directly responsible for what happened. In the sense of inheriting our history, we can say we owned slaves, we branded slaves, that is why I believe we must actually recognise our history and offer an apology."[32]

On my visit to Cape Coast, Ghana, in 1996, atop the dungeons where the newly captured enslaved were held awaiting the ships to transport them, still stands a branch of the church. White, Christian men were worshiping, while, in the dungeons below, the captured ancestors of Jamaicans were chained and waiting to be transported as human cargo.

The heroes of the British Empire, some of whom were pioneers in the acquisition and transportation of African enslaved people, leave their mark on the landscape of the colonies, even today, as statuary. Part of the movement for restorative justice is to redefine the criteria for recognition, which would, of necessity, exclude many British "heroes."

To correct the misconception that those who fought for the termination of slavery and against the tyranny of postslavery colonialism in Jamaica were wrongdoers, in 2017 the Jamaican Parliament tabled a law to remove the criminal records of Samuel Sharpe, Paul Bogle, and William Gordon. It was Sam Sharpe, a Baptist deacon, who was tried and hanged for the 1833 slave revolt, which deeply influenced the move to end slavery in Jamaica. Bogle and Gordon were also hanged for their roles in the Morant Bay uprising in 1865, twenty-seven years after the abolition of slavery, when the brutal colonial government executed four hundred others. This legal move by the Jamaican Parliament represents a necessary step to right the wrongs of the past when those who fought on the side of the oppressed were treated as criminals.

The consequences of centuries of apartheid and self-hate still appear in modern-day Jamaica, even 180 years since the abolition of slavery. Numerous dark-skinned Jamaicans are now taking to chemically treating their skin to acquire a lighter shade. The health risk notwithstanding, the practice has become widespread. On a plantation, social stratification was quite plain. The white master was at the top, the mulatto (half African, half white) in the middle, and the African enslaved at the very bottom of the social ladder. Today, the bleaching of skin—a practice deeply rooted in the desire of Black Jamaicans to acquire the skin color of former slave masters for social acceptance—is not the only attempt to mirror them. Almost 60 percent of African Jamaican women straighten their hair to have it look more Caucasian than African. Since abolition, women with straighter hair have found themselves more successful in attaining employment than those with naturally kinky hair. Up until 2003, convicted Rastafarians who grew dreadlocks were trimmed at the commencement of their incarceration in Jamaican prisons. It may be said that today's African Jamaican hair and skin, to a large extent, portrays the deep psychic vestige of enslavement best described as "self-hate." It is not uncommon for a Black Jamaican to describe another as ugly simply because they are Black or to describe a person as attractive as if this can only be so in spite of their Blackness.

In 2017, in recognition of the primacy of the issue of reparations, the University of the West Indies launched the Centre for Reparation Research. The center is the first of its kind in the region and is the brainchild of Professor

Hilary Beckles. It promotes research on the legacies of colonialism, native genocide, enslavement, and indentureship in the Caribbean, and focuses on bringing justice and positive transformation to these legacies. This is, indeed, a welcome move by academia, as the past incorrect interpretation and presentation of the history of enslaved Jamaicans has been mainly created by European writers.

As a member of the National Council on Reparation, I join with my colleagues in calling upon Britain to come to the table to participate in settlement discussions. The idea of restorative justice is a process whereby all parties with a stake in a particular offense come together to resolve collectively how to deal with the aftermath of the offense. It is a different way of thinking about crime and conflict. It focuses on holding the offender accountable in a more meaningful way. It repairs the harm caused by the offense, helps to reintegrate the offender into the civilized community of nations, and helps to achieve a sense of healing for both the victim and the community. For, in the words of Martin Luther King Jr., "injustice anywhere is a threat to justice everywhere."[33]

Caribbean states have penned letters of demand for compensation to the former slave-owning European countries. A 2016 letter to Prime Minister Cameron made the claim on behalf of several former British-held islands.[34] The European countries denied this claim for reparation, "en bloc." In fact, in Cameron's rejection of the claim, he quoted Foreign Secretary William Hague, who made it clear that the British government "does not believe that reparations are the answer."[35] These denials of the claims for reparations have now escalated the issue. We are now in the dispute stage with European countries, and therefore, a decision will have to be made about the intervention of an international judicial body.

It is in the interest of this healing for both the British and their victims that we ask to embark together on the rehabilitation necessary for the redemption of Jamaica's ailing economy. This can only be corrected by those who are indebted to us, by injecting capital into health care and education, among other priorities that are set out in the CARICOM Ten Point Action Plan for Reparation.[36] Jamaica's high rate of crime is directly linked to the high rate of unemployment, and the idle hands and hopelessness that unemployment created in 1838 is a yoke the country has not been able to fully shed. We need to stop the need for more prisons by fixing the despair slavery created in the first place.

The call for reparations will not go away. We, the descendants of the enslaved, are surrounded by clear evidence in the Caribbean of the scars and
vestiges of a period of cruelty too painful to disregard, too deeply embedded
to forget, and too horrific to turn the blind eye of indifference without being
guilty of complicity with those who perpetrated the most horrendous crime
against humanity recorded in recent history.

CHAPTER 5

The University and Slavery: Reflections upon the History and Future of the University of the West Indies

Sir Hilary Beckles

The mass chattel enslavement of more than 15 million Africans in the early modern transatlantic economy was a principal and active project of emerging academic and university communities. The enslaved, throughout colonial America, and in imperial Europe, constituted a subject that preoccupied "thought leaders" in their roles as shapers of public opinion, and as private and corporate investors. Everywhere, professors, priests, and pundits rose and wrote in support of African enslavement, placed their private and institutional money behind their mouths and manuscripts, and celebrated the profit at the business end of their pens.

Prominent academics, both as footloose freelancers and as tenured administrators of academies, alongside other collegial caretakers, included philosophical and financial support for slavery in their arguments about the institutional sustainability of universities. They provided pedagogical rationalizations for enslavement and sought significant endowments to enable universities to serve investors. As enslavers, college administrators and professors built the colonial and national higher education agenda upon the legal platform of property rights to enslaved Africans.

The enterprise of Black enslavement, furthermore, was embedded in the deepest conceptual underpinnings of Western colonial design, which was articulated most clearly and persuasively by persons recognized as academics. John Locke, for example, was celebrated in mid-seventeenth-century Britain and its colonies as the celebrity writer and philosopher of the idea of human liberty. More than any other author, Locke was extremely influential in legitimizing and incorporating transatlantic slavery as the bedrock of British investment in human property. Not only did he provide the state with legal, ethical, and administrative ideas and guidelines to promote enslavement, he was in his own right a significant financial investor in slavery, and served as the corporate secretary to the Royal African Company when it was established in 1672. Under his considerable academic influence were hosts of lesser legal and judicial minds, and cohorts of colonial administrators who networked and managed slave-based communities from Rhode Island to the sugar islands of the Caribbean.

Academics like Locke, then, were locked into African enchainment in ways that promoted the chattel proposition, which, by 1700, had made Caribbean sugar producers the richest farmers in the Americas. Universities and law schools that sprung up on the mainland as pillars of the world slave owners had made were umbilically linked through the thinking of Locke to Caribbean slave-based wealth accumulation. Their institutional roles were to reproduce an effective slave-owning class, and sustain the economies they managed. Academia, then, was as pivotal a partner in slavery as were banks, insurance companies, and commission agents.

An entourage of economists in the late seventeenth century entered the door pushed wide open by philosophers and jurists. Charles Davenant and Josiah Child, for example, proponents of the concept of economic growth propelled by trade in enslaved Africans, wrote extensively about the role of academic ideas in Western colonial culture. The legal and financial commodification of Africans by these proto-scholastic ideologues effectively fused political economy and colonial commerce, thereby establishing the emerging episteme of the plantation paradigm.

The University of the West Indies is deeply rooted, in every sense, in this production and pedagogical tradition. Its slavery legacy is at once physical and philosophical, constituting an inescapable cosmology that defines its parameters in relation to both its physical place and the identity of its educational vision and mission. There are few universities in the Black Atlantic as deeply attached to the political economy of slavery. Everywhere within the spaces it occupies, the signs and symbols of slavery constitute an imposing iconography and represent hegemonic heritage expressions. The universality of Black slavery and the identity of the university in these "West Indies" provide the potential for a powerful pedagogical program of educational action.

Established in 1948 by the discredited and retreating British Empire, the University of the West Indies was planted in Jamaica as an institution to promote elite democratic freedom on plantation lands still moist with the blood, sweat, and tears of thousands of enslaved Africans and their surviving progeny. The British, never without a sense of irony in their perception and treatment of history, chose to site this school for "the best and brightest" on the scene of enslavement. The juxtaposition of slavery and academic liberty was meant to symbolize a notion of rupture with roots, and a moving on with the new message of mass emancipation.

The first campus of the university was constructed on the sites of the Mona and Papine sugar plantations, enterprises that had been notorious in slavery days as cruel consumers of African life. The records of the plantations resonate with the reasons why enslavement had so enriched British entrepreneurs at the genocidal expense of Africans. Situated in the fertile valley that defines the Blue Mountains overlooking the city of Kingston, the plantations were more than sites of sugar production. They were places where African people without rights were laid to rest in unmarked graves, erased from history without dignity and identity, and buried deep in dirt not earmarked for agriculture.

The souls of the enslaved, it seemed, could not be contained by soils not consecrated. Their spirits, it is said, called out to campus administrators, as ancestors do to their descendants. The convergence of history and horror, learning and liberation, came with the decision to construct a state-of-the-art medical faculty complex on the campus. The site was skillfully chosen and was surveyed with the precision of experts with no purpose other than the pursuit of professional perfection. Jamaican engineers and architects entered the designated area in celebration of their expertise, as Chinese contractors rolled on the heavy equipment to tear the turf in order to lay the foundation.

As the machines ripped through the earth, the bones of boys and girls, men and women, long bundled and buried, rose to the surface and presented their faces. Tractors were stopped in their tracks. Contractors stared at the sight. The campus community, mostly survivors of the enslaved, called for a ceremony of recognition and celebration.

The roof of the plantation's unmarked burial ground had been ripped off, and the university came face to face with its history in the most spectacular, yet humane, fashion. The history of production on the plantation was well researched; but the people whose labor drove the business had not been a subject of the search. Now, they revealed themselves. They spoke with their bones. The site was made solemn. The campus memorialized the identities of all those enslaved persons whose names were found in schedules of accounts and itemized in lists of the emancipated.

The Mona message was not lost upon the medics. The faculty had built its pedagogy from the outset on public health, establishing for itself an impressive reputation in the discipline of community medicine. The performance achievement of professors originated in their earliest attempts to clean up the colonial mess, expressed forcefully in the chronic, endemic public health disaster of dying colonialism. Ill health and sickness were the universal Caribbean norm for the descendants of the enslaved. The medics had responded before the bones had spoken. Pathologists, historians, and archaeologists, for the first time, were engaged together, thanks to the eruption and excavation.

The idea of an elitist university had been part of the imperial response to workers' anticolonial revolution across the region during the 1930s. Colonies, one by one, became battle sites for popular democracy. The Black community, now a century into the "faked emancipation" of 1838, violently took on the imperial order. The Empire responded by offering a "small university" for the few, a decade later, as an act of social appeasement.

In 1962, the colonial institution, built on the base of Black debasement, was decolonized and entered a period of nationalist intellectualism. But the plantation paradigm was persistent. Before the end of the decade, Walter Rodney, historian of Africa, and graduate of the Mona Campus, had returned to his source. Rodney wasted no time taking the content of his courses beyond the campus perimeter into the communities of marginalized, oppressed descendants. The history had come home to roost. The young professor with Guyanese citizenship, after a short teaching and advocacy engagement in Canada, was denied re-entry to Jamaica by the government. The offense was that his taking of African history and epistemology to the community had created a volatile public political circumstance that rendered him a national security risk. Grassroots rebellion shook Kingston. The university was the epicenter. The Mona plantation had no plans to yield fully to the Mona Campus. The history and the future clashed in the classrooms, and the communities beyond.

Neighboring the campus, beyond its boundary, is a community that carries the name "August Town." The antislavery legislation of 1833 had made a provision to emancipate the masses of enslaved Africans on August 1, 1834. Liberated laborers all over the Caribbean celebrate August 1 as a crossroad in their journey. The village of enslaved Africans on the plantation emerged as August Town, an edifice to emancipation.

Rodney's research had conflated African and diaspora histories and blurred the boundary between campus and community. The bones that spoke fifty years later, it was said, had risen in celebration of his violent death two decades after his "deportation" in 1968. Mona, the ancestral home of the now multicampus university, continued to be a torn and turbulent cosmology in celebration of the freedom denied those who labored in its killing fields. There should be no surprise, therefore, that its epistemic pinnacle is a place occupied primarily by professors dedicated to the advocacy of social justice.

While colleagues at Mona were busy putting to rest the bones of ancestors, those at the Cave Hill Campus in Barbados were on an altogether very different mission. Theirs was one of archival discovery. The crumbling pages of plantation records had spectacularly delivered the history of one who was to be enshrined as an inspiration to all within the campus community.

As part of the celebration of the campus's fiftieth anniversary, the decision was taken to conduct research into the history of the space it occupies. It was generally known that the ninety acres of land that host the learning community had once been occupied by enslaved Africans trapped on small cotton, sugar, and cattle farms. Unlike Mona, whose historic identity was linked to large-scale slave owning and sugar production, Cave Hill's reputation was located at the other end of the wealth spectrum—the small, marginal white men and women who sought their salvation in the owning of a few Africans. Woodville Marshall, celebrated expert of the island's people and production, went in search of the campus's testimony. Among the many manuscripts examined in detail, he encountered an enslaved African man, the quintessential Cave Hill inhabitant, Quaw.

Captured in "Guinea" as a child less than ten years old, and sold in Barbados as a "bonus" on the auction block in the 1790s, Quaw began his life of enslavement as the property of a slave owner who owned the western portion of the Cave Hill lands. The child became a man of "substance" on the small plantation and, after acquiring literacy and freedom, was offered the prestigious occupation of sexton at the newly constructed Anglican Church adjacent to the property. There he taught the recently freed Black children, building a reputation as a respected teacher and school coordinator. The enslaved child who became a church curator was the first teacher in the community that became a college campus. Quaw is now celebrated as a pioneering educator, representing an intellectual insurrection that drove the campus to confront the crimes against humanity perpetrated within its vicinity.

The erection of a monument to Quaw was part of the university's attempt to engage in creative ways the legacy of slavery that still shapes its community. The realization that spaces that were once fields of violence, but now classrooms for discourses about humanity's finer values, constituting the richest imaginable sites for learning and teaching, has been politically empowering. By looking back, the future came into clearest view. Walking hand in glove with history created an intense harmony that serves as a conveyance of individual consciousness and community action.

Then there was the major matter of activism in the face of the new knowledge. Justice deplores silence and is best repaired with reason that leads to restitution. Campuses of the university became sites of spikes in consciousness in ways that now refuse to rest in peace without calls for reparatory justice. The bones that rose at Mona, and the character that called out at Cave Hill, created a coalescing of community action around the quest for acknowledgment—the core concept in reparatory justice politics.

In 2017, the University of the West Indies established a Centre for Reparations Research. It followed three years after the Caribbean Community Heads of Governments had instituted a Commission for Reparations. It was expected that the center would serve as the research arm of the policy-based commission. The location of the center within the Office of the Vice Chancellor was in part a remit from the region's political directorate, who had come to recognize the extent to which the legacies of slavery continue to militate against the region's best efforts to achieve sustainable economic and social development.

Linked to the Black enslavement legacy of the slave plantation system is the haunted heritage of indigenous genocide that typified the imperial colonizing project. The British took military possession of Barbados in 1625. Planting the flag on behalf of King James I, colonizers informed him that the island was devoid of inhabitants, but houses could be found everywhere surveyed. During the prior century, Spanish and Portuguese imperialists in Mexico and Brazil, respectively, had been slave raiding the island. The mines of Mexico, and the latifundia of Brazil, needed enslaved labor, and the in-

digenous community of Barbados was targeted. Those who survived fled to
the neighboring islands, which, unlike Barbados, contain mountains that
served as sources of survival, resistance, and rebellion.

Chattel slavery on the sugar plantations had not spared the indigenous.
They were integrated into the labor gangs as a minority within the majority
slavery status. Enslavers cared little for the color of their chattels, and more
with their capacity to cultivate crops. The brutalization of Natives resided
alongside the terrorism of Africans, who, in the Windward Islands especially,
formed joint military actions against their common oppressors. The lands
occupied by the Cave Hill Campus continue to yield archaeological evidence
of Native habitation, and subsequent genocide. Household technologies and
consumer items abound in the community as evidence of an existential reality that lurks inches beneath the slave-based surface. Indigenous and immigrant, "brown and Black," their cultures commingle in the world of
artifacts now displayed in faculty facilities.

Consistent with the consciousness inspired by the activism of reparatory
justice, campus leaders, in an effort to legitimize their occupation of the
violated space, have offered a pipeline to prosperity for these holocaust survivors. From their officially allotted "reservations" in Dominica, for example,
and from St. Vincent, where they have congregated in resilient communities,
cries from indigenous peoples of a claim for social integration and economic
empowerment were heard by the university. Indigenous peoples' scholarships were offered, leading to the growth of a student community that rede-
fines campus life. African descendant students in Barbados for the first time
were able to meet and greet indigenous people. The chains of history and
legacy were broken. Imperial myths about race and identity were shattered.
The campus, again, served as a convergence community that confronted the
horrors of history in order to forge a future without fear.

In addressing the lead role they played in the conception and development of African enslavement in the Black Atlantic, therefore, universities now
have ample opportunities to commit to the corrosion and eradication of the
cultural legacy that constitutes a determining racist force in postslavery society. The roots of racism were planted deep in the colonial discourses that
still constrain the community cosmology of democracy. These sunken pillars still serve as aquifers that irrigate the inhumane ideology of white supremacy assumptions and actions. The university, then, was in the garden of
the original sin, and should take matured responsibility for planting seeds
to enable leaves of love to blossom and fruits of freedom to flourish.

The pedagogical perspective adopted by the University of the West Indies calls for recognizing that academic excellence should embrace ethical conduct. The excellent academy must be an ethical ecology. An ethical university does not ignore, deny, or suppress its uncomfortable truths, especially if they are as terrible and disgraceful as crimes against humanity that chattel slavery was and is considered to be. Indeed, ethical academies stand up to their dastardly deeds and redirect discourses that counter the culture of hate and harm. Whatever was embraced in the colonial curriculum, and became the basis of popular tutelage, can be rejected and unlearned.

The progressive path to a shared future can be defined by new, integrative intellectualism signposted by monuments and effigies that stand for a more humane education mandate. The mission of ethical and excellent academies, then, should include the removal of celebratory symbols of slavery. Each institution should muster the courage to confront its own history of crime and cruelty. But none should stop short of calling for an ecosystem dedicated to education that promotes humanity's finest instincts rather than celebrate the shared history of slavery's shame.

CHAPTER 6

French Justice and the Claims for Reparations by Slave Descendants in Guadeloupe

Mireille Fanon Mendes France

La question est grande, on vous demande de toucher à des sociétés complexes, de ne pas les laisser telles que le passé les a faites ; on vous propose d'entreprendre par la loi une réforme sociale : c'est une œuvre que d'ordinaire accomplissent seules les révolutions.

The task is great, we are asking you to intervene in complex societies, to change the way the past has fashioned them; we are inviting you to achieve by law a social reform: it's a task usually accomplished only by revolutions.

—Charles de Rémusat, rapporteur on the Colonial Council, House of Representatives, 1838

All the decisions made during the transatlantic slave trade, enslavement, and colonialization could only be upheld because they were always made outside the framework of the common law. And that has never been repaired. Thus, we could state, like Eric David, that when "there is no closure for the event, it lasts again and forever, here and now, it is forever and again our contemporary."[1] Enduring proof is the situation of Afro-descendant people, and, among all the violations that afflict them, there is one that bears witness to the lasting consequences of enslavement: the issue of land. The descendants of slave owners own this land, but only because the real owners cannot provide title deeds and history of land ownership. They own it by hook or by crook. To the slave descendants, "this land is the sweat of our ancestors."[2] The land also represents the blood of thousands of indigenous people exterminated when the colonists arrived, mixed with the blood of the newly enslaved individuals. Most of the agricultural workers I have encountered recall seeing their great-grandparents, their grandparents, and their parents work this land, and clear the fields for planting, for as long as they remember. So, to whom does land in colonized and enslaved countries belong?

In a report to the prime minister of the French government, dated March 6, 2018, the Court of Auditors reviewed the collection of taxes in France's overseas dominions between 2011 and 2016.[3] It concluded that 45 percent of the property tax was collected illegally. The Court of Auditors estimated the financial loss to the state at around €500 million. Noting the difficulty of identifying taxpayers (individuals and businesses) and the gaps in cadastral data, the court recommended solving the problems generating property tax confusion by tackling "the problem of property deeds." This amounts to formalizing the property of the descendants of settlers, because they are almost the only ones able to provide such an act obtained with the complacency of justice. These lands were acquired from them by theft and crime. The state, in doing so, allows the consequence of the crime to continue and formalizes it. It should also be noted that some farmers have deeds of ownership that can sometimes be challenged at the time of a sale, their validity not being recognized.

Agricultural workers in the Sainte Rose region of Guadeloupe have long demanded real agricultural reform, arguing that their colonizer or slave-owner ancestors acquired the territories of many self-declared landowners through crime and theft. As a result, the agricultural workers have argued, the current ownership of these lands has no legitimacy. Rather, they contend, the state has concealed the theft of these lands by replacing colonizers' actions with unilateral decisions.

Both the colonizers' descendants and the state have failed to acknowledge this culpability. As a result, and given the willful rewriting of history to suggest that the current situation reflects a lawful transfer of land ownership, the farmers, now unionized, decided to take possession of a few contested acres.[4] Hubert de Jaham, the "apparent" owner of the contested land, to quote the terms used by the Court of Auditors, relying on a judgment in his favor, asked the state to intervene and uphold his property rights.[5] He claimed that these lands were his because they had belonged to his family since the era of enslavement and colonization. In August 2018, on the prefect's initiative, a unit of 150 gendarmes, assisted by a helicopter, dismantled the fences installed by the farmers of Daubin-Sainte Rose.

The farmers' claims were legitimate for two reasons: first, because the lands in question did not belong to either the colonists' descendants or to the state; second, because the Civil Code of 1805 recognizes the property rights to a piece of land of any person who cultivates and takes care of that land for thirty years, by virtue of the application of the rules of adverse possession.[6] This right was never recognized during enslavement, since in 1835 enslaved had no rights.[7] The 1789 Declaration of the Rights of Man and of the Citizen never acknowledged equality for enslaved.

Local people did not obstruct the August 2018 gendarme operation. But once the police forces were gone, Hubert de Jaham took advantage of the bulldozers brought to the site by the gendarmes. With the help of nine others, he demolished four of the outhouses that had been built, without any legal authorization a few years later. Alerted by the syndicat de défense du Patrimoine agricole (SPA), the gendarmes came back and arrested Hubert de Jaham. The SPA filed a complaint with the District Attorney in Pointe à Pitre, but, as of this writing, no charges have been filed against Hubert de Jaham.

The Court of Auditors' report on tax revenue from France's overseas territories (referred to by the French acronym DROM) (Overseas Departments and Regions) painted a bleak and heavily partisan picture. Presenting the situation as "very bad in Guadeloupe and Martinique, and even worse in Guyana and Mayotte," the court emphasized "the insufficient civic responsibility in reporting taxes."[8] Not only does this analysis gloss over the historical context of colonial land grabbing, but it also stigmatizes whole populations living on the territories. It is the expression of the collective subconscious of a state that continues to subscribe to its history of colonization, one still mired in its racial politics, and the ongoing refusal to acknowledge this legacy. This behavior is not specifically French: colonist and slave states continue to defend the criminal rather than the victim.

The institutional anxiety created around the quality of the tax revenue, its control, and its collection in the DROM as opposed to the "rest of the country," is particularly revealing when related to the statistics that describe the social and economic situation of those populations whose "insufficient civic responsibility" is criticized. According to the *Dom Tom News* in Polynesia, "nature is endangered by the lack of civic responsibility" of its inhabitants, who destroy the landscape by dumping unauthorized waste on the roadsides.[9] But while the *Dom Tom News* criticizes the local population, it ignores the fact that the biggest sources of local pollution were the more than one hundred nuclear tests conducted by France in the territories between 1966 and 1974. According to reporting by *Le Parisien*, Tureia, the closest atoll to Mururoa, "has been touched by thirty-nine radioactive fallouts," yet no site cleanup or medical follow-up to investigate possible genetic effects of the nuclear testing have been conducted.[10] Christian Sueur, a pediatrician who worked in Polynesia,[11] noted that one out of four children there suffers from a form of thyroid cancer. He also noted that, out of three hundred people, around twenty suffer from chronic illnesses, possibly from radiation exposure. During the decade of colonization by France, a dark decade for Polynesia, it was the government that clearly demonstrated "insufficient civic responsibility" toward a part of its population. By conducting nuclear tests far from the French homeland, the government violated the right of the Polynesian population to live in a healthy environment, attacking this population's physical and genetic integrity. No redress has ever followed.

In a detailed report on the economic and social state of DOM-TOM, Victorin Lurel, a former representative from Guadeloupe, emphasizes that "except for the particular case of Saint Barthélemy, the level of wealth among the population is significantly lower than the national per capita GDP."[12]

The statistics listed in Table 6.1 illustrate other dramatic discrepancies.

One explanation for these statistics is that the agricultural workers in the relevant territories not only have too little land to satisfy their basic needs but also that their economic activity is controlled by the government. They are forced to produce sugarcane[13] or bananas, crops still tied to a colonial model of production that does not yield adequate profits and thus aggravates the workers' situation. Forced to participate in a system of large-scale export that does not cover their most basic economic needs, they become reliant on a range of exploitative power brokers, including the state, the large commercial groups, and the landowners from whom they lease the land. This situation is reminiscent of the total reliance of slaves on their owners.

The French state has granted land ownership to the offspring of the former slave owners. Meanwhile, the agricultural workers, descendants of the former slaves, have been deprived of the right to own the land cultivated by their families for more than four hundred years. This situation has led to distinctions, exclusions, and preferences founded on national descent or so-

Table 6.1 Inequalities Make a System

	Réunion	Guadeloupe/ Martinique	Guyane/ Mayotte	Rest of the country
Institutional strength/control and collection of taxes	acceptable	damaged	very damaged	
National GDP deviation	38%	31% (Guadeloupe)	73% (Mayotte)	
Unemployment rate	28%	25% (Guadeloupe)	21% (Guyane)	10.5%
Poverty rate	49%	49% (Guadeloupe) 58% (Martinique)	92% (Mayotte)	
Reading readiness among youth < 18 years old	27.7%		74.6% (Mayotte)	10%
Infant mortality		8.3% (Guadeloupe)	16.1% (Mayotte)	3.6%
Interdecile Range[a]	5.4	6.7 (Guadeloupe)	10.7 (Guyane)	3.6

[a] This indicator measures how many times more the richest 10 percent receive compared to the poorest 10 percent of the population.
Source: Data from "Substantive Equalities in Overseas," Victorin Lurel, Report, March 2016, https://www.vie-publique.fr/sites/default/files/rapport/pdf/164000180.pdf.

cial origin, all of which have the effect of destroying equal access to employment. This situation constitutes a violation of Article 2 of the International Covenant on the Elimination of All Forms of Racial Discrimination.[14]

In 1848–49, in an act of direct discrimination, the French state decided to compensate slave owners:

- by systematically refusing any procedure that could lead to compensations/reparations for the victims of slavery;
- by maintaining, against the economic realities, the system of exporting sugarcane;
- by refusing to implement a plan to fight against enslavement;

- by forcing the victims of enslavement to forget the past, to go back to work without calling into question the social order, and to be forever grateful to the Republic for having emancipated them; and
- by ruling out the possibility of any reparation.

To these direct discriminations, we could add the indirect discrimination of a state that promotes the unity of the French nation while supporting measures that benefit only a part of the population. Why wasn't the principle of unity applied when they compensated the former enslaved owners? The reality that lies beneath the surface claims of egalitarianism is that the French Antilles and the other French colonies were forced to accept that their future depended entirely on France. Otherwise, why would France be afraid to allow its former colonies economic independence, thus respecting its international obligations with respect to sustainable development, the right to sovereignty, and self-determination?

This fear perfectly illustrates the way a state acts with regard to land, and more specifically to the right to sovereignty. It is easier to pursue a discriminatory policy than to acknowledge the rights of the Afro-descent population, in the name of a unity that is nothing more than the expression of indirect economic discrimination, based, since the emergence of the French Republic, on "unequal equality." This shell game persists with respect to enslaved descendants or people of African heritage. One cannot ignore that the colonizers involved in the 1492 "discoveries" not only committed genocide against the indigenous people living on lands that the newly arrived declared "deserted," but also a crime against humanity, by tearing millions of people away from villages on the African continent.

Since 1492, the "discoveries" represent the biggest demographic and ethical catastrophe known to humanity, as underscored by Nelson Maldonado Torres.[15] They completely changed the direction of human intersubjectivity and alterity. The establishment of policies about "race," a socially constructed concept aiming to justify the hierarchies between humans, completed the project of the colonizers who arrived in the wake of these "discoverers." This catastrophic dislocation of the course of humanity is still unrepaired today, including, for example, in the choice and implementation of public policies that reinforce the paradigm of domination. Ironically, these policies were adopted in the name of "equality." The signs of this treatment are visible in the management of land distribution.

After their emancipation, the newly freed citizens were given the option of leasing land from their former masters, by signing a lease agreement called "share-cropping." The agreement forced them to give a portion of their crop to their lessor and to grow only what the lessor wanted. Meanwhile, on mainland France, agricultural workers could sign a farming lease and were free to decide on their crop and harvest. Share-cropping was only abolished in 2010. Most of the workers interviewed by this author confirmed having found the lease signed by their parents. Some have continued to sign it, while others have refused to point to the lessor's inability to prove that they were the real owner of the land.

This colonial land management has reinforced the ownership of the former enslaved owners, while completely excluding the slave descendants from owning land. This situation is similar to the compensation system after the abolition of 1848. If today the state decides to grant a title deed to 45 percent of "apparent owners" without making an effort to consider those who have been excluded, this decision only marks the coloniality of power of the state, decreeing that one part of the population is less important than the other.

In this context, the negative lexicon—any harmful tax leaks, the fight against overseas fraud, the many disorders that are caused by the weakness of the titration of overseas land—used by the prime minister in his answer to the Court of Auditors' report insinuates that the state's colonial identity has never been set aside.[16] For example, the government refuses to consider the indirect economic discriminations against Afro-descendant agricultural workers, as underlined by the International Labor Organization in Convention 111.[17] If agricultural workers in Guadeloupe and the other overseas territories and departments were refused their rights as victims of crimes against humanity in the nineteenth century, the twenty-first century should offer an examination of this discriminatory and flagrant gap between lessors and lessees. Instead, the state continues to recognize a vast majority of descendants of former enslaved owners as legitimate landowners today, although they have no legitimate right to the land, apart from having unilaterally declared it theirs.

The issue of lack of title, mentioned in the Court of Auditors' report, cannot be treated separately from the historical recontextualization of the "discoveries" of 1492 and the lasting persistence of colonialism. As mentioned in the report, parts of the land affected by alleged irregularities in tax collection belong to the state, which acquired them as a matter of private law.[18]

The prime minister's observation in his response about "the numerous buildings erected on land belonging to the state or to local collectivities" should be examined through the lens of the law, but also through the same historical perspective as his proposal to make "the fight against overseas fraud one of the structural axes of government policy." Instead, the only serious issue is to establish who owns the land, instead of "rewarding" 45 percent of the apparent owners—if we only consider Guadeloupe—by legalizing their ownership, as the report suggests. Still, on what basis would this ownership be decided? If the state was to follow through on the proposal to thoroughly investigate land titles, would it not risk being in a delicate position from the point of view of the principles established by the administration concerning property taxes?[19]

It is regrettable that the government has required occupants without title (descendants of slaves, that is) to regularize their situation only in order to block a possible contestation; the people concerned could bring a financial action, demanding the reimbursement of some €500 million, which would result in a considerable loss of resources by the state, since it is a sizeable owner of the land in question, as noted by the Court of Auditors: "the DGFIP estimates that 30 percent of the taxations carried out against occupants without legal title (53 million euro per year) concern goods owned by the State."[20]

This dysfunction in the collection of property taxes in the overseas territories forces us to pay close attention to the way Martinique, Guadeloupe, La Réunion, and French Guyana moved from the status of sovereign and autonomous territories to the status of private property. We should recall that, through the Charter of 1626, Richelieu ordered two adventurers, Pierre Belain d'Esnambuc, the lieutenant of the buccaneer of Urbain de Roissey, and Urbain du Roissey, the seigneur of Chardonville, born in Paris, to found a company to establish a colony in the West Indies and to bring their spoils to the Association of the Lords of the Western Isles. This would be the foundation of the colony of Saint-Kitts (Iles de Saint-Christophe) and the beginning of the systematic and planned extermination of the Caribs. In Martinique, after seven years of violence and as a result of the first "peace treaty" (signed on December 21, 1657), the Caribs were relegated to only half of the island. But as the colonists wanted bigger properties, they started the 1658 war, as a means of ethnic cleansing. This allowed the colonists to declare that the newly acquired territories were uninhabited, or that only a few savages were living there, before declaring themselves official owners of these lands.

Under Louis XIII, the Charter of 1635 had solidified these kinds of claims to ownership. The colonization of the West Indies and of those islands that "were not yet inhabited by Christians" would be assured in perpetuity by private companies, thus offering a legal framework for an offensive against the Caribs. In 1643, the first slaves arrived in Guadeloupe. From this period on, these territories belonged to the crown. In March 1645, the king imposed the Custom of Paris on the islands, which opened the way to colonization by the monarchy, who proceeded to install a de facto direct administration in the colonies.[21] In 1648, the Company of the American Islands went bankrupt, was placed into liquidation and sold in batches in Paris by a notary. Thereafter, Louis XIV scolded the private owners for not "apply[ing] themselves enough to populate the islands in order to cultivate them and to establish a substantial trade, as they do in foreign countries ... and that they did not provide enough vessels to bring to France all the necessary items that its inhabitants need."[22] Later he ordered all the shareholders of the company to turn in their licensing titles. This opened up a new period of colonization, facilitated by the 1664 Charter,[23] which gave the Company of the West Indies (Compagnie des Indes Occidentales) the mission of expanding to Guyana, North America, Canada, Newfoundland, and to the coast of Africa from Cape Verde to the Cape of Good Hope.

With this series of charters, the Caribbean region found itself at the forefront of the transatlantic slave trade.[24] By the Edict of December 1674, the French monarchy revoked the Company of West Indies, turning Guadeloupe and Martinique into French colonies.[25]

During the French Revolution, these power relationships were continued: the judicial decrees of November 22 and December 1, 1790, replaced dominion by the monarchy with domination by the nation.[26] Though the law of April 4, 1792, recognized the political equality of mulattos, tensions remained high between white colons, mullatoes, free Blacks, and slaves. The 1794 Convention declared the abolition of "slavery of the Blacks in the colony; accordingly, [France] declares that all people, without distinction of color, residing in the colonies, are French citizens, and will enjoy the benefits and the rights in accordance with the constitution."[27] Abolition, yes, but without the reallocation of lands or the implementation of a reparations system for the former enslaved.

When Martinique, Santa Lucia, and Tobago were returned to France following the Treaty of Amiens (March 1802), enslavement was restored by the law of May 20, 1802, after a sizeable displacement of enslaved people.[28] In

Guadeloupe, which had belonged to France again since 1794, this restoration was the effect of a simple consular order on July 16, 1802, that, legally, could not have repealed the laws issued before abolition. When the Civil Code came into effect in Guadeloupe on November 9, 1805, its dispositions only affected the "French"; the other "populations" continued to be governed by the Code Noir (Black Code). In the first part of the twentieth century, these territories became overseas departments after the adoption of the law: "The colonies of Guadeloupe, Martinique, Réunion and French Guyana are set up as French departments."[29]

Returning to the precarious tax collection in Guadeloupe, the situation is clearly illustrated in Table 6.1 above. Should we attribute the enormous economic inequalities to the descendants of the colonist landlords, and to the way their ancestors acquired these lands through blood, crime, and theft? Or should we attribute it to the descendants of slaves, who were victims of crimes against humanity? Or maybe to the indigenous people who lived on these lands when the first colonists arrived? Let's add the state to this list—did it not become one of the main owners of the lands acquired through crime? According to the Penal Code (Art. 321-1), it is considered a crime to " conceal, hold, or provide an object, or to act as intermediary for its transfer, if it is known that the said object originates from a crime or an infraction." Ownership of these lands was the result of concealment, a process whereby someone benefits "in full knowledge of the facts, and by every possible means, of the product of a crime or an infraction." Is this not the case of the state, which did everything in its power to prevent reparations to the victims of slavery, despite the degrading and inhumane treatment that was inflicted on them for centuries? The state did not do anything, during the second abolition of 1848, to prevent the newly freed from facing the choice of either becoming precarious laborers of their former masters or being forced away from their homes, their housing, the only residence that they and their families had known since their arrival. This oppressive choice would once again present itself, this time to the descendants of slaves, when the state decided to only endow 45 percent of the agricultural workers with a title deed, forcing the other 55 percent to leave their ancestral homes.

And yet, this is the preferred solution, to put an end to the payment of the property tax by people who should not be in this position, and to avoid a large movement of protest against the state. This contestation would force the state to reimburse the taxes wrongly collected, to find itself owner of all these lands that are, in fact, reserved for private use, and to assume all the expenditures incumbent upon an owner, among others to sign leases and to settle claims; this would also, as already noted, make it impossible for the state to collect the property taxes.

In order to understand why the former enslaved have never received reparations for the crimes against humanity to which they were subjected, or why the indigenous people have never received compensations for the genocide perpetrated against them, it is important to remember the historic conditions under which the imposition of enslavement and colonialization took place. These include the legislative provisions articulated in the decree of April 27, 1848, concerning the abolition of enslavement in the French colonies and settlements.[30]

The famous abolitionist Victor Schœlcher was one of the decree's principal authors. His investment in abolition was dictated by moral and compassionate principles rather than political convictions: "The Whites cannot remain masters, since the Blacks no longer want to be slaves. This must end." But his first concern was to save the monarchy, and therefore the security of the landowners: "The Blacks would have freed themselves if the mainland had not freed them. The monarchy, once and for all collapsed, would have given power to the rightful ones, and what good could a handful of masters have done against a mass who knew the Republic was proclaimed?"[31]

He also wanted to save the plantations that were on the verge of failure: "Any delay would have given rise to the Blacks' revolt. . . . The interim government has foreseen it. It realized everything, and acted quickly, but not lightly, and it emancipated the slaves in order to save the masters."[32] It is in this context that the former owners received financial compensation, while the consequences of the mass crime that lasted more than three centuries were never addressed. Abolition was, on the one hand, a way of cushioning white domination in the colonies when the economic model of enslavement was running out of gas, and of developing policies of social control (domestic passports, diversifying crops beyond taxed sugarcane, mandatory school for children older than twelve). On the other hand, abolition was a way of providing new endowments for the industrial and financial capitalism that looked toward the African continent as an expansion of territories and a source of natural resources for the new French colonial empire.

The National Assembly approved the compensation arrangements proposed by the act of April 30, 1849. This meant retrospective ratification of the decree of April 27, 1848, particularly Article 5, according to which "the

National Assembly will set the value of the compensation to be granted to the colonists."[33] At the same time, the decree of 1848 repealed the act of 1802 that reinstated enslavement, and granted the most fundamental rights, like the right not to be enslaved, following the Declaration of the Rights of Man and Citizen.

The conditions for the compensation for former masters were debated in three National Assembly sessions on January 19 and 23, and April 30, 1849. The focus was on saving the economic system, as the finance minister (Hippolyte Passy, minister of finances, among others, in the first cabinet of Louis Napoléon Bonaparte [December 20, 1848–October 31, 1849]; during the debates on abolition, he had proposed a gradual abolition of slavery: freedom of children at birth and emancipation by redeeming) admitted: "[We don't want to] deal specifically with knowing by what legal right we will grant compensations to the former landowners. . . . What we need is to restore their credit. This is the first of the colonial needs that we need to maintain. Only this credit will give back to the colonies their life, their activity, their necessary dynamism." For the government, the abolition of slavery, through the choices made, enshrined the application of a special type of justice that exists outside the common law. This specific application of the law endures to this day, a situation that raises not just moral but political questions.

Economic rather than legal considerations drove the decision to compensate the former masters. Cash flow was needed to assure the plantations' economic growth. In Guadeloupe, Governor Layrle reminded people that "the compensation of landowners is legitimate," and he asked the newly freed to "pull themselves up by work" and to "enrich the country," concluding that "all his attention and all his efforts will be devoted from now on to secure a legitimate compensation to the owners. Vive la République."[34]

The historical record demonstrates that a double-trigger system was established, giving immediate compensation to the colonist-owners in the amount of 6 million francs, and, in addition, an annuity of 6 million francs for a period of twenty years (for a total of 120 million francs), registered in the general ledger of public debt.[35] Part of this fund was supposed to transit through colonial banks, which later played a major role in confronting the established order.[36] During the same period, a total of 248,000 enslaved were freed. But no reparations have ever been considered for the victims of exploitation, genocide, and crimes against humanity.

Compensation for the former enslaved owners, mentioned in the decree of April 27, 1848, and summarized in Table 6.2, consolidated the commodi-

Table 6.2. Variation of slaves' market value, statutorily established

Martinique	Guadeloupe	Guyane	Réunion
425.34F	469.53 francs Compensation for freeing of 87,087 slaves: 1,947,164.85 francs Annuity: 38,943,296 francs	624.66 francs	711.59 francs
TOTAL	40,890,461 francs		

Source: Data from Alain Buffon, "L'indemnisation des planteurs après l'abolition de l'esclavage," Société d'Histoire de la Guadeloupe, number 67–68, 1986, https://id.erudit.org /iderudit/1043814ar.

fication of people, contrary to basic tenets of French law. Repairing the crimes of slavery and colonialism, and their current consequences, would have necessitated getting the French Constitutional Council to repeal the laws of 1848 and 1849, because the relevant laws were contrary to France's international commitments, "its obligations to assure the respect of international conventions by the public authorities." That implies an obligation "to compensate for all the damage inflicted by the intervention of a law passed in disregard of France's international commitments."

However, reparations proceedings should not be limited to financial compensation. In the case of land ownership, they should question the way land deeds have been acquired since colonialization and how the law has been used to strip the victims of any rights. This preoccupation is not new. During the 2009 social conflict "contre la profitasyion,"[37] France made a commitment to assure "the economic development of the overseas territories"; one of the initiatives was to "collect and analyze all the elements needed to inventory the land and real estate without title deeds," but also to "establish a connection between a property and a person, in an effort to create, or to recreate, the title deed."[38] To date, this policy has not been implemented in Guadeloupe.

If the goal of the Court of Auditors was to determine the conditions for ensuring full and complete equality concerning property tax collection, it should have forced the state to investigate the fundamental inequalities sustained by persons of African descent. The state could have implemented a system of land redistribution by taking into account historical and judicial data, including the fact that the 1848 and 1849 laws were only aimed at shoring up colonial rule. The management of land tax collection reveals elements of the government's enduring colonialism, including its perception of otherness. Structural racism, often unconscious, has a real impact on the entire French society. That is why reparations must have as their objective the end of these elements of colonialism, the end of the influence exerted by the former slave owners, and the introduction of a form of social peace where the horrors of the past are not hidden and forgotten or replaced by a simple reconciliation of memories.

With these aims in mind, agricultural workers, union members from Guadeloupe,[39] and the Franz Fanon Foundation took legal action, in 2014, against the French state. The litigation's first goal was to repeal of the law of 1849 and of Article 5 of the decree of 1848. The latter provided the legal framework that has prevented victims from receiving any reparation or other judicial remedy, perpetuating the harmful effects of the state's criminal legacy.[40] For a long time, the people from Guadeloupe have claimed their fundamental rights, but these two laws have blocked their claims.

Article 5 of the 1848 decree violates the principle of equality by compensating certain people at the expense of other people who are reduced to the status of personal property.[41] It also violates the principle of respect for human dignity and the right to resist oppression by forbidding any form of access to the law.[42] It supports the impunity of the criminal by denying justice to the victim. It also infringes on the principle of ownership by legalizing the property of the person who committed the crime, and on the principle of sustainability by imposing a regime of colonial exploitation, by ruining people, in contravention of Article 6 of the Environmental Charter of 2004, which requires states to promote sustainable development designed to further social and economic progress.

In its September 8, 2016, answer to the union, agricultural workers, and the Fanon Foundation, the Board of State Court dismissed the petition on the following grounds: "If the law of May 21, 2001, *symbolically* recognizes slavery and the slave trade as crimes against humanity, this will not have force as a matter of criminal law justifying a conviction by virtue of the principle of non-retroactivity. . . . The Highest Court of Appeals considered that because the crime was not committed by the Axis parties during the Second World War [which could have been covered by the Nuremberg International military tribunal] . . . French law cannot assign criminal culpability."[43]

In the meantime, since the organizations were expecting this outcome to the first petition, they introduced a second petition, this time concerning the July 2010 law, concerning the switch from sharecropping—which reinforced land ownership—to farm renting, which had replaced sharecropping since 1946 in mainland France.[44] This new petition questioned the compliance of Article 10 of this law with the principles of law and equity, and more generally with the fundamental principles of the Declaration of the Rights of Man and Citizen.

The objective, particularly for the agricultural workers, was to secure agrarian reform and end the perpetuation of the crime. Their petition urged more sustained attention to the crime against humanity that has allowed the continuation, in the collective unconscious, of the idea that humanity is divided in two by the politics of race: one group free of political constraints, "the beings," and the other, because of the color of their skins, relegated to the status of "non-beings." The petitioners are still awaiting a decision, but during arguments before the court, the prosecutor acknowledged, after presenting the facts, that the situation of land leasing raises the very serious question of to whom the land belongs.

Certain intellectuals or political figures prefer silence or even the erasure of this historical period, as if to blot out its memory. These practices confirm the colonizing domination of the people in power. For example, in 2016, some parliamentarians belonging to Socialist Party, in the National Assembly, proposed an amendment during discussions on a bill about equality and citizenship.[45] The amendment called for "a moral reparation of the damages incurred by the slaves, by repealing the provisions regarding the compensations of the colonists."[46] They asked for moral reparations, whereas the perpetrators of the crime had earlier received land and money. This amendment, initiated by an Afro-descendant (Victorin Lurel, representative of Guadeloupe, former overseas minister), passed. But the amendment states that it doesn't "claim any willingness to compensate the victims of slavery." That issue must still be raised. The erasure of the period of enslavement adds another level to the crime. The victims are dismissed again as Non-Beings. By refusing, once again, to acknowledge that there has been a transgression of the concept of humanity, these representatives confirm the status of perpetual victim to the enslaved and their descendants.

In the view of this conceptual failure and of this willingness to erase the memory of the crimes against Africa and its millions of enslaved people, it is essential to set humanity back in the right direction, and to reaffirm the principles of intersubjectivity, equality, and protection of human dignity. There are no other ways but to overcome the impunity of the criminal and to clear the way for the victim to access justice and the right to sovereignty. Contrary to the preference of certain governments, institutions, and organizations, it is obvious that, since the second abolition, this work of rebuilding equality can only be realized through a consideration of the close relationship between justice and history, and an analysis of the role of the legal processes in the colonial system. This chapter is based on research completed in April 2019.

PART II

Reparations: Precedents
and Lessons Learned

CHAPTER 7

History on Trial: Mau Mau Reparations and the High Court of Justice

Caroline Elkins

On a brisk, spring morning in 2011, five elderly Kikuyu stood on the steps of London's High Court of Justice where the sun's brilliance combined with the glare of countless television cameras to create an atmosphere of disorienting optimism. More than a century had passed since Queen Victoria had opened the imposing gothic structure, which was a physical testament to her nation's commitment to the rule of law, both at home and in the empire. At the time, she presided over nearly a third of the world's land mass and some 500 million people. Britain's civilizing mission, with all of its uplifting rhetoric, was the cornerstone of Britain's imperial endeavors, and had become part and parcel of how many Britons understood and internalized the entwined institutions of nation, empire, and monarchy.

The rule of law, however, had taken on a different meaning in yesteryear's empire than in London's contemporary High Court of Justice. In Britain's colonial possessions, denials and subversions of rights expanded as colonial administrations became more entrenched and increasingly faced local populations who demanded equal protections under colonial rule and, eventually, independence from the crown. Particularly in the years after World War II, such demands often turned violent, with protests, insurrections, and states of emergency erupting in locations ranging from Bengal and Malaya to Nyasaland and Cyprus. In each instance, British officials labeled those insisting upon rights, not to mention independence, as terrorists, while highlighting real and fictitious indigenous acts of violence and simultaneously dismissing any claims of colonial repression as either exaggerated or unfortunate one-offs. Such a carefully honed, exculpating narrative carried forward into the construction of Britain's official archive, and with it the writing of imperial histories and the future accounts of what the British Empire meant to the nation itself.

Yet, in 2011, on that brilliant spring morning on the steps of London's High Court, the symbolic meaning of the five elderly Kikuyu standing beneath Queen Victoria's gothic shadow was unshakeable. Their very presence shattered several long-held truths about Britain and its empire. Together, the three men and two women from Kenya's rural foothills were poised for their first courtroom appearance since filing their claim some two years earlier. The charge: state-directed, systematic torture and violence in Britain's 1950s colonial detention camps in Kenya. Rooted as it was in historical revisions of past imperial actions, the case was unprecedented in Britain. For the very first time, the British Empire was on trial.[1]

That it was former Mau Mau adherents leveling charges of systematic abuse was astonishing for most Britons, particularly those who had lived through Kenya's state of emergency (1952–60). For many, Mau Mau—with its ritual oath taking and method of killing with *pangas*, or machetes—was synonymous with atavistic savagery. Not since the "Black Hole of Calcutta" had a phrase from empire entered into the English language with such ominous effect. Mau Mau adherents had used violent means to achieve their goals, including hamstringing cattle and murdering European settlers and African colonial supporters. The movement, however, had legitimate grievances and demanded *ithaka na wiyathi*, or land and freedom. Like many end-of-empire conflicts, Mau Mau was an anticolonial and civil war. In Kenya, this civil dimension was contained largely to the Kikuyu who constituted some 20 percent of the colony's population and were the most impacted by British rule. To suppress Mau Mau, the colonial government enacted nearly 150 pages of emergency regulations. These regulations legally enabled the colonial administration to launch a full-on assault against the Kikuyu civilian population in order to break its intransigence and passive wing support for the 20,000 Mau Mau insurgents who were fighting a guerrilla struggle against British military and colonial forces. By war's end, the British government had detained nearly the entire Kikuyu population, subjected detainees to punishing forced labor routines, and pursued policies of food denial and systematic torture to save "civilization" from the specter of so-called Mau Mau terrorists.

Some fifty years after the uprising, the Mau Mau claimants faced an up-hill battle against a determined and well-funded British government, which vowed to fight the case to the bitter end. While insisting that there was no validity to the allegations of systematic torture and abuse, Britain's courtroom defenders turned to legal technicalities to dismiss the case. As for the claimants, they relied on the revisionist expertise of historians, together with the surgically parsed and reassembled evidence that was crucial to the case's success. So, too, they depended on a legal team of human rights lawyers in London and Nairobi and their abilities to integrate highly specialized historical knowledge with the legal arguments necessary to win a case that few believed had much chance for success.

Ultimately, the Mau Mau case hinged on a triangulation between history, archives, and the law. As revisionist history was put on trial, so, too, was the near-century-old tradition of writing imperial history and, with it, long-held beliefs in what constitutes an official archive and usable historical evidence. For the Mau Mau claimants to succeed, battles over history that were playing out in the academic and public intellectual worlds would need to be recast in the positivist universe of the courtroom. There, the High Court judge would, at once, cast judgment on the fate of the claimants' allegations as well as the historical profession's account of the past and, with it, the present and future understandings of the British Empire.

Archiving and Writing History

Historians of empire have had a particular, and powerful, role to play in how the public and its politicians have viewed and shaped the world. Save for a few marginalized thinkers, often called radicals, British imperial historians ordered their narratives to conform to the dominant worldview, and offered explicit ideological defenses of ongoing British endeavors throughout the colonized world. For decades, Anglo-Saxon trusteeship, and the fairness if not humility with which the "white man's burden" brought humanity and civilization to the "lesser races" of the world, were the watermarks that ran through nearly every page of writing on Britain's imperial past. Then, there was a dramatic shift in historical perspective that took place after World War II. It was within this context that the many historians from Oxbridge and Kings College, London, in particular, no longer offered explicit moral claims about imperialism; instead, they scripted new interpretations of Britain's past that centered on the "official mind" of imperial expansion and retreat. Yet, as Richard Drayton has noted, "this post-1950 anti-ideological moment was itself a kind of ideological position."[2] Britain was no longer the story's selfless hero; nor was it the villain. In effect, imperial history now avoided the terrain of moral claims. To do so, it turned its head away from the ugly business of empire, leaving the questions of colonial violence, racism, and exploitation, and their meanings unasked, and therefore unanswered. Moreover, these historians spurned the claims of nationalist movements throughout the empire, minimizing their intentions as well as their effects. Drayton continues, emphasizing, "It was the perfect form of Imperial history for a British nation no longer so confident of its imperial role . . . and the School equally allowed the British nation to escape the scene of the crime."[3]

It is here that we see a striking coincidence in timing. Historians were shifting focus away from the "scene of the crime" at the exact moment when British colonial violence was approaching its most unbridled state. With imperial retreat came long, drawn-out end-of-empire wars. Beginning in Palestine and then moving to Malaya, Kenya, Cyprus, Aden, Northern Ireland, and elsewhere, the British initiated some thirty states of emergency in the years after World War II. In the case of Kenya, newspaper headlines at the time chronicled the allegations of torture and murder in Britain's detention camps and the colonial government's bonfires incinerating documents on the eve of decolonization. So, too, did the media cover Colonial Office insistences that nothing was awry behind the barbed wires of detention, and nothing of historical value was being destroyed with the archival purges.

Unlike the emerging postcolonial critique, for this new era of imperial historians and their descendants the neutrality, if not sanctity, of the British official archives was crucial. Written documents have been the only form of trusted evidence for doctrinaire historians, despite the fact that many knew for decades that the colonial archives, in particular, were missing crucial sets of files. Moreover, for many in the historical profession, oral testimonies were the stuff of anthropologists or area studies, particularly if they were taken from Black or brown people; reading archival ashes was the voodoo of critical theorists. But, without the glue of alternative sources, the fragments of evidence in the archives would remain just that, fragments. The power of the archive—despite the myriad ways in which the British government sought to control its contents for decades, as witnessed in the document incinerators of Kenya—shaped the ways in which the future understood the British imperial past. Over time, layers upon layers of historical accounts privileged the official narrative of the state as contained in its official records. The historical profession, with all of its claims of neutrality, has been deeply implicated in the reproduction of so-called archival realities and, with it, the British government's end-of-empire fictions, so carefully created and tended for decades.

In 2005, all of this began to change when the historical spotlight was turned on colonial Kenya. There, illuminated using the ashes and fragments of evidence, were the original crime scenes of the Mau Mau detention camps, emergency villages, and screening centers. Behind the barbed wire, hundreds of thousands of Africans were subjected to forced labor, systematized coercion, and unspeakable tortures. The book that reconstructed this history was my work, *Imperial Reckoning: The Untold Story of Britain's Gulag in Kenya*. At its most basic level, the book was an act of historical reconstruction. It was the first full account of the processes of detention during 1950s Kenya, processes that would witness some 1.5 million Kikuyu rounded up without trial and placed behind barbed wire in one of some one hundred camps or eight hundred wartime villages. The lack of previous systematic historical enquiry into this topic was, in part, a reflection of its politically charged nature. There was also the absence of evidence. Entire department files—like those of the Police Department—were missing from the national archives in Nairobi, and Britain's national archive at Kew was similarly plagued with an incomplete set of records.

In response, I developed an expansive research toolkit that included a thorough excavation of official sources. This included secondary and tertiary file series; private archives such as those at Rhodes House Library, Oxford, and various Christian missions in Kenya; memoirs and newspaper accounts; and hundreds of hours of original interviews with survivors of the detention camps and emergency villages, former colonial officers, missionaries, and European settlers, among others. Ultimately, the book drew upon these multiple sources to create an evidentiary mosaic, which, when completed, was still missing pieces but whose image was boldly evident, nonetheless. It was an image of extensive colonial violence, cover-ups at the highest levels of British government, and the subsequent complicity of many historians who had turned away from the ugly business of empire and produced histories that, at best, suggested, like the British colonial government at the time, that these episodes were one-offs rather than anything endemic and systematic to the British colonial project at the end of empire. These same historians penned some of the most scathing critiques of *Imperial Reckoning*, focusing particularly on uses of evidence, including the book's perceived lack of written documentation and overreliance on the alleged faulty oral testimonies of old men and women claiming victimhood.

History, Archives, and the Law: A Case for Reparations

When five elderly Kikuyu claimants filed suit against the British government in the spring of 2009, *Imperial Reckoning* would soon find itself in the middle of a triangulated battle between the law, the archives, and the historical literature on empire.[4] The Foreign and Commonwealth Office (FCO) was the named defendant for the British government, with the Honourable Mr. Justice McCombe presiding. The London law firm of Leigh Day, with the support of the Kenya Human Rights Commission, represented the Kenyan claimants. Together, they officially engaged my expertise and the historical evidence of *Imperial Reckoning* beginning in 2008. As the case progressed, the claimants' attorneys engaged, in late 2010 and early 2011, two other historians, David Anderson and Huw Bennett, whose work covered other areas related to the case.

Rather than contest directly the merits of the claimants' allegations, the FCO sought, instead, to strike down the case on legal technicality on two separate occasions, once in April 2011, and then in July 2012. The first strike down attempt centered on the question of the colonial state and liability. Throughout the case, the FCO expended considerable effort distinguishing between the colonial government based in Nairobi, which acted "in right of Kenya," and the colonial government based in London, which acted "in right of Britain." In effect, while the colonial government in Kenya was only notionally independent from the metropole, the FCO, for the purposes of this case, sought to draw an unambiguous line of separation between the colony and metropole in the 1950s. In so doing, it sought to distance the British colonial government at home from colonial officials' decisions and actions in Kenya and, with it, any liability that may have arisen due to systematized violence and torture in the detention camps during the Mau Mau uprising. In essence, if the Nairobi government acted "in right of Kenya," then any liability that may have incurred due to its actions was passed to the independent government of Kenya with the transfer of power in December 1963, according to FCO logic in defending itself in the case.

The British government's line of reasoning, while not without merit, was problematic. For certain, an overarching ethos of "trust the man on the spot" dictated British colonial governance in its far-flung empire. As a matter of practicality, it would have been impossible for the metropolitan government to micromanage day-to-day colonial rule. Be that as it may, the FCO sought to impose a kind of order, or a clearly delineated relationship between the colonial government in Kenya and Britain, that did not exist. In practice, the colonial government in Kenya and elsewhere was a state within a state. This is because the colonial government in Nairobi governed Kenya, and was governed by Britain.

The first strike-down hearing lasted nearly two weeks, and was a mini-trial unto itself. Together with mounting a defense against issues of the colonial state and liability, the claimants had several other high-water marks to reach to prove their claims had merit and were worthy of a full trial. First, they had to demonstrate, using extensive historical evidence, that the British colonial government in London knew of the abuses in the detention camps, did nothing to mitigate the abuses once they became known, and, furthermore, was complicit in systematizing the abuses. Looking ahead to a possible full trial, the claimants also had to demonstrate that there was enough extant historical evidence for the British government to defend itself. In other words, the British government, some fifty years after the events in question, had to be guaranteed a fair trial. Given the fact that many of the witnesses were dead, documentary evidence—and substantial amounts of it—were crucial to the claimants' case.

I produced two witness statements for the first strike-down hearing, the first and most lengthy of which was filed in February 2011. The court also required that I prepare a comprehensive statement "to explain the documentary material" to accompany my submission.[5] My February 2011 witness statement was, in effect, a trimmed-down version of *Imperial Reckoning*, technical in its reference to archival documentation throughout and, as much as it was possible, devoid of interpretation. In fact, my evidence was the topic of some debate in October 2010, the outcome of which would govern the nature of my work and that of the other historians once they joined the case. In effect, our roles as historical experts aligned with the conventions of our profession insofar as they were based on the identification of sources, though they also deviated from our conventions insofar as we were, in theory, to provide no analysis or interpretation. On this point, Justice McCombe was clear:

[The previous judge] dealt with the position of evidence which the claimants wish to call. That was the evidence of Professor Elkins. She had written one of the seminal texts in 2005. He accepted that her evidence was relevant in identifying documents or other material, but should not be admitted as expert evidence (that is evidence of opinion) as to what was to be inferred from those documents taken as a whole. Because of her familiarity with documents, she is thus able to identify documents which are likely to be of greatest interest in the arguments of the respective parties. She has a greater facility for this than do the parties themselves because of her great experience gained over some ten years of looking through archives in the course of which she researched a text in which she has interest. Plainly she makes efficient the process of identifying documents and material.[6]

To produce my witness statement, I relied upon the some six hundred footnotes of archival evidence contained in *Imperial Reckoning*, together with multiple other documents accumulated during my ten years of research for the book. The witness statement contained no transcripts from oral interviews. Instead, it analyzed, through the narrative arc of the witness statement, the institutional structures and practices of detention, the mounting allegations of abuses and deaths, the knowledge of colonial officials of these instances of torture and death, the systematization of colonial violence over time, and the efforts on the part of the colonial government in Nairobi and London to cover up abuses and sidestep any independent investigations. Put another way, using the techniques of historical narrative and embedded argument, the witness statement offered implicit analyses and interpretations, despite the court's directive.

The court also charged me "to identify, where possible, the extent of, and reasons for, document destruction and/or removal prior to independence by the British Colonial Government."[7] I detailed in my witness statement observations of archival gaps similar to those that I put forward in *Imperial Reckoning*. Missing from the archives in Kenya were, among other files, the Police Department and Special Branch files relating to interrogations and/or screening; District and Provincial Commissioner files and, with them, material related to villagization; and individual detainee files. Of course, thousands of documents remain in the official archives in London and Nairobi, many of which pertain to the more mundane practices of the camps, including their bureaucratic structures and functions. This evidence is not unimportant, as it is crucial to the reconstruction of the system of detention. As for the more sensitive documents, while many had clearly been removed or destroyed, I note in *Imperial Reckoning* that "even the most assiduous purges, however, often fail to clean up all of the incriminating evidence."[8] This evidence that escaped the purges—including hundreds of letters written by detainees at the time of the emergency, chronicling in detail the abuses and deprivations in the camps; colonial officials' acknowledgment and cover-up of forced labor in the detention camps; the official sanctioning of the dilution technique in the Mwea camps in spite of the colonial government's knowledge that the practice resulted in detainee abuse and death; and the creation of legal mechanisms to enable the use of force in the camps—was submitted with my witness statement.

To the surprise of the FCO and other observers, three months after the first strike-down hearing, the justice dismissed the FCO's motion, paving the way for the case to go forward to a second strike-down hearing, this one on the issue of statute of limitations. Importantly, Justice McCombe issued a lengthy historic ruling with his judgment on the first strike down that did not equivocate on several key issues. With regard to the question of liability passing to the independent Kenya government at the time of decolonization, McCombe stated that such an argument was "dishonourable." And, when addressing the question of the written historical evidence documenting systematic abuses and a cover-up, Justice McCombe was clear in his Approved Judgment: "The materials evidencing the continuing abuses in detention camps in subsequent years [1954–55] are substantial, as is the evidence of the knowledge of both governments that they were happening and of the failure to take effective action to stop them."[9] In effect, through the positivist lens of the court, academic critiques of *Imperial Reckoning*— which, in efforts to discredit the work, overlooked the hundreds of footnotes pointing to archival evidence, and instead focused on a perceived overreliance on oral testimonies—were put to rest. So, too, was the FCO's misguided belief that it could dismiss the Mau Mau victims' claims as meritless.

The Hanslope Disclosure

The production of historical evidence in the Mau Mau case proved a two-way street. Just months prior to the first strike-down hearing in 2011, and weeks before my first witness statement was due to the court, the FCO made a stunning announcement. As a result of the claimants' persistent requests for disclosure, the British government "discovered" some 300 boxes containing approximately 1,500 files of previously undisclosed documents. British colonial officials had packed up and removed these files of documents from Kenya at the time of decolonization in 1963, and they had remained under British lock and key, in various locations in and around London, ever since. When discovered, the boxes took up nearly one hundred linear feet of storage space in Hanslope Park—a Fort Knox–like building located in Buckinghamshire. Also known as "Spook Central," it is the site of some of Britain's deepest secrets, including those related to MI5 and MI6. The FCO also disclosed that, next to the Kenya boxes, they had similarly found some 8,800 files from 36 former British colonies that had also been spirited away from the various colonies at the time of imperial retreat.

The "Hanslope Disclosure"—as referred to by the court—is an extraordinary discovery by any standard. In the context of the Mau Mau case, and armed with the power of judicial disclosure, the court sought to evoke further evidence from the Hanslope files to understand which colonial state—that in Nairobi, that in in London, or both—oversaw the creation and execution of structures of violence in Kenya; to what degree this violence was systematized as opposed to the unfortunate doings of a few "bad apples"; and to what degree the colonial state in London was complicit in destroying and removing evidence at the time of decolonization. Indeed, these were the key interrelated issues at the heart of the Mau Mau case. That is, to what degree was abuse and destruction of life and property part of a calculated and systematic policy in Kenya and either overseen or, at the very least, condoned by the colonial state in London? It is here that the documents contained in the Hanslope Disclosure shed important additional light not only onto the nature of systematic violence at the end of empire but also on the degree to which the colonial governments in London and Nairobi were implicated in the selective process of how the past has been documented and remembered.

In the context of the Mau Mau case, excavating the Hanslope Disclosure was a massive, time-consuming exercise. To prepare my witness statement for the July 2012 hearing, I pulled together a group of Harvard students who, along with me, went through some 30,000 pages of new documents that were scanned and uploaded onto a searchable database. The British government, however, did its best to make our job difficult. The FCO first culled the files and released to the court those that it believed to be relevant to the case, and removed those it deemed to be either irrelevant or allegedly sensitive due to national security interests. Consequently, an ongoing struggle ensued, with the claimants' team demanding the release of relevant files not contained in the database, the FCO being slow to respond, and, when it finally did, making the releases in a piecemeal fashion, rendering our work, at times, similar to my previous efforts at Kew and elsewhere. That is, we had to make sense of the fragments and understand better what was missing, and why.

My third witness statement, based on the new evidence, ran over two hundred pages in length, notwithstanding exhibits, and pointed to thousands of pages of relevant new documents. Though none of the files contained in the Hanslope Disclosure fundamentally changed either the premise of the case or the arguments that I had made in *Imperial Reckoning*, they did offer substantial additional written evidence of British colonial violence. The documents that the British government either lost or hid for decades provided pages and pages of additional evidence validating the legal claims of the case and, with them, the historical claims that had originally been put forward, using a mosaic of historical fragments, in *Imperial Reckoning*.[10]

The new layers of additional written evidence were crucial to the claimants' success in overcoming the FCO's second strike-down motion. For nearly two weeks in July 2012, the British government argued that the claimants long exceeded the three-year limit for filing a claim and therefore the case had no standing in the court. Moreover, the FCO's attorneys vigorously defended Her Majesty's government's right to a fair trial and suggested over and again that too many eyewitnesses were dead and the amount of written evidence was thin, at best, and was certainly not enough for the British government to mount a reasonable defense to the claims of the case.

Once again, the claimants—and their historians—faced a very high burden of proof. We had to demonstrate, first, that the claimants could not have filed their case prior to the publication of *Imperial Reckoning* in 2005. In other words, the claimants had to prove that it was not until the historical reconstruction contained in *Imperial Reckoning* that they had enough detailed evidence to support their claims of widespread systematic abuse and hence a case against the British government. Second, and of equal importance, the claimants had to demonstrate that there was enough evidence available—in the form of both written documents and live witnesses—for the British government to defend itself against the charges. In both instances, the additional evidence contained in the Hanslope Disclosure was immensely important. Not only did the new documents provide thousands of additional evidentiary pages supporting the claimants' case but they also offered written evidence that chronicled the destruction and removal of documents from Kenya at the time of decolonization. In other words, for the very first time we, as historians, had documents documenting the document destruction in Kenya, and massive amounts of them.

By both legal and historical standards, the new evidence pertaining to document destruction was, and is, extraordinary. This evidence reveals in extensive detail the degree to which the British colonial government directed and orchestrated—at home and in Kenya—the purging of evidence pertaining to the formulation and use of systematized violence in the 1950s, the ex post facto attempts at providing legal coverage for British colonial agents who committed abuses, and the manipulations of investigations into these abuses and abrogations of law at the time. When read together, the new documents told a story of increasing destruction that paralleled the narrative of cover-up detailed in *Imperial Reckoning*.

According to the files in the Hanslope Disclosure, beginning as early as the fall of 1958, the Kenyan government began a process of downgrading and destroying documents. This process would become more elaborate and fine-tuned in the years ahead. Methods of transmission of secret documents were developed whereby a Secret Mail Office received materials, lockboxes were created, and safe rooms were expanded. By the end of 1959, the Kenyan government had developed a matrix that outlined the full extent of the files to be destroyed, and the method of their destruction, which included either burning by fire or by incinerator. There was also a contingency plan should "emergency destruction" prove necessary. In total, it was estimated that some three and a half tons of documents from various departments and ministries were slated for destruction.[11]

Two key documents found in the Hanslope Disclosure, both from May 1961, further outlined the destruction and removal process. The first is a memorandum from the colonial secretary in London titled, "Disposal of classified records and accountable documents." This memorandum outlines clearly the Colonial Office's policies for the "disposal of documents on independence," stating that no documents are passed on to the independent government that:

    (a) might embarrass Her Majesty's Government or other governments;
    (b) might embarrass members of the Police, military forces, public servants or others (such as Police agents or informers);

(c) might compromise sources of intelligence;

(d) might be used unethically by Ministers in the successor government.[12]

Ten days later, the Kenyan permanent secretary for defence, G. J. Ellerton,
circulated widely the second key memorandum entitled, "The Designation
Watch."[13] Ellerton's directives, based upon the earlier orders from the colonial secretary, would guide the selection process for document destruction
and removal through the final days of Britain's colonial rule in Kenya.
Known as the "Watch" system, all documents in all ministries and departments were to be divided into two categories: "Watch" and "Legacy." Those
documents to be designated as "Watch" were "those papers which must only
be seen by 'authorised' officers, and which will ultimately have either to be
destroyed or to be removed to the United Kingdom." Those papers constituting "Legacy" material were "all those other papers which may safely and
appropriately be seen in the course of duty by persons who may not fit the
definition of 'authorised' officers, and which will eventually be inherited by
the independent Government." Later, this definition was further honed to
mean "important background and in some cases, historical material, with
no security, political or individual personal implication." Enclosed in Ellerton's circular was a "W" stamp, which authorized officers were to use in demarcating a "Watch" file, leaving a "W" imprint on the top right corner of
each and every document selected for removal to Britain, or destruction. As
Ellerton noted, the process for "purging" is tedious and time consuming and
"may well cause you to tear your hair out."[14]

What is particularly striking is the choreographed nature of the "Watch"
system. This was by no means a haphazard process. Instead, it was one that
reflected the bureaucratization of social control that was characteristic of Britain's counterinsurgency efforts, particularly in the latter years of the Mau
Mau Emergency.[15] The orchestration of the "Watch" system was also very
much under the purview of the Colonial Office in London. There are numerous files in the Hanslope Disclosure documenting the minutiae in which the
Colonial Office—and the colonial secretary himself—were involved, including checklists of which papers were being burned, who precisely was hand-
carrying documents back to the UK and on which flight, and what RAF
planes contained which materials.[16] Moreover, overseeing the whole operation
on the ground was a hand-selected group of the government's most-trusted

officers. This included Terence Gavaghan, the chief architect of Britain's systematic torture in the Mau Mau detention camps.[17] In effect, known for executing the systematic destruction of bodies and minds in Kenya's detention camps, Gavaghan was now rendering to ash documents in colonial incendiaries, while ensuring others would be permanently held under lock and key. The British colonial government's chief torturer in Kenya became one of its chief archivists in the final days of British rule.

There exists in the Hanslope Disclosure a forty-five-page document line-itemizing specific files and collections of documents to be destroyed.[18] In addition, there is clear evidence that a particular procedure was to be followed for all documents destroyed. That is, Destruction Certificates were to be filled out and submitted for each document destroyed in accordance with Rule 3 (iv) of Colonial Office secret circular dispatch No. 1282/59. According to this procedure, copies of all Destruction Certificates were to be sent to the Colonial Office, where they were to comprise a permanent record.[19] In theory, there should exist thousands, if not tens of thousands, of Destruction Certificates that would have been sent to the Colonial Office on the eve of decolonization. In the official archives at Kew there existed not a single Destruction Certificate until the Hanslope Disclosure.[20] Such a wide-scale absence of documentation suggests the degree to which official archives in London have been culled and purged in a manner similar to the colonial archives in Kenya.

In the context of the Mau Mau case, the evidence in the Hanslope Disclosure appeared to demonstrate the degree to which the British government—having choreographed the archival cleansing operation—was complicit in its own defense. The FCO, however, having dumped hundreds of files related to document destruction upon the claimants' historical experts, took a different view. Conceding that, yes, in fact, some three and a half tons of files were destroyed at the time of Britain's decolonization from Kenya, the FCO then argued that those colonial administrators, "acting in right of Kenya," took the Colonial Office's directives too far. In effect, the FCO suggested that the colonial government in London, "acting in right of Britain," in no way suggested such extensive document destruction. Moreover, according to the FCO, as the claimants' historical experts had so ably demonstrated, this overzealous file destruction had, in fact, taken place. As a result, there was no possible way the contemporary British government could have a fair trial; therefore the judge should have no choice but to adhere to the statute of limitations.

With the FCO's argument dramatically unfolding for the first time in the context of the second strike-down hearing, an immediate burden arose for the historians not only to find documents in the Hanslope Disclosure proving centralization and systematization of document destruction but also to place these files in their broader historical context. It is here that the evidence in *Imperial Reckoning* proved valuable. Colonial officials in London were issuing sweeping document-destruction orders for Kenya at precisely the same time that they were covering up abuses in the camps and lying to the media and Parliament about these same abuses. Such instances of cover-ups were well documented in *Imperial Reckoning* and therefore were linked to the new Hanslope documents that chronicled the document destruction in order to illustrate the colonial government in London's state of mind as well as the broader political context in which its officials oversaw the document-destruction orders. Put another way, when the new Hanslope documents were integrated with *Imperial Reckoning's* evidence, it was clear that the colonial government in London was issuing its document-destruction orders at precisely the same time that it was engaged in a massive cover-up at home over its deployment of systematic violence in Kenya's detention camps and emergency villages.

Ultimately, the second strike-down hearing again rested on questions of legal technicality and the degrees to which historical evidence could be deployed to undermine the FCO's defenses. In fact, by the time of the second strike-down hearing, the British government no longer contested the claimants' allegations. That is, in one of the most dramatic moments in the case, when each of the claimants took the witness stand to testify to his or her abuses, the FCO's Queen's Counsel, or QC, did not challenge the veracity of the abuses they had endured. Rather, by the end of the second strike-down hearing, the British government relied fully on its position that the British government could not receive a fair trial due to the widespread destruction of documentation—documentation that could have exculpated the government, if it still existed—and therefore rested its case on the presumption that the judge would not take the near-unprecedented step of waiving the statute of limitations some fifty years after the alleged crimes had taken place.

Much to Her Majesty's government's surprise, therefore, and to that of many in the historical and legal professions, three months after the July strike-down hearing, Justice McCombe intervened with another historic ruling. This time, he again found in favor of the claimants, using his discretion to waive the three-year statute of limitation rule and opening the way for a full trial. The FCO vowed to appeal this ruling, though behind the scenes it was moving rapidly toward a settlement. The initial five claimants to the suit expanded to more than five thousand during the course of the next several months, as Leigh Day and the Kenya Human Rights Commission, together with the FCO, interviewed thousands of possible victims and, through a mutually agreed upon set of parameters, decided which victims had substantiated claims and therefore would be part of the final settlement. Then, on June 6, 2013, Britain's foreign secretary, William Hague, rose in the House of Commons and announced that the case had been settled. He offered the Kenyan claimants a formal apology in the form of a statement of "sincere regret" read into Parliamentary record as well as some £20 million in damages and the British government's funding of a memorial in Nairobi to commemorate "the victims of torture and ill treatment during the colonial era in Kenya."[21]

Conclusion

What changed the Foreign and Commonwealth Office's course in the Mau Mau case? There were several factors at play. One was Justice McCombe's ruling that lifted the statute of limitations: the British Empire would have been on trial not for weeks, but for months, at which time the revisionist evidence would be on full display. There was also the mounting public pressure coming from multiple corners, including the claimants' high-profile and vocal supporters such as Archbishop Desmond Tutu.

Then there was the evidence. The surgical way in which the fragments of historical evidence had been reassembled—first from archives in Britain and Kenya, and later from the Hanslope documents—rendered the British government's defense increasingly unsustainable. By the time of the second strike-down hearing, the FCO no longer contested the claimants' allegations of torture, a stunning and unprecedented admission of guilt; instead, the FCO cast its entire defense into the realm of legal procedure. Nonetheless, even in its turn to the statute of limitations, the FCO still needed historical evidence, or the lack thereof, to prove its case. Yet, its methodological sleights of hand and historical bluster—all of which had been part and parcel of the counterclaims to charges of systematic colonial violence in Kenya in the academic and public intellectual worlds when *Imperial Reckoning* was first published— had no place in Justice McCombe's courtroom. Instead, London's High Court was only interested in facts and acts, for which the FCO found it had fewer and fewer answers in its defense, and for which no historian was willing—no matter how pointed their critiques of *Imperial Reckoning* had been—to step into the courtroom to offer the British government a defense grounded in historical evidence.

Finally, there is the Mau Mau case's establishment of legal precedent. The question remains, then, why haven't there been multiple other claims filed against the British government similar to those in the Mau Mau case? Here, there are three interrelated issues at play. First, because of the peculiarities in British law, no case can be filed in the courts concerning incidents of alleged systematic violence in the empire that took place prior to 1948. As such, cases such as the massacre at Amritsar and the Arab Revolt in 1930s Palestine cannot be brought to the courts. Second, even if the 1948 law were not an obstacle, the claimants, like those in the Mau Mau case, must be present in Queen Victoria's High Court of Justice. In other words, the right to sue the British government for alleged acts of torture does not, under British law, pass to an individual's successor. Once victims pass away, so do their potential claims.

Last, but not least, there is the question of revisionist histories. To date, there does not exist an *Imperial Reckoning* for other parts of the post–World War II empire. Other potential cases are challenging to levy and even more difficult to execute successfully without revisionist histories, and copious amounts of written historical evidence supporting them. For some, the new evidence that came to light with the Hanslope Disclosure and the subsequent public release of its files—now termed the "Migrated Archives"—to the British National Archives generated enormous excitement for revisionist potential. In the end, however, there was little in the new document releases, other than those pertaining to Kenya, that offered any proverbial smoking guns or incriminating evidence with regard to systematic British violence in its empire. Perhaps this absence of evidence in the Migrated Archives is due to the fact that such documentation never existed; that is, Kenya was an exception to an otherwise successful British civilizing mission elsewhere in the empire. Or, what is much more likely, given all that we now know from a range of nonofficial sources about myriad theaters of postwar imperial violence, the British government extensively culled and curated the Migrated Archives for the other thirty-six colonies before their release to the public.

Such continued, careful maintenance of the official public record is in keeping with decades, if not centuries, of British archival practices. Indeed, it was because of the power of judicial orders mandating document disclosure that historians in the Mau Mau case successfully forced the release of some—though not all—of the documents discovered at Hanslope Park. At the time of the case's settlement, hundreds of additional document requests were under the court's scrutiny; these requests went away with the case's settlement, and most, if not all, of these requested files remain under the British government's lock and key. This, despite the fact that at the time of the Hanslope Park discovery, Foreign Secretary William Hague staged a series of public news events in which he pledged himself and his office to a new era of transparency and, with it, a release of all "irregularly held" files, subject to sensitivity review, as quickly as possible.[22] Such performative acts, however, were in keeping with years of imperial performances and cover-ups—cover-ups in which historians have, for decades, had a shared complicity. Ultimately, until such time as historians stop reproducing official narratives, even in part, and focus their efforts on reassembling the mosaics of evidence for other parts of the post–World War II empire, there is little possibility of the filing of another successful High Court claim similar to that of the Mau Mau victims.

CHAPTER 8

A Critical Assessment of Colombia's Reparations Policies in the Context of the Peace Process

Kathryn Sikkink, Douglas A. Johnson, Phuong Pham,
and Patrick Vinck

The case of Colombia is important for a volume on reparations for a number of reasons, not the least of which is because the Colombian reparations program is the most ambitious in the world to date, in terms of its size and scope. In the context of the 2016 peace agreement, Colombia has moved ahead on a wide range of policies for addressing state and nonstate accountability for human rights violations. The reparations program, however, predated the peace agreement and, in fact, ran parallel to the peace process, both preparing the ground for parts of the peace process and providing some evidence of the government's commitment to its responsibility to victims as it engaged in peace negotiations.[1] The reparations program was also very much a response to human rights and social justice organizations' community advocacy and litigation in Colombia that had long called for remedies for the many collective injustices of the conflict.[2]

In Chapter 15 of this volume, volume editors Margareta Matache and Jacqueline Bhabha write, "Governments have proved reluctant, with few exceptions [most notably post-Holocaust Germany], to engage seriously with demands for reparations." The Colombian government, responding to community advocacy, is certainly another exception to this statement. A visionary piece of legislation in 2011 defined a broad set of beneficiaries, established a requirement of finding and registering those victims, and enumerated a set of benefits to which they were entitled. Presidential decrees and rulings of the Constitutional Court further refined these requirements. Each of these was not only groundbreaking in the conception of society's commitment to repair the harm of fifty years of civil war but also expanded the expectations of what the fledgling institution charged with reparations policy should do, without, however, the strategic guidance and priorities that would allow it to fully succeed.

The Colombian peace agreement addressed a half-century-long conflict between the Revolutionary Armed Forces of Colombia (FARC) and the Colombian government. During the conflict, Colombia's security forces, right-wing paramilitary groups, the FARC, and a handful of other smaller revolutionary groups killed more than 200,000 Colombians, more than 80 percent of whom were noncombatants.[3] There is also evidence that Afro-Colombian communities disproportionately suffered in the Colombian conflict.[4] The fighting also displaced approximately 6 million people, out of a population of more than 48 million, and led to a wide range of other human rights violations and war crimes.

Colombian president Juan Manuel Santos initiated formal peace talks with the FARC in 2012, the year after the Colombian government had established its ambitious reparations program. For this reason, the reparations program was well under way by the time the peace agreement was signed in September 2016. The unit in charge of the reparations program, Unit for Comprehensive Attention and Reparation of Victims (Unidad para la Atención y Reparación Integral a las Víctimas), or Victims Unit (VU), constructed a registry of victims, in which by 2018 more than 8 million individuals were enrolled. The process of creating the reparations program and enrolling victims drew new attention to the diverse victims of the conflict. Eventually, in an unprecedented move for peace negotiations, victims' groups actually participated in peace negotiations in Havana, Cuba, presenting their stories and concerns in high-profile panels. While there was widespread support for reparations in the peace process, the most difficult parts of the agreement to negotiate were the provisions for some form of retributive justice with regard to the FARC's human rights violations.[5]

After four years of negotiations, the government and FARC leaders signed a three-hundred-page peace agreement in a ceremony highly publicized both nationally and internationally. The Nobel Committee awarded Santos the Peace Prize shortly after the agreement was signed.[6] But when the government submitted the peace agreement to a plebiscite in October 2016, 50.2 percent of the voters rejected it, with 49.8 percent voting in favor.[7] Many factors contributed to the vote outcome, including bad weather on the coast that kept many voters from the polls. But one of the key disputed issues was the belief held by many voters that FARC leaders were not going to be held sufficiently accountable for human rights violations.

Following the referendum, the government and the FARC modified some of the language and the terms of the peace agreement to respond to the concerns of the citizens who voted "No."[8] Rather than a second referendum, the government opted instead to seek approval from Congress, a provision entirely consistent with Colombian law and the terms of the agreement. In November 2016, both chambers of the Congress, which Santos's governing coalition controlled, voted unanimously to pass the new agreement; opposition legislators boycotted the vote.[9] President Santos and the FARC leaders managed to turn what appeared at the time to be a devastating defeat into an eventual victory for peace. The process, however, led some segments of the Colombian population associated with former president Alvaro Uribe to question the legitimacy of the peace agreement.

The peace agreement began to be implemented in December 2016, and mainly completed its first phase, the demobilization and disarmament process for the FARC, over the course of the next six months.[10] But it was still far from ensuring the reintegration of former combatants into Colombian society. The transitional justice provisions of the peace agreement included a truth commission, a special new tribunal for peace, and an office for missing persons. As of this writing, some are still in the process of being set up. For example, the Missing Persons Search Unit (UBPD) was not fully operational until 2019. The reparations process thus differed from the transitional justice provisions of the peace agreement, in that it had its work well under way before the peace agreement.

In this chapter, we draw on diverse research methods to provide a critical assessment of Colombia's reparation programs in the context of the peace process. Reparations were intended to assist victims to overcome or alleviate the damage they suffered, to restore their dignity, and to provide assurance that the harms they suffered would not happen again. Moreover, the government hoped that reparations could also contribute to the peace process; change how individuals interacted with others, their community, and the state; build confidence in state institutions; and strengthen the rule of law. These claims about how reparations policies contribute to both macro- and micro-level outcomes are, however, largely untested and lack empirical evidence.

In the course of our scholarly research on transitional justice, the authors of this chapter were part of a multilevel, mixed-method evaluation that was carried out between late 2014 and early 2015 to assess the efforts of the Victims Unit to implement the comprehensive reparations measures called for in Law 1448.[11] In our evaluation, we combined diverse methods of inquiry because each revealed multiple truths that needed to be taken into account when assessing the impact of transitional justice.

Background of the Reparation Program in Colombia

International standards on reparations expressed through international treaty law or international guidelines and principles are still developing.[12] The nonbinding 2005 UN Resolution 60/147 is an inflection point in emerging norms toward a more expansive view of reparations, one that includes not only compensation and restitution but also rehabilitation, satisfaction, and guarantees of nonrepetition. The Colombia program is based on the expansive view of reparations in the 2005 UN resolution as well as on the work of the Inter-American human rights system, which has "without doubt, developed the most innovative jurisprudence of reparations."[13]

The Colombian government established the reparations program in 2011. Reparations Law 1448 provides for:

> [A] set of judicial, administrative, social, and economic measures, both individual and collective, to benefit the victims who individually or collectively have suffered harm for events that occurred as of January 1, 1985, as a result of violations of international humanitarian law or of grave and manifest violations of international human rights law provisions, which occurred on occasion of the internal armed conflict within a framework of transitional justice, that make possible the effective enjoyment of their rights to truth, justice, and reparation with guarantees of nonrepetition.[14]

Although the Colombian conflict is often seen as beginning as early as 1948 or at the latest in the early-to-mid-1960s, the reparations policy "only" begins in 1985. But it is one of the most historically comprehensive world programs to date. During the peace negotiations, the FARC requested that the dates of the reparations program be extended to an earlier start date, a proposal that did not gain government support, perhaps because, by that time, the size of the victims' registry was already unprecedented.

The law and subsequent Presidential Decrees and Constitutional Court rulings took expansive views of temporal coverage, coordination of benefits, eligibility criteria for victims, and forms of reparations. They defined a broad set of beneficiaries, including all possible injury types (e.g., physical, emotional, economic, and fundamental rights), a requirement of finding and registering those victims, and a set of benefits to which they were entitled, not just to repair tangible harms but to restore victims to full citizenship. Although reparations were primarily intended for individuals and their families, there is also a list of more than three hundred communities that are subjects for collective reparations, nearly half of which are Afro-Colombian groups or indigenous groups.

To coordinate and implement this comprehensive reparations program, the law created the Victims Unit (VU). In addition to directly providing reparations, part of the VU mandate was also to coordinate various public and private entities that also had roles to play in the delivery of reparations. Because of the large number of victims and the comprehensive reparations to which they were entitled, the demands on the VU were immediate. The VU did not have the luxury of developing its services on a small scale, adapting and perfecting them from tests of everyday experience before creating the institutional capacity needed for scale-up. Rather, it has had to design, construct, and navigate its vehicle, all at the same time.

Our 2015 evaluation of the Colombian reparations program included three levels of analysis: (1) a macro-level benchmarking study comparing the Colombian program to other reparations programs around the world; (2) an institutional analysis of the VU's reparations and coordination functions; and (3) a micro-examination, via a large randomized survey, of the VU's implementation of reparations measures from the perspective of its beneficiaries and, more broadly, victims of the armed conflict. We draw on the knowledge gained in this evaluation, as well as in our previous research on transitional justice, in the sections below.

Macro-Level Comparative Analysis

We undertook the macro-level analysis through a process of "benchmarking" that compared Colombia's laws, institutions, and the results to date of the reparations program to other reparations programs around the world. We conducted a broad comparison of the Colombian reparations program with forty-five other reparations policies in thirty-one other transitional countries in the world. We then undertook a more in-depth comparison of the Colombia program with policies in a reference group of reparations policies in five other comparable countries: Guatemala, Indonesia, Peru, South Africa, and Morocco.[15]

This evaluation found that the Colombian reparations program is unprecedented and unique in a number of ways. First, it aims to serve a far larger number of victims than any other reparations program in the world, both in absolute terms and relative to population size. But in addition to being the most ambitious program, as of 2016, Colombia's reparations program had already been the most effective because it had already compensated more individuals than any of the other reference countries, while at the same time still having a much larger number of victims to compensate in the future than any other program.

The VU uses a larger list of different kinds of human rights violations than any other country on record, including murder, threats, forced disappearances, sexual violence, and other grave harms. Colombia moved quickly to create a National Registry for Victims (RUV), and that registry grew dramatically over time to include 7 million victims by 2016. By 2018, the number of victims on the RUV had grown to more than 8.5 million.[16] Because of the age and composition of the RUV, which integrated four previous lists of victims, the actual number of targeted reparations victims who could be reached was smaller than the number listed in the registry, because there was some duplication in the lists, because some victims and family members had died, and because it was impossible to locate others.

The VU's preliminary evaluation in 2016 placed the total number of victims capable of receiving support under Law 1448 at that time at close to 5.7 million persons, a number of whom had already received reparations. Even with this adjustment, in terms of scale, the Colombian reparations program is of historic proportions. The very existence and work of the RUV in Colombia is in and of itself an accomplishment. Two of the other cases we examined—Indonesia and Morocco—did not even have registries, and Guatemala and South Africa had lists from their truth commissions, but not full-fledged registries. Of the reference group, only Peru has a registry. The creation of the registry and its ability to register more than 8 million victims is one key stage of implementation of the reparations program in Colombia.

No other case of reparations comes anywhere close to the number of victims listed on the Colombian registry. The Colombian victims' registry now includes more than 15 percent of the current population of Colombia; none of the other forty-five reparations programs in the world have registered or repaired more than 1 percent of their populations. The differences between the Colombia program and the other reparations programs are largely the result of the huge size of the displaced population in the country and the Colombian Constitutional Court's decision to expand the original legislative mandate of the reparations program to include displaced people. Since the peace agreement, new displacement in Colombia has diminished significantly.[17] But, by the end of 2016, Colombia was still the country with the highest total number of internally displaced people (IDP) in the world, ahead of Syria.[18] If displaced people had not been included in the Colombia program, the size of the registered victims would have been approximately 2 percent of the population, still twice the size of other large reparations programs. Because of these unique challenges presented by the Colombia program, the VU faced multiple dilemmas as it scaled up.

Colombia also had quite an open eligibility process for reparations victims, initially setting few limits on when and for how long victims could register for monetary benefits. This is the reason for the growth from 7 million to 8.5 million victims on the RUV between 2016 and 2018. While this dramatically reduced barriers for victims—and follows some international guidelines of not imposing burdensome limits on victims for registration—the long window made Colombia more vulnerable to organizational "scale-up" issues, as the VU faced significant challenges meeting the needs of its constantly growing constituency.

Colombia was one of the few countries in the world that defined different classes of victims and compensated differently based on those classifications. For example, the families of individuals who had been killed receive different compensation than people who have been displaced. The VU has worked to tailor reparations to the needs of the victims through the creation of an individual reparations plan, known as a Plan for Comprehensive Attention, Assistance, and Reparation (PAARI; Plan de Atención, Asistencia y Reparación Integral a las Víctimas). The PAARI results from a consultation with a VU staff person on an individual's needs to be matched with the available services in the area that would help the individual move from a state of vulnerability to independence and self-reliance. So, for example, the PAARI for a victim who had been directly subject to violence and also displaced would be different than the PAARI for a victim of direct violence who had not been displaced.

Each community entitled to collective reparations also worked with the VU to draw up a tailored plan for that community, called a Comprehensive Plan for Collective Reparation (PIRC; Plan Integral de Reparacion Colectiva).

Other countries that tried to define different classes of victims and compensate based on those classes were eventually overwhelmed economically or administratively by the effort and felt obliged to return to less differentiated solutions. By 2018, however, the Colombian program has managed to provide differentiated reparations for large numbers of different types of victims, and to work with communities to draw up plans for collective reparations. This may have been possible because the Colombian leadership was determined to be in the forefront of reparations programs and the Colombian reparations program was designed taking into account the critiques of other reparations programs when compared to international norms.

It has been difficult for other large and complex reparations programs to implement and comply with their goals. Given the ambitious nature of the Colombia program and its massive and unprecedented size, such implementation and compliance challenges are also in evidence. The implementation of the Colombian program is discussed below in the institutional analysis.

The macro-level analysis provides an overview of the Colombian reparations program and the big picture of implementation. A year before the peace agreement was signed, the VU had already been very efficient in delivering compensation to victims compared to other cases in the world. None of the other reference group countries have compensated so many individuals. Only Indonesia came near to providing reparations for the number of people to whom reparations were delivered in Colombia by the end of 2015, and it did so mainly by delivering lump compensations to communities rather than payments directly to individuals.

Not only had the VU compensated more victims, but also had done so in a relatively short period of time. But, when we compared the number of individuals already compensated to the total size of the pool of victims, it became clear that Colombia still faces a huge task to provide reparations for the individuals in its registry.

The macro-analysis raises the question of why a developing and conflict-ridden country like Colombia innovated with this remarkably ambitious and forward-looking reparations program. President Santos and the early leaders of the VU, including Paula Gaviria Betancur, deserve credit for their vision, but the vision of a handful of key policy makers cannot by itself explain an undertaking of this magnitude. Among other possible explanations, we would signal that the Colombian program is the last in an increasingly ambitious and integrated set of reparations programs throughout Latin America in the context of democratic transitions and transitions from conflict. In this sense, Colombia learned from the experiences and successes and failures of neighboring countries, including Argentina, Chile, Peru, and Guatemala. The Colombian government also took into account innovative jurisprudence on reparations of the Inter-American human rights system in designing and implementing its program. But the international influences and pressures are only part of the explanation. No international organization or foreign government pressured Colombia to adopt this program. Rather, the Colombians themselves chose to exercise leadership in this area, aiming to set a new global model of integral and transformative reparations. In this, they were responding to domestic constituencies and institutions, both nongovernmental organizations and their own judicial sector. In recent years, Colombia is gaining recognition for the far-reaching jurisprudence of its judicial system, especially the Constitutional Court, and so the domestic judicial system itself exercised influence on the reparations program.

Ultimately, while the macro-level comparison confirms the remarkable ambition of the Colombian program, it yields relatively little understanding about how the reparations programs were actually being implemented in Colombia. The institutional and micro-level analyses help clarify what such ambition has meant in practice—both in terms of the capacity of the VU to live up to its mandates as well as the consequences for the program's reception by the public and victimized populations.

Institutional Analyses

To understand the reparations process in Colombia, it was necessary to look more closely at the institutional issues that influenced the granting of reparations and, in particular, at institutional developments within the VU, and relations between the VU and other government agencies. We focus on an institutional analysis of the VU's work in the delivery of a set of reparations measures, specifically indemnification of individuals and community-level or collective reparations. The VU's direct delivery of reparations was only one small part of its work. It was also responsible for the coordination of the

interagency task force of thirty-nine governmental units and thirteen allied organizations that have responsibility for pieces of the reparation puzzle
created through national legislation and Presidential Decrees.[19] Of these,
seven ministries had specific responsibilities for meeting the reparations
goals.

The VU's institutional dilemmas derived in large part from the very nature and scope of the reparations program. The sheer numbers of victims registered turned out to be much larger than initially anticipated. The Colombian
government's thorough planning process, including the assignment of resources, was built on a much smaller estimate of numbers of victims. The
legislation also divided up the reparations objectives between multiple agencies and created the VU to provide some of those outcomes but also to coordinate the efforts of other agencies, although the VU did not always have the
political power to coordinate them. And all of these reparations were supposed to be delivered by 2021. The VU faced unprecedented challenges. To
meet them, it would need additional time and a massive influx of resources.
The situation became precarious since the election in 2018 of center-right
candidate Ivan Duque as president of Colombia, who has cut funding for
reparations.

In this context, one fundamental problem the VU faced was how to strategize and prioritize its work. The leaders and staff at the VU demonstrated
great creativity and commitment to developing new ideas and methods for
delivering reparations to victims. But the VU also established more than four
hundred goals with no apparent hierarchic structure indicating either priorities or expected timing or assignment within specific units with responsibility for outcomes. Such a vast, undifferentiated list of goals indicated a lack
of strategy that would help the organization focus its energies, leadership, and
operations on measurable outcomes. Indeed, the VU compounded the problem by not doing enough to control the rising expectations of victims—and
their disappointment with the government when its lofty goals remained un-
met.

Even so, the VU met 98 percent of its milestone goals for compensation
of victims by the end of 2014 and exceeded its goals for the compensation of
children and adolescent victims and those transitioning to adulthood. But,
by 2016, the VU had barely started addressing reparations for victims of displacement. The number of displaced people alone made the task daunting,
since 85 percent of the victims registered in the national registry are victims
of displacement.

The reparations program acted on the belief that certain communities had been specific targets of organized violence and their collective needs could not be repaired through reparations to individual members only. It thus included an important component for collective reparations. While the VU had met its goals in delivering compensation to individuals at the time of the 2015 evaluation, it had been less successful meeting its goals on the delivery of collective reparations, many of which were targeted for Afro-Colombian or indigenous communities, with others focused on specific social organizations, like those representing journalists. The national planning bureau, CONPES, established goals for the VU of creating 833 comprehensive collective reparations plans for geographically and socially based communities, of which 417 were to be plans for ethnic communities. It did not, however, establish goals for the actual delivery of such reparations. Only other actors, such as national ministries, could deliver many of the services demanded by communities. The preferences of these diverse constituencies have often been in conflict, putting the VU in the challenging and undesirable position of having to expend significant resources trying to seek acceptable compromises. The VU's task was to *produce* collective reparations plans. The VU interpreted its obligation to produce collective reparations as a mandate to work with communities to generate lists of projects desired by the communities as part of reparations. Other ministries had to be persuaded to collaborate. So, for example, the Health Ministry needed to build a new health clinic or develop a psychosocial program for that community. But the Health Ministry had not been included in the collective reparations planning process. As a result, communities complained that their expectations were not always met as anticipated. They criticized the VU staff for their attitudes or the slow pace of the implementation. In May 2015, for example, there was a collective victims' protest in Bogota in which protesters demanded the dismissal of certain functionaries for "demeaning and abusive treatment," particularly of collective victims.[20] But the problems were not just due to the VU bureaucracy attitudes and staff turnover but also to the very way the reparations process was conceived and organized, in which the VU did not have the power to implement the collective reparations lists.

Each of these Comprehensive Plans for Collective Reparation can include measures of restitution, financial compensation, physical and psychosocial rehabilitation, satisfaction measures, such as truth and memory, and guarantees of no repetition. This is similar to individual reparation plans, but with particular attention to recognizing and dignifying collective subjects,

reconstructing the collective life plan or ethnic development plan, addressing psychosocial recuperation of affected groups, rebuilding institutional
rule of law, and promoting reconciliation and peaceful coexistence.[21] Developing the plan in a participatory manner was therefore an important step
that the VU supported. Highly customized measures have, indeed, been
developed in community plans.

So, for example, an individual reparations plan might include provisions
for psychological therapy, but a community might require the creation of a
clinic in the community. Similarly, in terms of memory work, collectivities
may be best served by public memorials. Some communities that were isolated by the violence and excluded as a result might require the construction
of roads to assist their reintegration into the nation. The VU believed these
collective reparations needed to be tailored to each community and the planning process should widely engage the community.

One component of the planning process was a diagnostic phase during
which organizations explained what happened to them in the context of the
armed conflict. That process was largely seen positively, especially among ethnic communities. About half of the communities and organizations that
were interviewed praised the participatory nature of the process. There were
various benefits of the planning process. VU staff reported that their work
in creating plans with communities led to very moving conversations, drawing them closer to the lives of the victims, and motivating the staff. In the
surveys we conducted, collective subjects cited their recognition as victims,
and the respectful treatment received, as important achievements of this
collective reparations planning process. At the time of our evaluation in
2015, however, not a single collective reparations plan had been completed.

While the community processes might have temporarily increased the
legitimacy of the VU in the eyes of community members, this could turn to
disappointment and disillusionment if results were not commensurate with
their raised expectations.

The VU helps to sustain the credibility of the national project by creating a strong narrative of the impact of the systemic violence on Colombian
communities and of victims' needs to become fully active citizens. Still, this
is not sufficient to maintain, much less build, the national public consensus.
The VU is embedded in a complicated social system comprising victims,
political entities and processes, and citizens. The VU must evolve its current
strategies and tactics so that it can transform the social system in which it
is embedded from one of resistance to one of collective mobilization. For

example, if the VU could involve representatives of other agencies and ministries to work with the communities in the collective reparations planning process, it could potentially mobilize more political will and resources for collective reparations.

Victims' and Beneficiaries' Perspectives on Reparations and the VU

The third component of the study examines the VU's implementation of reparations measures from the perspective of its beneficiaries and, more broadly, victims of the armed conflict. In addition to the individual and group interviews with key stakeholders discussed above, team members designed a randomized survey of 3,136 Colombian adults, including both victims who had received reparations and those who had not yet received reparations. The data collected provide a comprehensive resource for analyzing victims' perspectives about the VU's efforts to implement comprehensive reparations measures.

The survey focused on three groups among the population: (1) the general population; (2) victims in the registry (registered respondents); and (3) victims who had registered and who had received at least one form of reparation, usually financial compensation (repaired respondents). We use the term "repaired" to refer to respondents who received reparations, although we understand this may sound odd at first in English, because it is the way Colombians refer to the process in Spanish and how they translate it into English. We cannot use other more common synonyms in English, such as "compensated" or "indemnized," because these refer specifically to financial payments, and Colombian reparations are more diverse than that.

The goal of the survey was to answer a number of research questions from beneficiaries' perspectives. In general, we sought to capture victims' self-reported perceptions of the program's various reparations measures. More specifically, we sought to gauge the program's successes and challenges in terms of social cohesion and what the VU defines as "transformative" reparations, that is, overcoming moral, emotional, and physical damages, and contributing to socioeconomic stabilization. Because this is a state-based program, and because attitudes toward the state and its role in the conflict vary quite dramatically in Colombia, we also sought to measure victims' and citizens' confidence in the state and perceptions of the rule of law in

Colombia, and to analyze their relationship to the reparations program. Finally, because Law 1448 outlines both individual and collective reparations measures, we sought to identify the effects that collective victims (such as ethnic groups or institutions like schools) report. These include participation in diagnosis of damages, the formulation of a collective reparations plan, the strategy for rebuilding social fabric, and the implementation of collective reparations plans.

The sample of the general population was split nearly evenly between male and female respondents. The registered and repaired populations contained many more female respondents than males, because when victims of homicide and/or disappearance ("indirect victims of homicide") were randomly selected from the RUV's database, a close relative responded to the questionnaire, frequently a female relative.

In terms of racial diversity, among the general population, most respondents self-identified as mixed (48%) or white (30%). The repaired population was roughly similar, with 52 percent self-identifying as mixed and 23 percent as white. The registered population exhibited slightly more diversity, with 40 percent identifying as mixed, 23 percent as white, 13 percent as Afro-Colombian, and 10 percent as Black.[22] The general population reported on average a higher level of education than the registered and repaired populations, with 22 percent having only primary education or less, compared to 46 percent for the registered and 48 percent for the repaired.

There were high levels of violence and victimhood among the individuals surveyed, even among the general population. Forty-five percent of the adults among the general population reported having experienced some form of conflict-related violence either directly or indirectly, and 26 percent of the general population considered themselves victims of the armed conflict. Among registered and repaired victims, almost everyone reported having experienced direct forms of violence, including experiencing the killing of a household member, having been forced to abandon land or experience destruction of goods/properties, or having experienced harassment by armed groups. With respect to perception of harm, registered and repaired respondents described the harm they suffered overwhelmingly as psychological/mental or emotional, but also as material/economic, moral, physical, and social. Respondents among the general population who suffered some form of violence or self-identified as victims of the conflict also categorized their harm in roughly the same proportions. These are self-reported results and the veracity of those claims cannot be asserted. However, perceived victimization underlies perceptions and attitudes about reparations.

The survey revealed attitudes about the definition of reparations and how they should be administered. Law 1448 of 2011 embodies a complex definition of reparations involving compensation, rehabilitation, restitution, satisfaction, and guarantees of nonrepetition. A majority of survey respondents, however, defined reparations as a general form of compensation (financial, material, or symbolic). A smaller number (26% of the general population and 11% of registered victims) defined reparations as the restitution of land and housing. The majority of all three groups responded that reparations should be given individually, while 17 percent of registered, 19 percent of repaired, and 29 percent of the general population felt that reparations should be given collectively. About two-thirds of respondents indicated that having some form of official recognition of victims was important or very important, and a majority also found it important to very important to establish memorials for what happened during the armed conflict.

More than two-thirds of the respondents in the general population (69%) indicated being aware of the existence of a state program providing reparations and assistance to victims of the armed conflict, compared to 81 percent among registered victims, and 88 percent among repaired victims. We are uncertain exactly how to interpret these numbers. On the one hand, it seems puzzling, in particular, that only 88 percent of repaired victims are aware of a state program of reparations. This could be due the fact that the VU was responsible both for distributing humanitarian assistance as well as reparations to victims of the conflict. It may be the case that registered and repaired victims who were receiving both humanitarian assistance and reparations from the VU may not have understood the distinction between the two. On the other hand, from the point of view of research on name recognition from other fields—either market research for firms or research for political campaigns—these numbers suggest that the Colombian reparations program has received a relatively high level of awareness and name recognition in a rather short period of time. Nevertheless, lack of knowledge was cited as a frequent barrier to registering for reparations. For the general population, the media was the main source of knowledge of the victims' law and the VU. Registered and repaired victims most frequently reported that they had learned about the victims' law and the VU from friends, family members, and neighbors.

The survey also assessed victims' perceptions of their right to participate in the formulation, implementation, and monitoring of the state's
victims' policies. The vast majority of respondents in each group did not
participate in such processes, generally because they were not aware of opportunities to participate. Only a third of the respondents thought the state
had provided space for victims' organizations to participate in the formulation, implementation, or monitoring of the state's victims' policies.

We have argued above that it is essential that the VU prioritize more
clearly which tasks it will undertake first. The survey supports this call for
clear prioritization and clear comunication about priorities. In qualitative interviews, respondents noted that they felt the state's current system of pri-
oritizing victims for reparations was random or based on luck. Two-thirds
or more of the three sampled populations said that those most in need should
be prioritized. The respondents did not define clearly what they meant by
need, and such definitions might vary greatly. Nevertheless, there is genuine
support for the idea that the VU should prioritize based on need.

The Colombian government had hoped that reparations would be an effective means of increasing confidence in the government and decreasing the
demand for justice by victims. One of the most positive findings in terms of
stated goals of implementing reparations is that repaired victims, and to a
lesser extent registered victims, tend to have more positive views about the
state in general and the state's recognition and support to victims in particular. While no causal link can be established, the results are suggestive of
some association between reparations and positive perception of the state,
in the sense that respondents were more likely to have trust in the state and
feel that the state cared about them. This association, however, could be stronger. The difference between repaired and registered respondents was still
relatively small considering that repaired respondents had already benefitted from compensation. Furthermore, more than half of repaired victims did
not consider their compensation payments as a form of reparations and two-
thirds said these payments had not delivered justice.

One of the most paradoxical findings of the survey is that respondents
perceived that there were relatively high levels of corruption in the reparations process, but very few of them reported that they had actually been asked
for a bribe or had paid one.

The survey shows that victims' self-reported psychological needs appear
as grave as their material needs, especially for indirect victims of homicide,
whom the VU targeted for early compensation. Ideally, compensation awards

should be accompanied by counseling and other measures to ensure that victims distinguish them from general humanitarian assistance and to maximize their reparatory effect. The VU's ability to deliver psychological follow-up and monitoring, however, is limited. In the Colombian reparations program, the Ministry of Health was given the major responsibility for provision of health needs of victims, including their psychological needs, and it has not yet been able to adequately respond to these needs. Likewise, the VU does not have the mandate or capacity to follow up on victims' needs, especially in light of the finding that four-fifths of repaired victims responded that they were never or rarely followed up on by the VU.

Conclusions

We conclude by highlighting the main themes present throughout this chapter: the major accomplishments of the Colombian reparations program, the huge challenges Colombia faces in delivering integral reparations to so many people, and thus its need to prioritize clearly. Among its accomplishments, the Colombian process is now the cutting edge of reparations programs worldwide and will be seen as a model for other countries in the future. The Colombian case suggests that reparations programs can be effective means of incorporating marginalized groups in society and building more trust in government institutions. But it also raises many possible challenges for the VU in terms of the size of the expectations such a complex and complete policy generates, and the difficulty in meeting such expectations. In order to manage these challenges, the VU and the Colombian government must work to prioritize the delivery of reparations and strategize how to do so within the limits of available resources related to state budget and human capacity.

Colombia has made an impressive commitment to repairing victims of conflict and human rights violations. It has done so through Law 1448 of 2011; the creation, staffing, and funding of the VU; and through the peace agreement. The VU is an expression of a countrywide commitment to repair victims. In order for the VU and other parts of the Colombian government to carry out this mission, they will need to continue to receive the necessary financial resources and political support. To provide such a massive and unprecedented number of reparations, the country needs to think about how to integrate reparations policy into its broader political economy. In order to repair 15 percent of the Colombian population, the government as a whole will need to incorporate reparations policy into its macro-economic policy. In future years, reparations will need to be considered in any discussion of political economy in Colombia. The financial resources necessary to success-fully complete the mandate of the reparations program may need to come from additional sources. So the central government needs to develop greater partnerships with local governments, civil society, and the private sector to carry out its ambitious state-sponsored program. No amount of effort by the VU or other institutions of the Colombian state will be able to sustain this reparations program without financial and political support from the gov-ernment and from the society as a whole. In the context of a society still deeply divided over the peace agreement and its transitional justice provisions, it is not clear that such financial and political support will be forthcoming.

CHAPTER 9

Justice Beyond the Final Verdict: The Role of Court-Ordered Reparations in the Struggle for Indigenous Peoples' Human Rights in Guatemala

Irma A. Velásquez Nimatuj and Aileen Ford

Racism and Violence Against Indigenous Women in Guatemala

The crimes that the women of Sepur Zarco denounced in their quest for justice reflected the confluence of racism, sexual violence, and economic exploitation of indigenous peoples in Guatemala during the genocidal period of the internal armed conflict (1975–88).[1] Racism and violence against indigenous women—often expressed through sexual violence—were part of the state's ideological terror, which resulted in the planning and execution of disappearances, massacres, and rapes during this period of Guatemala's history. In a larger sense, the sexual violence and slave labor that the state perpetrated in Sepur Zarco were also a continuation of the illegal, centuries-old disparagement of indigenous women's inherent human dignity, for which the state has yet to answer.

With the imposition of the Spanish colonial regime in the sixteenth century, early examples of racism emerged in the form of geographic segregation and subordination of indigenous peoples through a caste system: the Leyes Nuevas of 1542 declared indigenous peoples "free subjects" of the Spanish king if they agreed to live concentrated in *pueblos de indios*.[2] Catholic evangelization pressured indigenous peoples to "forget the errors of their past rites and ceremonies," including their ancient cosmologies and religion.[3]

The work of historian Severo Martínez Peláez and sociologist Marta Elena Casaús Arzú elucidates how European and criollo elites relied on racist stereotypes, characterizing indigenous people as lazy, conformist, and drunken.[4] These stereotypes persisted for centuries, and eventually combined during the years of internal armed conflict with epithets such as "subversive," and "traitor, satanic and, once again, irredeemable and degenerate."[5] According to the legal scholar Miguel Ángel Curruchiche Gómez, during the implementation of the colonial system in Guatemala, this racist ideology facilitated "the physical action of stripping away lands from their legitimate owners [indigenous peoples] in different stages and with diverse justifications, among which the *encomienda* stands out for its cruelty and inhumanity."[6] The *encomienda* labor system laid the foundations of land tenure in Guatemala, and one of its primary characteristics was "the monopoly of the Spanish over the most productive and extensive lands (*latifundio*), whose products will be commercialized to satisfy external needs, and a minimum amount of land necessary for the survival of the indigenous labor force (*minifundio*)."[7]

In addition to facing the usurpation of their lands, the devastation wrought by diseases introduced by Spanish colonizers, and the destabilization of their prior ways of life, indigenous peoples were forced into slave labor to serve the Spanish in their homes, churches, and in public works projects. Indigenous women were particularly affected by the systematic destruction of their social nucleus, and were subjected to frequent rape, separation from their own families while they nursed the children of Spaniards, and enforced labor spinning cotton into thread (and replacing any missing material at their own cost).[8] These circumstances effectively reproduced a social hierarchy headed by white elites who dominated Mayan, Xinka, and Garífuna peoples. The racism of Spanish colonizers functioned through the propagation and institutionalization of biological and cultural forms of discrimination that categorized indigenous peoples as distinct and inherently inferior to Europeans and their criollo descendants in Guatemala. Meanwhile, indigenous peoples "maneuvered these institutions [e.g., *encomienda*, *pueblos de indios*, the Catholic Church, etc.] to resist, protest, transgress, survive, and reproduce themselves under extremely adverse conditions."[9] The writer Juan Fernando Cifuentes Herrera documents some of the many uprisings, protests, and other forms of resistance that Mayan peoples organized throughout the history of Guatemala to defend their rights and protect their autonomy.[10]

Guatemala's independence from Spain in 1821 did little to alter the relative position of indigenous peoples in Guatemalan society. In the new republic, criollo and ladino elites replaced Europeans at the top of the social hierarchy, but they solidified their power through the continued oppression of indigenous and Afro-descendant peoples.[11] Liberal governments enacted an economic and political agenda that included expropriating and distributing the Catholic Church's latifundios, and selling or gifting state lands after declaring them vacant. This retooling of the colonial power structure often resulted in the dispossession of indigenous peoples' communal lands.[12]

Throughout the nineteenth century and into the middle of the twentieth, a series of dictators ruled Guatemala, perpetuating an oppressive oligarchic structure with devastating social consequences for the country's indigenous and rural populations.[13] Over a period of years, however, protests and political organizing among indigenous and nonindigenous communities increased in scope and intensity and eventually led to a revolution on October 20, 1944. Constitutional reforms followed, challenging existing inequalities. They included a reversal of the 1934 vagrancy law known as the Ley contra la Vagancia, instituted by the dictator Jorge Ubico, and reversals of the day laborer regulations that had forced landless indigenous and ladino people to work 150 days a year on the latifundios of larger landowners or on state infrastructure projects.[14]

Only ten years after the 1944 revolution, Guatemala was again in the throes of dramatic political upheaval, as a counterrevolution that began in 1954 reversed the recent political gains, replacing them with oppressive socially and economically conservative policies. Key actors behind this were the U.S. Central Intelligence Agency (CIA), conservative sectors of the Guatemalan oligarchy, and the upper hierarchy of the Catholic Church.[15] This authoritarian rule, and the related closure of democratic political channels, fomented a confrontational social situation, which eventually grew into a brutal thirty-six-year armed conflict between the repressive forces of the totalitarian government and the popular resistance movement. The civil war formally ended with the signing of the Peace Accords in 1996.

The Genocidal Period, 1975–88

Throughout the 1970s and 1980s, the Guatemalan state experienced a crisis of legitimacy that had grown since the 1954 coup d'état against democratically elected president Jacobo Árbenz Guzmán. As elsewhere in Latin America during the latter part of the twentieth century, a series of military governments assumed power in Guatemala by means of fraudulent elections.[16] Everyday life in the country became militarized, public debate was stifled, and repression was brutally imposed by autocratic rulers on all sources of real or imaginary opposition. Popular movements made up of union members, students, professionals, workers, teachers, or peasants that demanded social change were the targets of violence and brutality.[17]

The sociologist Carlos Figueroa Ibarra identifies three general waves of state repression that took place in Guatemala after the onset of the 1954 counterrevolution, the first in 1954, the second between 1967 and 1971, and the third between 1978 and 1983.[18] He describes the first wave of state repression as an anticommunist "witch hunt" that filled prisons with political prisoners.[19] The second wave was characterized by the use of extrajudicial killings and enforced disappearances, with a geographic focus on the capital city and the eastern region of the country, where the guerrilla forces were based at the time. These areas, which tended to have larger ladino populations, reported the highest number of terror victims up to that point in the armed conflict.[20] The third wave of repression began at the end of the 1970s. One of its defining characteristics was the state-sponsored hunt for "internal enemies" and sources of "subversion," which included indigenous peoples living in rural areas as the primary targets.[21] After 1978, state violence increased to unprecedented levels, with particularly vicious episodes of violence inflicted on Mayan communities. At the same time, selective violence in the form of kidnapping, torture, rape, and enforced disappearances continued to cause terror among ladinos and mestizos living in the capital and other municipalities. During this third wave of repression, violence against the indigenous population in the countryside was widespread and indiscriminate.

During their presidencies, General Fernando Romeo Lucas García (July 1, 1978–March 23, 1982) and General José Efraín Ríos Montt (March 23, 1982–August 8, 1983) set out to create a new counterinsurgent state. The driving ideology of this new state was its defense of the traditional privileges of the oligarchy and the protection of the vested economic interests of large landowners, a legacy of colonial power relations in the country. Ríos Montt spoke of the need to save Guatemala from what he described as the "diabolic possession" of the communist insurrection.[22] Thus, historic disdain for indigenous peoples merged with the state's anticommunist fight and Evangelical religious ideology to justify the dehumanization of indigenous peoples.

The political anthropologist Jennifer Schirmer and sociologist Julieta Carla Rostica offer evidence to support this analysis. They suggest that "racism continues to be a central key to interpret genocide in Guatemala."[23] Drawing on old stereotypes and prejudices in its descriptions of indigenous communities and peoples as ignorant, easily manipulated, savage, and subhuman beings susceptible to the guerrillas' promises, the militarized state unleashed the full force of its counterinsurgency strategy on communities whether or not they were involved in the popular uprising.[24]

With the objective of destroying challenges to prevailing power structures in Guatemala, the state planned and executed a series of repressive acts through the army's campaign plans Victoria 82, Firmeza 83, and Reencuentro institucional 84, along with operations plan Sofía.[25] Under the cover of an anticommunist strategy within the general context of the U.S.-backed Cold War, the Guatemalan state implemented a campaign of terror, which included the physical extermination of any person or community it believed to be a communist or communist sympathizer. State terrorism combined with the historical fear and hatred of localized indigenous rebellion. These two drivers led to attacks on entire regions, with some areas like Sepur Zarco becoming targets of indiscriminate violence disproportionately directed against the indigenous Mayan population. What ensued were disappearances, collective murders, and mass rape—in other words, acts of genocide.[26]

In 1999, the Commission for Historical Clarification (CEH, in its Spanish acronym), under the auspices of the United Nations, published the results of a wide-ranging study documenting the violence and crimes committed during the internal armed conflict period in Guatemala (1960–96). Its conclusions were authoritative and devastating: The Guatemalan state was responsible for 93 percent of all human rights violations and acts of violence documented. In particular, state forces committed 626 massacres against Mayan children, women, elderly persons, and men in communities across the country.[27] What is more, through its scorched-earth operations, the state destroyed entire villages, including homes, crops, clothes, tools, animals, and everything that survivors possessed. Members of the army and its paramilitary forces systematically raped Mayan women and girls—often before murdering them—as part of a genocidal project to attack not only the women's bodies and spirits but also the families and communities whom the Guatemalan state was intent on demoralizing, destroying, and ultimately controlling.[28] As a result of these crimes against humanity, entire villages had to relocate, their inhabitants forced to flee to the mountains, live in concentration camps, or seek refuge in Mexico. The Guatemalan state monitored and controlled these concentration camps, organized into so-called model villages or development poles where the population's every move could be controlled, even altered.[29]

The Guatemalan state attacked all twenty-two Mayan peoples in the country. The Achi, K'iche', Ixil, Kaqchikel, Q'eqchi', and Q'anjob'al peoples were the targets of the most severe human rights abuses, abuses that resulted in an estimated 200,000 murders and disappearances, and more than a million internal and international displacements.[30] The history of the Sepur Zarco community is intimately connected to this larger reality.

Sepur Zarco Trial and Sentence

The Mayan Q'eqchi' community of Sepur Zarco inhabits a region of the Polochic Valley located between El Estor municipality in the eastern department of Izabal and Panzós municipality in Alta Verapaz department. The area has a long history of land conflicts and dispossession of indigenous peasants.

According to the land rights scholar Laura Hurtado Paz y Paz, Q'eqchi' families from San Pedro Carchá, Cobán, and Senahú migrated to the area of Sepur Zarco and its neighboring communities from the 1950s onward.[31] Their numbers grew during the 1960s as they migrated to escape the extreme exploitation and miserable living conditions they suffered as laborers on regional coffee plantations.[32] From 1978 onward, peasant farmers in the region, including adolescent and adult men from Sepur Zarco, organized themselves into committees to seek legal possession of the lands they occupied by applying for property titles through the National Institute for Agrarian Transformation (INTA, in its Spanish acronym).[33] Tensions in the area increased, as did the mobilization of indigenous peoples to secure their land tenure after the Panzós massacre on May 29, 1978, a massacre during which the army opened fire on Q'eqchi' peasants who had gathered to assert their land rights, killing up to 140 women, children, and men.[34] Simultaneously, a group of self-styled local plantation owners—whose claims to land ownership were disputed by the locals—encouraged the Guatemalan army to intervene to protect their interests and quash the indigenous mobilization that was taking place.[35]

As a result of that invitation from nonindigenous plantation owners, the Guatemalan army established a military outpost in the communities of Sepur Zarco and Tinajas in August of 1982 under the command of then-president General Ríos Montt.[36] The connection between the army's repression and local plantation owners' organizing to secure the capture of indigenous land was incontrovertible, as security forces arrived with lists of community leaders whom they captured and disappeared. Demecia Yat, one of the surviving women of Sepur Zarco who came forward to denounce her husband's disappearance and the sexual violence she experienced at the army's hands during 1982–83, stated:

> I'm sure that my husband was a member of the land committee. He used to talk about the land, but I didn't care to remember [no me importaba guardar la memoria]. Now I know to remember. What I remember is that, when he was alive, he would participate in meetings in the community. He didn't go outside [Sepur Zarco], but in the community, he would attend meetings. When they grabbed him, they accused him, "You're part of the guerrilleros, you're one of the people that come down from the mountain," or "you're mountain people" [sos gente del monte]. They accused him of passing food [to the guerrillas].[37]

The installment of the Guatemalan army in 1982 marked the beginning of a six-year period during which a series of brutal acts were committed against the women who lived in Sepur Zarco. That year, security forces tortured, disappeared, and murdered most of the men and teenagers participating in local land committees.[38] In the communities surrounding the military outpost, they also systematically raped not only the wives of community leaders but also numerous women and girls of all ages and in different stages of pregnancy, while other women fled to the mountains.[39] The army then forced the remaining survivors to relocate to the area surrounding the military outpost, where the wives of the disappeared men, whom the army called "the widows," had to take turns going every three days to the post to "serve" the troops who came there to rest on a rotating basis from larger military zones in Cobán and Puerto Barrios. This so-called service included domestic slavery in the form of cleaning, preparing food for an average of four hundred soldiers, and washing soldiers' clothes in the nearby Roquepur River. It also included sexual slavery, as women experienced constant and massive rapes by soldiers and officials during their turns in the military outpost, their homes, and the river.[40]

Although the outpost ceased to operate in 1988, the trauma and stigma surrounding these crimes led survivors to remain silent for years. After the signing of the Peace Accords in 1996 and the benefit of some psychological support, some women began to speak about what they had endured during the armed conflict.[41]

It was not until 2011, however, during the First Tribunal of Conscience Against Sexual Violence Toward Women during the Armed Conflict in Guatemala, that women's organizations, activists, and survivors began to build a case against former military commanders of the outpost and surrounding area. That year, a group of fifteen Q'eqchi' women formed their own collective, called Jalok U, meaning "change" or "transforming" oneself in Q'eqchi'. The goal of their collective struggle was to hold accountable some of those responsible for the crimes they had lived through. When their case finally went to trial in February 2016, the fourteen surviving Q'eqchi' women sat in open court with their faces covered for security reasons. In their testimonies, the women recounted the degrading torture that the soldiers subjected their husbands to, as if they were animals, before "disappearing" them. Some recalled their time in the mountains, watching their children die from disease, malnutrition, or machete wounds that the army and civil patrollers inflicted upon them as they fled for safety. They lamented how they could not give their loved ones a proper burial, because they were in hiding and under constant persecution from the security forces. They also recounted the multiple times that the soldiers and military commissioner had raped them in the military outpost, by the river, or in their homes in front of their small children. They reported on how the military forced them to take contraceptives while performing their "service" so that they would not become pregnant from these ongoing rapes by countless men. The women shared how the army made them buy their own cleaning and cooking supplies, and even after their formal military "service" ended, they still had to deliver tortillas, firewood, and six pounds of corn to the outpost daily, even if this meant starvation for their families.

Speaking for the thousands who remained silent or had died, the women talked amid tears about the methodical way the army had violated them, destroyed their family structure, and altered their overall way of life. As a result of their testimony, on February 26, 2016, the three-judge panel of the High-Risk Tribunal "A" in Guatemala City found retired lieutenant colonel Francisco Reyes Girón and former military commissioner Heriberto Valdéz Asij guilty of crimes against humanity in the form of sexual violence, sexual and domestic slavery, humiliating and degrading treatment, forced disappearance, and murder.[42] The court sentenced Reyes Girón to 120 years in prison and Valdéz Asij to 240 years.[43]

The initial reaction to the court's verdict was very positive. According to María Ba, member of the Jalok U collective and Sepur Zarco survivor: "When the verdict came, I was pleased. I was sitting with my face covered. I was praying, and I thought, 'Hopefully, justice is done.' This is all my life; this is all my story. Everything I lived through was very painful. I don't want other people to live what I lived through."[44]

Carmen Xol Ical, another member of the Jalok U collective, described her reaction in the following way: "At the moment and hour when the judge issued the verdict, I was excited. That was what I wanted, for justice to be done. So, my struggle was to tell my story. I didn't go to lie. I went to tell everything I saw, everything I lived, and justice was done. I told all that I held in my heart, and justice was done. For me, justice is that no one else lives through all that we did. That women don't suffer, especially the young women today, [and] that what I suffered first-hand doesn't repeat itself."[45]

Likewise, legal professionals and activists who had accompanied the Sepur Zarco women expressed their satisfaction with the final verdict as well as the trial's larger significance for survivors of sexual violence during the internal armed conflict. Hilda Pineda, attorney in the Human Rights Division of the Public Prosecutor's Office (Ministerio Público) said, regarding the potential impact of the Sepur Zarco case, that:

> One of the biggest achievements for the Human Rights Division, in the Internal Armed Conflict Unit especially, was that the women said what they had suffered—sexual violence. For many years, there had been open [court] proceedings, but women hadn't dared to speak about the sexual violence they had suffered. This [case] has allowed many women who suffered sexual violence during the internal armed conflict to currently come forward to the Division and be prepared to declare and say that, indeed, they have suffered sexual violence. So, this is incredibly important so that more victims have access to justice.[46]

For Ada Valenzuela of the National Union of Guatemalan Women (UNAMG, in its Spanish acronym): "The development of the Sepur Zarco case is a historic fact that sets precedents in Guatemala and the world. The women spoke, they were heard, and every voice woven in their testimonies corroborated the enormous pain that the women and their communities lived through during the war."[47]

The women of Sepur Zarco overcame the challenges of aging, illness, and fierce opposition to demand publicly an end to these abuses and the state's role in perpetuating them. Their victory was momentous because it was the first time in Guatemalan history that national courts had collectively tried acts of sexual violence and sexual and domestic slavery committed during the internal armed conflict.[48] Indeed, Sepur Zarco was the first time "that a national court *anywhere* in the world had ruled on charges of sexual slavery during an armed conflict—a crime under international law."[49] However, as the aftermath of the trial showed, the hard part of transitional justice cases is making sure reparations result in structural benefits for those affected.[50]

"Transformative Reparation" Measures for Sepur Zarco

As part of its verdict, the High-Risk Tribunal "A" issued a series of specific "transformative reparation" measures that had the objective of providing "dignified and holistic" paths for the women of Sepur Zarco and their communities.[51] At the state level, the court first ruled that the Ministry of Education (MINEDUC, in its Spanish acronym) should improve the infrastructure of schools in the Sepur Zarco, Poombaac, and Esperanza communities; establish a bilingual secondary school for girls, youth, and women; award scholarships for all three levels of education for the entire population of Sepur Zarco; and include a description of the Sepur Zarco case in school textbooks. Second, it stated that the Ministry of Culture and Sports should develop cultural projects for the women of Sepur Zarco and their larger collectivity, create a documentary film in collaboration with MINEDUC about their case, and translate the case's verdict into the twenty-two Mayan languages.

Third, it directed the Ministry of Public Health and Social Assistance to build a well-equipped health center in Sepur Zarco, stocked with all the necessary medicines. Fourth, the court ordered the Ministry of Defense to incorporate topics about women's human rights and legislation for the prevention of violence against women into military training courses. Fifth, it declared that the Guatemalan state should, through the appropriate agency, continue the process of legal allocation of land to the indigenous community of Sepur Zarco and to nearby communities, carrying to completion processes that had been initiated before the army disappeared community members during the internal armed conflict. Finally, the court ordered the state to coordinate security measures to protect the plaintiffs and their family members through its Interior Ministry.

The court also ruled that the municipality of El Estor, Izabal, should not only build, within one year of the judgment, a monument honoring the struggle of the women in the Sepur Zarco case, but also that the municipality should work with development committees from Sepur Zarco, San Marcos, Poombaac, and La Esperanza to ensure the provision of basic public services to these communities and to the women there in particular. The office of the Public Prosecutor, for its part, was required by the court to continue investigating the final whereabouts of those still missing from Sepur Zarco and its surroundings. Finally, the court stated that the concurring plaintiff organizations (*querellantes*) should make efforts to have February 26 declared a commemorative "Day for Victims of Sexual Violence and Sexual and Domestic Slavery," and that they should undertake the necessary actions before the Guatemalan Congress related to the Law on Enforced Disappearance. Although the court did not designate a specific time frame or budget for compliance with these reparation measures, Mujeres Transformando el Mundo (MTM), an organization that promotes strategic litigation to eradicate violence against women, coordinated periodic institutional roundtables involving representatives from the different ministries, the Attorney General's office, the national Land Fund (Fondo de Tierras), and the Public Prosecutor to promote dialogue, cooperation, and monitor the progress of implementation.[52]

As of the writing of this chapter, there has been limited progress related to implementing these reparations measures, and the majority of that progress has been in the areas of education and health care. In September 2017, UNAMG presented its publication of a thirty-eight-page illustrated text about Sepur Zarco called *La luz que vuelve*, with the backing of MINEDUC.[53] Likewise, during the summer of 2018, representatives of MINEDUC presented a pedagogical guide and audiovisual material entitled "The Experience of the Path to Justice (Sepur Zarco case)" to a group of educators and community leaders from Izabal and Alta Verapaz.[54]

Beyond these measures, progress has been difficult for various reasons. Although some ministers and public servants in the state have shown an inclination to comply with their respective reparation responsibilities, budgeting and legal constraints, construction challenges, and unresolved land possession issues—among other factors—have interfered with the roll-out of plans.[55] Unless land is owned publicly, for example, construction cannot begin for a permanent health center or high school; in practice, the relevant land is currently private. In the interim, the Ministry of Health and Social Assistance has installed a mobile health clinic at the women's insistence. With respect to access to cultivable land, the eight official property owners of Sepur Zarco's territory had not, as of October 2017, established with the Secretariat of Agrarian Affairs (SAA, in its Spanish acronym) an acceptable price to sell the land.[56]

Aftermath of the Trial

While the primary objective of the court-ordered reparation measures was to transform the conditions of vulnerability and marginalization in which the women of Sepur Zarco and their communities lived, these women continue to face many of the same challenges today. Living conditions in Sepur Zarco are a testament to how insidious oppressions continue to affect indigenous war survivors.[57] Dirt access roads to the community are in poor condition, winter storms washed away a key bridge in 2017, the Polochic River routinely floods and makes local transportation precarious, and there are no potable water or drainage systems for residents.[58] Sepur Zarco has a primary school, but the state provides no other education for youth; as a result, many young people migrate to different parts of the department or the capital city for better paying work.[59]

In 2017, MTM published a baseline diagnostic report that demonstrates the utter lack of state engagement that continues to affect community members' lives more than a year after the trial's verdict and supposedly transformative reparations order.[60] The report's statistical results echoed the words of a Sepur Zarco woman: "We hope they give us what we asked for, what we agreed to. But there's nothing. What we want now are agrarian solutions. . . . We asked for schools. We asked for health centers. Of course, there's one, but it's not enough. . . . We wish for compliance already. We want to see it while we're alive to be able to leave a better future for our children, so that they can study. That was what we asked for from the institution. They should listen to us. We have rights."[61]

While the Sepur Zarco case offers some hope in matters of justice and human rights, it also exemplifies the shortcomings of court-ordered reparations as a strategy to address structural issues of racism and discrimination. As the case so clearly demonstrates, the Guatemalan state has done very little in matters of transitional justice and reparations for the victims of state-sponsored crimes during the war. Moreover, reparations in the Guatemalan context often include commitments that should already be the responsibility of the state. As noted, in the case of Sepur Zarco, some of the transformative reparations measures have yet to materialize, including the construction of a permanent health center and housing for the women, and scholarships for youth in the community to attend middle and high school. These are basic obligations that the Guatemalan state should already be providing to guarantee the welfare of its citizens.

The fundamental issue of land tenure for the Q'eqchi' people—one of the principal reasons why the military murdered and violated them in the first place—remains unresolved. Without a formal offer from the current landowners, or a plan from the state to pay for and distribute the territory in question, the women of Sepur Zarco remain under the constant threat of losing their land and means of economic survival. Demecia Yat, a member of the Jalok U collective, said: "I want my children and grandchildren to be at peace, to be calm, and have land to plant like we had before the conflict came. We were all right before. We had some of everything to eat. We planted yuca, chile, [and] beans. We were all right. Now everything is money; you must buy. That's why I want my grandchildren to have a place to plant, like we used to do."[62]

The women of Sepur Zarco may have blazed a trail that inspires other survivors to break their silence and seek justice for the sexual violence endured during periods of internal armed conflict. However, life in the region has not fundamentally changed, as poverty and state abandonment remain the norm.[63] In Guatemala, court-ordered reparations measures typically involve multiple ministries and, as a result, significant interinstitutional coordination and political will are necessary to execute them appropriately and effectively.

Complicating the panorama for transformative justice is the fact that, to this day, the military retains disproportionate influence over the country. Political, military, and economic sectors in Guatemala continue to challenge the reparations proceedings related to Sepur Zarco.[64] For example, during the Sepur Zarco trial, the Association of Military Veterans of Guatemala placed posters outside the court defending Reyes Girón and Valdéz Asij and accusing the Q'eqchi' women of being prostitutes, an argument the defense lawyer also included in his closing statements. Furthermore, through institutions created and focused on the "peace process," the Guatemalan state has been responsible for obstructing access to files related to the armed conflict; spreading a culture of silence about the past; promoting the remilitarization of the country, especially in many communities fighting to protect their land and natural resources; and denying that genocide occurred in Guatemala.[65] The economic elites of the country, fearing that the course of justice will reveal their direct involvement in crimes against humanity due to their role in financing the military's scorched-earth campaigns, have joined these military associations in their efforts.

Conclusions

Given this larger context, it is important to place the legal proceedings of the Sepur Zarco trial and verdict within both a jurisprudential and political framework. For Guatemala as a nation and for Mayan women in particular, the court's verdict in the Sepur Zarco case represented an historic victory. Through their valiant testimonies, the Q'eqchi' women of Sepur Zarco managed to move the Guatemalan justice system. As a result, the High-Risk Tribunal "A" handed down convictions for homicide, enforced disappearance, and crimes against humanity. Thanks to the women's efforts, the court also decided that the crimes that retired lieutenant colonel Francisco Reyes Girón and former military commissioner Heriberto Valdéz Asij had committed had violated international humanitarian law. The Sepur Zarco verdict remains a valuable precedent for young people and future citizens to enable them to build a world that rejects and punishes any attempt to repeat such acts of sexual and domestic slavery against unarmed indigenous women.

While this litigation has generated important precedents, it has had mixed impacts for the individuals it directly affects, who live in extreme poverty and for whom justice is long overdue. The Q'eqchi' women who gave their testimony—most of whom are illiterate and do not speak Spanish—achieved with their courage what indigenous professionals or academics have been unable to do. They reclaimed the dignity not only of the indigenous peoples of Guatemala but also of more than 5 million indigenous peoples worldwide who, in different moments of history, have faced genocide and other crimes against humanity. That said, the struggle for justice does not end when the trial does. On the contrary, survivors must keep fighting against a society and a state that continue to dehumanize and criminalize them.

Overseeing the implementation of the reparations measures is the executive branch of government, which includes the Ministries of Education, Health and Social Assistance, Defense, Interior, and Culture and Sports. If reparations measures fail to address the root causes of the violence against Q'eqchi' women, their communities, and so many other indigenous people that occurred during the internal armed conflict, including by engaging with the tasks of improving school and health infrastructure and recognizing indigenous land rights, it will be impossible to achieve truly reparative justice.

The problems associated with realizing the promise of reparations do not diminish the value of pursuing legal justice, which represents a hard-fought and significant step in the right direction. However, it is vital to reckon with the complexities and limitations in creating necessary structural changes. Guatemala is still a patriarchal society, and indigenous communities are not immune to discrimination and violence. Likewise, the events of the internal armed conflict still affect internal relations within these same communities. The fear and stigma surrounding sexual violence force many women to remain silent about what they have experienced, even with their own husbands and families. As a result, most indigenous women victims of sexual violence have yet to come forward, and in the interim, tragically, many have died.

To achieve long-lasting structural changes, it is imperative to continue dismantling the deeper causes of the violence that the state unleashed upon the inhabitants of Sepur Zarco, including racism, patriarchy, unequal distribution of wealth, concentration of land and natural resources, ideologies of terror and authoritarianism, and pacts among corrupt economic and political elites to raid the country.[66] Transformative reparations, while difficult to achieve, are necessary for a country as socially and economically unequal as Guatemala. Transitional justice processes are crucial so that, one day, the official narrative that continues to criminalize the survivors—labeling them communists, guerrillas, terrorists, revenge seekers, and freeloaders—will change. Hopefully, the trials currently taking place in Guatemala will finally lead all citizens to accept that historically embedded racism is among the primary forces that have driven the state, its security forces, and elites to commit inhuman acts against indigenous people.

CHAPTER 10

Colonial History at Court: Legal Decisions and Their Social Dilemmas

Nicole L. Immler

Introduction: The Legal Paradigm

The year 2011 saw a landmark decision in the Civil Court in The Hague. For the first time, the statute of limitations blocking liability for mass executions by the Dutch military in the decolonization war in Indonesia (1945–49) was partially suspended. As a result, the Dutch government had to apologize and give compensation to the victims. In 2013, a similar historic court judgment (discussed by Elkins in Chapter 7 in this volume) forced the UK government to pay reparations and apologize to some of the victims of their colonial policies in Kenya.

Though court rulings in favor of the plaintiffs signal success for human rights and transitional justice, the strictly legal framing of these processes is fraught with problems. In particular, court cases address individual claims even where, as in the contexts under discussion here, the core issue motivating the litigation is the structural and systemic violence pervading a whole society. Lawsuits targeting historical injustices are part of a larger trend. Since the Nuremberg trials, it has not just become "thinkable to put history on trial, it has juridically become necessary to do so. . . . It has become part of the functions of trials to repair juridically not only private but also collective historical injustice."[1] Literary scholar Shoshana Felman points to the flaws inherent in this process of staging the voices of the oppressed: Many injuries cannot be narrated in the language of law, and frequently efforts to right the injuries and injustices of the past instead repeat and reproduce the trauma they are attempting to heal, what she called the "juridical unconscious."[2] This *juridification of politics*, a specific fusion of history, memory politics, and litigation, has proliferated since the late 1990s, dominated by the reckoning with the Holocaust. Instead of initiating criminal proceedings, advocates seeking justice have advanced civic restitution lawsuits, including in U.S. federal courts.[3] Some historians have critiqued the historical representation of the Holocaust advanced through these lawsuits, pointing to the way in which cases have, for example, highlighted individual cases of theft instead of focusing on the fact of mass murder.[4] Others, however, have welcomed what they consider a "fruitful model" through which the judge encourages much-needed historical investigation.[5]

A similar debate, centred on the merits of ongoing colonial lawsuits, is taking place in the Netherlands. Some historians argue that legal cases have finally brought scholarly and public attention to the violence of the decolonization period.[6] But others argue that truth needs to be established before litigation is initiated, to avoid the danger of securing forms of "justice" without truth finding.[7]

Lawsuits advanced in a postcolonial setting confront another key challenge: Who has the right to determine what counts as justice and repair? Or, as the Indonesian historian Bambang Purwanto has put it: "Is it up to the Netherlands to decide what price must be paid for our freedom?"[8] He fears that those legal cases "keep both countries in the grip of guilt and penance," and that they thereby perpetuate rather than overcome problematic colonial power hierarchies. But some historians disagree, suggesting that lawsuits can clarify the perpetrator-victim position, providing a forum for entering into a relationship and into a (historical) dialogue.[9] According to historian Selma Leydesdorff, for widows from Srebrenica who lost their husbands and sons to ethnic cleansing at the end of the Bosnian War (1992–95): "The law can be a beginning for reconnection, but . . . can never be more than a partial response to the survivors' needs."[10] Some have argued that the lawsuit-dominated discourse of transitional justice concentrates on bringing these litigation efforts to fruition, to the detriment of careful monitoring of medium- and long-term effects and of victims' needs.[11] This chapter follows up on these demands for *localizing transitional justice*, emphasizing the empirical over the normative approach to the topic.[12]

However, assessing recognition is not just an empirical problem; it is also a conceptual one.

Recognition—A Critical Theory Approach

The issue of recognition is a pressing one in transitional justice practices but also in theoretical scholarship on social and political theory. There is an enduring concern that certain types of recognition procedures stabilize identities and naturalize certain power relations (*affirmative recognition*) instead of contributing to their transformation (*transformative recognition*), to borrow the terminology of philosopher Nancy Fraser.[13] Problematizing forms of recognition that affirm primarily identities, Fraser emphasizes instead the question of economic redistribution.[14] How the symbolic and the monetary relate to one another is indeed a key question in transitional justice, including in the cases examined in this chapter. Is monetary compensation meant to add a purely symbolic weight to apologies or should this compensation have a transformative power? We see a similar move in transitional justice toward transformative justice to get more grips on the actual effects of those recognition procedures.[15]

This chapter argues that to better understand and optimize the recognition process we need to broaden the way dialogue functions in transitional justice mechanisms. Examining colonial injustice through the lens of a court case generates two main protagonists: the perpetrators (the former colonizer) and the victims (the formerly colonized). This corresponds to the classic idea of recognition being a process between two opposing parties, the simplistic victim-perpetrator or, in this case, the colonized-colonizer binary. My research, by contrast, reveals a dialogue with multiple players on multiple levels. It is a dialogue within families and local communities and with postcolonial diasporas.[16] Conceptualizing an approach to dialogue that entails more fluid concepts of identity can generate a more profound understanding of both the essentializing and transformative aspects of recognition procedures. First, I describe the Dutch-Indonesian case. I then touch on another instance where litigation addressing colonial crimes illustrates how the dilemmas explored in the main case are not unique. I conclude by reframing recognition as a dialogical practice—by making use of Hartmut Rosa's notion of recognition as "resonance"[17]—to address more clearly how the social practice of reparations and their normative character are intertwined.

Framing Justice Through Litigation

The court case of the so-called widows from Rawagede started in 2009. It concerns Indonesian women from a small village in West Java whose husbands were summarily executed by Dutch military forces in 1947 during the de/recolonization war (1945–49).[18] The widows' representatives filed a claim against the Dutch state in the Civil Court in The Hague, and—surprisingly—two years later they won their case. More than sixty years earlier, on December 9, 1947, nearly all the men from their village, Rawagede, were killed in one day because they were alleged to be resistance fighters.[19] The Dutch colonial rulers were fighting to regain the colony they had lost to Japanese occupation during World War II in 1942 and then to Indonesian independence on August 17, 1945. The colony, the Dutch East Indies, had been under Dutch rule for 350 years since it was annexed by the Dutch East India Company in the seventeenth century. Anxious to re-establish the old order, the Dutch military had returned to Indonesia and tried, in so-called police actions, to recolonize their old possession. International pressure and the realization that the war could not be won pushed the Dutch finally to formally acknowledge Indonesian sovereignty in December 1949.

Though Dutch military violence in the Dutch Indies during the decolonization war was already known to both the Dutch government and the UN, it was a veteran's testimony in 1969, followed by an official government report known as *Excessennota*, that elevated the issue into a nationwide concern. There followed documentation of other "excesses" (seventy-six in all), but despite photographic evidence and press attention, these revelations had little impact on public or scholarly attention or on justice-related advocacy. This changed with the court cases: initiated by the Dutch-Indonesian Committee for Dutch Debts of Honour,[20] Liesbeth Zegveld, a Dutch lawyer specializing in human rights and war crimes litigation,[21] represented the one male survivor and the nine widows of men executed during the massacre in Rawagede petitioning the Civil Court in The Hague to claim recognition. These advocates advanced a range of different arguments on behalf of their clients. They included the severity of the crimes (unlawful summary executions), the long-standing passivity of the state in the face of well-documented

atrocities, the illegitimate use of the statute of limitations to bar the widows'
from presenting their case to the courts, the availability of firsthand witnesses, and a compelling comparison with the Jewish case. These claims, coupled with the overarching point that they related to "a period in Dutch history
that has not yet been settled," generated a convincing case before the court.[22]

Two years later, in 2011, the Dutch government was ordered to take responsibility for "wrongful acts of the state,"[23] turned into an apology, and
pay €20,000 in compensation to the one survivor and the nine remaining
widows. The claims of survivors' children were denied, as the court called
them "descendants" and considered them to be "less directly affected."[24] On
December 9, the Dutch ambassador issued the first official government apology at the heroes' cemetery in Rawagede. Payments into the widows' newly
established bank accounts followed two weeks later. The Rawagede case, publicized on national television, prompted many new claims by widows of men
summarily executed in other regions.

A New Standard: Apologies and Compensation

In 2013 an informal agreement with the Dutch state promised a similar form
of recognition to Indonesian widows in the former Dutch East Indies, including those from South Sulawesi, whose husbands were shot dead without any
form of trial during "cleansing operations" under Captain Raymond West-
erling (and others) in 1946–47. The recognition took the form of a more informal apology announced at the Dutch embassy in Jakarta.[25] Because the
state actors were slow in making payments, some widows died during the process. Because it was an informal agreement, their children could not step into
the process and take over as heirs to their mothers' claims, a procedure that is
guaranteed only in a legal process. Therefore, Zegveld once again took up the
applicants' cause in front of the court, and again she and they met with success.

In 2014, children of executed men in the villages of Suppa and Bulukumba
in South Sulawesi claimed "equal treatment" and filed claims; the child victims
in Rawagede followed.[26] They argued that it was unfair that the widows alone
received acknowledgment, because losing a father was as devastating a loss.

In 2015, the court held the Dutch state liable to pay compensation to both
the widows *and* the children of men who were summarily executed in the
former Dutch East Indies.[27] While the Rawagede decision served as a
general model for the Sulawesi widows, for child victims the regulation

differs: The court held that the same lump sum of €20,000 was not applicable, instead, assuming adequate evidence was presented to the court, the state would only be liable to cover the children's lost living expenses. Zegveld's 2017 request presented to the Ministry of Foreign Affairs for a collective arrangement to cover the claims of more than five hundred child victims was rejected.

In 2016, the Dutch court held the state liable for war crimes other than executions, a first. These crimes included torture by electric shock perpetrated by Dutch soldiers in 1947, and the rape of an Indonesian woman by Dutch soldiers during a "cleansing action" in Peniwen in East Java in 1949. In the latter case, though the victim claimed damages worth €50,000, she was only awarded €7,500.

In 2017, 2018, and 2019, the Dutch state was successful in appeals against recognition petitions launched by applicants who had not filed their cases within the two-year limitation period since they received notice of the government's potential liability in their cases. While executions were considered too serious to be considered time-barred, this did not apply to the loss of property. In the same sessions, the Civil Court in The Hague heard dozens of new victims—survivors of mass executions and torture and child victims—in remarkable Skype interviews, all aimed at establishing evidence for unlawful actions by the Dutch military in the former colony. Skype hearings were a first for the court. So was the fact that the court started its hearings an hour earlier than usual, due to the time difference with Indonesia, to accommodate the very aged witnesses from Sulawesi.[28] But did those hearings serve the victims and the cause?

In 2013, I listened to three child victims who testified about their father's murder by the Dutch military. I was surprised by the amount of time the judge allowed for the victims to narrate their stories. Several years later, I sat in the same court-room, listening to those Skype testimonials. Though I was supportive of these efforts to ensure that victims had an opportunity to speak about their traumatic histories, I wondered about the extent to which they were really being heard. All testimonies are about mass violence; they clash with the defendant lawyer's search for individual evidences. Do Skype interviews really enable long-buried memories to surface in such detail? Are they conducive to justice for the victims?

In 2020 the court finally awarded compensation to three children, thereby rejecting the state's position that these war crimes are time-barred. Subsequently, the parliament decided not to pursue further litigation, but to come up with a general compensation scheme: a civil settlement of €5,000 for all children who can demonstrate that their fathers had been unlawfully executed by the Dutch army between 1945–49.[29]

At the time of this writing, nearly ten years have passed since the first claims against the Dutch state were filed. The first decision in 2011 was celebrated as a "milestone" for the human rights movement and the utility of international law as an instrument of accountability and justice for state crimes, as the statute of limitations was (partly) barred.[30] However, over time, it became apparent that litigation could not solve all the outstanding recognition issues and that alternative strategies for securing some form of justice were needed.

The Search for Alternatives

The victims' lawyer, Zegveld, described the adoption of a litigation strategy to address reparations and recognition issues as an emergency solution:

> We took the case to the civil court; why did we do that? The widows were not looking for time-consuming procedures, most were eighty-five or older. What is more, they were not motivated by resentment or anger. Rather, they were more looking for some kind of recognition, for someone who would reach out to them, perhaps saying sorry, and acknowledging what happened. At one point I really thought we could avoid litigation, there was a lot of media attention when we started thinking about this case. Public opinion was strongly in favour of the widows. At some point our then minister of development, Mr. Koenders, decided to donate €850.000 in development aid to the village, and I thought that this gesture perhaps could solve this matter, that the money might be used to build a school or a hospital, and that there could be a plaque attached to the building, commemorating the men of Rawagede. And I thought perhaps then it would be all right. I was not completely sure, but we discussed the issue along these lines. But the state was not willing to make any causal link between this money, which they termed development aid, and the events in 1947. And that really closed the discussion. All what remained was litigation.[31]

Once the government refused to accord symbolic meaning to the "development aid" paid, Zegveld commissioned the Amsterdam International Law

Clinic to research the chances of a claim. The clinic saw a possibility that the launch of legal proceedings could "be used in a wider campaign supporting the broader cause of the Committee: general awareness and recognition of the atrocities that took place in the village of Rawagede."[32] These legal efforts enabled colonial crimes to be addressed in a way they never had before. But in the process, the original political struggle for a state-to-state apology developed into a claim for recognition of civil victims and financial compensation for personal damages. The challenge became determining which kind of collective solution would be more appropriate.

The Challenges of the Legal: Bottom-up and Comparative Views

An empirical assessment of the meaning of the apology and compensation for the victims and the families in Indonesia who received these reparatory measures is instructive. In what follows I consider the findings of interviews I conducted in various villages with victims, their families, and activists involved in reparations processes on both the Indonesian and the Dutch sides.[33]

Justice Needs to be Tangible

Was justice done? The answer depends on whom is asked. The widows—all in their late eighties and nineties at the time of the interviews—seemed happy with the recognition and the attention their cause received. As a result of the compensation, most were able to afford better living arrangements: They could buy the house they had been renting or invest in a house for themselves or their children; some were even able to help their children pay off debts. They also reported enjoying better quality food, at least for a while. Often their idea of repair was causally linked to what was lost. One widow not only lost her husband but also her house and wanted to rebuild it (she succeeded). The survivors listed desires that were very concrete: to be able to eat chicken (a symbol of being middle class), to visit Mecca (a wish all the women had, but none could fulfill), and to gain some independence ("I want my own house"). The apology by the Dutch ambassador—a ceremony at the graveyard,

the place most dear to them—was a symbolic gesture described as highly meaningful by the village head. However, without money or other concrete forms
of compensation, many would not have been satisfied. As some of the child
victims said in response to a question about the value of apology, it would
have been "an empty gesture." The apology must be tangible, "shaking hands
only is not enough."[34]

Revictimization: Sharing on One's Own Terms

The material benefits also generated social tensions. In Rawagede the widows
were forced to share half of their compensation with the broader victim community, because they were considered the "representatives" of all 181 victim
families buried at the local cemetery.[35] The decision that compensation was
to be shared had not been clearly communicated beforehand, and the widows
and survivor family members had no clear say in the decision process. As a
result, they felt mistreated and robbed. Though they would have been willing to engage in some form of sharing, as community is considered important, and gift giving is highly respected, they expected to do this on their own
terms. The lack of transparency and agency associated with the process un-
settled both the families and the village as a whole for years.

In villages in Sulawesi, by contrast, social obligations became visible in a
different way. Here, extended family networks—such as the multiple widows
of local kings killed by the Dutch—disagreed over who could legitimately
make claims, reviving tensions over split family loyalties. Because compensation could threaten social harmony, it was decided that any funds received
would be invested in a mosque to reunite the family symbolically.[36] One already compensated widow invested the money received in a car used both
by her grandson but also by the community. In effect, she enhanced her own
mobility but also that of the villagers.[37]

"We Are Still Poor"

Money is always welcomed to improve living conditions. Some of the
(grand)children expected more from the outcome of the litigation. "Every-
body thought that we received *lots* of money, but we're still poor."[38]

One grandson was grateful that he was able to pay all his debts with his grandmother's money, but at the same time felt deeply ashamed that he could not protect her against the enforced sharing process by the village authorities.[39] It is a painful reminder of his weak position in the village's hierarchy.

Victims or Heroes?

In Rawagede these personal disappointments contrast with the sense of pride experienced by the younger generation as their village—thanks to the media attention afforded by the court cases, the infrastructure improvements funded by Dutch development aid, and the commemoration activities organized by the local widows foundation at the monument—became famous ("a place in Indonesian history") and a better place to live. We thus confront a paradox. In the Netherlands the widows are a symbol of a *colonial disaster*, but in Indonesia they represent a *heroic independence struggle*. Both these versions of history are memorialized at the very same cemetery. Does Indonesian nationalistic historiography, by turning victims into heroes, silence individual suffering? Or does the Dutch postcolonial narrative, by turning heroes into victims, deny survivors their agency and pride? Do survivors, by accepting "small money," undermine their own political agency and the dignity for which their countrymen fought?[40]

Comparative Views

Similar issues have arisen in other contemporary court cases involving decolonization struggles, such as the so-called Mau Mau case or the war of independence in Kenya (1952–59).[41] Here too, the legal process generated resentments, as some victims felt excluded by settlements paid out in 2012 by the British government only to applicants listed in the court cases. Here too, the UK government was not willing to countenance a debate on alternative, more collective, remedies.[42] Here, too, it is not a colonial reparations case; in the Kenian case it is on torture and in the Dutch case on executions, both in the context of the exercise of colonial rule.[43] Here too, the apology made to address the larger victim community was meant to compensate for the shortcomings of individual compensations. However, as the Indonesian case

showed, at a personal level the symbolic needs to be accompanied by a concrete gesture that materially benefits survivors. At the same time, individual
redress brings with it the risk of social frictions and revictimizations as divisions and jealousies within the survivor community emerge.[44] In Indonesia, some people expect more from their own state than from the former
colonizer; if asked, some would have preferred a hero's pension instead of a
victim payment. What for some is an attempt to address colonial injustices,
is for others another colonial act of "divide and rule," undermining the establishment of a collective consciousness fought for in the independence
war.[45] Both approaches, one might suggest, ignore facts that do "not suit local sensibilities," such as the collaboration of locals with the colonial administration or the use of the emergency "to settle old scores."[46] And, both in
the UK and in the Netherlands, scholars and media pay most attention to
the treatment of those claims at home, while the effects on the people for
whom they were designed remain underexposed.[47]

Reframing Recognition As a Dialogical Practice

The Dutch-Indonesian cases support the claim that dealing with colonial injustices requires greater vision in the transitional justice field than has been
explored so far. Legal procedures alone, necessary though they are for survivors and their descendants, are limiting. Some of the problems are inherent
in the transposition of large-scale structural violence to individual legal
cases. Other problems stem from the way in which legal processes reproduce pre-existing hierarchies, promising a kind of transformation while de
facto stabilizing hierarchies. In what follows, I offer some reflections on the
limitations of legal practice and on the possibility of advancing colonial reparations practices by engaging in a more "dialogical perspective."

The sociologist Hartmut Rosa labelled the courtroom a "resonance-
free" space, which is not about empathy, compassion, insight, or understanding, but about enforcing one's own claims against those of the other
side.[48] There we find rather a strategic communication than a resonant
dialogue. He describes legal recognition as a deaf institutionalized relationship with the world. In effect, being acknowledged by law does not
necessarily mean that victims feel seen or acknowledged.[49] Indeed, as this
research shows, for many of the victims the success of their claims is not

decided in the courtroom (when they win their cases), but when the decision is implemented (when the recognition or the money makes a difference in their life). This shifts the focus from the courtroom to the social settings.

Dialogue Within Families and Communities

Paying compensation for past injustices is not just a financial transaction and a symbolic gesture but a social process that evolves. This means, in villages such as Rawagede, that more attention is needed to ensure that former victims are not revictimized by the process, and that the decision-making and sharing is a self-directed process that creates agency and empowerment, not one that is imposed. This approach needs a form of anthropological research to establish survivors' wants and needs as well as local understandings of justice. It also requires clear communication and transparency in the procedures, so that they do not remain in the hands of a few activist individuals.

Recognition is a *relational experience*: the success of the process depends on whether the mediators who represent and communicate decisions to the claimants are accepted, whether there is a *resonant* context (a supportive environment), and whether the gendered nature of the experience is acknowledged, given that—as the interviews in the Indonesian villages showed—females' priorities (household, food, health) often differ from those of males (honor, representation, protection). In Rawagede, after the widows also the children of executed men claimed equal treatment, they were not only highlighting the fact that a selective recognition of individuals endangered the social fabric but also claiming co-ownership of the recognition process.

As Gready and Robins have noted in relation to compensation policies: "The potential for shifts in agency and power relations around reparations resides mainly in the fact that reparation campaigns usually evolve over time, from below, as a result of civil society and victim/survivor mobilization and in the face of official opposition. Herein lies the possibility for participation, constituency building and the acquisition of new skills, and fresh patterns of engagement with the state through and beyond reparation campaigns."[50] They call for a form of participation that transforms victimhood: "Transformative justice requires a radical rethinking of participation in transitional and transnational justice interventions. It seeks a form of participation that engages with but transforms victimhood."[51] Here participatory action and grassroots involvement are crucial to a transformative process, an essential element in transitional justice.[52]

Dialogue with the Diaspora

It is not just social aspects that are excluded from the courtroom, political factors are too. Originally the Rawagede case was a claim about the "recognition of August 17, 1945, as the *de jure* date of independence of Indonesia and a general apology from the Dutch Government."[53] It turned into a struggle for compensating victims. What has looked in the courtroom like an engagement with the colonial past in Indonesia has been, from the very beginning, an engagement with the present-day postcolonial Netherlands. Those court cases were initiated by a member of the Indonesian Diaspora living in the Netherlands (Jeffry Pondaag, chair of the Committee for Dutch Debts of Honour), who translated his sense of the neglect of colonial history as shared history into a claim on behalf of the formerly colonized.[54] For him it was not just about *injured citizens* during colonialism but also about himself, and his feeling (as an Indonesian) of still not being accepted as an *equal citizen* in Dutch society today.[55] His claims, and those of an increasing postcolonial movement,[56] therefore, go far beyond the acknowledgment of historical injustice and relate to disappointments in a Dutch society that has not yet come to terms with its postcolonial legacy—a society in which many postcolonial migrants still do not feel like fully acknowledged members.

Recognition as Dialogue

While the Rawagede and the follow-up court cases can be interpreted as a kind of "reconnection" with the colonial past, providing new facts on the re/decolonization war but also a value judgement, both stimulating a scholarly and public debate, a key dilemma of those legal cases also becomes evident: a discussion in which the categories colonizer and colonized are constantly repeated. This also stabilizes hierarchies.

While the classic idea of a "struggle for recognition" is seen as an inherently emancipatory practice that tends to continually call into question oppressive social arrangements,[57] critics show how recognition can easily become an essentializing tool, as the other is placed in an "otherized" position from which to be recognized. Kristina Lepold has called it an "ideology critique of recognition" to stress that recognition can "be implicated in the reproduction of problematic social orders,"[58] An example is the gender-blindness of many recognition procedures; another example is the "format" of many colonial apologies: following Tom Bentley they rest "on the colonizer voicing a narrative, while the colonized remain less audible . . . maintaining hegemonic narratives and speaking positions [rather] than overturning them."[59] Recognition in this context is not so much enabling as constraining.[60] To address this, Nancy Fraser distinguished between *affirmative recognition*, naturalizing certain power relations, and *transformative recognition*, which restructures "the underlying generative frameworks and relationships."[61]

This chapter suggests that making use of Hartmut Rosa's idea of recognition as "resonance" could help exploring further what qualifies as transformative recognition. Rosa defined "resonance" as a dynamic process of encounter in which opposing sides intersect and transform. He sees the precondition for resonance in a kind of "participatory parity" so that "we hear each other and speak to each other as 'equals.' . . . Social actors can only establish resonant relationships (and hence parity of participation) when they take the stance of listening and responding on equal terms."[62] Only then is a transformative act possible. Rosa argues that recognition is felt only when a mutual transformation has taken place, when it has enabled *both* parties to overcome their original positions.

Looking at current Dutch debates on independence, decolonization, violence, and war in Indonesia in 1945–50, a key question is whether there will be a space created in which Dutch and Indonesian voices are equally represented to find a broader truth rather than being constrained into performing colonial role patterns. If recognition measures could function as a space in which dominant readings of histories and alternative readings of history meet and make room for more fluid identities, allowing people to leave narrow "victim" or "perpetrator" identities, this might help to deconstruct the dichotomized (and also legal) logic of "who acknowledges" and "who is acknowledged," of "who gives" and "who receives," which in itself carries the signature of historical violence and power relationships. So far, the Dutch have determined what price to pay, as the Indonesian historian Purwanto has put it.[63] In its place, "to learn from the bottom," to paraphrase Gayatri Spivak, would provide a plurality of voices and therewith "a broader truth" and also different answers to what justice is about.[64] Hearing those different answers could qualify as resonant dialogue.

Future Research Agenda

The lawyers behind the colonial reparations cases are aware that legal action is constrained. One is also increasingly aware that the monetarization of the debate tends to overstate the value of money.[65] While financial compensation is just an instrument to achieve recognition, it has become a means in itself. However, by *expanding the law*, they hope to initiate a "much broader political solution."

But, what kind of solution? How can one improve existing recognition and compensation processes so that no secondary victimizations take place? How can one translate anthropological or oral history research results into legal and/or extra-legal procedures that can then be followed up by local initiatives that do more justice to the experiences and needs at the grass roots, within survivor communities themselves? More broadly, how can the legal cases be used as a starting point to stimulate a process of transformation in postcolonial societies that takes the historical legacy of colonialism into account? This might require further scrutiny of the concept of recognition as a desirable good, whether it can do justice to the multiple voices and identities people have and need to have in our globalized societies. These are questions that need to be investigated further, not just in Indonesia, Kenya, or Namibia but also in Europe. Being more aware of the limitations of legal processes will feed thinking about additional, supplementary, instruments, and create awareness that those legal cases indicate a possible shift in hegemonic structures, a shift that has not yet been made.

PART III

====

Outstanding Issues:
Unrepaired State-Sponsored
Collective Injustice

CHAPTER 11

Unhealed Wounds of World War I:
Armenia, Kurdistan, and Palestine

Rashid Khalidi

The centenaries of the beginning and end of the World War I were widely commemorated by solemn ceremonies in 2014 and 2018, respectively, mainly in Europe, but also elsewhere around the globe. In contemplating this hideous conflict, wherein the most modern industrial means of the day were employed for the systematic taking of over 15 million lives, most people think primarily of the trenches of the Western Front. It was there that the largest number of battlefield casualties were suffered, and there that lethal military innovations such as poison gas, aerial bombardment, and the use of tanks were first previewed on a massive scale.[1] Because of its unprecedented violence, its murderous outcome, and the societal upheavals it produced, for generations thereafter this terrible war traumatized the European societies that were engaged in it. It is also common knowledge that World War I completely redrew the map of Central and Eastern Europe, that it brought down three great European dynasties, the Habsburgs, the Romanovs, and the Hohenzollerns, and that it helped to bring the Bolsheviks to power in Russia.

Less attention has been given to the fact that, although its main protagonists and theaters of battle were European, World War I was not only a European war. It was, as its name indicates, a world war, one fought across large swaths of Africa, the Middle East, and the Pacific. Indeed, of all the major combatant nations, the population of a mainly non-European state, the Ottoman Empire, suffered the highest proportion of military and civilian wartime casualties. As much as 15 percent of the Empire's total population, or about 3 million people, perished during World War I, one-fifth of the war's entire death toll.[2] The next highest proportions among all combatant nations were for France and Germany, which each lost about 4.3 percent of their total populations during the war, or over 4 million people between them, mainly young male soldiers

These horrific casualties among the peoples of the Ottoman Empire—I will return to some of the grim peculiarities of these losses—are only one reason for paying attention to the extra-European aspects of World War I. Another is that among the forces of the Entente powers in particular were millions of colonial soldiers. These came both from so-called white colonies, like Australia, New Zealand, Canada, and South Africa and ex-colonies like the United States, and also from the British and French colonial armies raised among the subject peoples of South Asia, North and West Africa, and elsewhere around the globe. The colonial powers mobilized around 4 million of the latter, mainly by conscription.[3] Historians of decolonization have traced the explosion of nationalist demands in these nonwhite colonies during the post–World War I era in part to the exposure to the horrors of this war of soldiers raised among the African, Arab, and Asian colonial populations. This was thereafter compounded by their continued discriminatory treatment by the white European powers, in spite of the great sacrifices many of them made on the battlefield. These are issues of great sensitivity to this day. On the hundredth anniversary of the war, there was intense controversy in both France and Algeria over the Bastille Day parade in Paris on July 14, 2014, in which Algerian soldiers participated, alongside others from all the countries allied to France. The Algerian troops who marched in that parade represented more than 175,000 of their compatriots—the equivalent of twelve divisions of infantry—who fought and died for their colonial overlord, France, more than a hundred years ago, mainly in the trenches on the Western front. Equally large numbers of other colonial troops, especially Indians (1.5 million), North Africans (more than 210,000), and West Africans (more than 160,000) made similar sacrifices.[4]

Among the other reasons for the importance of World War I's extra-European results, several seem particularly pertinent today. They have to do with what I call the unhealed wounds of World War I: in particular the wounds of Armenia, Kurdistan, and Palestine. In Western Europe today, some of the main enmities that helped to produce three wars between 1870 and 1945, including the two world wars—notably, the intense hostility between France and Germany—are seen to have ended. Indeed, a desire to avoid the recurrence of such wars was central to the creation of the European Union and its precursors. In some areas of Eastern Europe and the Balkans, similar reconciliations seem to have taken place, while elsewhere in these regions, problems dating back to 1914 and before continue to simmer, as in Bosnia and the Ukraine. As the EU expanded, it appeared to provide a sense of closure regarding conflicts in some of these troubled regions, although not in all of them. Meanwhile, it has recently become clear that the EU is far from being the panacea for Europe's problems that some once saw it as being.

There has been no such sense of closure, no such resolution of enmities, in the Middle East. There, the scars of earlier conflicts are still raw, and borders and the entities created by the victors of World War I and its sanguinary postwar sequels are still a source of vigorous, sometimes violent, contestation.[5] These imposed borders, and the artificial nature of the states created within them by European colonial measures like the Anglo-French 1915–16 Sykes-Picot Agreement, have produced periodic conflicts between states, and civil wars within others. These include bloody decades-long Kurdish insurgencies in Iraq, Turkey, and Iran; the Lebanese civil war of 1975–90; the 1990–91 war over Kuwait; the Syrian civil war cum proxy war that is still ongoing at the time of this writing, and the festering hundred-year struggle over Palestine.

One dramatic example of such contestation was the categorical rejection of the borders between Iraq and Syria, and of other inter-Arab borders, by the so-called Islamic State in Iraq and Syria, also known as ISIS, or by its Arabic acronym, *Da'esh*. Notorious for its many spectacular atrocities, this entity purported to transcend and erase these hated borders. At the end of June 2014, the "Islamic State" proclaimed a revived Islamic caliphate encompassing these two countries and claiming the territory of many others and pronounced its sovereignty over all Muslims. This was not the first instance in modern Arab history of the rejection of these artificial, European-drawn borders, which Arab nationalists have opposed for generations, but it was certainly the most radical one.

One of the first announcements of the presence of the Islamic State as a territorial entity was an English- and Arabic-language video showing the dynamiting of a just-captured border post between Iraq and Syria. These are two of the states created within borders that were largely determined in 1915 and 1916 by the Sykes-Picot partition. This arbitrary procedure produced zones of influence with no reference to local conditions or the wishes of those affected, but rather solely to suit Anglo-French imperial interests. These zones were established by the negotiators of these accords, Sir Mark Sykes and

Francois Georges-Picot, often by drawing long straight lines across the desert that are still visible on modern maps. The entities thereby created became the nuclei of at least five of the existing states of the Middle East today.

However, the impact of World War I in the Middle East goes far deeper than the capricious imposition of borders, and the creation of artificial states. While psychic traumas undoubtedly persist as a result of these divisions and partitions that were engendered by colonialism in the Middle East, in other areas of Africa and Asia similar traumas seem to have been largely overcome. In fact, in spite of their questionable origins, like scores of nation-states in Africa and Asia that are in whole or in part the creation of colonial mapmakers, most such Middle Eastern states have taken on a life of their own. They are examples of the way in which in postcolonial situations, the state left behind by the colonial power eventually plays a part in engendering a new nation. Indeed, many of the nation-states that have grown up inside such arbitrary borders appear to be going concerns, for better or for worse.

This chapter, however, focuses neither on the successes of the different European colonial experiments in the creation of new states in the Middle East, nor on the problems created by this arbitrary and largely externally driven process of state-formation. It is, rather, concerned with those cases where peoples-in-formation were not allowed to form states, where nation-states were prevented from developing, and where a sequence of tragic events during and after World War I has continued to have repercussions until the present day, leaving behind wounds that are still unhealed.

The three outstanding Middle Eastern cases in this category are those of the Armenian, Kurdish, and Palestinian peoples. Each one is quite different from the other two, and the national movement of each people has its own unique history and its own specificities. Moreover, each people is facing quite different circumstances today. What they share, however, is the common World War I and postwar experience of cruel disappointment of their hopes for self-determination and independent national development. In spite of various commitments in this regard that were offered by the victors of that war, notably Great Britain, in the end none of these commitments were honored. As a result, these three peoples ended up as perhaps the greatest losers of the postwar settlement in the Middle East.

Let me take first the case, which was the most tragic during World War I but the only one in which the people in question today enjoy any form of national independence and self-determination, however precarious and partial. This is the Armenian case. It is the most tragic because, during World

War I, the Armenian people suffered the most of the three peoples I am discussing. At the outset of the war, Armenians in Eastern Anatolia were caught in the midst of an epic series of battles between the Ottoman and Russian armies, and they thereafter were subjected to a genocidal exile from most of their ancestral homeland, which killed as many as a million and a half of their people.[6]

A full examination of this genocide would involve a detailed discussion of the prewar and wartime circumstances that led the leaders of the Committee of Union and Progress (CUP), who had untrammeled control over the Ottoman Empire, to perceive the entire Armenian people as an enemy of the Ottoman state, and to decide that they had to be extirpated. Such a discussion would neither justify nor extenuate the crime against humanity that they committed. It would only provide a historical context, in particular regarding the fateful clash between nascent Turkish and Armenian nationalisms on the same terrain within a multinational state, a context that is far more complex than many are prepared to admit on both sides of what has become a great historiographical divide.

At the same time as the genocidal outcome of this clash constituted the most tragic of the three cases I will be discussing, it is also the only one that has resulted in any form of independence on any part of the homeland of the people in question. Neither the Kurds nor the Palestinians are independent today, unlike the Armenians. This independence was gained only in part of the homeland Armenians consider their own (many areas of which they in fact originally shared with other peoples, including both Turks and Kurds). It was only gained after the most awful sacrifices during the war and then in the post–World War I era, as the nascent Armenian state had to fight desperately for its very existence, eventually to be swallowed up by the Soviet Empire as the Armenian Soviet Socialist Republic. Only after the fall of the Berlin Wall and the dissolution of the Soviet Union did a small but truly independent Armenia see the light.

This history is well known, if still disputed, but there is an element that complicates this story, and links it directly and integrally to the other two recounted below. This involves the wartime and postwar role of the imperialist European powers, notably Russia, Germany, Great Britain, and France, in exacerbating the plight of the Armenian people. After the war began, Tsarist Russia treated the Armenians as pawns as its troops advanced into the territory of the Ottoman Empire, with the aim of expanding its imperial domains further southward. We know from the diplomatic correspondence between the Western allies that Russia sought to annex large swathes of Ottoman territory, as well as the Turkish Straits. However, when Russian troops eventually withdrew from Eastern Anatolia, they callously exposed that region's innocent Armenian population, as well as Armenians elsewhere in the empire, to the ruthless vengeance of the CUP regime.

Similarly, imperial Germany, which had long been allied to the Ottoman Empire, completely failed to protect the Armenians when units of the Ottoman army, which German officers had long advised, and in some areas commanded, advanced eastward and retook Ottoman territory from the retreating Russians in 1915. As the Ottoman forces advanced, they and their auxiliaries wreaked havoc on the defenseless Armenian population, who were treated as collaborators with the Russian enemy. The entire Armenian population of Eastern Anatolia was deported in 1915 and 1916, and, in the process, most Armenians there and elsewhere in the empire were massacred. Only a pitiful remnant survived to reach the cities of Syria. In spite of the dependence of the Ottoman military on German support, and notwithstanding German officers' and diplomats' full knowledge of the extent of the atrocities that were taking place, which the diplomatic archives indicate they had faithfully reported back to Berlin, the German government did nothing: Its alliance with the Ottomans was too important.

Finally, there are Britain and France. Britain witnessed these agonizing episodes at a distance during the war. Afterward, when its forces and those of its allies were in occupation of Istanbul and large areas of Ottoman territory, Britain made far-reaching promises to the Armenians that it would support an independent Armenia on extensive territories that had formerly belonged to the Ottoman Empire. Like Russia and Germany, Britain was acting in furtherance of its own imperial interests, and the Armenians were no more than a pawn in their game. The British Empire had no more concern for the Armenian people per se than had the Russian or the German empires. As British statesmen showed repeatedly at the Versailles Peace Conference and afterward, they were by no means apostles of the self-determination of oppressed peoples. Indeed, as that conference convened in Paris in the spring of 1919, British troops were engaged in shooting down Indians and Egyptians who were demonstrating for their freedom in Amritsar, Cairo, and elsewhere in India and Egypt.

Soon after the end of World War I, in response to the occupation and partition by the imperialist European powers, and the hideous human losses that the empire had suffered (over 1.5 million subjects of the empire perished during the war, in addition to the 1.5 million Armenian victims), the pre-cursor of the modern Turkish Republic arose in Ankara. Its leaders quickly rallied much of the populace and the remnants of the Ottoman army and bureaucracy to the Turkish national cause. Their forces began to push back the occupying allied armies, first the French (who had come to rely on Ar-menian military auxiliaries in their occupation of Ottoman territory), then the Greeks, and then the British, from what eventually became territory of the Turkish Republic. When this happened, neither Britain nor France lifted a finger to help their erstwhile Armenian allies, who were besieged by mul-tiple enemies. The Armenian civilian population once again suffered the cruel consequences. In the end, Armenia survived on a small parcel of the territo-ries formerly inhabited by Armenians, first as a satellite within the orbit of the USSR, and then as an independent but impoverished, embattled, and land-locked state, still struggling with traumas that date back to World War I.[7]

The second case, that of the Kurds, is very different from those of both the Armenians and the Palestinians. The Kurdish national movement was later in developing than those of the Turks, Arabs, Greeks, Armenians, and several other peoples of the Ottoman Empire. Like the Armenians, the Kurds lived in many areas among populations of other ethnicities, who spoke other languages and had conflicting aspirations. By the time World War I broke out, their language had not yet been modernized or homogenized and unified, as Turkish, Arabic, and Armenian had begun to be during the late nineteenth century through the widespread expansion of the press, publish-ing, and various educational initiatives. Nevertheless, Kurdish nationalism had already begun to develop in the prewar period, with the growth of the first Kurdish clubs, newspapers, and other early precursors of a modern na-tional movement. When the war ended, and with President Woodrow Wilson's proclamation of the principle of national self-determination, many Kurds, like Arabs, Indians, Koreans, and numerous other peoples, believed that the moment of national independence had finally dawned.

Remarkably, when the Kurds appealed to the British to support their de-mands for independence, British officials responded positively, making promises to the Kurds similar to those that had been made to the Armenians.[8] Indeed, by some accounts, the British promised to the Kurds certain regions that they had promised to the Armenians. This should not surprise us: Dur-ing and after World War I the British were commonly charged with duplic-ity in making contradictory promises to different parties. In the case of Palestine, they made conflicting commitments to the Arabs, the French, and the Zionists, which led to that country being described as the "thrice promised land." Whatever the case regarding these British promises, the result for the Kurds was the same as for the Armenians. When the moment of truth arrived, and the British commitment to support them was tested as Turkish nationalist forces expanded their area of control in Eastern Anatolia to include areas claimed by the Kurds, the British did nothing. Thereafter, the chimera of Kurdish independence vanished for decades. Like the Armenians before them, in vain did Kurdish representatives try to put their case before the Versailles Peace Conference, which simply ignored their claims and those of most other peoples who had similar demands for self-determination.

In the end, Kurdistan was partitioned between independent Iran and Turkey, British-controlled Iraq, and French-controlled Syria. Most Kurds today still live mainly in those four states. Their history since then has been one of struggle to maintain and develop their national identity, to unify what is still a deeply divided national movement, and to avoid becoming pawns of the regional and international powers that succeeded the great European imperialist states. They revolted many times against the national oppression they were subjected to, first in Turkey during the interwar period, and then repeatedly in Iraq in the decades after World War II. These revolts were brutally suppressed with air power, overwhelming force, and, in the case of the Iraqi Baathist regime, the use of poison gas. Again and again, the Kurds were cruelly abandoned by powers that had been happy to support them in furtherance of those powers' own aims. Thus, the short-lived Kurdish Mahabad Republic in northwestern Iran was left to its fate by its Soviet backers in 1946 once they reached a deal with Britain and the United States for the withdrawal of all foreign forces from Iran, and most of its leaders were executed by the Iranian authorities.[9] Similarly, the United States, which together with Iran and Israel had backed the Kurdish revolt against Iraq in the 1970s, immediately abandoned the Kurds when U.S. ally Iran made an advantageous deal with Iraq in Algiers in 1975. This was the occasion for the immortal words of Dr. Henry Kissinger to a horrified chair of a congressional committee, Otto Pike, who remonstrated with him about this betrayal: "Covert action should not be confused with missionary work."[10]

There have been many other such betrayals of the Kurds, and many other similar abandonments. To this day, the Kurds are largely dependent on the kindness of untrustworthy strangers for such autonomy as they have been able to secure, as in parts of northern Iraq since the 1990–91 war there. More recently, they achieved a precarious autonomy in broad areas of Iraq and northern Syria as these two states disintegrated under the pressure of sectarian civil wars, the first provoked by the American occupation of Iraq, its dismantling of the Iraqi state and installation of a Shia-dominated sectarian regime (whose constitution was perversely modeled by its American framers on that of Lebanon), and the challenge of the Islamic State. But, as elsewhere, this autonomy is threatened by suspicion of Kurdish claims to autonomy, and possibly independence, on the part of the four nation-states among whom they are divided: Turkey, Iraq, Iran, and Syria. It is threatened as well by the inconstancy of would-be allies like the United States and other Western powers that profess sympathy for them. Facing constant pressure from Turkish military forces in occupation of parts of Northern Syria and abandoned by its erstwhile American allies, this autonomy was also under attack—and may be again—by the Islamic State in Kurdish-inhabited areas of Syria and Iraq dominated by different Kurdish paramilitary forces. The Islamic State abhors the nationalism of the Kurds, which is an affront to the transnational Islamic sovereignty that this entity proclaims, as it abhors the secularism of the political movements that incarnate Kurdish nationalism. Like Armenia, Kurdistan is land-locked and embattled, and it continues to face an uncertain future, just as it has ever since World War I.

This brings us finally to the case of Palestine. It is only possible to sketch out some of the ways in which this too constitutes one of the unhealed traumas of World War I. Here we have another people to whom pledges were made by Britain during World War I. Here too we have betrayal, as the fine words of wartime British promises of Arab independence, in the Husayn-McMahon correspondence and several other public British pledges, were shown to be hollow in Palestine and indeed throughout many other parts of the region. However, it was not only Britain but the entire League of Nations that made commitments that, in the case of the Palestinians, were not kept. These pledges were enshrined in the League's Covenant, which in its Article 22 described the former Arab provinces of the Ottoman Empire as territories whose "existence as independent nations can be provisionally recognized."[11]

Insofar as Palestine was concerned, the Balfour Declaration, issued in November 1917, flatly contradicted this solemn pledge. This document proclaimed that there was only one people with national rights in Palestine, the Jewish people, and that the overwhelming Arab majority of the population of the country, not named or described in the declaration, were only to enjoy "civil and religious rights," not political or national rights. This language was incorporated verbatim into the League of Nations Mandate for Palestine, adopted in 1922, which thereby denied the Palestinian Arab majority of the population the independence the covenant had promised them. The British knew perfectly well what they were doing. In a memo that remained secret for decades, Lord Balfour wrote in 1919: "So far as Palestine is concerned, the Powers have made no statement of fact which is not admittedly wrong, and no declaration of policy which, at least in the letter, they have not always intended to violate."[12]

This is the origin of the long odyssey of the Palestinians, exacerbated by the policies of the British colonial authorities in fulfillment of the commitments that had been made to political Zionism in the Balfour Declaration and the Mandate for Palestine. It was compounded by the UN General Assembly, which voted to hand over most of Palestine to a Jewish state for the Zionist-led 33 percent Jewish minority of the population, which then owned just over 6 percent of the land. The United States and the USSR, the superpowers that pushed for passage of the partition resolution, then left the Palestinian Arab state that was also supposed to be established by this resolution to be strangled in its cradle by a combination of the might of the new Israeli state, the collusion of Jordan and Britain, and their own indifference. The United States and the USSR were determined to create a Jewish state and were much more concerned with their rivalries with one another, and with supplanting the declining power of Britain, than they were with the fate of the Palestinians.

In my writings on the history of Palestine, I have elsewhere provided more detail on the specific traumas suffered by the Palestinians, particularly as a result of the massive ethnic cleansing of 1948, known as the Nakba, or "catastrophe," which involved Israel's expulsion of more than 750,000 of their number, the majority of the Arab population of Palestine.[13]

Together with the Kurds and the Armenians, the Palestinians are among the great Middle Eastern losers of World War I and its aftermath. There is one more common characteristic of all three peoples. All of them suffer not only from the consequences of the specific events just traced that are rooted in World War I and its immediate sequels but also from something that has caused these wounds to remain raw: This is the impact on all three peoples of systematic policies of denial and erasure.

All have thus been victims not only of specific material indignities, of wide-scale massacres, of organized ethnic cleansing. The effect of all these hurts has been amplified and has been made to resonate, generation after generation, by the denial by the powerful nation-states that have dominated the Middle East for the past half century—notably Turkey, Iraq, and Israel—that these things happened, or that they happened as the victims knew very well that they did. The collective memory of these peoples, the testimony of the victims, and that of the survivors and the refugees, has been largely ignored as part of this wholesale denial.

Worse, all of these peoples have been told that they do not exist, or should not exist, and material vestiges of their past in their homelands have been extirpated or appropriated. The Kurds were long told by Republican Turkey that there was no such thing as a Kurdish people, that they were no more than "mountain Turks," and they were forbidden to use or teach their language. The links of the Armenians to most of their ancestral homeland were downplayed, and their contributions to the societies they had once formed a part of were ignored. Meanwhile, the very existence of the Palestinians as a people was denied. This denial was most famously expressed in 1969 by Golda Meir, who scoffed, "There is no such thing as a Palestinian people. It is not as if we came and threw them out of their country. They didn't exist."[14]

Beyond this, in these three cases it is the victims who have been blamed, and the losers who have been scapegoated by the victors. The victors have done this partly by successfully deploying the broad brush of "terrorism." By some legitimating sleight of hand made possible by sovereignty, states are never described as engaged in terrorism, whether they are killing innocent civilians by using phosphorus, poison gas, nuclear weapons, or any other means of mass destruction. Meanwhile, entire peoples can be condemned and treated as pariahs, effectively excluded from the human community, and subject to any form of inhuman treatment if this label can be successfully attached to some of them. This is what has happened in these three cases.

Finally, with the exception of tiny Armenia, the very names of the countries of these peoples have been erased from the map, just as the victors tried to erase all signs of their presence, whether by the destruction of villages, as in Palestine, or by other means. Physical erasure, archaeological legerdemain, divide-and-rule tactics, all of these have been utilized to make the evidence of the existence of these peoples go away. Thus, today there is no Kurdistan and no Palestine on the map, and while a small state of Armenia exists, it is the exception.

All of these tools in the arsenal of the victor have been employed at different times. The net effect has been to compound the original injury, and to keep these wounds from healing. It takes generations to overcome mass historical trauma in the best of circumstances. The case of the lasting trauma of the trench warfare of World War I on the populations of France, Germany, and Britain is a perfect example. As only one illustration, at the center of nearly every French village and town is a monument bearing the long list of names of its sons (often inscribed "A nos enfants") who died on the battlefields of that awful war. This is an attempt to assuage the trauma caused by these terrible losses, and to show respect for those veterans who survived. But when there is denial that trauma even occurred, when it is asserted that the victim has no cause for complaint, or even that the tormentor is the real victim, then the trauma caused by material and physical hurt is compounded and magnified.

Thus, if we ask why the Armenian, Kurdish, and Palestinian wounds just described are unhealed, there is something beyond the genuine grievances, something beyond the grave and complicated political issues still to be resolved. There is also the hard issue of remapping the way in which these conflicts are understood, especially by the victors, but also by the victims and by the rest of the world, so as to undo this cruel denial. This may be as difficult to achieve as the resolution of the political issues themselves, so deeply embedded is this stubborn denial of the national trauma of the Armenians, the Kurds, and the Palestinians in the national narratives of several of the powerful and successful nation-states of the Middle East.

CHAPTER 12

Nakba Denial: Israeli Resistance to Palestinian Refugee Reparations

Michael R. Fischbach

Introduction

The public signing of the 1993 Oslo Accords between Israel and the Palestine Liberation Organization (PLO) brought the issue of how to resolve the
Palestinian refugee problem, which dated from the 1948 Arab-Israeli War,
to renewed global attention. Indeed, this issue was and continues to be one
of the most vexing dimensions of any attempt to resolve the Israeli-Palestinian
conflict peacefully. As a result of fear, Israeli expulsions, and other factors,
approximately 750,000 Palestinians were uprooted and became refugees
because of that war, a war Palestinians call the Nakba (Arabic: catastrophe).
Israel never allowed wide-scale return of these refugees, leaving them
stranded in exile for decades. The most well-known dimension of the refugee problem has been the steadfast Palestinian insistence upon the refugees'
right of return to what is now the State of Israel as a form of reparations, and
Israel's equally steadfast refusal to allow this. Yet various other elements of a
reparations regime besides return have been claimed over the years, including property compensation for those refugees who were forced to abandon
property, per capita payments to all refugees as compensation for refugeehood, and moral reparations in the form of official Israeli apologies or at least
acknowledgment of refugee suffering. None of this has occurred to date.

All the talk of the refugees and the peace process, however, belies the reality that the greatest challenge to any movement on reparations is that for
decades Israel has denied responsibility for the Nakba. Thus, the entire

question of reparations for Palestinian refugees faces an immense hurdle: how to prompt Israel to agree to reparations when it refuses to admit any guilt or culpability in the creation of the refugee problem in the first place. Israeli resistance to reparations has long played the defining role in demarcating the rather limited diplomatic boundaries of the peace process and, with it, the terms of a final reparations regime. It therefore is incumbent upon both scholars and negotiators to understand the history behind Israel's Nakba Denial to grasp current thinking on the question of Palestinian refugee reparations.

This study examines Israel's attitude toward the Nakba and Palestinian refugee reparations in two parts. The first details what occurred during the first Arab-Israeli War of 1948, notably the displacement of a massive percentage of the Arab population of Palestine during (and after) the fighting. It also discusses Israel's confiscation of refugee property and early commitment to paying compensation for some of this property, as well as its various attempts to reduce financial exposure on this front. The second part examines the various forms of Nakba Denial and the ways that Israel and its global supporters have used this counternarrative in recent years to deflect calls for other types of refugee reparations, notably moral reparations.

The Nakba

The first Arab-Israeli War broke out in British-controlled Palestine during the final days of November 1947, giving rise to the Palestinian refugee problem and lasting, formally, until armistice agreements were signed between Israel and four Arab states in 1949; the Palestinians were not included in the armistice agreement. The war itself was the result of the decades-long competing national ambitions of Palestinian Arabs and Zionist Jews. The population of Palestine was 90 percent Arab and less than 10 percent Jewish when the British wrested the area from the Ottoman Empire in 1917–18 during World War I and established the British Mandate for Palestine. Formally supported by Palestine's new rulers through the Balfour Declaration of November 1917, the Zionist movement, which since the late 1890s had been dedicated to solving the problem of global anti-Semitism by creating a state for the Jewish people, brought more and more Jewish immigrants into the country during the course of the three decades of the British Mandate in Palestine.

Zionist political ambitions to build a Jewish state not surprisingly clashed with the political goals of the Palestinian Arabs who wanted to be free from both Britain and any Jewish state created in their homeland. Arab-Jewish violence and violence from both sides directed against British targets eventually prompted the British to announce their withdrawal from the country and to turn over the problem of what to do next to the newly formed United Nations in 1947. The UN voted on November 29, 1947, to partition Palestine into a Jewish state, an Arab state, and an international zone around the holy shrines in the Jerusalem area. Not including the international zone, the Jewish state would make up some 56 percent of the country, and the Arab state 43 percent—despite the fact that, by late 1947, Palestine's population stood at one-third Jewish and two-thirds Arab, and Jews owned only about 20 percent of all arable land.[1]

Fighting broke out almost immediately after the vote. The war between Jewish forces and the Palestinians, assisted by foreign Arab volunteers, widened six months later, with Israel's declaration of independence in mid-May 1948, and the subsequent entrance into the fighting of units from the armies of several Arab countries in support of the Palestinians, as well as foreign Jewish (and some non-Jewish) volunteers in support of Israel. The fighting lasted until late in 1948 and led to a huge Israeli victory and the creation of a Jewish state occupying some 77 percent of the country. The remaining 23 percent, consisting of areas known thereafter as the West Bank and Gaza, came under Jordanian and Egyptian control, respectively. No Palestinian Arab state emerged.

The result was a tremendous victory for Zionism and the new state of Israel, and a bitter political defeat for the Palestinians and the Arab World. Worse still for the Palestinians was the resultant demographic revolution. Approximately 750,000 Palestinians, more than half the population of the country and 80 percent of those who had lived in what became Israel, found themselves refugees from the 1948 war, and stranded across hostile borders and cease-fire lines from their homes, fields, houses of worship, and places of business. In the process, the refugees had to leave behind hundreds of villages as well as homes in mixed Arab-Jewish cities such as Jerusalem, Haifa, and Jaffa. Some of them fled, but others were expelled deliberately by Jewish forces. Regardless of how they left their homes, Israeli authorities confiscated the land and property they left behind, destroyed their villages (somewhere between 360 and 427 villages were destroyed), and barred them from returning.[2] The Nakba was catastrophic for all Palestinians, but was a particular

socioeconomic and psychological disaster for the refugees who ended up living in the West Bank, Gaza, and the surrounding Arab countries, surviving
largely on UN food rations. The refugee problem was born.

Palestinian Refugee Property Losses

One issue related to reparations emerged right away after the 1948 war: the
fate of the large amount of land and other property that the refugees left
behind. In ad hoc fashion, prestate Jewish civil and military authorities had
begun to confiscate moveable and immoveable refugee property in the spring
of 1948, even as the war raged. Eager both to lay its hands on as much property as possible and also to shore up the authority of the new state, the provisional Israeli government after May 14, 1948, began pursuing legal strategies
to confiscate the property. For example, it enacted the Abandoned Property
Ordinance No. 12 on June 21, 1948, and three days later, the Abandoned Areas Ordinance, to extend the state's control over conquered areas and properties. The cabinet then created the Ministerial Committee for Abandoned
Property in July 1948. On August 20, 1948, this committee decided on a plan
to confiscate the refugees' property formally by transferring legal title to the
property to the Finance Ministry but giving the Agriculture Ministry
the power to use it. It also created a new office to take possession of the refugees' property: the Custodian of Abandoned Property.[3]

The provisional government followed up on this by enacting the sweeping Emergency Regulations (Absentees' Property) Law on December 2, 1948.
The regulations placed all confiscated property belonging to refugees—what
the law called "absentees"—under the control of the Custodian of Abandoned
Property. The regulations were based on Indian and Pakistani laws enacted
in 1947 to address the property that Hindu, Sikh, and Muslim "evacuees" left
behind as they fled during the massive population exchange between India
and Pakistan. On March 14, 1950, the Israeli Knesset (parliament) adopted
the Absentees' Property Law, an expanded version of the earlier Emergency
Regulations. It not only led to the Custodian of Abandoned Property changing its name to the Custodian of Absentee Property but also authorized the
Custodian to sell the confiscated refugees' property to a Development Authority.[4]

One reason the government wanted legal cover to sell the property was
that it already was working on selling most of it to the Jewish National Fund

(JNF), a Zionist land-purchasing agency. This eventually took place in January 1949 and October 1950, with the JNF agreeing to pay the equivalent of $250,380,718 in Israeli currency for 2,373,677 dunums of land.[5] The JNF intended to use the land to build housing for new Jewish immigrants. During the first several years after the fighting ended, the government worked with the JNF and the Jewish Agency, a Zionist organization tasked with settling new Jewish immigrants in the state, to destroy remaining structures on the refugees' land and create in their place settlements for new immigrants. From 1948 to 1958, a total of 467 new Jewish towns and settlements were built.[6]

Given its intimate role in the conditions leading to the war, the United Nations actively monitored both the 1948 fighting and the refugee plight. The UN General Assembly eventually issued Resolution 194 (III) on December 11, 1948, which made direct reference to Israeli responsibilities regarding the refugees, stating that the: "refugees wishing to return to their homes and live at peace with their neighbours should be permitted to do so at the earliest practicable date, and that compensation should be paid for the property of those choosing not to return and for loss of or damage to property which, under principles of international law or equity, should be made good by the Governments or authorities responsible." Resolution 194 also created the United Nations Conciliation Commission for Palestine (UNCCP) to effect a peaceful resolution of the Arab-Israeli conflict. Despite this resolution, Israeli authorities categorically refused to allow the refugees to return to their homes or consider restitution (return) of their property.

Israel did tell the UNCCP, however, that it would pay compensation for some of the vast amount of confiscated refugee land it had expropriated. An official Israeli committee in 1948 determined that the refugees left 2,008,114 dunums (one dunum = 1,000 sq. m.; approximately one-quarter of an acre) of land worth $328,445,000 (this and subsequent figures are in 1948 U.S. dollars).[7] By 1950, the Custodian of Absentee Property determined that he controlled more land than that, 3,299,447 dunums, but estimated that it was worth only $36,681,935.[8] In 1962, the Ministry of Justice offered no figure for the scope of the land but proffered a monetary figure of over $564,200,000.[9]

By contrast, other contemporary estimates of property were considerably higher. Syrian-Palestinian economist Yusif Sayigh determined in 1966 that the refugees had owned 6,611,250 dunums of land—twice as much as the highest Israeli estimate—worth $1,625,702,000.[10] Palestinian Sami Hadawi, who worked as a land valuator for the pre-1948 British government in

Palestine, collaborated with the Lebanese economist Atif Kubursi in 1988, and came up with an estimate of 19,031,012 dunums of land worth $2,131,467,000; their study included the vast desert lands of the southern Beersheba district of Palestine, which accounts for the greatly increased scope.[11]

Finally, UNCCP itself carried out a massive effort from 1952 to 1964 to document refugee property losses. It finally determined that it could document 6,057,032 dunums of individually owned refugee land worth $824,780,808, although it conceded that there was more land that it could not document.[12]

One reason why the Israeli estimates historically have been lower is that Israel insisted it would only pay for specific categories of refugee land. As early as the Lausanne Conference that the UNCCP convened in 1949, Israel stated it would pay compensation only for land that had been cultivated prior to the refugee exodus. In other words, it would not pay for any other type of land or real estate, including pasture/grazing lands, threshing floors, mines, rock quarries, or marginal land, even though the Israeli government put such confiscated land to use and profited from it.[13] Israel eventually further limited its compensation offer to cultivated lands that had been individually owned, as opposed to any type of common or collectively owned farmland; the UNCCP later estimated in 1962 that the value of communally owned Arab land stood at $56,000,000.[14] Israel would refuse either to pay compensation for the Arab share of any government property that the British Mandate had previously controlled, or for any public land.

From the beginning, Israel also refused to pay any compensation for moveable property that refugees left behind, such as furniture and household goods, vehicles, farm equipment and animals, warehouse inventories, and factory machinery. This, despite the fact that the Israeli government generated money from the sale of such moveable property. Estimates of the value of moveable refugee property have varied. The UNCCP came up with estimates in 1951 and 1961 ranging from $70,122,000 to $169,538,070, depending upon methodology.[15] In 1966, Sayigh estimated the value of such losses at $453,375,000.

Early Israeli Efforts to Minimize Compensation Liabilities

Although Israel agreed to pay compensation to the refugees as part of a peace settlement, it simultaneously tried to reduce its refugee compensation liabilities by raising counterclaims, not against the Palestinians, but against the Arab World as a whole. At the 1949 Lausanne Conference, Israeli negotiators first broached the idea that the Arabs owed Israel compensation for war damages. They placed fault squarely at the feet of the surrounding Arab nations, arguing that Jewish suffering during the war was a direct result of the Arabs' invasion of Israel. By December 1950, Israeli authorities had collected claims to damage in towns and cities, as well as agricultural losses, together totaling nearly $37,000,000.[16]

For its part, the UNCCP decided by October 1949 that its mandate only included discussing refugee property compensation, not compensation for "ordinary war damages," which fell "outside the scope of the resolution [194] of the General Assembly."[17] It therefore would not consider war damages claims against Arab armies and fighters as part of its mission to deal with refugee property compensation. Interestingly, an internal Israel committee, the Lif Committee, determined a few months later that the Israeli government's counterclaims for war damages were illegal, and that Israel legally could not shift the burden of war damages claims against the Arab states to the refugees and their property compensation claims.[18]

By far the Israeli government's most serious effort to reduce Palestinian compensation was the linkage of any such future payments with the property losses that Jewish immigrants from Arab countries sustained during and after 1948. It was the mass immigration of Jews from Iraq in 1950–51 that first prompted Israeli Prime Minister Moshe Sharett to declare in March 1951 that "we shall take into account the value of the Jewish property that has been frozen in Iraq when calculating the compensation that we have undertaken to pay the Arabs who abandoned property in Israel."[19] Yet, beyond the asymmetry of the claims—holding Palestinian refugees financially liable for what the Iraqi and other Arab governments did to their Jewish citizens—the inability to determine such Jewish losses with any degree of precision has bedeviled Israeli policy. Based on immigrant estimates, the Israeli government tried to register claims for property left behind in Arab countries; however, by February 1956, it had managed to register only $103,373,485 in claims—less than one-quarter of what Israel estimated it owed the Palestinians.[20]

In the end, the talk of compensation and counterclaims did not matter. Given the failure of its peacemaking efforts at the Lausanne Conference, and again at the Paris Conference convened from September to November 1951, the UNCCP suspended its active peacemaking measures and thereafter worked on specific, technical issues relating to the refugees. The UN General Assembly passed Resolution 512 (VI) on January 26, 1952, stating that "the governments concerned have the primary responsibility for reaching a settlement of their outstanding differences in conformity with the resolutions of the General Assembly on Palestine."[21] The subsequent decades of war and diplomatic nonrecognition rendered the question of Palestinian refugee reparations irrelevant until the onset of the Oslo peace process between Israel and the PLO in 1992–93 brought the refugee problem back to center stage. Yet the question of reparations came up against a solid wall of resistance: Israel's steadfast refusal to accept responsibility for the refugee problem and therefore agree to a wider reparations regime.

Nakba Denial

The question of reparations to Palestinians has been an extremely sensitive one for Jewish Israelis. Israel received reparations from the government of West Germany from 1953 to 1966 for Nazi crimes against Jews during the Holocaust. The thought that the Jews of Israel, too, were guilty of acts requiring reparations during the 1948 war for Israel's independence, therefore, has been repugnant. Also, Israel has long maintained that it was not responsible for the tragedy of the refugees. Throughout the years, it maintained its willingness to compensate the refugees for some of their lost property, as noted above, but that only amounted to a retroactive property purchase devoid of any sense of guilt, or moral or political liability. Beyond that, Israel and its supporters worldwide have gone to great lengths to create a Nakba counternarrative. This Nakba Denial does not simply deflect calls for further reparations but goes further by denying moral culpability for the refugee problem more broadly.

Nakba Denial stems from two political imperatives: to resist reparations and shore up Israel's foundation myths. The first deals with tangible dimensions of any final Israeli-Palestinian peace deal—refugee return and/or the payment of reparations—while the second addresses the intangible, moral, and psychological dimensions of such a settlement.[22] Central to this has been a counternarrative that posits that, while regrettable, the tragedy of the refugees was not Israel's fault and that the continued plight of the refugees therefore is a problem for the Arab World and the United Nations, not Israel. This narrative rests on several arguments.

War Is War

One familiar argument in Nakba Denial is that the refugees fled as part of the chaos of war. "War is war," and tragic events inevitably occur. This narrative asserts that the 1948 war was a defensive one; Palestine's Jews fought to defend their new state against neighboring Arab states invading on May 15, 1948. Any resulting Arab dislocation, however traumatic, was, therefore, the Arabs' fault and now their responsibility. Israel should not be singled out for any kind of reparations to Palestinians beyond the specific issue of property compensation.

This ideological reading of history overlooks the fact that the war began long before the Arab states became involved in May 1948. Localized Jewish-Palestinian conflict broke out shortly after the UN's partition plan was adopted on November 29, 1947. Jewish forces had already seized portions of the UN-mandated Arab state by the time the Arab states entered the fray nearly six months later. As a result, there were already more than 200,000 Palestinian refugees by the time neighboring Arab armies entered the war. These refugees included some who had fled in fear after the much-publicized massacres of Palestinian civilians, such as the one that occurred in the village of Dayr Yasin in April 1948.

Israeli historian Ilan Pappé has jettisoned the "war is war" narrative, and instead labeled the prestate Israeli actions a case of "ethnic cleansing."[23] In fact, beginning in the 1980s, a number of scholars, called the "New Historians," including Pappé and fellow Israeli scholar Benny Morris, plumbed declassified Zionist archives and challenged the "war is war" narrative. Their research revealed that Jewish soldiers carried out a number of other massacres of Palestinians besides the well-known case of Dayr Yasin that provoked refugee flight. Moreover, they documented how Zionist military campaigns included the systematic depopulation of conquered Palestinian towns and villages. The largest single incident of expulsions was the forced depopulation of more than 50,000 Palestinians from the cities of Ramla and Lydda and their forced march to Jordanian-controlled territory in July 1948.[24]

Scholars such as Pappé and Nur Masalha conclude that Palestinian expulsions were neither an accident nor merely an unfortunate consequence of the fighting ("war is war"). According to these historians, the actions of Jewish forces were the culmination of decades of Zionist thinking about how to rid Palestine of its Arab population. Long before 1948, Zionist officials zeroed in on a major demographic conundrum facing the Zionist movement: how to build a Jewish state in a country that was already populated by an Arab majority. Zionism sought to build not just a place where there were Jews, but a Jewish place. In practice, this always meant a state with an overwhelmingly Jewish demographic majority. What, then, was to be done with Palestine's Arabs? In fact, as far back as the early days of the British Mandate, many senior Zionist officials both spoke and wrote about the need to "transfer" the Palestinians to the surrounding Arab World, that is, to "de-Arabize" Palestine.[25]

During the latter years of the British Mandate, Zionist officials went beyond mere discussions about moving Palestine's Arabs out of the country to formulating transfer plans. In 1937, the Jewish Agency established a transfer committee.[26] In May 1948, senior JNF official Yosef Weitz proposed the creation of another transfer committee as the war was underway and as refugees already were being expelled.[27] One of the most knowledgeable Zionist land experts during the Mandate, Weitz was deeply invested both in the Zionist project and in the specific question of how to acquire land and assure a large Jewish majority in a future Jewish state. Following a December 1940 meeting to discuss the future of the Zionist project, Weitz confided to his diary: "It should be clear to us that there is no room in Palestine for these two peoples. No 'development' will bring us to our goal of independent nationhood in this small country. Without the Arabs, the land will become wide and spacious for us; with the Arabs, the land will remain sparse and cramped. . . . The only solution is Palestine, at least Western Palestine [Palestine without Transjordan], without Arabs. There is no room here for compromise!"[28] Although the provisional Israeli cabinet did not authorize him to form his transfer committee in 1948, Weitz formed the committee anyway. He wrote in his diary on May 20, 1948, that the refugee exodus then underway would create "a complete territorial revolution. . . . The State is destined to expropriate . . . their land."[29] He thereafter issued a memorandum on "retroactive transfer" that he presented to provisional prime minister David Ben-Gurion on June 5, 1948.[30]

The long history of Zionist discussions about the "Arab Problem," including talk of transferring the Palestinians to another country, along with documented incidents of expulsions in 1948, refutes the Israeli narrative that most of the refugees simply fled or followed their leaders' orders to leave. The massive de-Arabization of the new Jewish state in 1948 was fully in line with pre-1948 thinking about how to build a Jewish-majority state. Zionist leaders, in fact, exulted in the Nakba. Provisional foreign minister Moshe Shertok (later Sharett) wrote in June 1948 that "the opportunities which the present position [the refugee exodus] open up for a lasting and radical solution of the most vexing problem of the Jewish State are so far-reaching as to take one's breath away."[31] Israel's first president, Chaim Weizmann, boasted, shortly after the war, to the American ambassador to Israel that the flight of the refugees was a "miraculous simplification of our tasks."[32] Weitz wrote, "I cannot imagine how we would have shaped and stabilized the state had the Arabs remained. . . . The flight of the Arabs came like a gift from heaven, and we should not belittle it."[33]

Those who insist that there was no Zionist master plan to expel Palestinians has been uncovered and that Israel, therefore, did not commit ethnic cleansing in 1948 still must grapple with a key fact: Regardless of how and why the refugees fled, the provisional Israeli cabinet took a decision on June 16, 1948, to bar their return. Top Israeli officials insisted on this point during the cabinet's discussions that day. Ben-Gurion, who had received Weitz's memorandum on "retroactive transfer" just eleven days earlier, stated clearly, "I believe we should prevent their return." Were the refugees to return, he argued, "and the war is renewed, our chances of ending the war as we wish to end it will be reduced." Shertok agreed that Israel must take advantage of the ongoing de-Arabization of the country. "Can we imagine a return to the status quo ante? . . . They will not return. [That] is our policy. They are not returning."[34] Even if the Israeli government was not responsible for the refugees' flight, and therefore currently is not liable for their exodus, it certainly is responsible for the fateful June 1948 decision not to allow them back in the country, a demand that the UN has advanced since December 1948. Israel must accept responsibility for the fact that this has still not occurred all these decades later.

The Population Exchange Thesis

A second feature of Nakba Denial involves the population exchange thesis. This narrative equates the experience of Palestinian refugees with the experience of Jewish emigrants from Arab countries.[35] The goal has been to neutralize Palestinian demands, including the right of return, by claiming that, regardless of the refugees' reasons for leaving (and regardless of whether or not Israel was responsible), an irrevocable Jewish-Arab population exchange occurred in the Middle East after 1948. During and after that year, approximately 800,000 Jews left Arab countries, from Iraq to Morocco, for various reasons. Most of them ended up immigrating to Israel, and many were settled in new towns built on the ruins of abandoned Palestinian villages that Israeli and Jewish Agency authorities had destroyed. In recent decades, many Israel supporters have tried to deflect calls for Palestinian refugee return and compensation by claiming that a massive, permanent population exchange between Israel and the Arab World had occurred: most of Israel's Palestinian Arabs and their property for most of the Arab World's Jews and their property. Israel resettled these Jews at great cost, the argument goes, and the Arab World must resettle the Palestinians. Any further Israeli financial obligations regarding Palestinian refugee reparations, therefore, are out of the question.

The population exchange thesis first emerged publicly in the late 1970s, when Israel was involved in peace negotiations with Egypt. A group called the World Organization of Jews from Arab Countries (WOJAC) was formed in November 1975, with financial support from both the Jewish Agency and the Israeli Ministry of Foreign Affairs. WOJAC promulgated the exchange thesis early on in its existence. In a 1978 publication, WOJAC official Mordekhai Ben Porat noted that the group "emphasizes that the exchange of populations which took place in the Middle East between Jews and Arabs is an accomplished and final act."[36] In the wake of the failed Camp David II and Taba negotiations between Israel and the PLO in 2000–2001, both the Israeli government and supportive Zionist organizations began preparing for the day when substantive Israeli-Palestinian negotiations would resume and they would have to defend Israel's refusal to accede to refugee return and wide-scale reparations. Part of these efforts was to revive the population exchange thesis.

Israeli and global Zionist figures once again were quite clear about why they were championing this narrative in the 2000s: blunting Palestinian claims. A September 2002 document that the World Jewish Congress (WJC) produced, entitled, *A Population and Property Transfer: The Forgotten Exodus of Jews from Arab Lands*, noted: "In the period surrounding the birth of the state of Israel, there were two refugee movements: one into Israel and one out of it. In effect, there was an exchange of populations. . . . Israel seeks no 'right of return' of the Jews to Arab lands. Likewise, it rejects a 'right of return' for Arabs to Israel."[37] In November 2002, the WJC and the Canadian Jewish Congress (CJC) sponsored a conference on Jews from Arab countries at which Keith Landy, president of the CJC, described the goal of the WJC's "forgotten exodus" campaign. "To be crass," he said, "it's a bargaining tool at the table with Palestinians when it comes to negotiating a settlement in the Middle East."[38] Later, in August 2003, Nimrod Barkan, director of the Israeli Foreign Ministry's World Jewish Affairs Bureau, noted, "Since Palestinians insist on bringing up the so-called Palestinian refugees' right of return, we will continue to raise the issue of justice for Jewish refugees."[39]

A Claims Commission and the "End of Claims" Clause

Nakba Denial also manifests itself in Israel's insistence that any compensation payments be made not to individual refugees but rather to some kind of international fund. Moreover, Arab Palestinian acceptance of such compensation constitutes a legally binding "end of claims" declaration. Since 1949, Israel has insisted that any compensation payments it makes would be paid out in global fashion, not to individual refugees. This reflects its rejection of any individual or even collective obligations to Palestinians as refugees, or even as persons. Israel would pay into a fund and not to individual refugees. Why? One reason was that Israel long has claimed that the refugees' ownership rights to their property have been legally severed.[40]

The particular question of whether or not Israeli laws actually allowed the state to take control of legal title to the refugees' land initially proved vexing to Israeli authorities. Israel told the UNCCP in early 1949 that it was willing to pay compensation but claimed that it had taken over all legal rights to the refugees' properties, including titles. Shertok told the UNCCP, "We are definitely ready to accept in principle, that property has to be compensated. What we do not accept is the question of the individual juridical rights."[41] However, the Committee to Examine the Issue of Compensation for Absentee Property (known as the Lif Committee) issued a report on March 17, 1950, noting that Israeli legislation up to that point had not, in fact, allowed the state legally to pass title to the property onto the state. The Knesset settled the matter by adopting the Absentees' Property Law just three days before the Lif Committee's report was delivered, a law that authorized the state to take over legal title of the property and sell it to a Development Authority.[42] In the state of Israel's eyes, the refugees lost control of legal title to their property in 1950.

As for Israel making payments not to individual refugees but rather to an international fund, in the wake of the 2000 Camp David talks, both Israeli and Palestinian negotiators, not to mention the United States, generally have accepted the notion that refugee reparations would be paid out through some kind of international fund to which both Israel and other countries would make payments. The fund, or some other type of international mechanism, would then do the heavy lifting of determining who is eligible for reparations payments, ascertaining the validity of such claims, and so forth, relieving Israel of this arduous responsibility.

Another key Israeli demand is its "end of claims" clause. Such a clause would affirm that any reparations made in accordance with a peace deal would constitute a final resolution of all Palestinian refugee claims. None could be lodged thereafter; the refugee problems would be solved officially. Regardless of whether or not a specific refugee agrees with the final deal that Palestinian and Israeli negotiators hammer out, she or he legally would be bound to accept or reject the reparations regime proposed in the deal and would not be able to seek further reparations outside of that regime. This was expressed clearly in the Israeli negotiators' position at Camp David, which was that a refugee's acceptance of compensation would constitute a waiver of any future claims against Israel: "Transfer of compensation to a claimant shall be conditioned by such claimant's waiver of further proprietary claims. . . . Israel shall have no further commitment or obligation emanating from the Refugee issue beyond those specified in this agreement."[43] Ultimately, the "end of claims" waiver is integral to the broader Nakba Denial modus operandi in that it would absolve Israel of any lasting financial responsibility and, by extension, moral obligations to the refugees.

Some experts on the subject have maintained that refugees possess individual rights to redress of their grievances and are not legally obliged to receive reparations as part of an en masse settlement. In any event, they do not give up those rights if they reject such a settlement, and are free to pursue individual redress later. For example, in 2013, the Royal Institute of International Affairs (Chatham House) in London convened a workshop of experts involved in the question of Palestinian refugee negotiations. Based on this, Chatham House subsequently published a study that questioned the international legality of Israel's demand for an end of claims clause: "A key Israeli demand in previous negotiations on the refugee issue has been that an agreement represent an 'end of claims' and a definitive resolution of the issue. A number of participants questioned whether this is legal and mentioned that even if an agreement were to stipulate an end to claims, individual refugees could still pursue their rights in courts and other forums. It would then depend on those courts and forums whether or not they would uphold the finality of the agreement."[44]

Rejecting Moral Reparations

One of the key ways that the Nakba Denial narrative has impacted Israel's stance toward reparations is its insistence that Israel owes the refugees compensation for certain types of refugee land and nothing else. Put another way, there will be no "moral reparations" or other payments or statements that might constitute an admission of responsibility or guilt. This has collided with a key Palestinian demand that Israel admit responsibility both for the Nakba and the decades of refugee exile since 1948. At the January 2001 Taba negotiations, Palestinian negotiators presented a demand that Israel agree to a statement along these lines: "Israel recognizes its moral and legal responsibility for the forced displacement and dispossession of the Palestinian civilian population during the 1948 war and for preventing the refugees from returning to their homes in accordance with [UN General Assembly] Resolution 194."[45] Israeli negotiators apparently presented a proposal that offered a statement of regret for the refugee problem but little else.[46] The lack of substantive negotiations thereafter has meant no real progress on this point.

Is this an important point? For Palestinians, it certainly is. First of all, wider reparations beyond just property compensation are immensely important to the refugees. UNCCP and UNRWA (United Nations Relief and Works Agency for Palestine Refugees in the Near East) studies point to the fact that only about 40 percent of refugees actually owned land in Palestine, not including individual refugees' shares in communally owned land.[47] So moral reparations, whether in terms of "refugeehood," loss of livelihood, pain, and suffering, or even just intangibles such as a statement of responsibility, are important to all refugees, but especially those who cannot claim property compensation. Experts on the subject also back up Palestinian insistence upon some sort of moral reparations from Israel. The same 2013 study by Chatham House included a statement on the importance of including an element of "symbolic justice" in any final resolution of the refugee problem: "The success of a compensation mechanism hinges on also addressing normative issues of responsibility, moral acknowledgment and recognition. Without addressing these issues, anticipated levels of financial compensation will be inadequate to provide real closure to the refugee issue."[48]

The experts also noted that: "The refugee issue cannot be resolved solely through financial and technical solutions, and that, rather, the normative aspect is essential. . . . There was also broad agreement among the participants that any form of refugee compensation should be accompanied by at least a degree of moral acknowledgment that the Palestinian people had been wronged, since this would carry a lot of value and would be important for closure of the issue."[49]

Yet, it is important to point out that even if Israel someday does concede partial responsibility for the refugee tragedy, or expresses "regret" for Palestinian refugee suffering, the narrative of Nakba Denial precludes it from accepting full responsibility for the refugee problem. Furthermore, any such statement of regret will be balanced by Israel's recent insistence since the 2001 Taba talks that Palestinians concede the post-1948 Jewish demographic majority by recognizing Israel publicly "as a Jewish state" or by recognizing "the Jewish nature of Israel." Zionism understands Israel as a Jewish state, for the Jewish people. Arabs might be tolerated within that state—indeed, one out of five Israeli citizens today is a Palestinian Arab—but it is not their state. This Israeli demand is designed to block any Palestinian insistence for the right of refugee return; in Zionist eyes, the return of refugees would threaten Jewish demographic preponderance and thereby the "Jewish nature of Israel."

Israel has worked hard in recent years to concretize this position in law. The Budget Foundations Law (Amendment No. 40) of 2011, often called the Nakba Law, effectively criminalizes the act of publicly mourning the Nakba on Israel's Independence Day. The law allows the Ministry of Finance to reduce state expenditures or other support to any institution that commemorates the Nakba on that day. The law also allows the state to withhold support for any institution that rejects "the existence of the State of Israel as a Jewish and democratic state."[50] In May 2014, Israeli prime minister Binyamin Netanyahu followed up by pushing for another law that would enshrine Israel as the "nation state of the Jewish people." He told his cabinet that "the state of Israel provides full equal rights, individual rights, to all its citizens, but it is the nation state of one people only—the Jewish people—and of no other people."[51] His emphasis on "individual rights" to all citizens, but not "national" or "cultural" rights, was telling. So was Netanyahu's open statement of what many of his fellow Israelis believe: Despite the twenty-first-century philosophical challenges to the idea that states should be set aside for one ethnic or religious people only—and that others, from immigrants to minorities, are therefore effectively disenfranchised—the idea of "ethnocracy" is alive and well in Israel.[52] The Israeli Knesset ended up adopting the controversial nation-state law in July 2018.

The problem with asking the Palestinians to recognize the Jewish nature of Israel as part of a final reparations regime is that Israel essentially is demanding that the Palestinians admit and acknowledge the obvious: They lost, the Israelis won, and the land now officially belongs to the Jewish people (wherever they live), even if Palestinians live there. Even if the Israelis, in return, offer a statement of regret for Palestinian suffering, it still amounts to victors' justice. The victors demand recognition that they won, and in return perhaps will acknowledge the losers' sorrow.

Palestinian scholars and activists have been particularly engaged in recent decades in challenging Nakba Denial by placing the Palestinian case for refugee reparations before the international public. The BADIL Center for Palestinian Refugee and Residency Rights in Bethlehem has provided detailed legal analysis and advocacy for Palestinian refugee rights, as has the Institute for Palestine Studies in Beirut and Washington, DC. The London-based Palestine Land Society has carried out in-depth activities documenting the Nakba, including historical and spatial mapping. So has Zochrot, a group in Israel that includes Israeli Jewish activists. Al-Awda—the Palestine Right of Return Coalition—has mobilized refugees and their supporters around the world in defense of refugee rights. Among other things, such advocacy work has demonstrated to negotiators, notably those from the PLO, that refugee reparations demands cannot be bargained away willy-nilly and must be suitably addressed if the refugees are to "buy into" any final Israeli-Palestinian peace deal.

Conclusion

A problem facing any discussions of reparations in the wake of genocide, ethnic cleansing, war crimes, or other forms of organized violence is securing some type of reparations regime that is satisfactory to the victims of that violence. This has been easier in the case of countries that have been defeated in war or otherwise subject to international military and political pressure that weakens their resistance to such reparations than it has been for countries like Israel that have emerged victorious, whether de facto or de jure. A significant impediment to the issue of Palestinian refugee reparations has been Israel's reluctance to any form of reparations save limited compensation for certain categories of refugee property and, perhaps, some kind of statement of "regret" for the refugees' suffering. This Israeli resistance to wider reparations stems both from practical concerns about costs and from its political and ideological reluctance to challenge its foundation myths by admitting responsibility or guilt for the seven-decades-long Palestinian refugee problem. This has driven Israel and its partisans to adopt various stances to minimize reparations and create a counternarrative of Nakba Denial to stiffen the resolve not to submit to the kind of reparations regime that Palestinian negotiators have envisioned over the years. Beyond being the vastly more powerful player in Israeli-Palestinian peace talks in the past quarter century, Israel also has benefitted from the near universal support of the United States in its insistence on narrowing the limits of refugee reparations.

The study of reparations and resistance to reparations must balance any focus on international law and historical case studies of successful reparations systems with an examination of cases like the Israeli-Palestinian conflict, where a confluence of forces has led to a greatly diminished vision of what a postconflict reparations regime might look like. Such an examination is likely to determine not just that the victorious are less likely to concede guilt but also that victory emboldens their ideological reluctance to concede wrongdoing, despite the obvious suffering of the victims of the conflict.

CHAPTER 13

Repairing Colonial Symmetry: Algerian Archive Restitution As Reparation for Crimes of Colonialism?

Susan Slyomovics

Since Algeria's independence from France in 1962 after 132 years of colonial rule (1830–1962), claims and counterclaims for reparations have continually resurfaced in a variety of legal forums and public spaces. A brutal war of decolonization (1954–62) brought an end to France's settler colony in Algeria, instigating incompatible and ongoing demands for repatriation, restitution, and reparations.

There has been no closure about the definition of crimes of colonialism leveled by Algerians just as there is still no agreement about where and how the archives of French Algeria can be uncontroversially deposited. The affective intensity surrounding human rights arguments about crimes of colonialism is embodied in disputes about restituting a formerly colonized nation's archives—the site for its history and self-narratives—as a form of reparations. These tangible physical documents, records, and archives exist in association with a complex set of actors, actions, and motivations resulting in "dynamics of how records spiral and appear and reappear through time and space, generating affect, accruing interpretations, and resulting in new archival formations and re-formations."[1] Since the archive of French Algeria remains largely in French hands, there is no escaping historical linkages between France's settler colonial project in Algeria and ongoing disputes about archival sovereignty, provenance, and digitization.

This case study focuses on reparations in relation to French destruction and appropriation of objects, such as artifacts and documents, taken from Algeria to France beginning with the French conquest in 1830 through Algerian independence in 1962. Algeria demands an officially sanctioned return of all objects as one form of French reparation, while at the same time rejecting French proposals to digitize collections. Currently, the countries are at an impasse, as French solutions for compensation and satisfaction confront Algerian demands for restitution and repatriation as implacably opposed remedies, even though both comply with the 2005 United Nations guidelines solutions toward reparation.[2] Who physically possesses the actual archive therefore raises issues about the afterlives of settler colonialism in the metropole, and human rights definitions of reparation, restitution, and the "right to know." In the context of former French Algeria, ongoing disputes related to the colonial archive highlight theoretical, affective, and historical arguments and also serve as a real and symbolic proxy for unresolved claims against the former French colonial state over crimes its agents perpetrated during its period of conquest and rule in Algeria.

Crimes of Colonialism

Since independence in 1962, Algerians have demanded reparations from France for the crimes that former French colonizers perpetrated against the local population and its archives, architecture, and property. Colonial violations include land dispossession and resettlement, massive internment, torture, forced labor, and genocide.[3] Such allegations reflect competing histories of French colonial rule in Algeria. Houari Boumédiène, postindependent Algeria's second president, was the country's first head of state to demand an apology and acknowledgment from France for the despoliation of land, people, and resources. In 1973 he cited centuries of colonialism as justification for financial indemnifications. The occasion was the fourth summit of the Non-Aligned Movement (NAM), hosted in Algiers. Focused on the search for a new world economic order of cooperation and development, Boumédiène took up an activist stance by linking reparations to NAM's existing principles: "Hasn't the time come to rearrange the rules of international law in accordance with the data of the contemporary world and in view of the natural right of peoples to recover their wealth and dispose of them without being penalized, those who robbed and exploited them for decades, even centuries, and logically owe them reparation?"[4]

Such efforts gained little traction, and decades later the question of French acknowledgment of colonial crimes, let alone reparations, persisted. In fact, the heroic French narrative was nearly inscribed into law in France. In 2005, an attempt was made to mandate that instruction on colonialism's beneficial civilizing mission should be required for French secondary school students.[5] In response to that effort, Algerian president Abdelaziz Bouteflika swiftly demanded an official state apology from the French government, raising the issue of "crimes of colonialism." Ultimately, French president Jacques Chirac vetoed the 2005 law, and Bouteflika's demand for an apology for crimes of colonialism was never addressed. Instead, the "memory wars," in the words of historian Benjamin Stora, have continued unabated.[6]

The roots of these "memory wars" can be traced in part to the Algerian leadership's linkage of colonial crimes to acknowledgment and reparations. Frantz Fanon, who joined the Algerian National Liberation Front in strong support of the right to political independence, inspired some of their ideological and financial demands. Although his book *The Wretched of the Earth* was written before Algerian independence, Fanon argued for a "just reparation" for the crimes of colonialism and one marked by a "double realization." According to Fanon, the colonized must, on the one hand, articulate that reparations are their rightful and just due, and, on the other hand, colonizing capitalist powers must acknowledge the requirement to indemnify the formerly colonized: "The imperialist states would make a great mistake and commit an unspeakable injustice if they contented themselves with withdrawing from our soil the military cohorts, and the administrative and managerial services whose function it was to discover the wealth of the country, to extract it and to send it off to the mother countries. We are not blinded by the moral reparation of national independence; nor are we fed by it."[7]

Independence and self-determination, according to Fanon, are not merely necessary conditions but intrinsically moral forms of reparative justice. Moreover, his argument speaks directly to disputes over archives, records, and documents as sources for Algerian independence, self-determination, and self-knowledge. Centuries of colonialism and loss of Algerian records constituted cogent reasons for financial indemnification:

The wealth of the imperial countries is our wealth too. On the universal plane this affirmation, you may be sure, should on no account be taken to signify that we feel ourselves affected by the creations of Western arts or techniques. For in a very concrete way Europe has stuffed herself inordinately with the gold and raw materials of the colonial countries. . . . So when we hear the head of a European state declare with his hand on his heart that he must come to the aid of the poor underdeveloped peoples, we do not tremble with gratitude. Quite the contrary; we say to ourselves: "It's a just reparation which will be paid to us."[8]

Fanon was a key theorist linking crimes of colonialism to demands for reparations, as was Boumédiène, who launched an early campaign to recuperate Algeria's national archives from France. After establishing the country's first postindependence national archives in 1971, he declared it "a fundamental factor in safeguarding the constituent elements of a nation's personality [un facteur fondamental de sauveguarder des éléments constitutifs de la personnalité d'une nation]."[9] Records embody the character of the nation, according to Boumédiène, while archival studies scholar Anne Gilliland ascribes rights and protections to the archive as a legal personality epitomizing the nation's patrimony: "If we think of records as our juridical personae and therefore in some sense a shadow image of ourselves, as well as artifacts embodying our persona—physical, intellectual, and creative inscriptions (i.e., that some part of ourselves is transferred into the artifact through the act of making), then we are hurt not only legally but also affectively when those records are maliciously or even accidentally destroyed, lost, or denied to us."[10]

Yet simply determining what documents were taken, and how they were spirited out, is not fully known. For instance, it is difficult to trace the trajectories of short-hop military planes and trucks commandeered during the war to transport French Algeria's records out of Algeria to France via Algerian ports. It is clear, however, that at every bureaucratic level of the colonial administration, generations of documents from local Algerian archives found their way to France. French officials collected them from the upper echelons of the colonial Government General down to the level of the province, prefecture, municipality, town, and institution, such as prisons, banks, and businesses. Today, military and diplomatic archives pertaining to the Algerian War of Independence remain scattered in libraries throughout France, partly available to researchers but inaccessible in Algeria. Indeed, the aim of France's National Overseas Archives (ANOM), inaugurated for the metropole in 1966, was to conserve an array of colonial publications comprising books, newspapers, maps, architectural plans, brochures, and ephemera.

The volume of the ANOM Algeria holdings is estimated at 200,000 boxes, or more than 600 tons of documents.[11] French officials removed these documents in accordance with an official *circulaire*, or a government directive with the force of a command, that the French colonial bureaucracy headquartered in Algiers circulated on March 6, 1962. Known as "Circulaire n°2.AG.A534 DG AG," it mandated that "all archives without any exception, administrative, political, cultural, economic, and social of Algeria, must be brought to France."[12] A succession of Algerian governments has never ceased calling for the restoration of these physical artifacts and archives, many of which possess such intense actual and symbolic importance that French proffers of copies will not suffice. More recently, archival demands as a form of restitution has been grounded in Article 11 of the 2008 UN Declaration on Indigenous Rights: "States shall provide redress through effective mechanisms, which may include restitution, developed in conjunction with Indigenous peoples, with respect to their cultural, intellectual, religious and spiritual property taken without their free, prior and informed consent or in violation of their laws, traditions and customs."[13]

Irreconcilable Definitions of Repatriation, Restitution, and Reparation

One underlying problem is that France and Algeria have widely diverging definitions of the word "repatriation," let alone the mechanisms for redress. For Algeria, repatriation aligns more closely with UN interpretations and focuses on its material history currently residing in France and demands for its return to Algeria. In contrast, France's juridical deployment of "repatriation" after 1962 pertains to the return of former European settlers from the Algerian colony to the metropole. In the aftermath of Algerian independence, the French government provided money paybacks, as mandated by indemnification laws, to Algeria's European settler community that relocated to France. In effect, the French government deemed them "repatriated" to a French homeland that, for many, was never theirs. This former settler population was categorized "repatriated" (*rapatrié*) to France according to the law of December 26, 1961, which stated: "French, having to leave or considered forced to leave, as a result of political events, a territory where they were established and which was previously under the sovereignty, protectorate or trusteeship of France."[14] Those "repatriated" were compensated through several stages of restitution. Their first set of reparations was based on the law of July 15, 1970. This law was then modified in 1974 to increase payments; and it was further amended on January 2, 1978, with additional amounts, and yet again in 1984.[15] Importantly, French financial measures of the 1970s and 1980s were directed only to settler colonists, never to "natives," and always to compensate for the loss of French Algeria. These French financial measures that acknowledge settlers as returnees and repatriates who merit and qualify for indemnification encouraged further pursuits for compensation, including compensatory lawsuits for settler losses of Algerian properties. In fact, believing that French government financial gestures toward repair were unsatisfactory, those settlers who departed in 1962 have produced hundreds of legal cases in various courts against the independent Algerian state.[16]

The disputes over colonial archives, and with them, starkly competing notions of "repatriation," are thrown into relief against the backdrop of French compensation programs to former settlers. Labeled reparations by France, these indemnification protocols have kept alive the settler colonist category even as the former settlers were legally transformed into "repatriates" to France. Indemnity was dispensed after Algerian independence because European settlers (and the native Algerian Jewish community) were included in the colonizing social body of French Algeria once in France. In contrast, those Algerians Muslim relocated to the metropole were shunted aside. Such was the case of the *harkis*, or Algerian Muslims aligned with France against their compatriots, many of whom served in the French army. Those whom French authorities permitted to flee Algeria for France after Algerian independence (estimated at 85,000 auxiliaries, including families, plus 55,000 privileged Algerian Muslims) were granted lesser compensation and subventions.[17] Notwithstanding the anguish of the settlers' self-described "exodus" and "exile," decades of French financial reparations and other reparative measures facilitated their integration to France. They received recognition and parity for their Algerian educational degrees, and colonial work histories transferred seamlessly into the national education and social security systems. Decades of French reparation and indemnification practices did not compensate the colonized but rather reinvigorated the settler in the metropole and provided some assistance to *harkis* who supported them in Algeria.

Conflicting conceptions of "repatriation" link the fate of settlers with that of the colonial archives. In effect, French interpretations of "repatriation" were applied not only to people but also to the transferred colonial archives. Much like the settlers, the archives have a privileged home in France. The new building for the colonial library erected in Aix-en-Provence in the south of France for transferred archives reflects the massive construction initiatives to shelter the collectivity of European settlers, suggesting that repatriated colonial bodies and archives were not only returned home but also in need of actual physical homes. For the French, along with some six hundred tons of artifacts and archives, over a million people were successfully resettled, moving from south to north across the Mediterranean. For Algerians, the former French colonial-era archives of Algeria await their repatriation by means of a north to south voyage homeward.

Case Studies of Archival Destruction and Removal

Algerian claims and French counterclaims involving Algerian archives exported to France extend not only to the era of independence but also to that of the French conquest of Algeria in 1830. These two decisive moments are historical bookends to the demands for archival restitution. From the beginning of France's 1830 establishment of the Algerian settler colony until 1962, even the casus belli for subjugation was inscribed in the destruction of objects and property. Evidence for this comes from, among others, Alexis de Tocqueville, who bore witness to France's conquest and the first decades of rule. In his published letters from Algeria, he confirmed the Ottoman Algiers Regency's legitimacy, including its property and taxation regimes, religious institutions, traditions of higher learning, and manuscript libraries. While celebrating the conquest in his second letter dated 1837, he was attentive to the connections between conquest, legitimacy, and property, including archives:

> In order to make the vestiges of the enemy domination disappear, we first took care to tear up and burn all written documentation, administrative records, and papers, authentic or otherwise, that could have perpetuated any trace of what had been done before us. The conquest

was a new era, and from fear of mixing the past with the present in an irrational way, we even destroyed a large number of streets in Algiers so as to rebuild them according to our own method, and we gave French names to all those we consented to leave alone.[18]

Tocqueville made important factual links between archives and the concept of settler colonialism as a distinct imperial formation. A new colonizer society needed land, and settler colonialism depended primarily on access to territory—territory whose dispossession from local inhabitants took a variety of forms.[19] In Algeria, French officials destroyed ownership documents and taxation rolls, thus facilitating French sovereignty through possession based on the doctrine of *terra nullius* ("nobody's land"). The interrelated forms of violence toward Indigenous land, property, and documentation are the violations that have subsequently triggered Algerian calls for redress based on the Declaration of Indigenous Rights.

As the Algerian archives were being destroyed, one of Tocqueville's contemporaries, Jean-Toussaint Merle (1782–1852), famously hauled ashore a Gutenberg press to produce publicity releases in the midst of battle. This was the first recorded instance of a printing press in Algeria, which ensured multiple copies of French-language documents as the new order of the day.[20] In effect, a significant proportion of archives, records, Arabic manuscripts, Ottoman Turkish bureaucratic paperwork, and land maps went up in flames at the same time that the new colony's first French newspaper made its inaugural appearance. In the heat of battle, colonial authorities both destroyed records and sought to erase their memories through acts of removal and replacement.[21] In short order, new archives were organized to underwrite the paperwork needs of the new settler society.

Gabriel Esquer later picked up Tocqueville's mantle and wrote during Europe's interwar period about the destructive beginnings of the 1830 French conquest of Algeria. In 1920, Esquer was appointed chief archivist and paleographer at the National Library in Algiers.[22] His observations about the French occupation of Algiers drew on historical hindsight emerging from his lifework, which was to edit, preserve, and interpret the papers and correspondences of the various generals involved in the 1830 conquest. Based on voluminous military files, Esquer, like Tocqueville, concluded that French troops undertook conquest and occupation in great disorder. He recounted the French failure to collect administrative documents and described soldiers lighting their pipes with Ottoman government papers. However, Esquer came to a different conclusion than did Tocqueville. According to the archivist, for the French to know the state of properties and public revenues, they had to trust the declarations of the local people involved.[23] Yet in spite of Esquer's conclusions, no French government official or early conqueror overseeing the local population ever did consult the local population, as such efforts would have potentially undermined French claims to land and other material possessions in Algeria.

Destroying the archival past eliminates Indigenous history and land records. The French, however, did not destroy all materials from precolonial Ottoman Algeria. Instead, they moved some of the archives to the metropole before 1962, where they remain inaccessible. In referencing the destroyed and removed material, Algerian archivists deploy the term "memoricide" and concepts of "killing memory" from the examples of the 1990s Balkan wars and attendant destruction of the libraries and cultural heritage of Sarajevo.[24] In the case of the former Yugoslavia, the International Criminal Court prosecuted for the first time the ruination of libraries, records, and cultural sites as crimes against humanity. Emotional intensity, absence of archives, absence of information, and comparative cases have fueled contentious disputes between Algeria and France. Controversy remains ongoing in part because Algerian archivists do not know what happened to all the archives, where they are, or who has them. This, in turn, has conjured an imaginary warehouse of materials—a warehouse that opposing sides insist that the other possesses and has willfully occluded.[25]

In the case of Algeria, the destruction, replacement, and transfer of archives began with the conquest of 1830 and ended through systemized archival destructions that marked the French colonial retreat. Two days after Algeria's independence, French secret operatives torched the university library of Algiers, which functioned as the country's second-largest library, using phosphorus bombs to inflict maximum damage. The library contained some 600,000 volumes, of which approximately 200,000 to 400,000 documents and books were either damaged or destroyed. The bombing was attributed to the Secret Army Organization, or Organisation armée secrète (OAS). Comprising the OAS were French settlers, including librarians, who were supported and armed by military elements opposed to the imminent loss of French Algeria. Still, what was destroyed is not entirely clear. Only in 1985, for example, at the twenty-three-year mark of Algerian independence, could Mahmoud Bouayad, chief conservator of the National Library, declare that many Arabic manuscripts believed destroyed in 1962 had, in fact, been transferred to France, where he believed they remained. Algerian librarians also noted that their scorched library was not included in the comprehensive 1996 UNESCO report of the twentieth century's numerous destroyed libraries and archives.[26] The result is that Algerian assertions about destruction, removal, and inaccessibility are intertwined with deliberately obfuscated information about the archive. Once again, the French grip on the colonial archive as "repatriated" dovetails with settler colonial identity in interesting ways. In this instance, "repatriated" people deny and sidestep discussions about "repatriated" objects in much the same way that the French government officials, down to the present day, obfuscate in answer to questions about archival destruction and removal. Yet, in fascinating ways, missing archival records reappear from time to time as token gestures in French diplomatic exchanges with Algeria.

The Gift, Not the Transfer, of the Archive

Although the Algerian government demanded immediate repatriation of their archival materials, instead, for over sixty years, France has, on occasion, released a handful of documents to coincide with French diplomatic missions to Algiers. For example, in 1967, there was one lot of 450 registers, in 1975 a lot of 153 registers, and in 1981 a lot of 183 registers. When French president François Mitterrand came to power in 1981, however, he halted such archive transfer practices and proscribed discussions about Algerian archives in France.[27] It is not a coincidence that, by 1982, Mitterand granted full pardons to the French generals imprisoned as members and leaders of the OAS. They had been held responsible for the Algiers library bombing as well as the failed overthrow of Charles de Gaulle's government. Indeed, de Gaulle was the French president who brokered Algerian independence, and the generals were tried and sent to prison for their coup attempt. Mitterand, having amnestied and released the generals from prison, would reintegrate them (the French term is "revised") into the armed services, and indemnify them as a form of reparations with fully restored and retroactive military pensions and benefits.

Despite Mitterand, French practices of releasing selective documents as diplomatic pickings to Algeria were never entirely abandoned. On October 21, 2007, the French embassy in Algeria issued a press release with little fanfare announcing that General Jean-Louis Georgelin, chief of staff of the French armed forces, officially relinquished to his Algerian counterpart, General Ahmed Gaïd-Salah, the French army plans for mines that had been placed along the length of the Challe and Morice Lines between 1956 and 1959.[28] The Morice Line, named after the French minister of defense André Morice, was an electrified, mined fence running 460 kilometers along the Algerian-Tunisian border and another 700 kilometers along the Algerian-Moroccan border. In sections on the western Moroccan frontier, the Morice Line was doubled by the creation of a second and parallel mined, electrified fence called the Challe Line, after Maurice Challe, the French general and member of the OAS involved in the Algiers putsch of 1961 to overthrow Charles de Gaulle. The Algerian side of the frontier had included a patrolled track, manned by 80,000 French soldiers along three parallel north-south physical barriers to provide effective coordinated deterrents with electronic systems, mines, alarms, radars, searchlights, and armed men. Along both frontiers—Morocco in the West and Tunisia in the East—French authorities buried 11 million antipersonnel mines during the Algerian War of Independence, extending minefields forty-five meters on each side. Between 1963 and 1988, postindependent Algeria succeeded in defusing 8 million bombs and returning some 50,000 hectares of land to their original agriculture and pasturage, leaving approximately 3 million mines to cause disproportionate numbers of injuries and deaths, especially among children and transhumant locals. Since independence, estimates range from the French figure of 3,000 to the Algerian figure of 80,000 dead and wounded along Algeria's borders.

France's most recent diplomatic gift, which French president Emmanuel Macron offered in 2017, is the promise to return the skulls of nineteenth-century Algerian resistance fighters—the result of decapitation and shipment to France for scientific study. Stored in the Musée de l'Homme in Paris, and similar to the cases of Indigenous groups globally, their existence has triggered demands for restitution and repatriation of native remains.[29] Macron's proffered Algerian skulls, a gift embedded in Franco-Algerian social exchanges, inevitably raised the stakes for reparations when Algerian authorities in late 2017 formally requested not only the skulls but also all of their archives. Finally, three years later on July 3, 2020, France restituted twenty-four skulls from several hundred still held in their museum. Flown to Algiers by an Air Algérie plane, the skulls in caskets draped with Algerian flags were solemnly borne by soldiers along a red carpet flanked by dignitaries. Their arrival in Algeria was the occasion for deeply felt performances of sovereignty and postindependence mourning practices to memorialize national heroes returned from forced exile. The fierce, prolonged nineteenth-century resistance to the French conquest became fused to the country's 1962 independence victory. On July 4, the closed caskets were publicly displayed in the Algiers museum. On July 5, Algerian independence day, a ceremonial burial service held in the capital's Martyrs Cemetery laid to rest the human remains. As of this writing, bodies but no archives have been returned.[30] Moreover, Macron's commissioned and influential Sarr-Savoy report of 2019 that advocates for restitutions to Africa specifically excludes Algeria (and Egypt) on the grounds that both countries require different legal adjudications.[31]

The "Right to Know"

The International Council of Archives (ICA), representing the international archives community, has formally adopted a position on archival claims that stresses the inalienability of official records and the need for restitution. Microfilming copies is one proposed solution, but it remains mutually unacceptable to France and Algeria. Such a move protects states with similar archival disputes over the question of ownership of the original—in the case of France, the originals remain in France. However, the ICA's position does not address the reasons as to why the French government has a legitimate claim to control the repository of Algerian materials, nor does it satisfy the formerly colonized claims to the actual physical record. At stake, among other things, is the "right to know," a phrase that French jurist and legal expert Louis Joinet authored and that appeared in a much-quoted UN document published in 1997. He linked his opposition to impunity for perpetrators of human rights crimes to a subsection he entitles "the right to know"; it has become a credo for archivists worldwide and is known as the Joinet principles:

> Item 17: This is not simply the right of any individual victim or closely related persons to know what happened, a right to the truth. The right to know is also a collective right, drawing upon history to prevent violations from recurring in the future. Its corollary is a "duty to remember," which the State must assume, in order to guard against the perversions of history that go under the names of revisionism or negationism; the knowledge of the oppression it has lived through is part of a people's national heritage and as such must be preserved. These,

then, are the main objectives of the right to know as a collective right. Item 18: Two series of measures are proposed for this purpose. . . . The second is aimed at preserving archives relating to human rights violations.[32]

Beyond restitution disputes, the laws and practices governing French archives also contravene Joinet's principles. The pre-1962 Algerian archives held in France were to be closed for a fifty-year period. However, five years prior to the archive's anticipated opening, the French Senate adopted an amendment increasing the declassification period to seventy-five years. Such a move was yet another indication of France's desire to control the production of knowledge emanating from the Algerian archive. In addition, the perennial disagreement between the right to know and the right to individual privacy was also at play.[33] In practical terms, for archival users, the right to know is dependent on the on-the-spot decision making of individual archivists. Based upon my experience in the French military archives, archivists may declare documents closed due to the 2008 law on privacy because jailers, police, and judges mentioned in Algerian wartime paperwork are still alive.[34] In fact, ministers spoke up on behalf of France's Algerian War veterans when advocating for a delay in opening archives. In so doing, these ministers referred to France's 1994 law recognizing crimes against humanity, which retroactively could be applied to those living with criminal involvement in wartime French Algeria.[35]

French Archival Legacies for Algeria

The French legacy of archival science in Algeria encompasses practices specifically constructed for the colonial context but that extend beyond it into independent Algeria. In addition to the known removal of French archives from Algeria, according to Fouad Soufi, former head of Algeria's National Archives, the new Algerian state inherited and maintained destructive protocols from their former colonial administrators. Soufi points to a major French colonial concept reserved primarily for Algeria that reached its zenith in 1960, perhaps in anticipation of independence two years later. The colonial administration deemed archives for which it saw no further utility as "dead" archives, and marked them for destruction. In contrast, "living" archives, or *archives vivantes*, were documents useful to France's proper and good administration of the Algerian colony. French concepts of best archival practices in the metropole were partly exported to the colonies to maintain those documents deemed of historical importance to the French colonial project and, therefore, labeled *archives nobles*.[36] The result has been a lamentable state of the archives, which Gabriel Esquer, the colonial administrator and head of the library, took note of as early as 1912: "For offices, it was a tradition to throw in the cellars [the administrative papers] which they considered cumbersome: It was what was called to 'transfer to the archives' [*verser aux archives*]. Later, it became clear that colonial trade goods were embedded in administrative documents. This was what determined with some delay the creation of an archive service in the General [colonial] Government."[37]

In practice, massive numbers of files about Algerians who were caught in the courts and prison system during the some 130 years of French rule list such details as names, judgments, and prisoner transports, but little about torture, killings, and mass graves.[38] Such a lacuna has become all the more evident as, since independence, an outpouring of books, films, and newspaper articles based on Algerian oral testimonies has appeared, which, in turn, casts further light on the lack of colonial documents publicly available. In addition, researchers on Algeria believe that records, films, and tapes do exist, because they, too, have been the subject of incremental release.

While bureaucracies everywhere selectively destroy (or "deaccession") materials and documents if only in the interests of space, it matters who decides, and which sovereign entity determines, what is kept or discarded. The postcolonial practices of creating but also pruning the archive of French Algeria have been infused with the "cultural semantics of a political moment" and according to terminologies, classifications, systems of surveillance, and images of the "native" that determine the pervasive militarism, sexism, and racism of the colonial archive.[39] For example, researchers seeking documentation about traditional forms of land ownership, or Islamic mortmain (*waqf*), seek recourse in methodologies that include reading against the grain of the colonial archive, oral interviews, and deploying far-flung Ottoman archives and writings in languages other than French. When Soufi deplores the ways in which colonial practices continue into the postindependent decades, he is pointing to archives generated by, and for, an independent Algeria whose history demands better and more comprehensive documentation than the French ever afforded. He notes that the concept of "living" archives generates adverse consequences whenever paper documents are privileged or assumed to belong not to the nation but to whichever bureaucratic entity produced them. Therefore, not only French colonial bureaucrats but also those of postindependence Algeria saw little reason to submit to a newly created Algerian National Archives, or even local and provincial Algerian archives. This continuity in archival practices between the colonial and postcolonial era continues to frustrate both archivists and those seeking to access records of the past.

Respect des fonds, or the integrity of record groupings, is another impediment to Algeria's demand for the repatriation of its archives. In practice, the Ministry of the Interior holds great sway over the record groupings, or *fonds.* Thus, the science of archives is embedded in the administrative entity typically responsible for policing and surveillance, emergency management, national security, registration of identity cards, supervision of local governments, and public administration. Such control reaches back to the nineteenth century, with the April 24, 1841, publication of a circular that archivist Michel Duchein designates the "birth certificate" of the idea of *fonds d'archives*: "to gather together by fonds, that is to unite all the deeds (i.e., all the documents) which come from a body, an establishment, a family, or an individual, and to arrange the different fonds according to a certain order.... The documents which only make reference to an establishment, a body or a family must not be confused with the fonds of that establishment, body, family."[40]

The integrity of record groupings is sustainable within the framework of a national archive. Issues arise, however, when the concept is applied to a former colonizing state confronting decolonization. Exceptions to the *respect des fonds* have occurred during archival gifts or wholesale transfers from state to state, especially when new states are formed through independence. Duchein, however, raises the issue of the principle of territoriality to highlight that the fate of archives depends on the fate of the territory in which they reside, which in this case means France. Presumably, he would argue against incremental releases of documents moving across the Mediterranean because, although expedient, they compromise archival integrity and the *respect des fonds.*

According to the French government, artifact and document collections are nontransferable and in the public domain. This belief in inalienability, beginning with former French royal collections, applies to public museums and archives. It moves seamlessly from France's 1566 Ordinance of Moulins to its iteration in Article L.451-5 of the French Code du Patrimoine.[41]

Nonetheless, in 2002, even longstanding principles of inalienability were overturned, allowing for a process to declassify archives and objects, and with this process the legal capacity to transfer them elsewhere. The code of patrimony, amended in 2002, empowered a national scientific commission (Commission scientifique nationale des collections) to overrule the principle of inalienability. According to American historian Todd Shepherd, such disputes highlight his distinction between archives of administration and archives of sovereignty.[42] To circumvent new possibilities of potential document transfers, archivists like Duchein invoke principles of territoriality and archival integrity. To this day, archivists' opposition to Algerian demands for restitution of all colonial administrative and military archives is grounded in the *respect des fonds* framework.

Archive digitization will not resolve Algeria's claims. Abdelmadjid Chikhi, current director of Algeria's national archive center reports that his French counterparts offered a compromise: Algeria would be given access to copies of disputed items if Algeria abandons its claim to archives in France. Chikhi refused, with these words: "We're not going to give up our right. We're not going to give up our property, quite simply because it's something that belongs to us. What's mine is mine. I'm not going to sign away our national heritage."[43] In all, according to Chikhi, France still has about 50,000 manuscripts taken from Algeria, as well as large numbers of other historical artifacts. Included in the archival caches are documents that could shed light on Algerian sovereignty before French rule in 1830, a historical fact that France disputes. For his part, Chikhi asserts bad faith on the part of the French government: Records may be property according to law, but the law allows for redress only in cases of illegal seizure of property, which, according to Chikhi, was the case in Algeria.

The field of archival science has devised two arguments in support of Algerian claims. First, rebutting France's legalistic interpretations, laws enabling *replevin* justify the recovery of goods obtained through wrongful seizure. Second, rebutting French claims that France was the creator of the Algerian archive, archival scholarship introduces the concept of co-production and co-creation for the entirety of French Algeria's records. This argument entails support for equitable, participatory practices in the current management and disposition of the records.[44] In 1966, the two countries reached an agreement, although it was for copies, as opposed to originals, of certain, and not all, Ottoman documents. Since this agreement, there has been political deadlock. France argues that French officials collected these archives and artifacts when Algeria was not a colony of empire but rather made up three provinces that were integrally part of France. Having originated with civil servants, police, and military, the archives fall under French law and are, therefore, sovereign and nontransferable. Insofar as digitization is concerned, Algerians reject it for themselves, but promote it for the French. Even in the digital era, physical possession and ownership of documents are crucial, and thus the conflict remains between the two states at the archival, political, and diplomatic levels. Indeed, in 2012, when Chikhi was offered digitized copies of Algerian documents in French libraries, he renewed demands for restitution of transferred national archives by citing the 1963 UN Charter, adding: "The French didn't want to leave any symbols of the state, and the archives are a symbol of state. In any case, if a document or artifact originated on Algerian soil, it is Algerian property. And no one asked us if we wanted to be ruled by France."[45]

The Years 2018–20: The Turn to Tangible Restitutions?

Settler colonialism is alive and well in France today. According to historian Lorenzo Veracini, the presence of former settlers in France vitiates the possibility of transforming sixty-six years of claims, counterclaims, justifications, and disclosures:

Quite significantly, however, where decolonisation takes the form of a settler collective exodus, as happened in Algeria, Libya, Kenya, Angola, Mozambique, North and South Rhodesia/Zimbabwe, South West Africa/Namibia, and more recently, in the Gaza Strip (evacuated of Israeli settlers, but not yet of colonial control), the decolonisation of territory is not matched, even symbolically, by an attempt to build decolonised relationships. Indeed, settler departure conceptually mirrors and reinforces settler colonialism's inherent exclusivism and confirms a "winner takes all" settler colonial frame of mind that demands that settler sovereignties entirely replace Indigenous ones (or vice versa). By denying the very possibility of a relation between coloniser and colonised after the discontinuation of a settler colonial regime, settler departure produces a circumstance where decolonisation cannot even conceptually be construed as a relationship between formally (yet not substantively) equal subjects.[46]

However, in recent years, France has witnessed several changes, both politically and legally, that have resulted in a newfound extension of reparative
rights to the formerly colonized noncitizens of France. Indeed, 2018 was a
watershed year, with President Macron acknowledging French culpability in
the torture of Maurice Audin, an anticolonial activist who disappeared after
the French army arrested him in 1957 in Algiers. This announcement came
in the wake of Macron's 2017 campaign statement that the French colonization was a "crime against humanity," although the international legal term
"crimes of humanity" did not exist in French law until 1994.[47] Such political
gestures have seen parallel changes in the legal realm. Until 2018, to be eligible for French reparations, an individual had to be a French citizen. This
requirement was codified through Article 13 of Law no. 63–778 (July 31, 1963)
that excluded all claims by the "Algerian Muslims of French Algeria"—the
colonial terminology that made them French subjects but not citizens.
France's constitutional court reversed this law by quoting Article 6 of France's
1789 "Declaration of the Rights of Man." In early 2018, a French court decided
that non-French citizenship was not a basis for denying reparations, pensions, or indemnification to Algerians harmed or tortured during the Algerian War of Independence.[48] This opens new avenues for individual Algerian
claimants to confront the French state about torture and harm. It should also
reignite another round of archival imaginaries, the right to know, and
claims to restore documentation and artifacts about and from Algeria currently held in France. As of this writing during the summer of 2020, the
French National Assembly is examining the first draft of a law that legis-
lates that specific items known to have been looted must be returned permanently to their places of origin within one year. Significantly, if passed, it
will amend the French legal principle concerning the "inalienability" of the
country's national collections, making deaccessioning archives legally possible. Could it be argued in a court of law that taking and withholding the
colonial archive can be interpreted as harmful either to an individual Algerian or to the national body politic? It is worth imagining that the right of
reparations for crimes of colonialism would include restituting the Algerian archive.

CHAPTER 14

The Romani Genocide During the Holocaust: Resistance and Restitution

Ian Hancock

A deliberate effort to diminish the Romani experience in the Third Reich—
to deny that Romanies were targets of the Final Solution, and thus of the Holocaust itself—occurred in both academic and political arenas at a time
when no contradictory scholarship had yet emerged to challenge it. By the
time a number of researchers and politicians began to acknowledge the Romani genocide during the Holocaust, schoolbooks, academic literature, documentary films, and Holocaust centers were already memorializing the
Holocaust without reference to its Romani victims. This chapter attempts to
explain why recognition of the Romani experience during the Holocaust, and
responses to it, have been very slow to reach public awareness, despite the
fact that Romanies as well as Jews were two racialized peoples singled out
for extermination by the Nazis. The chapter does not address the plight of
people with mental and physical disabilities, Germans among them, who
were also systematically eradicated in order to "cleanse" the Aryan gene pool
of defective elements, being singled out for their "dangerous" inheritable genetic characteristics.[1]

The first English-language account of the Romani situation during the
Holocaust appeared on the eve of the Second World War. Written by Harvard scholar Cyrus Sulzberger, the main foreign correspondent for the *New
York Times*, it consisted of a front-page piece accompanied by photographs
for the August 23, 1939, issue of the British *Evening Standard*. It was entitled
"Nobody Wants These Wandering Gypsies,"[2] and made reference to Romanies' precarious position in Hitler's Europe. Even before World War II had

ended, Rafael Lemkin, the person who coined the term "genocide" and successfully fought for an international legal treaty prohibiting and criminalizing it, wrote that Romanies, like Jews, too, had been victims of genocide.[3] This important assertion was barely noted. Only the *Journal of the Gypsy Lore Society* (*JGLS*) covered the situation of Romanies in the Third Reich, and then only after Liberation, publishing essays by Frédéric, Kochanowski, and Maximoff in 1946, and by Molitor and Cowles in 1947. But the *JGLS* had a very limited readership, and while the official Yugoslav reports on the camp at Jasenovac did a great deal more than the *JGLS*, the world at large remained unaware of the fate of Europe's Romani population.[4] Other early essays were by Philip Friedman (1951), Pauwels and Bergier (1960), and Joseph Schechtman, who wrote "in the Nazi scheme and practice, Gypsies came next to the Jews" and noted that "contrary to the Jews, who shortly after their liberation started to write down the history of their persecution, the Gypsies largely failed to do the same, and only much later was the world informed of this people's tragedy."[5]

There were a number of reasons for such scant awareness. Unlike the Jews, Romanies were, for the most part, powerless and illiterate, lacking a national territory or a government. Earlier efforts by Romanies in the 1930s to organize internationally had been thwarted by the war and were slow to re-emerge.[6] Second, centuries-old racism had marginalized Romani populations everywhere, a social barrier maintained by Romanies themselves. Third, especially for the English-speaking world, the word "Gypsy" evoked images of a particular social behavior rather than of a people, so that Romani problems were not taken seriously. This was the case when, in 1984, the United States Holocaust Memorial Council's chairman, Rabbi Seymour Siegel, told the *Washington Post* that he doubted whether "gypsies" really constituted a distinct ethnic people, asking whether "there really is such a thing."[7] Also, in June 1985, Richard Feen, director of Public Affairs and Community Outreach for the council, walked out of a presentation that I gave on the Romani genocide during the Holocaust but later admitted that he "had no real idea of who or what Gypsies were, or what their part was in the Holocaust."[8]

Postwar Germany labeled Romanies asocial (and thus "behavioral") rather than a specific people. As a result, they did not qualify as victims of genocide, and reparations for survivors were not discussed. Similar racist attitudes prevented Romanies from speaking on their own behalf at the Nuremberg trials. Viada Vojvod, a Romanian Romani leader, attended the Eichmann trial in Israel, but could not give evidence. Other commissions compounded this exclusion. The United Nations did nothing to assist Romani survivors following the Liberation. Also, while some independent refugee agencies helped displaced persons, including Roma and Sinti, the U.S. War Refugee Board failed to make any mention of them, even though the War Crimes Tribunal in Washington was aware of the crimes committed against Roma as early as 1946. The record of a meeting between Justice Minister Otto Thierack and Josef Goebbels on September 14, 1942 notes: "With regard to the destruction of asocial life, Dr. Goebbels is of the opinion that the following groups should be exterminated: Jews and Gypsies unconditionally, Poles who have served 3-4 years of penal servitude, and Czechs and Germans who are sentenced to death. . . . The idea of exterminating them by labor is best."[9]

Insofar as Romanies were mentioned at all, then, it was as "Gypsies," a mere footnote to the Jewish tragedy, along with "other" persecuted groups that included, inter alia, LGBT people, political dissidents, and Jehovah's Witnesses. An example of this listing of "leftovers," with the Romani victims in the last place on his roster, is found in Stewart Justman's *The Jewish Holocaust for Beginners*: "In addition to the Jews, the Nazis murdered prisoners of war, innumerable Russian civilians, political prisoners, common criminals, Jehovah's Witnesses, homosexuals, vagrants and some 100,000 gypsies, among others."[10] Nevertheless, a point deploring this narrative was made most forcibly by Stefan Wutzke: "With regard to the Roma, to rank the attempted extermination of an entire people on the same footing as the imprisonment of political dissidents [e.g., in the category of 'others'] is egregious and a distortion of history."[11]

As details of the Romani extermination were uncovered, "Gypsies" were increasingly referred to as "Sinti and Roma," following pressure from Sinti in Germany who demanded that distinction, but "genocide" or "the Holocaust" were yet to be words associated with the Romani victims.

Along the way, there have been three types of denials: (1) denial that there was a "Final Solution of the Gypsy Question," (2) denial that Romanies were the victims of genocide during the Holocaust, and (3) denial that the Nazis even had a "Gypsy Law."

First, for Jews and Romanies, the various proposed "solutions" for dealing with each differed over time.[12] An early reference to "the final solution of the Jewish question," found in a Nazi Party document from 1931, concerned the possible use of Jews as forced labor to drain areas of swampland.[13] In 1937, one SS memo recommended the mass drowning of Romanies by towing them out to sea and scuttling the boats, but for both Romanies and Jews, the

solution moved inexorably toward a single goal—complete physical extermination.

In his 1938 address to the German Association for Racial Research,
Dr. Adolph Würth of the Racial Hygiene Research Unit said, "The Gypsy
question is a racial question for us today. In the same way that the National
Socialist state has solved the Jewish question, it will also have to settle the
Gypsy question once and for all. The race-biological research on Gypsies is
an unconditional prerequisite for the Final Solution of the Gypsy Question."[14]
In March of the same year, a letter to the "Imperial Leader of the SS" from
Dr. Werner Best, head of the Nazi Security Police, addressed the "initiat[ion
of the] Final Solution to the Gypsy problem from a racial point of view."[15]
The first official publicly posted party statement to refer to the Final Solution
of the Gypsy Question was signed by Himmler.[16] He also ordered the Bureau
of Romani Affairs to be moved from Munich to Berlin.[17] The Auschwitz Memorial Book has "the final resolution, as formulated by Himmler in his 'Decree for Basic Regulations to Resolve the Gypsy Question as Required by the
Nature of Race,' of December 8, 1938, meant that preparations were to begin
for the complete extermination of the Sinti and Roma."[18]

A conference on racial policy and to decide, inter alia, upon the Final
Solution of the Gypsy Question, was held in Berlin on September 21, 1939,
and organized by Reinhard Heydrich, who was head of the Reich Main Security Office and the leading organizational architect of the Nazis' Final Solution of the Jewish Question. An express letter sent by the Reich Main
Security Office on October 17, 1939, to its local agents stated that "the Gypsy
Question will shortly be regulated throughout the territory of the Reich." At
about this time, Adolf Eichmann made the recommendation that the "Gypsy
Question" be solved simultaneously with the "Jewish Question."[19]

On January 24, 1940, a memorandum from Leonardo Conti, secretary of
state for health in the Ministry of the Interior, which was sent simultaneously
to the Main Office of the Security Police, to the Kripo headquarters, and to
the Reich Health Department in Berlin, read: "It is known that the lives of
Romanies and part Romanies are to be regulated by a Gypsy law [Zigeun-
ergesetz]. . . . I firmly believe, now as before, that the final solution of the
Gypsy problem can only be achieved through the sterilization of full and part
Romanies." On July 31, 1941, Heydrich also included the Romanies in his
"final solution" shortly after the German invasion of the USSR, ordering
the Einsatzkommandos "to kill all Jews, Romanies and mental patients."[20]

He informed the Reich commissioner for the East, Hinrich Lohse, of this inclusion of the Romanies in the "final solution," and on December 24, 1941, issued the order that the Romanies "should be given the same treatment as the Jews."[21] Himmler signed the order dispatching Germany's Sinti and Roma to Auschwitz on December 16, 1942. The "Final Solution" of the "Gypsy Question" had begun.[22] Scholar Erika Thurner adds:

> Heinrich Himmler's infamous Auschwitz decree of December 16th, 1942, can be seen as the final stage of the final solution of the Gypsy Question. The decree served as the basis for their complete extermination. According to the implementation instructions of 1943, all Romanies, irrespective of their racial mix, were to be assigned to concentration camps. The concentration camp for Gypsy families at Auschwitz-Birkenau was foreseen as their final destination . . . opposed to the fact that the decision to seek a final solution for the Gypsy Question came at a later date than that of the Jewish Question, the first steps taken to exterminate the Romanies were initiated prior to this policy decision; the first gassing operations against Romanies did indeed take place in Chelmno as early as late 1941/early 1942.[23]

Second, despite the fact that the term "genocide" appeared in the title of one of the very first essays on the Romani Holocaust, Holocaust historian Stephen Katz claimed that the murder of Romanies in the Third Reich did not qualify as genocide. He wrote that "the only defensible conclusion, the only adequate encompassing judgment . . . is that in comparison to the ruthless, monolithic, meta-political, genocidal design of Nazism vis-à-vis Jews, nothing similar . . . existed in the case of the Gypsies."[24] The same denial is found in Guenther Lewy's widely relied-upon book, in which he argues that "the various deportations of Gypsies to the East and their deadly consequences do not constitute acts of genocide"—a claim he has maintained in some of his lectures.[25] In a blame-the-victim statement he also wrote "prejudice alone, I submit, is not sufficient explanation for the hostility directed at the Gypsies . . . certain characteristics of Gypsy life tend to reinforce or even create hostility."[26] Roald Dahl once said something similar about Jews and was rightly and roundly castigated for it. Lewy's book is on sale in the United States Holocaust Memorial Museum's bookstore and was listed in Judah Gribetz's 1,000-page report on Holocaust victims' claims as one of his two sources on Romanies, but neither the store nor Gribetz includes any of my own books, which contain overviews of the Porrajmos (the Romani word for the Nazi genocide of Romanies).[27]

Third, Nazis did have "Gypsy Laws." However, in her presentation at the 2014 Yom Ha-Shoah commemoration in Tulsa, Oklahoma, former United States Holocaust Memorial Museum (USHMM) fellow Nadine Blumer stated that "the Nazis never had a comprehensive law against the Roma, as they did with the Jewish Question," as though (if it were even true) it made the genocide less deadly.[28] Her only source was probably Michael Berenbaum's book *The World Must Know*; there he wrote that "Gypsies had been subject to official discrimination in Germany long before 1933, but even the Nazi regime never promulgated a comprehensive law against them," a statement which—as the wording would indicate—he seems to have taken in turn from David Luebke, who wrote that "no comprehensive 'Gypsy Law' was ever promulgated."[29] This was no doubt based on a loose interpretation of a statement made by Eichmann during his trial in Israel, that he was not sure whether any directives "existed for Gypsies as they existed for Jews. . . . He could not remember the details very well . . . but that Gypsies, like Jews, were shipped off to be exterminated he never doubted."[30] Regardless, a Nazi document drafted under the direction of State Secretary Hans Pfundtner of the Reichs Ministry of the Interior on March 4, 1940, did address the creation of a "Gypsy law" (Reichzigeunergesetz) to deal with "the introduction of the total solution of the Gypsy problem on either a national or an international level."[31] It was evidently already on the table before then, for a fortnight earlier (on January 24) a memorandum from the secretary of state for health in the Ministry of the Interior (Reichsgesundheitsführer) Leonardo Conti sent to the Main Office of the Security Police in Berlin read:

> It is known that the lives of Gypsies and part Gypsies are to be regulated by a Gypsy law [Zigeunergesetz]. . . . I firmly believe, now as before, that the final solution of the Gypsy problem [endgültige Lösung der Ziegeunerproblems] can only be achieved through the sterilization of full and part Romanies. . . . I think that the time for a legal resolution of these problems is over, and that we must immediately try to sterilize the Gypsies and part Gypsies as a special measure, using analogous precedents. . . . Once sterilization is completed, and these people are rendered biologically harmless, it is of no great consequence whether they are expelled or used as labor on the home front.

Blumer's statement evidently reflects what she assumed must be true, but it is in fact false: "No direct or indirect evidence . . . has been delivered which could prove the existence of a formal written order by Hitler to start the mass extermination of the Jews."[32] It is revealing that this same "no law" argument has been made by revisionists in the case of the Jewish victims. In a rebuttal in which all arguments are equally applicable to the Romani victims, Melvin Salberg and Nat Kameny of the Anti-Defamation League write:

> There is no single Nazi document that expressly enumerates a "master plan" for the annihilation of European Jewry. Holocaust denial propagandists misrepresent this fact as an exposure of the Holocaust "hoax." In doing so they exercise a fundamentally misleading approach to the history of the era. That there was no single document does not mean that there was no plan. The "Final Solution"—the Nazis' comprehensive plan to murder all European Jews—was, as the Encyclopedia of the Holocaust observes, "the culmination of a long evolution of Nazi Jewish policy. The destruction process was shaped gradually: it was borne of many thousands of directives. At the same time, the development and implementation of this process was overseen and directed by the highest tier of Nazi leadership, including Heinrich Himmler, Reinhard Heydrich, Adolf Eichmann Hermann Goering and Adolf Hitler.[33]

In a talk given at the Weiner Library for the Study of the Holocaust and Genocide in London on May 12, 1989, the late Donald Kenrick noted that in the early years after 1945 it was generally accepted that the "destruction of the European Jews," as Raul Hilberg (1961) called it, was part of the same operation as the destruction of the European Gypsies. The Nazi officer Ohlendorf, leader of the Einsatzgruppen, at his trial in Nuremberg was in no doubt: [He said] "there was no difference between Gypsies and Jews."[34] SS Officer Percy Broad, who worked in the political division at Auschwitz, wrote that the Central Office was aware of the intent to exterminate the Romanies, following an order that appears to have come directly from Hitler himself.[35]

By the late 1970s, Nazi documentation relevant to the genocide of the Romanies during the Holocaust was neither inaccessible nor sparse, and one must therefore conclude that the failure to give it its due place in the historical record was deliberate, or—perhaps worse—simply reflected a lack of concern. Professor Jan Rataj, a history professor at Charles University in Prague, most recently said that the Romani Holocaust, "to a significant degree, is a so-called 'unknown,' even though today this is rather due to society's lack of interest in it than to a lack of accessible information sources about it."[36] This dismissiveness has been a constant factor in the Romani struggle to have the genocide during the Nazi regime, its consequences, and the factors leading up to it properly acknowledged.

Moreover, it is important to underline that the actions taken against the Romani people in German-speaking lands long predated Hitler's rise to power. In September 1888, the German Imperial Ministry of the Interior issued an order stating that "the main duty of the authorities in fighting the Gypsy Plague must be a unified, cooperative action, involving not only the police, but also the heads of community administrations." In the early 1890s the Swabian parliament held a conference on the "Gypsy Scum" (Das Zigeunergeschmeiss), at which the military was empowered to apprehend and document Romanies. In March 1899, under the directorship of Alfred Dillmann, the Bavarian police created a special Romani affairs unit in Munich, later to be named The Central Office for Fighting the Gypsy Nuisance, to regulate the lives of Romanies.[37]

Dillmann's *Zigeuner-Buch* appeared in 1905, paving the way for what was to befall Romanies in the Holocaust thirty-five years later. Nearly 350 pages long, it is in three parts, the first an introduction stating that Romanies were a "plague" and a "menace" against which the German population had to defend itself using "ruthless punishments" and that warned of the dangers of mixing the Romani and German gene pools. The second part was a register of all known Romanies, giving genealogical details and criminal records, if any; and the third part was a collection of photographs of those same people. Dillmann's ideas about "race mixing" later became a central part of the Nuremberg Laws in Nazi Germany. In February 1906, the Prussian Central Ministry issued special instructions to the police to "combat the Gypsy nuisance," and a register was started to keep a record of Romani activity. Increasing anti-Romani terrorism in Germany led to an influx of Romanies from that country into Western Europe. Two years later, a policy statement from the House of Commons in Vienna, capital of the Austro-German Alliance, was sent to the ministers of the Interior, Defense, and Justice "concerning measures to reduce and *eliminate* the Gypsy population" (emphasis added).[38]

In 1920, the psychiatrist Karl Binding and the magistrate Alfred Hoche argued in their jointly authored book, *Allowing the Destruction of Life*

Unworthy of Life, for the killing of those who were "Ballastexistenzen," that is, whose lives were seen to be simply dead weight within humanity. The second of the three groups that they maintained were "unworthy of life" were the "incurably mentally ill due to genetically inherited diseases," and it was to this group that Romanies were considered to belong, "criminality" being seen as a defective criminogenic (i.e., "racial") condition.[39]

In Baden, in 1922, requirements were introduced that all Romanies be photographed and fingerprinted. A 1926 Bavarian law "to combat Gypsies" came into effect, and its Provincial Criminal Commission endorsed a law to control the "Gypsy Plague." In 1927, legislation requiring the photographing and fingerprinting of Romanies was instituted in Prussia, where eight thousand were processed in this way. Bavaria instituted laws forbidding Romanies to travel in family groups or to own firearms. Those over sixteen were liable for incarceration in work camps, while those without proof of Bavarian birth began to be expelled from Germany. A group in Slovakia was tried for cannibalism, which Phillip Friedman interpreted as part of the growing media campaign against the Romani population.[40] After April 1928, in direct violation of the Weimar Constitution, which guaranteed equal rights for all citizens, Romanies in Germany were placed under permanent police surveillance. In the same year, Professor Hans F. Gunther wrote that "it was the Gypsies who introduced foreign blood into Europe."

In April the following year, the Munich Bureau's National Center jointly established a Division of Gypsy Affairs with the International Criminology Bureau (Interpol) in Vienna. Working closely together, they enforced restrictions on travel for Romanies without documents and imposed up to two years' detention in "rehabilitation camps" on Romanies sixteen years of age or older. When Hitler became chancellor in 1933, there were dozens of anti-Romani laws—though not one anti-Jewish law—already on the books. He had no need to incite public hatred against Zigeuners ("Gypsies"); that was already in place. Romanies are not mentioned in *Mein Kampf*, for example (and Poles are scarcely mentioned).

The Great Divide

At Donald Kenrick's 1989 talk in London, he said "I don't yet know when the movement started to make the destruction of the Jews a separate unique event, different from that of the Gypsies. . . . It was a surprise to me." Moreover, at his talk in Russell Square, he asked, rhetorically, "What does it matter if the Jewish genocide under the Nazis is unique or not? If it was unique, then it won't ever happen again. But if it wasn't unique, then we must be on our guard against it happening again, and modern science can make any genocide a holocaust; there was no unique Jewish Holocaust. Similar mass genocide has happened before, is happening now, and will happen in the future unless some supranational force can stop it." He later elaborated upon this in two essays that were both published in 1996.[41]

A concern that Kenrick voiced more than once was that the exclusive categorizing of just one victimized group in this way smacked uncomfortably of Hitler's own vision of a higher-ranking Germanic "master race," his Herrenvolk. In their classic *Manufacturing Consent*, Edward Herman and Noam Chomsky introduced the opposing categories of "worthy victims" and "unworthy victims," the former "merit(ing) lavish attention and concern, [unlike] unworthy victims, whose fate is ignored or denied."[42] This is central to the work of Carolyn D. Dean, who argues that "popular and scholarly attention to the Holocaust has led some observers to conclude that a surfeit of Jewish memory is obscuring the suffering of other peoples," cautioning that "anyone concerned with human rights [must] recognize the impact of cultural ideals of 'deserving' and 'undeserving' victims on those who have suffered".[43]

The idea that the Jewish case was unique seems to have been initiated by Yehuda Bauer of Yad Vashem in his 1978 book, *The Holocaust in Historical Perspective*. Sybil Milton, then senior historian at the USHMM, described Bauer's position as "the most extreme example" of the "uniquist" claim.[44] In 1979, Elie Wiesel, in his report to the president, wrote that the Holocaust "was essentially a Jewish event; the Jewish people alone were destined to be totally annihilated."[45] The following year, the journal *Midstream* published two essays about the Jewish uniqueness of the Holocaust, one by Edward Alexander, entitled "Stealing the Holocaust," and another by Yehuda Bauer, entitled "Whose Holocaust?" in which he referred to "a certain paradoxical envy on the part of non-Jewish groups directed at the Jewish experience of the Holocaust ... [which] would seem to be an unconscious reflection of anti-Semitic attitudes."[46] Yet, Sigmund Strochlitz referred to envy from Jews in his comments at the USHMC's memorial for the "Gypsy victims of Nazi genocide" in Washington, DC, on September 16, 1986. With a remarkable lack of tact, Strochlitz, chairman of the Council's Days of Remembrance Committee, said that there were "feelings of envy" on the part of the Jewish prisoners at Auschwitz-Birkenau because of the existence of the family camp where "Gypsy families ... were living together [and] playing together."[47] A similar stereotype-driven description of the Romani camp at Auschwitz-Birkenau as a "vast playground, an ongoing carnival" was imagined by authors Lucette Lagnado and Sheila Cohn Dekel.[48] Historian Ulrich König makes it very clear that the "family camps" were not created out of any humanitarian motive or desire to bestow special privilege, but because the Romanies became completely unmanageable when separated from family members.[49] Michael Zimmermann adds to this:

> The Nazi institutions involved with the persecution of the Romanies knew about the particularly close family ties in this ethnic group. If these family ties were not taken into account, as happened in part with the deportation of 2,500 Sinti to Poland in 1940, there were certainly difficulties for the police, which were recorded negatively. To this extent, the Reichssicherheitshauptamt [State Security Office] order of 29 January 1943 to deport the Sinti and Roma to Auschwitz "in families" reflected efforts to keep the friction and resultant bureaucratic problems associated with the deportation and internment as small as possible.[50]

Romani families were not kept together everywhere, for example, in the case with those shipped to camps elsewhere in Poland; it seems to have been a policy enacted at Auschwitz-Birkenau in particular, since Jews brought there from Theresienstadt in September 1943 were also allowed to remain together with their families.[51]

Finkelstein reports, "During the USHMM's planning stages, Elie Wiesel, along with Yehuda Bauer, led the offensive to commemorate Jews alone ... defer[ring to Bauer] as 'the undisputed expert on the Holocaust period.'"[52] Tina Rauch, a former graduate student at the University of Texas, attended the "Children of the Holocaust Second Generation" conference on March 20, 1988, in San Antonio. When she asked Wiesel, the keynote speaker, why he had made no mention of Gypsies in his talk, he told her, "We must not let the Holocaust get away from the Jews." Professor Wiesel was awarded the Prix Médicis, the Presidential Medal of Freedom, the U.S. Congressional Gold Medal, the French Legion of Honor, and the Nobel Peace Prize. No Romani scholars or activists, long silenced in public, could compete with those credentials.

Perhaps because the Romani experience was similar to that of the Jews, it presented the greatest threat to the centrality, and hence uniqueness, of the Jewish genocide. The London *Times* journalist Melanie Phillips addressed this on her website, Melanie: "Although the Nazis targeted various groups for persecution, only the Jews were singled out for genocide; being 'inclusive' misrepresents what the Holocaust was. By downgrading this *unique* victimization, it inescapably diminishes the Holocaust itself" (her emphasis).[53] Israeli prime minister Benjamin Netanyahu also said in February 2018 that "the Holocaust was designed to destroy the entire Jewish people and not any other peoples."[54]

It has been argued that by "sharing" the Holocaust, the Jewish right to a homeland as a form of reparation is thereby weakened. Zygmunt Bauman explicitly referred to the way in which Israel "tries to employ the tragic memories as the certificate of its political legitimacy," and Pieter Lagrou has written of the Holocaust's being "gradually integrated as a cornerstone of Israeli national identity," while Norman Finkelstein, more bluntly, wrote that "to increase Israel's negotiating leverage the Holocaust industry increased its production quota."[55] The belief that the Jews alone were singled out for the Nazis' genocidal intent spread quickly. In 2009, Democratic state assemblyman Dov Hikind told the New York *Daily News* that "The Holocaust is a uniquely Jewish event . . . [the other victims] are not in the same category as Jewish people with regards to the Holocaust . . . it is so vastly different."[56]

Another example of "sanctification by repetition" based on guesswork or a failure to go to the primary sources concerns the number of Romani deaths in the Holocaust, which is most often given as half a million.

The count of half a million Sinti and Roma murdered between 1939 and 1945 is too low to be tenable; for example, in the Soviet Union, many of the Romani dead were listed under nonspecific labels such as Liquidierungsübrigen [remainder to be liquidated], "hangers-on" and "partisans." . . . The final number of the dead Sinti and Roma may never be determined. We do not know precisely how many were brought into the concentration camps; not every concentration camp produced statistical material; moreover, Sinti and Roma are often listed under the heading of "remainder to be liquidated," and do not appear in the statistics for Gypsies.

Bernard Streck had already drawn attention to this ten years earlier:

> Attempts to express Romani casualties in terms of numbers cannot do justice to the physical and psychological damage endured by those who survived. Any numbers we have cannot be verified by means of

lists, or card-indexes, or camp files; most of the Gypsies died in eastern and southern Europe, shot by execution troops or fascist gang members. The numbers of those who actually died in the camps have only partially been handed down to us; almost all the files were destroyed when those camps were evacuated.[57]

The Auschwitz State Museum Memorial Book has stated:

Unlike the Jews, the overwhelming majority of whom were murdered in the gas chambers at Birkenau, Belzec, Treblinka and all the other mass extermination camps, the Gypsies outside the Reich were massacred at many places, sometimes only a few at a time, and sometimes by the hundreds. In the Eastern Territories alone, 150 sites of Gypsy massacres are known. Research on the Jewish Holocaust can rely on comparison of pre- and post-war census data to help determine the numbers of victims in the countries concerned. However, this is not possible for the Gypsies, as it was only rarely that they were included in national census data. Therefore, it is an impossible task to find the actual number of Gypsy victims in Poland, Yugoslavia, White Ruthenia and the Ukraine, the lands that probably had the greatest number of victims.[58]

British Holocaust historian Robert Dawson notes that the documentation (in Hebrew) of the interrogation of Adolf Eichmann at his trial in Jerusalem includes his estimate of 500,000 as the number of Romanies that had been transported to the death camps in the year and a half between January 1943 and September 1945 alone, apart from the Romani losses from the previous decade.[59] Several published estimates put the figure in excess of 1 million deaths, and even thirty years ago Pauwels and Bergier listed it at 750,000.[60] That perhaps an even higher number of Romanies were murdered in the fields and forests where they lived than were murdered in the camps has been recognized for some time. A reference to this appeared in the (London) *Financial Times*, noting that "between 500,000 and 750,000 were killed in the German death camps during the war, and another million may have been shot outside."[61]

New information continues to reach us that is pushing the death toll upward. Paul Polansky of the Iowa-based Czech Historical Research Center has reported on the hitherto unrecorded concentration camp at Lety u Pisku in the Czech Republic that was used for the disposal of Romanies. Later used as a pig farm, Lety and a chain of other camps processed mainly Romanies, killing them on the spot or sending them on to Auschwitz. These numbers, like those from the Romani camps in northern Italy documented by Thurner, have not yet been figured into the estimate.[62] Probably the most reliable statement regarding numbers was made at the first U.S. Conference on Romanies in the Holocaust, which took place at Drew University in November 1995, when Sybil Milton, then senior historian at the U.S. Holocaust Research Institute in Washington, stated that "we believe that something between half a million and a million and a half Romanies were murdered in Nazi Germany and occupied Europe between 1939 and 1945."[63] Significantly, the same figure appeared again in a November 2001 report issued by the International Organization for Migration (IOM), which was commissioned to locate and compensate surviving Romani Holocaust victims. The brief states that "recent research indicates that up to 1.5 million Roma perished during the Nazi era."[64] It is certainly a fact that interviews in the past four years by trained Romani personnel who have obtained testimonials at firsthand from claimants throughout central and eastern Europe have already shed startling new light on this issue; in May 1992, I flew to Chicago to meet with Anya Verkhovskaya and Haim Cohen, two of the IOM personnel who had traveled throughout eastern Europe to find and register Holocaust survivors. They told me that the number of Romani survivors they located far exceeded any previous estimation, and that they wanted to produce a documentary film about their findings, but that they were strictly discouraged from doing so.

In Greece, fifty Romanies were murdered for each German casualty. In Croatia, between 80,000 and 100,000 Romanies are estimated to have perished at the hands of the Ustaša, mostly at the Jasenovac camp, "the Yugoslav Auschwitz."[65] Moreover, personal property stolen from Romanies in Serbia, in particular at Jasenovac, was sent to the Vatican by the Ustaša (a Croatian fascist, ultranationalist, and terrorist organization that was active as one organization, between 1929 and 1945), handed over to them by the Catholic monks who ran that camp. It was claimed at the London Conference on Nazi Gold—an international conference held in London in December 1997—that nearly $2 million in gold coins and personal jewelry was confiscated from the more than 28,000 Romanies who were murdered there. The Vatican refused to respond to this and other charges leveled at it during that conference.[66] As of now, the Vatican has denied ever possessing any funds obtained from Nazi sources and has not provided any reparations to any victims.

The extent of the Romani losses has been noted by other specialists who, as is relevant when documenting genocide, considered percentages rather than numbers. Margot Strom and William Parsons wrote "the Nazis killed between a fourth and a third of all Gypsies living in Europe, and as many as 70 percent in those areas where Nazi control had been established longest."[67] Heger asked, "How many people in Britain and America today are aware that the Gypsies of Europe were rounded up by the Nazis and sent to their death in almost similar proportions to the Jews?"[68] And, in a letter to Elie Wiesel written on December 14, 1984, (to which he received no reply) Simon Wiesenthal protested the exclusion of Gypsies from the U.S. Holocaust Memorial Council (USHMC): "The Gypsies had been murdered [in a proportion] similar to the Jews; about 80% of them in the area of the countries which were occupied by the Nazis."[69] For the first time, the U.S. national press, in 1989 in *Newsweek*, acknowledged the extent of Romani losses, writing "Germany had exterminated roughly 70 percent of Europe's Jews and an even higher percentage of its Gypsies."[70] Finkelstein wrote, "Justifying preemption of the Gypsy genocide posed the main challenge to the Holocaust Museum. The Nazis systematically murdered as many as half a million Gypsies, with proportional losses roughly equal to the Jewish genocide."[71] Regarding the USHMM's advisory board's assurance that America, as a democratic civilization, "is the enemy of racism," Romanies have in fact a far more demonstrable claim to a "racial" identity than do Jews; this latter has been the subject of many studies.[72] A report on the health of the Romani American population by a team of Harvard geneticists, which appeared in the prestigious medical journal *The Lancet*, confirmed that analysis of blood groups, haptoglobin phenotypes, and HLA types establish the Romanies as a distinct racial group with origins in the Punjab region of India. Also supporting this is the worldwide Gypsy language Romani, which is quite similar to Hindi.[73]

William Safire, the *New York Times Magazine*'s "On Language" columnist from 1979 to 2009, raised the issue of the "uniqueness of Jewish suffering" in that publication, read by millions, and referred to "the [mistaken] notion that not only Jews ... but gypsies were chosen by the Nazis for annihilation," while rejecting at the same time the word "holocaust" because it "has been used to encompass more than the murder of Jews [such as ...] the wholesale murder of gypsies in World War II."[74] Adam Kirsch's *New Yorker* review of a new book on the Nazi concentration camps listed the victims as

"Communists, criminals, dissidents, homosexuals, Jehovah's Witnesses and Jews," and, in the *New York Times Book Review*, Roger Cohen called the book a "monumental study . . . a work of prodigious scholarship . . . with agonizing human texture and extraordinary detail."[75] Kenedi Janós wrote, "The mass media, in a veiled and often less-veiled form, goad opinion in an anti-Gypsy direction," seldom helping promote an empathetic view of Romanies. In one news analysis headline, the *New York Times* asked whether Roma were a "primitive" people.[76]

The definition of "Holocaust" on the Anti-Defamation League's website states: "The Holocaust was the systematic persecution and annihilation of more than six million Jews as a central act of state by Nazi Germany and its collaborators between 1933 and 1945. Although millions of others, such as Romani, Sinti [*sic*], homosexuals, the disabled and political opponents of the Nazi regime were also victims of persecution and murder, only the Jews were singled out for total extermination."

Wiesenthal recounts that, in 1985, Werner Nachmann, president of the Jewish Central Council in Germany, repeatedly refused to allow Romani participation in a ceremony commemorating the liberation of Bergen-Belsen.[77] At the same time, Darmstadt city mayor Günther Metzger told the German Council of Sinti and Roma that it had "insulted the honor" of the memory of the Holocaust by wishing to be associated with it.[78] In that year's *UNESCO Yearbook on Peace and Conflict Studies*, Bauer wrote, "Roma were not Jews, therefore there was no need to murder them all," a statement he repeated almost word for word at the 1988 "Remembering for the Future" conference at Oxford, at which this writer was present, and where he was berated publicly by Wiesel for asking him to include Romanies in a forthcoming BBC interview.[79]

In 1988 Steven Katz wrote, "The only defensible conclusion, the only adequate encompassing judgment . . . is that in comparison to the ruthless, monolithic, meta-political, genocidal design of Nazism vis-à-vis Jews, nothing similar . . . existed in the case of the gypsies. . . . In the end, it was only Jews and the Jews alone who were the victims of a total genocidal onslaught in both intent and practice at the hands of the Nazi murderers."[80] Bauer echoed this view, arguing that "the whole gypsy 'problem' was for Himmler and most other Nazis only a minor irritant."[81]

Edward Alexander shared William Safire's objection to the too-liberal use of the word "Holocaust" when he wrote that "ignorance and arrogance are in full flower; 'Holocaust' has been used to encompass more than the murder of the Jews, from the casualties in our Civil War to the wholesale murder of gypsies in World War II."[82] Hard on his heels came Richard Breitman's statement that "whatever its weaknesses, 'Final Solution' at least applies to a single, specific group defined by descent. The Nazis are not known to have spoken of the Final Solution of the Polish problem or of the gypsy problem."[83] The California State Board of Education obviously believed this too when it compiled its Model Curriculum for Human Rights and Genocide for use in the schools in that state; while it included Jews as victims of genocide in the Holocaust, "gypsies" were relegated only to a ragbag of "people who have suffered from totalitarian policies."[84] Those who began to publish in opposition to the uniquist position, writers such as Papazian, Stannard, Churchill, Young, and, Sodaro were swiftly challenged.[85] The Stockholm International Forum in January 2000, at which this writer was a presenter, was to coordinate an international task force intended to "preserve memory of the Holocaust [and] expand education about that disaster"—but its published 239-page report contains not a single reference to Romanies.[86]

In 2014, the Texas Holocaust and Genocide Commission made a formal request that that College Board include the Holocaust in its AP World History curriculum; until then, "the AP History curriculums did not require any knowledge to be tested about the Holocaust or genocide."[87] The College Board replied to the commission on December 17 to say that they had agreed to insert the sentence "The Nazi government in Germany undertook the annihilation of Jews from the whole continent (the Holocaust), as well as the murder of other targeted groups of Europeans" as "Key Concept 4.1." As a member of that commission, I objected to Romanies being, once again, an unnamed "other," and asked for it to query this; I had already provided materials to various College Board members with whom I was independently in contact. It became evident that the College Board was, in fact, taking its direction from the USHMM; in an e-mail dated December 2, 2014, Allison Thurber, then senior director of the College Board's History Curriculum and Content Development, wrote: "Lawrence [Charap, senior director, Curriculum, Instruction, and Assessment] and I will continue to work with Kristin and Christina from the Holocaust Memorial Museum to find ways to reach a greater audience among AP History teachers for the rich archival and teaching materials they offer."

Their final wording was "World War II decimated a generation of Russian and German men; virtually destroyed European Jewry; resulted in the murder of millions in other groups targeted by the Nazis including Roma, homosexuals, people with disabilities, and others; forced large-scale migrations; and undermined prewar class hierarchies."[88] The Texas Holocaust and Genocide Commission itself is unsure exactly who and what Roma are; the vocabulary listing for *Roma and Sinti* on its website reads "definition coming soon."

In the *Encyclopedia of the Holocaust*, which was published in 1990, just three and a half of its two thousand pages (a quarter of 1 percent of its total) are devoted to Romanies. *A Holocaust Curriculum: Life Unworthy of Life, an 18-Lesson Instructional Unit*, designed for schools, does not mention Romanies at all.[89]

The Rationale for Creating the United States Holocaust Memorial Museum

In the late 1970s, the advisory board responsible for detailing the mission of the USHMM in Washington, DC, stated that "this museum belongs at the center of American life because America, as a democratic civilization, is the enemy of racism and its ultimate expression, genocide." It took eight years after its creation before the first Romani-American member, William Duna, was appointed by President Reagan in May 1987. Until that time, a concerted effort had been made by several Romani leaders to initiate a dialogue with the USHMC's administrators, but the attitude they encountered was consistently either mocking—its then-chairman Seymour Siegel told a reporter from the *Dallas Times Herald* that Romani spokespersons were "cranks" and "eccentrics"—or else were patronizing: acting executive director Micah Naftalin told the *Washington Post* "the problem with Gypsies is that they're not well schooled. They're quite naïve and, to some extent, distrustful."[90] Leslie Doolittle, a reporter for the *Dallas Times Herald*, told me that she was warned by a council liaison officer to be careful when talking to me because I was a "wild man." When asked by Doolittle why none of the letters from Romani organizations were being answered, USHMC spokeswoman Marcia Feldman told her "it's difficult to know who's who in this world . . . we get bombarded by a lot of unusual mail." Feldman told *Los Angeles Times* reporter Edward Boyer that "[the Council's] members include Jews, Poles, blacks, an Armenian and representatives from trade union and women's groups"—none victims of Nazi genocide—but no Romanies. She added that the council would hire "a specialist in Gypsy affairs" and later reported that, after contacting the (non-Romani) Gypsy Lore Society, the council had "located a Jewish expert in Gypsy studies about doing a research project this summer."[91] In a critique of the council's ignoring the Romani victims, executive director of the

Jewish Federation Jackie Jacobs said that "to do otherwise [than appoint a Romani member to the Council] would give the Nazis yet another victory."[92]

It was in 1984 that a group of Romani Americans staged a demonstration in Washington, DC, wearing concentration-camp uniforms and carrying placards claiming racism; this protest was covered—with a photograph—by the *Washington Post*.[93] It took this protest, and a threatened discrimination suit, finally to prompt the above media responses. William Duna was replaced by this writer, who served for four years until the beginning of the George W. Bush administration, when none of the council's eleven Clinton appointees was retained. Implicit in the selection of federal appointments is the understanding that a candidate placed by the opposition party could be appointed if no qualified candidate was found by the party in power, but that didn't happen. Its director, Michael Berenbaum, made clear that "the United States Holocaust Memorial Museum [. . . is] not a Jewish institution, but a government institution"; it is thus maintained in part by taxpayers—including Romani Americans.[94] When it was established as an independent federal agency in 1980, it was provided with an annual budget of $800,000, increased in 1983 to $2 million a year.[95] There was a further period of twenty years during which there was no Romani representative member on the USHMC. It took until 2016 before President Obama appointed the third Romani member, Ethel Brooks from Rutgers University. Her appointment, however, came with the condition that she be able to raise and contribute $30,000 each year.[96]

In February 1987, the USHMC held an international conference on "Other Victims" of Nazism, which included a panel on the Romani situation, though no Romanies were invited to participate in its organization or were included in the program;[97] a similar conference took place in December 2002 at Tel Aviv University, again with no Romani involvement. In the following year, the Capitol Children's Museum in Washington, DC, established "a tribute to the victims of the Nazis," but adamantly refused to include Romanies.

Romani Responses in Europe

The first, fruitless, effort to obtain restitution was made soon after the war by a handful of Romani survivors:

> Survivors founded the "Committee of German Gypsies" in 1946 in Munich. They demanded authorization to represent the German

Gypsies, a prosecuting counsel at the Nuremberg Trials, recognition as victims of persecution during the Nazi regime and compensation. They also demanded to be recognized as an ethnic minority,
with the right to be treated equally in economic and cultural terms.
Their attempt to rehabilitate the persecuted Sinti and Roma was,
however, to no avail. In fact, the opposite was the case. The discrimination on the part of the police and authorities continued uninter-
rupted. The old law concerning the Gypsies and the work-shy was
still in force and it was not until 1947 that it was repealed by the
U.S. military government, on the grounds that it was not in accordance with legal principles [however . . .] the practices of registering and discriminating were continued, and Nazi files continued to
be used. It was not until 1970 that the law was finally repealed and
not replaced.[98]

Restitution claims continued to hit a brick wall. In 1950, the Württem-
burg Ministry of the Interior announced that "Zigeuners" were persecuted
under the National Socialist regime because of an asocial and criminal record and not for any racial reason, despite "race" being the Nazis' sole rationale for their genocide. Bauer used that argument when he wrote "the Gypsies
were not murdered for racial reasons, but as so-called asocials."[99] Lewy echoed
it: "Because there was no intent to kill all Romanies, and because policies against them were not motivated by Nazi race theory, their treatment
cannot be compared with that of the Jews and therefore they do not qualify for inclusion in the Holocaust—in sum because their treatment did not
constitute a genocide and it was not motivated by a policy based on Nazi
race theory."[100]

But history "makes it clear that the persecution of Roma and Sinti on racial grounds preceded the Nazi assumption of power," and equally clear is
that the "racial" component was central to Hitler's world view.[101] As soon as
he became chancellor in 1933, Hitler passed "the law for the prevention of
hereditarily diseased offspring," which ordered sterilization "specifically
[for] Gypsies and most of the Germans of black color."[102] Other laws issued
in the same year intended to "Prevent Offspring with Hereditary Defects."
Hans Globke, head of service at the Ministry of the Interior for the Third
Reich, who served on the panel on racial laws, declared that "in Europe, only
Jews and Gypsies are of foreign blood," and race-hygienist Robert Körber

wrote in an essay entitled "Volk und Staat" that "the Jews and the Gypsies are today remote from us because of their Asiatic ancestry, just as ours is Nordic."[103]

From 1937 onward, the Wehrmacht High Command began issuing decrees ordering the exclusion of all Romanies from military service for reasons of "racial policy." Himmler signed a new order based upon the findings of the Office of Racial Hygiene, which had determined that Romani blood was "very dangerous" to Aryan purity, and Tobias Portschy, area commander in Styria, wrote in a memorandum to Hitler's Chancellery that "Gypsies place the purity of the blood of German peasantry in peril," recommending mass sterilization as a solution.[104]

In 1938, Himmler called for documentation specifying the Romanies' "racial affinity . . . in the final solution of the Gypsy question." In his address to the German Association for Racial Research, Adolph Würth of the Racial Hygiene Research Unit said, "The Gypsy question is a racial question for us today. In the same way as the National Socialist state has solved the Jewish question, it will also have to settle the Gypsy question once and for all. The race-biological research on Gypsies is an unconditional prerequisite for the Final Solution of the Gypsy Question." Further, Kurt Ammon stated that the Nazi policy "views the Gypsy problem as being foremost a racial one." A letter was sent to Himmler from Werner Best, head of the Nazi Security Police, addressing the "initiation of the Final Solution to the Gypsy problem from a racial point of view."[105]

In 1939, an implementation order from the Reich Criminal Police Department was issued, which stated that "the aim of the measures taken by the state must be the racial separation once and for all of the Gypsy race from the German nation, then the prevention of racial mixing." In 1940, in a speech delivered to top-level Nazi party officials, Himmler said, "The Gypsies are a question in themselves. I want to be rid of them this year if it is at all possible. . . . They do great racial damage."[106]

In 1943, the president of the National Criminal Police Association issued the following statement: "Political preventative custody can be ordered to stop any further children of mixed blood issuing from the willful continuation of sexual union between Gypsies and Gypsies of mixed race, and those of German blood." A party bulletin entitled *Maintenance of the Race and the Genotype in German Law* stated that "pursuant to German racial legislation, Gypsies are of foreign blood. Their political, biological, cultural and vocational separation from the German race has now been effected by means of the elimination of those of foreign blood in the same way as was [done] for the Jews."[107]

Views on Romanies as "asocials" were "shared by many Germans after the war, including some of those responsible for compensation."[108] Members of the shattered postwar remnants of the surviving Romani population lacked the legal tools to challenge this statement, and no outside agency came forward to assist. A case in point from 1955 involved Erik Balasz, who had contracted tuberculosis while a prisoner in Ravensbrück and whose mother was shot there. The Compensations Claims Office in Detmold, using the "security-not-race" argument, denied his claim. Commenting on this at the time, the French medical genealogist Professor Montandon admitted a painful truth: "Everyone despises Gypsies, so why exercise restraint? Who will avenge them? Who will complain? Who will bear witness?"[109] And no one did.

In 1962, the newly formed Comité International Rom (later renamed the International Romani Union) was able to document several thousand petitions from Romani survivors in Germany and France and submit them in compliance with the terms of the Bonn Convention, which had provided France with funds to compensate French nationals: "But again Gypsies, handicapped by illiteracy, often found it beyond their ability to provide the proof required, [and] only a tiny percentage were successful. In one case, Paprika Galut received the derisory sum of £5 for the loss of her new-born child who had perished in Auschwitz."[110]

In 1971, the Bonn government stated that the surviving victims of war crimes were to be compensated under the terms of the Bonn Convention but freed itself from its responsibility to honor the Romani claims by once again using the argument that Romani deaths were strictly on the grounds of security and not race.

In 1980, the Bavarian minister of the interior, Gerold Tandler, a Christian Socialist, called Romani demands for war crimes reparations "unreasonable" and "slander[ous]." In 1985 Werner Nachman, president of the German Jewish Central Council, adamantly refused to allow Romani participation in a ceremony commemorating the liberation of Bergen-Belsen; he had the support of Darmstadt city mayor Günther Metzger, who told the German Council of Sinti and Roma that it had "insulted the honor" of the memory of the Holocaust by wishing to be associated with it. In the following year a report was issued by the German Ministry of Finance, which concluded that "all those victimized by Nazism have been adequately compensated . . . the circle of those deserving compensation need not be extended any further." Regardless, Romani efforts to seek justice continued to be made and continued to fall on deaf ears.[111]

In 1988, on the fiftieth anniversary of Kristallnacht, a campaign was launched to erect a Holocaust monument in Berlin to honor the Jewish victims of the Holocaust. Soon after the start of the campaign, the Central Council of German Roma and Sinti demanded that the Holocaust memorial be conceived to commemorate the common destiny of Jews and Gypsies, as many thousands of Roma and Sinti—men and women, infants and adults, young and old, healthy and sick—had perished in the concentration camps and killing centers of the Third Reich. In response, the original proponents, supported by the president of Germany's Jewish community, maintained that the singular quality and quantity of the Jewish torment called for a specific and separate monument. Besides, should Gypsy victims be admitted to the sanctum, other victims might have to be let in. In turn, the advocates of the Roma and Sinti community objected to Gypsy victims sharing a separate memorial in Berlin with an array of "lesser" martyrs: victims of euthanasia, Soviet prisoners of war, non-Jewish Poles and Russians, Jehovah's Witnesses, political prisoners, homosexuals. They also considered it humiliating to be offered a separate-but-not-equal monument on the remote and secluded grounds of what had been a Gypsy camp in southwest Germany.[112]

Romani advocates raised their voices against the Swiss government actions against Roma, too. Swiss immigration officials refused to admit the Romani refugees seeking asylum who had marched to Geneva from Germany in 1993, led by Rudko Kawczynski, following the German government's declaration—subsequently carried out—to return them to eastern Europe.[113]

Moreover, in 1996, the news broke that hidden Nazi bank accounts had been discovered in Switzerland, and, as it began to spread, it initiated an ongoing furor over who had claim to any part of it. Known as the "looted Swiss assets," these were monies converted from property stolen from the prisoners and secreted in banks in ostensibly "neutral" Switzerland.

This was not the first such deal involving Swiss banks. Some thirty-five years earlier, in 1962, after having consistently denied holding any victims' assets, a number of Swiss banks announced that they had "discovered" $7 million belonging to Jews killed in the Holocaust, which were then turned over to various Jewish charities. Responding to ongoing pressure from attorneys representing Jewish groups, they unearthed a further $28 million in 1995, although those attorneys claimed that as much as $7 billion still remained unaccounted for. "The downfall of the Third Reich did not halt the devaluation of Gypsy lives. Though West Germany paid nearly $715 million to Israel and various Jewish organizations, [as of 1979] Gypsies as a group received nothing."[114] Whether those millions were demonstrably only of Jewish origin or had in part been converted from property also taken from Romanies was not addressed at that time. Nor was Switzerland alone in its complicity, since some of the gold in its banks was then sent on by the Nazis to pay neutral countries, such as Sweden, Spain, Portugal, and Argentina, in return for war materials and supplies.[115]

The news that money confiscated by the Nazis was being held in Swiss banks was compounded by the discovery by a security guard the following January of Nazi-related bank records that were about to be destroyed. If enacted, this would have constituted a violation of a federal ban—and charges were made that the central bank had routinely been laundering the plundered gold for the Nazis throughout World War II. The response from the Swiss government was swift: It announced that restitution would be forthcoming to those who could present valid claims. The amount first mentioned was 5 billion Swiss francs (US$4.7 billion). In all of the ensuing international media coverage, Romanies were not once mentioned.

On February 12, 1997, the Swiss government agreed to explore with Jewish but not Romani groups the best way to compensate the Holocaust survivors. After meeting with representatives of the State of Israel and of the World Jewish Congress, the Swiss Minister of Foreign Affairs Flavio Cotti announced that as of March 1, 1997, a fund of $70 million would be set aside for reparations, donated by the Union Bank of Switzerland, the Swiss Bank Corporation, and Credit Suisse—Switzerland's three largest banks. On March 5, the Associated Press reported the Swiss president, Arnold Koller, as saying that his government would set up an additional fund of $5 billion to aid victims of the Holocaust and any other genocide or disaster and would finance it by selling off tons of gold over the next few decades.[116]

On April 16, 1997, the Swiss Federal Council announced that it had appointed a prominent Swiss businessperson, Rolf Bloch, to head a new committee to oversee the disbursement of the stolen funds. In consultation with the World Jewish Restitution Organization, an umbrella group of major Jewish organizations together with Israeli state representatives, selected three of its prominent citizens for membership to serve alongside the four members appointed by the Swiss government. The representative of one Swiss Romani association complained that they were treating the situation as though it were "purely a Swiss-Jewish concern"; indeed, a year later *USA Today* could still refer to the "$300 million in gold stolen from Jews."[117] The one Romani attendee, not named in the same article, despaired that arguments over who was to serve on the board "have eliminated a role for the Nazis' number two victims [since] . . . no Gypsies were named to the seven-member board."[118]

Several Swiss and non-Swiss organizations also created an international eighteen-member advisory council, which was to include representatives of various groups victimized in the Holocaust. "European Gypsies" were included in this proposal, and two were appointed: the late Rajko Djurić, then president of the International Romani Union, and Robert Huber, president of Radgenossenschaft der Landstrasse, the main Swiss organization of Romani and non-Romani travelers.

Furthermore, in 2003, a short-lived organization called Gypsy International Recognition and Compensation Action was created to help Romanies seeking compensation for claims of moral damage brought against IBM, stating that IBM was complicit with the Nazis since it supplied the regime with machines that enabled the identification of Romanies who were later killed in the concentration camps; but it was dismissed by the Swiss court.[119]

Elsewhere in Europe

In 1952, the new West German government offered to pay each Romani survivor five deutsche marks a day (about $1.20) for the number of days spent in the camps. "Many illiterate gypsies simply signed away their claims for compensation in exchange for trifling sums."[120]

The Berlin-based Erinnerung, Verantwortung und Zukunft (EVZ) ("Remembrance, Responsibility and Future") Foundation is an official German government body whose purpose is to make restitution available to surviving victims of Nazism. In September 2017, through a subcontracted agency called the Voice of the Roma Coalition, some seventy Romani survivors in Moldova were for the first time slated to receive help, not in the form of cash, but only of food and coal and only for a few months. EVZ's director, Marin Alla, said "there are now about 600 Roma who lived through the Second World War left in Moldova, but the funding from Germany is not sufficient to help all of them." He added that, for the past twenty years, Jewish Holocaust survivors in Moldova who were in camps, ghettos, and labor battalions had been receiving a pension of €336 (US$400) per month, as well as receiving help with home care, food, medicine, winter clothes and coal. According to Greg Schneider, the executive vice president of the Conference on Jewish Material Claims Against Germany, since 2013 almost seven hundred Jewish survivors in Moldova had received a one-time hardship fund of €2,556 (US$3,048).[121]

Thanks to the efforts of Petre Matei, a Romanian historian; Roma activists; and NGOs, a few hundred Romani survivors in Romania began to receive monthly pensions from Germany in 2016. Because the compensation came seventy years after the end of the war, very few of the survivors were still living. Yet, the Romani survivors have not started to receive their rightful pensions from the Romanian state due to biased bureaucracy and attitudes of state representatives.[122] The reason that the Romanies began to receive pensions decades after the Jewish survivors is because many were illiterate, their community disorganized, and still subject to considerable discrimination. "The problem for the Roma is that they can't read and write, and even if they could, they wouldn't be able to speak German," Matei said. "Also, to be anti-Semitic could be problematic, but to not like the Gypsies in Eastern Europe, it's not that dangerous."[123]

Ralf Possekel, head of quality management at the EVZ Foundation and human rights activist, said that because it was "hard to reach the Roma people . . . hard to include them," his organization would begin working directly through Romani organizations as their intermediaries, but "the budgets of these projects are small, and cash is not distributed to the survivors directly. EVZ funds food, home repairs and volunteer helpers for the elderly."[124] Following on from the initial project in Moldova, there are nine similar projects planned for countries including Ukraine, Russia, Bulgaria, and Serbia. In 2016, it was announced that Romani survivors in the Czech Republic would get a one-time payment of €2,500 (US$3,000) each as a result of months of negotiations between the Czech and German foreign ministries.[125]

Romani Responses in the United States

On June 25, 1984, the U.S. Romani Holocaust Council was created in Los Angeles.[126] It was an alliance of a number of regional Romani American organizations together with the International Romani Union, and the principal item on its agenda was to demand representation on the United States Holocaust Memorial Council. On July 20, a group of some fifteen Romani Americans, representatives from eleven states, gathered in Washington, DC, dressed in concentration camp uniforms to protest that exclusion from the USHMC, carrying placards reading "Justice for Roma" and "Why no Gypsy representation?" Being told that there was no vacant spot available, they asked whether one of the councilors might step down to make a place for them. Refusing, Executive Director Seymour Siegel told the press that "there are no openings in any case. They have some cockamamie idea, which I would not support, of asking certain members of the council to leave."[127] Perhaps because of this, the council created the post of "Special Advisor on Holocaust-related Gypsy Matters" in May 1985, and this writer was appointed. But when questioned a year later as to why my opinion had never once been sought, the council's then acting director, Micah Naftalin, told the *Washington Post* that it had only ever been an "honorary position."[128]

On September 16, 1986, Roma were allowed an official Romani remembrance ceremony in Washington, DC, and Elie Wiesel made a very brief appearance at that event, where he told us "I couldn't be here today, and yet I couldn't not be here.... We have not done enough to listen to your voice of anguish. We have not done enough to make other people listen to your voice of sadness. I can promise you, we shall do whatever we can from now on to listen better." Despite this assurance, Romani efforts to have a permanent representative appointed to the USHMC continued to be frustrated.

The situation was still unchanged three years later, when Simon Wiesenthal wrote to Seigel's successor, Wiesel, once again "with the suggestion that one of the more than thirty Jewish members of the Memorial Council might be replaced by a Gypsy. To this letter [he] received no answer at all."[129] At this time, the ten-member Romani-Jewish Alliance was incorporated to lobby for a common cause, but was ineffective.[130]

In 1995, The World Jewish Congress successfully won a suit against the Swiss banks that resulted in a settlement in a U.S. court for numbers of survivor groups, though none that included Romanies. In November 2000, the presiding judge, Edward Korman, approved a plan that placed funds amounting to $1.25 billion in the control of the Israeli Banking Trust, with the New York lawyer Judah Gribetz as the "Special Master" in charge of administering its disbursement.[131] By 2015, $1.28 billion had been distributed to nearly half a million claimants, though not to any Romanies.

Perhaps because of the increasing media attention being placed on Romanies, the Center for Holocaust Study at Drew University held the first-ever conference on the Porrajmos—the Romani Holocaust—in December 1995.[132]

In Warsaw in November that same year, as a member of the U.S. State Department delegation, I had addressed the Organization for Security and Cooperation in Europe, soliciting help in locating Romani survivors in Europe and support for their right to claim war crime reparations.[133] Efforts to become a part of the process were not particularly successful, to a large extent because Romaphobia was at an all-time high. As an example, the then chief prosecutor, Benjamin B. Ferencz, founder of Pace University's Peace Center in New York, decided not to recommend that the U.S. War Refugee Board include Romanies in their compensation payments to survivors, which amounted to several hundred million dollars. "Gypsies" are not mentioned anywhere in their documentation, and Ferencz has ignored all written and telephone requests for clarification.

When it was first formed by the World Jewish Congress, the so-called Gribetz Plan had required various claimant bodies to submit proposals detailing exactly why they believed that they qualified for reparation. The national bureau of the International Romani Union met with their Philadelphia attorneys to create a new body and to file claims for reparations on behalf of that organization. The Romani American Education Foundation (RAEF) was incorporated in New Jersey in 1996; its main legal representative was Ramsey Clark, former U.S. attorney general, and its board members included two state senators. Its purpose was twofold, first to create a proposal to submit to the Gribetz Plan, and secondly to locate survivors and the relatives of survivors who could prove their case. The general consensus among the various Romani organizations with which the RAEF was in communication was that only part of any restitution should go in the form of pensions to the survivors, while the rest should be used to improve the situation of Romanies in Europe today, particularly in the areas of human rights, health, and education. On this basis, the "Hancock Proposal" was drawn up and submitted by our attorneys, but its receipt was not acknowledged.[134] Besides including estimates of distribution of available funds—in percentages because of the unknown expected amount—the proposal was that "Romani Centers" be established in a number of major cities in Europe and in North and South America, each linked by computer to the digitized holdings of the Romani Archives and Documentation Center and to other Romani websites, that there be learning and social centers for students and others and disbursement points for scholarships and other funding. John Nickels, a Romani American leader from New Jersey, attended one of the meetings in New York supervised by attorney Judah Gribetz of the lawyers involved in the disbursement of the looted Swiss assets and was told by the judge not to speak. I phoned Judah Gribetz and was met with stunning rudeness and grossly unprofessional remarks about "gypsies."[135]

In December 1997, I prepared an official statement that was circulated at the London Conference on Nazi Gold, and Donald Kenrick of the Romani Institute in London was deputized to present the Romani case.[136] He gave an overview of the plight of Romanies in the Holocaust and reported that the International Romani Union was asking for a fund of $115 million to be created to help European Romanies. The request received no response. A very small number of Romani individuals reportedly had been given insignificant amounts of money (as little as $1,500) by way of compensation, and concerns were raised that this would be seen as sufficient compensation and acknowledgment on the part of the Swiss. Those individuals were likely pleased to receive any money at all and were not in a position to decline it in the hopes of a more equitable settlement, which to date has not been forthcoming.

Romani Americans were initially hopeful that greater recognition of the Romani case would come from the United States than had been so far evident in Europe, since the U.S.-based Executive Monitoring Committee, an informal network of more than eight hundred public finance officers, had been successful in getting the State Department to issue a joint U.S.-Swiss statement that reaffirmed the commitment of both governments "to address openly all issues related to the Holocaust and to its victims."[137] The ancestors of the overwhelming number of Romani Americans, who number about 1 million, arrived in this country several decades before the Nazi period and consequently have no direct link to the Holocaust. Only five survivors had been identified in the United States, and because of cultural restrictions on speaking of the dead, only a couple of those were willing to become involved in the campaign for reparations.[138] There are more eligible individuals among the post-1990 influx of Romanies from central and eastern Europe, but their sometimes illegal status makes them reluctant to come forward.

In 1998, Senate Bill 1900 created a federal Commission on the Swiss Gold, which included two U.S. congressmen, four senators, and the then-chairman of the USHMC, Miles Lerman. The bill provided for the appointment of individuals from the private sector and an effort was made to have John Nickels placed on that committee. It was not successful.

Change?

As more details of the Porrajmos become known, the harder it becomes to deny that it happened. Those who do so are being challenged publicly, as in the Czech Republic, where Romanies have called a member of parliament to account for denying the Romani plight during the Holocaust and, in a show of solidarity, a city mayor joined their demonstration in protest.[139] In the wake of this protest, the Norwegian government offered to finance the building of a monument at the Czech Romani death camp at Lety u Pisku. There are journal essays, theses, and dissertations documenting and questioning the efforts to exclude Romanies from Holocaust historiography.[140]

As the elderly survivors pass on, those who were there to tell their stories become fewer and fewer. The perspective is broadening to focus on the Nazi genocide in greater detail—what forewarning signals were being sent in the years preceding it that should have been recognized, and how are we to guard against the same signals apparent today?

Moves forward are still painfully slow; Romanies have just 1.5 percent representation among the sixty-five members of the USHMC despite losing about 70 percent of our people in Europe; there are still Holocaust memorials and commemorative events that exclude us. Treatises continue to be written that rank the victims of the Nazi genocide, as if doing so makes the deaths of the members of one group more or less bearable than the deaths in another.[141] Exclusion continues.

Fifty years ago, Grattan Puxon wrote, "How a total price can be put on that persecution I do not know. But presuming that it should be a sum relative to the very large amounts, I would maintain that the Romani people are due to receive about £30 million. Divided up among thirty million Romani children in Europe today it would work out at £10 a head—enough for a few school books."[142]

We are still waiting for the schoolbooks.

PART IV

Ways Forward for Reparations

CHAPTER 15

The Roma Case for Reparations

Margareta Matache and Jacqueline Bhabha

The call for reparations as a critical element in the quest for repair, healing, and accountability for state wrongs has mobilized many constituencies across the globe in the last few decades.[1] Scholars, advocates, and some governments have advanced widely contrasting arguments, coupled with a broad range of tactics, to press the case for reparations. Some have proposed *backward-looking* rights-based models of reparation, justified "as a compensatory right that cannot be outweighed by considerations of social utility."[2] Others have focused more on *forward-looking* utilitarian approaches, arguing for material accountability for past harm and reversal of an ongoing legacy of economic injustice and social exclusion.[3] Across a diverse range of political, geographic, and ethnic constituencies, and for distinct reasons, many actors—often in identity-defined silos—have called for reparations for harms suffered by their communities.

The most extensive reparations initiative, and in many ways the most iconic, is the German government's program establishing wide-ranging reparations payments to victims of the Holocaust. Yet, as Ian Hancock argues in Chapter 14 of in this volume, Romani victims of the Holocaust have been purposely and severely neglected, a highly revealing omission and a testament to the ongoing lack of Roma political and social power.

Colonial domination and other forms of oppression have been the basis of a plethora of other reparations claims. In Morocco, brutal repression of dissidents and political adversaries by the postcolonial Moroccan regime following independence has been the subject of a program of symbolic and financial reparations.[4] In the United States, several egregious forms of racially targeted state violence have been subject to successful compensation claims: in 2014 compensation was paid to some of the victims of forced sterilization during the twentieth century by the state of North Carolina.[5] However, one of the most dramatic instances of U.S. state injustice, centuries of enslavement, has yet to be the subject of government reparations.

In fact, enslavement represents another crucial theme in the exploration of the legacy and ethical breaches of past state-sponsored, collective injustice. To date, no reparations—legal, psychological, symbolic, or material—have been granted to the descendants of enslaved people in any of the countries where enslavement existed. The discussion about the need for reparations for enslaved and previously colonized populations is not new, but it has witnessed a dramatic recent and renewed visibility. Sir Hilary Beckles argued in a 2015 talk at Harvard Law School that a turning point was occurring in global attitudes to reparations for historical injustice.[6] Marian Mandache, the leader of Romani CRISS, a Roma rights organization from Romania, echoed this regenerated pressure for reparations for past wrongs with a call for Roma reparations and government accountability for Roma enslavement during a 2016 Harvard conference: "It's not about a crime committed in a dark alley and with the constraints of the law. It is about past and prevailing moral injustice. There should be no statute of limitations on resolving human suffering," he noted.[7]

The topic of reparations also remains intensely contested. Some authors have argued that "the rising of concern with the past overlaps so directly with the decline of more explicitly future-oriented politics."[8] Others have brought up objections based on historical complexity, the supersession of historical injustice, or intergenerational justice.[9] Governments have also proved reluctant, with few exceptions, to engage seriously with demands for reparations. Some representatives of victims or survivors, for their part, have also rejected reparations as a valid social justice strategy. Wary of the potential moral hazards involved, they have criticized the acceptance of "blood money" or what they consider an opportunistic use of the past.[10]

This chapter examines the concept of reparations in cases of enduring oppression, using the Romani people as a case study. Despite a history of enslavement, mass murder, extermination, and modern racism through school segregation, forced sterilization of women, hate crimes, and socioeconomic discrimination, reparations for injustice, past and enduring, have not been made to Romani communities. This chapter addresses this anomaly and explores strategies to repair the harm of anti-Roma collective injustice, past and present.

The Canons of Anti-Roma Injustice

Racist Ideas

Patricia Hill Collins discusses what she calls the "matrix of domination" in the organization of power in a society, arguing that power arises historically and socially through intersecting systems of oppression. Collins argues that such systems of oppression include four connected domains of power: structural, disciplinary, hegemonic, and interpersonal.[11] This theoretical framework is generative for understanding the Roma oppression case.

In what follows, we argue that diverse, evolving, yet intersecting forms of oppression and axes of power across Europe have perpetuated anti-Roma racism and recurring collective wrongdoing for one thousand years. Although recently most European state policies and interventions targeted at the Romani people have rejected legal discrimination against them, some governments have adopted some assimilationist and condescending agendas that continue to signal the racist idea of Roma social and cultural inferiority.[12]

When the Roma arrived in Europe, they found societies steeped in long histories of hierarchical ideology, something Benjamin Isaac has termed "proto-racism."[13] As some authors discuss, while scientific racism only emerged more powerfully in the nineteenth century, seeds of racialist ideas and "racist" ideology and practice had long been features of European civilization.[14] Isaac shows that in the fifth century, "Airs, Waters, Places," a treatise attributed to Hippocrates, influenced both Plato and Aristotle and advanced a form of racially inflected environmental determinism: "Those who inhabit low-lying regions, that are grassy, marshy, and have more hot than cool winds, and where there is hot water, those will be neither tall nor well-shaped, but tend to be stocky, fleshy, and dark-haired; they themselves are dark rather than blonde, more susceptible to phlegm than to bile," the Greek physician argued.[15] A forerunner of later bias, Aristotle advanced a theory of natural slavery and justified enslavement: "Humanity is divided into two: the masters and the slaves; or, if one prefers it, the Greeks and the Barbarians, those who have the right to command; and those who are born to obey."[16] Moreover, as Julia Ward discusses, "The connection between Western racist policies and Aristotle's theory of slavery in the modern period leads to the supposition that Aristotle himself forged a link between racial identity and slavery."[17] Such intellectual edifices laid the foundations for a pervasive system of structural oppression that manifested itself in different forms of racism, including genocide, discrimination, the enactment of separatist policies, and violent acts of rejection and physical hostility toward Roma. This legacy endures.

Donald Kenrick and Grattan Puxon argue that, upon the Roma's arrival onto European soil around 1100, their "blackness" positioned them straightaway as an inferior people. After Romani people settled in different regions of Europe, such as the Basque country, non-Romani residents refused them access to their churches; they could only participate in services by looking in from the windows. Albanians assigned Roma only at the back of mosques.[18] Spanish people would refuse to work with most Roma, except blacksmith and vintner Roma.[19] A 1560 decree from Archbishop Petri of Sweden stated that "the priest should not concern himself with the Gypsies. He shall neither bury their corpse nor christen their children."[20]

Discriminatory conduct had its narrative counterpart. Gadjo/non-Roma writers and scholars routinely described Roma as a criminal, inferior, ugly people who had to be excluded from mainstream social and civic life. In the 1400s narratives centered on Roma's "blackness" and "inferiority," describing their "most ugly faces, black like the Tartars," and pointing out that "the same sun makes the linen and the Gypsy black."[21] In the early 1600s, Spellman defined Romani people as "the worst kind of wanderers and impostors springing up on the continent, but yet rapidly spreading themselves through Britain and other parts of Europe,

disfigured by their swarthiness; sun-burnt; filthy in their clothing, and indecent in all their customs."[22] In France, Roma were described as "the poorest miserable creatures." A Spanish author wrote about Roma that "the men are all thieves, and the women libertines."[23]

The ideology of an inferior Romani race was also starting to take shape: in 1783, German author H.M.G. Grellman characterized Roma as a " idlers, cheats, and thieves."[24] Another early scholar categorized Roma in 1863 as "a distinct race, without religion and, perhaps, without morals also, who have for centuries lived among superior nations."[25] Other scholars talked about the "civilized" and "superior" nations of Europe in opposition to the "gypsy" or the "peculiar" race.[26]

Legalized Anti-Roma Violence, Executions, and Rejection

Institutional oppression, legalized violence, and genocide were pervasive, too. According to Kenrick and Puxon, between 1471 and 1637, anti-Roma laws existed in many places, including Spain, Holland, and Scotland. For example, in the 1500s, England under King Henry VIII, the government of Venice, and the Portuguese rulers all enforced anti-Roma laws based on a bigoted notion of their collective criminality.[27] Angus Fraser notes that in the fifteenth and sixteenth centuries, Roma were chased away from the kingdoms of Portugal and England, from the provinces of the Netherlands, and from the cities of Venice and Milan, among other places. In the same period, a series of laws mandated the death of all "Gypsies" or their leaders in England, Sweden, or Denmark. In the seventeenth century, France ordered the confinement of Romani women and children to "workhouses" and the shaving of hair on their heads. Romani women were targets of other rulers, too: in Moravia and Bavaria, they would cut off one of their ears. In the eighteenth century, the Dutch organized "Gypsy Hunts."[28] In Mainz, a 1714 law authorized the killing of all Roma, due to their "lifestyle," which is clear evidence of what would later be defined as genocide and genocidal intent.[29] In 1749, King Ferdinand VI ordered "the Great Gypsy Round-up," a law aiming "to arrest, concentrate, imprison and exterminate 'all the gypsies living within the kingdom of Spain,'" which culminated in many losses and the genocide of twelve thousand Roma (a quarter of the Spanish Romani population then).[30]

Separatist policies based on the alleged inherent inferiority of Roma intersected with assimilationist modes of thought that emerged in the late 1700s. This was a paradoxical but nonetheless deeply oppressive approach. One strategy was the forced removal of Romani children from their families (a practice considered genocide today) together with the provision of instruction in basic reading and writing skills to the children with the intent of freeing them from "the fetters of old customs and vices."[31] "You must begin with children, and not meddle with the old stock, on whom no efforts will have effect," Hoyland agreed, while reflecting on the assimilationist measures of Maria Theresa, the empress of the Hapsburg Empire.[32]

One of the most dramatic forms of institutionalized oppression of Roma was enslavement. From the 1300s, different axes of power coalesced to enforce repressive anti-Roma measures through the institution of slavery. A racist narrative of Roma criminality, and otherness justified the economic self-interest of the church, nobles, and the Crown to promote a system where tyrannical power yielded huge economic gains to enslavers in Walachia and Moldova for more than five hundred years.[33] It was not until the nineteenth century that the abolitionist movement, influenced in part by earlier Enlightenment reforms in Europe, created pressure for the abolition of Roma enslavement in 1855–56.[34] In a 1841 publication, the Swiss author Emile Kohly de Guggsberg described the Roma enslavement in the following terms: "Slavery is the country's greatest shame, a black stain in front of foreigners. . . . Will you dare to count yourselves among the civilized peoples as long as it is possible to read in your newspapers 'for sale: a young Gypsy woman'?"[35]

The Holocaust and Its Legacy

Old anti-Roma policies and laws were disassembled, only to be replaced by others deeply rooted in ideology of white racial superiority. In the nineteenth century, criminologists strongly influenced by adherents of biological determinism, such as Richard Liebich and Cesare Lombroso, used their "research" to claim criminality was inherent in the Roma character. Liebich, for example, argued that the Roma were "an unchangeable people of morally inferior thieves and frauds."[36] Alfred Dillman founded the Gypsy Information Service in Munich to fight the "Gypsy nuisance." Robert Ritter conducted extensive work identifying and classifying "Gypsies," with a clearly expressed intent: "What is the way to cause this traveling people to disappear? There is no point in making primitive nomads settle and their children go to school," Ritter would write in 1939 in the German state health journal.[37]

Deeply racist ideology, justified through scientific racism then, continued to inform the development of forms of structural oppression and violence across Europe, eventually culminating in the killings of between 250,000 and 500,000 (some scholars estimate that the number was more than a million) European Roma by Nazi regimes during the Holocaust.[38] Similar ideologies set the basis for state measures targeting Romani children, measures adopted and continued before and after the Holocaust. In line with eugenics ideology and starting in 1927, the government of Czechoslovakia adopted eugenics policies that resulted in the assignment of Romani children to special schools, allegedly because they exhibited mental disabilities.[39] This abusive placement practice, although not legal anymore, continues to this day, in both the Czech Republic and Slovakia. These schools prevent children from advancing to higher education. On average, according to the EU Fundamental Rights Agency's 2014 report, one Roma child out of every ten has "attended a special school or class that was mainly for Roma, even if only for a short period."[40]

School segregation has been pervasive across Europe. Communist regimes, including those in Hungary and Bulgaria, despite their assimilationist ideology, continued to foster the separation of Romani children in the school environment well into the late twentieth century, an ideological paradox in itself.[41]

Roma and other related groups, such as Yenish, were also targeted for child separation. Yenish children have also been subject to forced transfer from their families. From 1926 to 1973, Switzerland implemented the "Children of the Road" national policy, asking the Swiss organization Pro-Juventute to move Yenish children away from their parents into orphanages.[42] Instances of child removal from their families have also been documented very recently in countries such as Slovakia and the UK.[43]

Today, in Europe (and beyond) the legacy of state-sponsored violence and the power of whiteness continue to fuel and justify dehumanization, prejudice, and racism against Roma in many domains. In 2013, 60 percent of Hungarians still believed that criminality is in "gypsy" blood.[44] A 2015 survey by the Pew Research Center shows that Europeans hold strong anti-Roma prejudice: 86 percent of Italians, 60 percent of the French, and almost half of the Spanish, British, and German populations have unfavorable opinions about Roma.[45]

Dehumanization and the language of hatred fueled the extermination of millions of people during the Holocaust, and these are still used at the highest levels against Romani people. Zoltan Bayer, a founding member of Hungary's (now-governing) Fidesz Party, wrote in an op-ed that "a significant part of the Roma are unfit for coexistence. They are not fit to live among people. These Roma are animals and they behave like animals."[46] In the past few decades, hate crimes against Roma have proliferated across Europe. In 1992, Sima's Chetniks, a Serbian paramilitary group, killed twenty-seven Roma civilians from the villages of Skocic, Malesic, and Setic in northeastern Bosnia.[47] Yet, in June 2018, the Appeals Court of Serbia acquitted six defendants charged with war crimes.[48] Between 2008 and 2012, the European Roma Rights Center (ERRC) documented sixty-one attacks against Roma in Hungary.[49] In 2018, NGOs reported on the rise of hate crimes in Ukraine, including the murder of several Romani individuals by Ukrainian extremists.[50] After an attack against a Roma camp, which they filmed and posted online, a fascist group based in Ukraine said that they "'safely burned' the camp of makeshift tents, saying they were 'cleaning' Kiev."[51]

Romani communities across Europe are under threat, even more so now, when the enduring belief and the "racecraft" of Romani criminality are also exploited online as a weapon for anti-Romani violence.[52] Cultural and behavioral racism and the racist ideology of Roma inferiority and criminality continues to serve non-Roma as a perverse and false "moral" narrative that informs, inflicts, justifies, and reinforces anti-Romani racism.

Anti-Roma Law and Policy Proposals

Attempts and actions to institutionalize anti-Roma state measures continue across Europe, with no end in sight. In the past few decades, in spite of EU antidiscrimination legislation, policy makers in various parts of Europe have proposed, and on occasion implemented, overt anti-Roma laws and measures.[53] In 2010, France proposed a bill to fingerprint Romani EU citizens alongside non-EU migrant groups. "A biometric system will allow us to detect repeated requests for repatriation assistance and help us prevent the undue payment of return aid to people who come once, twice," proposed Martine Rodier, the minister of immigration and integration. Fortunately, the European Commission blocked this attempt to violate Roma EU citizens' entitlements because it breached the EU Freedom of Movement Directive, which protects the rights of all EU citizens to cross EU borders freely. France is not the only EU member whose representatives of state institutions have suggested anti-Roma measures. In 2011, Catalin Chereches, the mayor of Baia Mare, Romania, built a wall separating the Roma from the majority community.[54] In 2018, Italy's minister of the interior, Matteo Salvini, announced his intentions to conduct a national census of Roma, "a prelude to expelling those without valid residence permits," followed by a letter sent in July 2019 to provincial authorities requesting "a report on the presence of Roma, Sinti and Camminanti settlements" to "prepare a plan of clearances."[55]

In sum, racist, segregationist, and coercively assimilationist policies and practices have shaped European approaches toward the Roma across the centuries. Systems of racialized oppression and punishment, from enslavement to forced sterilization, child removal from families, police abuse, and school segregation, have generated "a series of catastrophes," both cultural and political for the Roma, in the words of Cornel West.[56]

Addressing past injustices and their violent legacies is a necessary precondition of creating a fairer future. Understanding and tackling present-day anti-Roma racism, not only from the perspective of socioeconomic oppression but also in relation to the historical and intersecting axes of power, oppression, and domination just discussed, is critical as a basis for tackling and reversing enduring injustice.

Legal and Other Responses to Collective Injustices

Long-standing and collective racist practices have endured despite test-case litigation and the antidiscrimination legislation upon which it depends, and remedies for historic racism have been nonexistent. In part, litigation could challenge this lacuna. A recent case illustrates a strategy that could be adopted much more broadly. In 2018, a German court in Cologne awarded compensation to Nenad M., a twenty-one-year-old Romani wrongly placed in a "special school" for children with disabilities for eleven years. According to Romea, "Judges based their ruling on the assumption that if he had been allowed to attend a mainstream school he would have completed all of the basic education requirements by the age of 16. By assigning him to 'special school' he was denied that opportunity, which has correspondingly had consequences detrimental to his professional prospects."[57]

This ruling provides a precedent, but there is no legal mechanism in place for generalizing its impact automatically to the large cohort of Romani children subjected to the same violations. And although the European Court of Human Rights has acknowledged that school segregation affects more than half the Romani children in some countries or regions, none of its judgments have generated reparations for the large pool of affected Romani children in some European municipalities. Moreover, whereas the "pilot judgments" procedure of the European Court—also seen as a form of class action—has the capacity to identify and address systemic problems, not enough cases

challenging the same human rights violations against Roma have been consistently brought before the court to date to justify application of this potentially helpful procedure.[58] As the European Roma Rights Center noted in
2010, to demand redress, "Roma rights advocates should seek to take advantage of this new approach by developing their argumentation under Articles
41 and 46 of the Convention and requesting that more specific wording is
included in judgments."[59]

European antidiscrimination measures thus fall short of what Amartya Sen has called the "idea of justice." Sen distinguishes between *Niti*
and *Nyaya*—Sanskrit terms that identify different aspects of justice. Just
procedures, rules, and institutions define *Niti*, whereas *Nyaya* indicates
the realization of justice, the outcomes of existing laws and institutions.
For Sen, justice depends both on the creation of certain types of laws and
procedures but also on the outcomes they produce for particular constituencies.[60] In many ways, his framework speaks to the realities of Roma in
Europe, where there exists a plethora of laws and policies (*Niti*) but nevertheless a failure to correct enduring forms of injustice and to secure just outcomes (*Nyaya*). Ongoing educational segregation illustrates this point.[61]

This is not to say that no cases of individual redress exist. Apart from the
case of Nenad M. cited above, a few dozen other Romani children have benefited financially from damages received after court judgments found they
had been unjustly placed in special schools for children.[62] Of course, $4,000,
the amount received by each of the seventeen applicants in the landmark
desegregation case *D. H. and others v. the Czech Republic*,[63] does not undo
the lifelong social, economic, and emotional impact of segregation in an educational system with an inferior curriculum. Moreover, it does not ensure
justice and remedies to the large number of Romani children facing similar
circumstances. Damages paid to a few Romani women coercively sterilized in
Slovakia and the Czech Republic during and after communism constitute another example of individual redress but, similarly, highlight the absence of
systematic reparations for all Czech and Slovakian Romani women affected
by these eugenics practices.

Given these limitations in collective legal redress, what alternative paths
to reparations exist? Howard Zehr, a prominent scholar on the topic of restorative justice, considers restorative justice an "alternative framework for
thinking about wrongdoing," especially in situations of very large-scale
wrongdoing. "The framework focuses on those who have been hurt and on
healing, through both material and symbolic remedies."[64] Zehr also argues

that both offenders and the direct victims of harm should be engaged in the process of redress. A third, broader constituency of affected community members, whom he calls "secondary victims"—akin to the "bystanders" whom Martha Minow, a celebrated author on the issue of reparations, considers key participants in processes of social repair—are also important stakeholders in the reparations process.[65] Restorative justice, Zehr notes, aims to heal, empower, and promote restitution or vindication through apology and recognition of the harm done. Of course, it is not, nor should it be viewed as, the only tool.[66] But restorative interventions need to address both the enduring experience of subjugation and hostility inflicted on generations of community members as well as the material structures of systemic and structural discrimination, inequality, rights denial, and other forms of oppression.

Toward Roma Reparations

Minow suggests three forms of reparations with complementary impacts on communities harmed by state violence: (1) monetary compensation, (2) restitution of misappropriated properties, and (3) apology. Zehr identifies four related but additional victim-oriented strategies relevant to a comprehensive restorative justice project. They include (1) access to information, (2) systematic processes of truth telling, (3) sustainable tools for victim empowerment, and (4) restitution or vindication.[67] International human rights frameworks refer to compensation, rehabilitation, restitution, satisfaction, and guarantees of nonrepetition as forms of redress.[68] In what follows, we set out several reparations strategies that have been utilized by other constituencies targeted by state injustice, and discuss how they may relevant to the Roma case. In addition to these models for reparations, and complementary to the arguments discussed in the previous sections, we include several additional approaches that we consider particularly relevant to the Roma case.

Truth Telling

Truth telling and a systematic collection of accurate historical information are important reparations strategies for establishing a comprehensive record of the past and generating a deep and enduring account of the *longue durée* of anti-Roma violence. As Zehr points out, victims need to comprehend "why it happened and what has happened since" the offense, and to tell "the stories in significant settings, . . . where they can receive public acknowledgment."[69] Consider the case of Romani women. Between 1935 and 1976, the Swedish government forcibly sterilized sixty thousand Romani women because of their "inferior racial types."[70] During the Holocaust, the Nazis targeted Romani women for sterilization experiments for similar eugenic reasons. Female sterilization was state policy in Czechoslovakia until the Sterilizations Directive was abolished in 1993. In 2003, a fact-finding report shed light on the stories of 230 Romani female victims of coercive sterilization from forty settlements in Slovakia, a large number of them forcibly sterilized even after Slovakia moved from state communism to a democratic regime.[71] A European Roma Rights Center report documents how the practice of sterilizing Romani women (and women with disabilities) against their will continued throughout the 1990s and 2000s.[72]

The European Court of Human Rights has found these measures to be human rights violations under international law, although it did not recognize the racist intent. But beyond individual awards in favor of the small number of Romani women complainants, no other reparations or formal healing processes have been instituted. Public discussion and access to fora that facilitate healing are critical tools for those still coming to terms with past trauma as well as for the society that enabled it.

Truth telling and information diffusion are equally critical for other past atrocities. Descendants of the victims and perpetrators of Roma enslavement, genocide, child removal, and other anti-Roma atrocities and state injustices need those subjects to be aired and captured as public knowledge. To date, despite Roma advocates' repeated attempts, state institutions have failed to establish robust structures, including archives, to enable comprehensive truth telling about the past.

Very little has been achieved in these domains. Romania has taken some initial steps to reverse centuries of institutional silence. In 2007, the Romanian government established a national commission to study Roma enslavement and its consequences; unfortunately, the commission was dismantled before it produced any record of its proceedings. In 2011, the Romanian Parliament declared February 20 a Romanian national day for commemorating the Roma enslavement. Some state institutions have issued public statements on this anniversary date to recall this long denied and ignominious chapter of national history. But these fledgling administrative moves, including a few public declarations on commemorative dates, have had little political or social impact to date on state institutions and non-Roma entities at the local or national level.

Memory can serve as "a political tool" for victim constituencies.[73] Its corollary, "forgetting," is a powerful tool for oppressors. So far, not enough progress has been achieved to create "historical consciousness" of past atrocities, including enslavement, among Roma and non-Roma alike.[74] The communities need to jointly participate in creating a shared sense of social responsibility and solidarity for past and present injustice. Open and easy access to archival information, relevant memorials, and public acknowledgment are all of vital importance for victims, perpetrators, descendants, and others. Incomplete past efforts to address the past, such as the Romanian commission on enslavement, need to be re-established. The revision of history textbooks and archives, the publication of complete historical records, the symbolic renaming of some city landmarks (parks, squares, streets) after Romani resisters and victims, and the mounting of exhibitions and other educational activities are urgently needed to maintain memory and generate broader public awareness of, and engagement with, these issues.

Memorializing Resistance

John Torpey argues that "reparations politics tends to invoke a conception of people as weak and as permanently damaged by adversity."[75] It is certainly the case that much reparations advocacy has an unduly privileged concern with victims over scrutiny of oppressor inhumanity and culpability. But the documentation of harm gives the power to advance healing, to generate an understanding of the past, and to develop a strategy for future harm prevention. In the Roma case, isolated counternarratives to official representations of Roma have begun to emerge as alternative histories, artistic works, and youth initiatives.[76] The story of Netoci, a semi-nomadic Roma who escaped from enslavement in what is today Romania and created their own self-contained and isolated communities in the Carpathian Mountains, is one example of an episode of resistance to slavery.[77] Another example shows up in records dating back to 1722 indicating that about a thousand Roma in Germany formed their own combat groups to oppose oppressive military forces.[78] During the Holocaust, Roma resisted German forces, including on May 16, 1944, now known as Roma Resistance Day.[79] Roma resistance also occurred in Czechoslovakia. As noted by *Romea*, the *After the Jews, the Gypsies* [Po

Židoch Cigáni], mentioned Ján Tumi, nicknamed "Koro," and Ladislav Petík as part of this resistance. Ladislav Tancoš also participated in the resistance with his military unit during an uprising, shooting dead a German guard at a military warehouse, taking grenades and rifles, and then escaping.[80] And so, a systematic history of Roma resistance has yet to be written.

In memorializing resistance, the participation of allies is as meaningful as the active engagement of the affected community itself. Several non-Romani intellectuals have allied themselves with Romani people as opponents of anti-Roma policies in Europe. Hancock makes reference to several key nineteenth-century figures, including Mihail Kogalniceanu, an intellectual abolitionist in Romania. In addition, there were scholars, such as Alexander Paspati and Jean Alexandre Vaillant, or princes, such as ruler Alexandru Ghica, who, under pressure from his daughter Natalia Balsch and his adviser, Edward Grenier, publicly declared: "Slavery has been abolished in all the civilized states of the Old World; only the principalities of Moldavia and Wallachia retain this humiliating vestige of a barbaric society. It is a social disgrace."[81] More than a century later, in 1993, President Vaclav Havel would also speak out: "The Gypsy problem is a litmus test not of democracy but of a civil society."[82] These people and others deserve a place in the history of national resistance to oppression and injustice as well as in the transnational history of Roma resistance to domination. Their legacy of courage and leadership calls for memorialization on a par with that of more established icons of liberation and independence struggles.

Strengthening the Voices of the Victims

According to Zehr, survivors of enduring attacks to "their properties, their bodies, their emotions, their dreams" should actively engage in justice processes.[83] Instead in the current case of the Roma, the opposite situation prevails. The Romani children unjustly assigned to special schools in Europe continue to miss out on educational opportunities and the employment trajectories that depend on the benefit of an education.[84] The stain of European racism and the complacency of government structures indifferent to their reparatory obligations continue to tar these children's lives and those of future generations. Even where school segregation is actively countered, its legacy on previously affected generations remains painfully intact. The voices of the Romani children and youth as well as their families' need to be heard and included in justice and healing processes, not only from a justice perspective but also to strengthen a sense of agency and the self-worth that is fostered by substantive engagement.

Offender Accountability

Minow argues that the rule of law should apply to cases of state-sponsored violations: "Those massive horrors should be treated as punishable criminal offenses perpetrated by identifiable individuals."[85] Many historical and juridical challenges arise in identifying responsible perpetrators capable of participating in reparations adjudications today, decades or centuries after the historical acts.[86] Several other chapters in this volume address this issue. But in the case of the Roma, recent harms with enduring consequences, such as forced sterilization or abusive placement of Romani in special schools, are also yet to be collectively addressed. To date, survivors and their descendants have lacked "direct or indirect access to offenders," such as teachers, schoolmasters, doctors, nurses, and so forth. Nor have they had access to any formal measures to apportion responsibility for harm. Moreover, perpetrators have yet to be involved in public proceedings that address the motivations and drivers of acts for which they bear responsibility, together with procedures for moving forward toward a sense of reconciliation and healing.

Restitution

Restitution, both material and nonmaterial, is widely considered an important element in the process of reparatory justice. As Zehr notes, "Restitution by offenders is often important to victims, sometimes because of the actual losses, but just as importantly, because of the symbolic recognition restitution implies."[87] Over the centuries, Romani people have been deprived of their homes, land, possessions, and other historical and social entitlements. However, little rigorous research documents the extent of the losses or the processes by which such takings were executed. As Hancock notes in Chapter 14 in this volume, the jewelry, artifacts, and other possessions of Romani families taken from them during the Holocaust have never been restored. Also, Kosovar Roma who lost their houses and properties during the 1999 war and were forced to flee to Serbia or other parts of the former Yugoslavia are still

attempting to ensure restitution of their properties.[88] These legitimate restitution claims need to become a government priority in the territories where
claims arise, just as other comparable restitution claims have been adopted
as government policy.

Apology

Apologies are fundamental to the process of reparations. As Minow underscores, through apologies perpetrators "acknowledge the fact of harms, accept some degree of responsibility, avow sincere regret, and promise not to
repeat the offense."[89] Though, to date, Romanian state institutions and the
Orthodox Church have failed to issue a formal and comprehensive apology
for the history of enslavement, some signs of progress toward the acknowledgment of Roma enslavement exist. As underlined above, in 2007, the Romanian government established a national commission to study Roma
enslavement. In 2011, the Romanian Parliament affirmed its commitment to
the official remembrance of enslavement by declaring February 20 the commemorative day of Roma slavery. A member of the European Parliament, of
Roma origin, placed a memorial plaque in the Tismana monastery, where the
first references to enslaved Roma were documented.[90] These symbolic measures signify welcome progress against the long backdrop of denial, even
though they are merely a prelude to the much-needed process of conducting
an effective, clear, and public apology for Roma enslavement by state institutions and the Orthodox Church. Apologies are also still required for other
forms of state-sponsored racism or genocide against Roma, from the
eighteenth-century genocide in Spain to the twentieth-century Holocaust
across Europe.

Reparative Compensation

Compensation constitutes a critical element in the reparations process. Where
a clear legal case can be made for attributing culpability, such payments seem
appropriate and just. But neither European nor national legal mechanisms
currently oblige counties such as the Czech Republic or Slovakia to acknowledge and repair the damage suffered by all victims as a result of forced sterilization or segregation in special schools. Little attention has been paid to

the question of compensations for opportunities squandered—the willful deprivation of educational opportunity, the trauma of forced sterilization, the legacy of abusive family separation, the quotidian damage of racial hatred and contempt. Though court decisions in the cases of forced sterilization of Romani women have indeed included pronouncements about improving future laws and reforming current and future practice, no compensatory obligations by states parties toward the class of affected Romani women have been established. In 2009, the government of the Czech Republic announced a bill to compensate Romani women unlawfully sterilized. The Czech prime minister "expressed regret but did not acknowledge the state-supported" role in the sterilization process. As Albert and Szilvasi note, "In September 2015, however, the Czech government added insult to injury by rejecting the compensation bill without public explanation."[91] Yet, in August 2019, state action on compensations progressed, as "the Chamber of Deputies' Commission on the Family, Equal Opportunities and National Minorities has called on the Czech Health Ministry to do so, and the ministry has agreed with Czech MPs Pastuchová and Válková to submit the necessary bill to do so."[92]

Turning to enslavement, nearly five hundred years of enslavement in the territory of contemporary Romania generated huge gains for key beneficiaries of the institution, among them the Romanian Orthodox Church, the nobility, and the state itself. But the profits derived from enslavement, the inherited capital generated by centuries of exploitation and accumulation, have never been redistributed. After abolition, in 1856, the 250,000 freed Roma (some scholars argue that the number was higher) were given no reparations. More than 160 years later, the same remains true for the descendants of enslaved Romani people—neither compensation, individual or collective, nor moral or legal acts have addressed the five centuries of cruel oppression.

Arguably, what is most essential in the case of past harms, including enslavement, is redress in the face of its enduring legacy. The collective disenfranchisement and marginalization of the Romani people need to be repaired, including through financial compensations. Also, social and economic measures to reduce the legacy of enslavement, including the wealth gap, and preventive measures to forestall further harm need to be complemented by a comprehensive and integrated process of societal repair and healing. Historical acknowledgment and symbols, infrastructural development, educational and training scholarship funds, affirmative action programming following constructive examples elsewhere, vigorous public antibias and antiracist measures in relation to issuance of birth certificates and other critical identity registration documents, allocation of public housing, provision of medical and related services, and employment inclusion are all programmatic investments that require purposeful political, fiscal, and social engagement over time.

Legal Measures

No corrective or reparatory obligations have been set by the courts or indeed by other state institutions to compensate for and apologize to the large numbers of children placed in special schools or sterilized women unable to file court complaints. Yet this is necessary to challenge the status quo, which, as Derrick Bell notes, seems "logically self-evident, objective, *a priori* valid."[93] A new, integrated, and radical approach, with legal and policy mechanisms, public pronouncements, and societal memorialization, is needed to correct collective injustice while also making a sustainable contribution to future healing and flourishing for the Romani people as a whole.

We are suggesting, therefore, a more holistic, antiracist, integrated, and corrective stance than the existing legal doctrines that focus predominantly on individuals, because the racial oppression of Roma is structural and the human rights violations tend to affect individuals belonging to minority groups in large numbers. Its efficacy, however, will in large part depend on active and sustained engagement with the issues of affected constituencies, their allies, and particularly the new generation of leaders and thinkers whom we hope to encourage. Ultimately, governments responsible, whether directly or as a matter of historical legacy, for the collective injustices we have described have an urgent duty to initiate these processes.[94]

Conclusion

The reparations agenda we have outlined in this chapter is an extensive, expensive, and ambitious one. It requires considerable resources of political will, institutional engagement, and public consciousness and mobilization. However, European institutions have shown little inclination to move in any of these directions despite vigorous advocacy attempts. To date, as this volume testifies, all-too-numerous victims of state-sponsored collective injustice receive no reparations, government accountability is weak or nonexistent, and institutions in a range of domains are not penalized for perpetrating or acquiescing in collective wrongdoing.

The reparations agenda we outline is both essential and feasible. Essential because the unaddressed legacy of Roma suffering and discrimination constitutes one of the most egregious vestiges of past cruelty within Europe, and feasible because a plethora of tools to achieve this end exist, including tools that we have outlined above. But we need to mobilize and organize to translate the reparations agenda into effective and transformative practice.

CHAPTER 16

What Justice for Starvation Crimes?

Alex de Waal and Bridget Conley

Introduction: Victims of a Lesser Crime?

The topic of reparations for acts of starvation—and more broadly, justice for those who suffer famine—has been neglected by scholarship, law, and human rights activism. An array of scholarly and legal resources is relevant to the intellectual project of understanding acts of starvation as crimes, and the ethical project of prohibiting them. This is a field wide open for exploration, and this chapter is an attempt to map this conceptual terrain.

There is today an implicit hierarchy for the victims of mass atrocity, in which those who perished of starvation, thirst, exposure, and exhaustion are not ranked on par with those murdered by violent means. Our first obligation is to recognize starvation crimes and their victims and survivors, thereby overcoming a long-standing oversight.

Evelyne Schmid opens her book *Taking Economic, Social and Cultural Rights Seriously in International Criminal Law* by quoting Hans Frank, the German governor general of Poland during World War II, "that we sentence 1.2 million Jews to die of hunger should be noted only marginally."[1] Frank was convicted of the crime of extermination, among other charges, in Nuremberg. But Schmid observes, "Frank's assessment remains accurate: other atrocities attract much more attention than deliberately starving people, which is often noted only marginally."[2] There were more than 6 million victims of starvation on the Eastern Front: in the Nazi prisoner of war camps, the siege of Leningrad, the starvation in Kharkiv and Kiev, and throughout the towns and villages of western Russia, the Ukraine, and Poland. Those aggregate numbers rival those who died of violence.[3] Contemporary writers such as Raphael Lemkin were preoccupied with the use of food deprivation as an instrument of genocide.[4] But starvation deaths are often little more than footnotes in the catalogue of atrocities committed in the Axis-occupied territories.[5]

Similarly, the genocide of the Armenians in 1915–16 is recognized internationally and has been extensively researched and documented. More Armenians died of hunger, thirst, exhaustion, and exposure than were violently killed. However, accounts of the genocide focus on the massacres and treat starvation deaths almost as incidental.[6]

A more recent case is Ethiopia under the military regime of Colonel Mengistu Haile Mariam, which used starvation as a weapon against insurgents and thereby ensured that a drought rapidly degenerated into a calamitous famine in 1983–85.[7] But when the subsequent government prosecuted senior officials for international crimes, the cases focused almost entirely on murders committed during the "Red Terror" of 1977–78, with no attention to the infliction of starvation.

A comparable experience marked the tribunal for Cambodia.[8] Prosecutors showed an interest in taking on international crimes involving starvation but lost enthusiasm when they were pressed to find quicker routes to convicting the men in the dock. The neglect of famine in transitional justice is the product of a mistaken understanding of famine as the product of nature, or only relevant to economic and social rights, which are a second-order concern within the international justice paradigm.

This chapter begins by developing the concept of "starvation crimes." This is a useful umbrella term that encompasses different kinds of acts prohibited under existing international regimes of law. Starvation crimes are a particularly heinous subset of political, economic, and military actions and policies that contribute to extreme hunger and famine, which must, in turn, be seen in the context of hazards such as drought and crop diseases. We delineate these distinctions to identify which acts of starvation would qualify for potential criminal prosecution and for the application of measures under the transitional justice umbrella.

What Kind of a Crime Is Mass Starvation?

The verb "to starve" has both transitive and intransitive senses. In the transitive sense, starvation is an act committed by one person against another.

In the intransitive sense, starvation is a physiological condition, which may be caused by a wide range of factors. When starvation is perpetrated on a large scale over a protracted period, the outcome is famine.

Famine is large-scale hunger, destitution, and elevated mortality. The definition of famine has changed from the scarcity of food to the failure of people to have sufficient economic, legal, or political entitlement to food.[9] Typically, as famines unfold over a prolonged period of months or years, people sell off their assets and deplete their social capital as they strive to obtain food. Hunger and its corollary of increased susceptibility to disease, along with social disruption and attendant crises of health and sanitation systems and the mass migration of distressed people, cause increased mortality. These factors intersect to create a vortex of collapse among the most vulnerable.

Famines are distinct from chronic hunger and malnutrition: They are spectacular and terrible outbreaks of extreme distress. Often they strike against a background of entrenched poverty and food insecurity. However, it is not always so: Famines such as the Dutch hunger winter of 1944 and the recent starvation sieges in Syria are striking examples of previously well-nourished populations rapidly reduced to famine.

Famines occur on a spectrum from those caused principally by natural calamity to those that are acts of genocide or extermination, with a range of manifestations in-between. When famine occurs in the context of war or violent repression, it is frequently accompanied by violence that intensifies and multiplies the harms done: violent death and injury, large-scale incarceration and displacement, destruction of houses and civilian infrastructure, stealing of assets. Belligerents often obstruct humanitarian aid, but the core processes that reduce a population to reliance on aid are the more salient factors in faminogenesis.

Famines cause long-term social and economic disruption. A population emerging from famine may be dispersed, demoralized, and divided. Children who suffer malnutrition may endure lifelong physical and mental deficits. However, famines also have their beneficiaries, such as those who gain from massive transfers of assets, including land, or who consolidate power.

Starvation Crimes

"Starvation crime" is a portmanteau term. Drawing on David Scheffer's coinage of the term "atrocity crimes,"[10] it does not refer to a legal category as such, but rather brings together a range of crimes under different provisions of international criminal law, in a manner that gives them political salience. It bears a resemblance to Diana Sankey's proposed term "subsistence harms,"[11] but is focused on the specific suite of acts that produce famine, or near-famine, conditions.

Starvation is already a criminalized act, named as such, under the laws of war. Attacks on "objects indispensable to the survival of the civilian population" are criminalized in International Humanitarian Law (Article 54 of Additional Protocol, Article 14 of Additional Protocol II, and relevant customary IHL). Similar prohibitions are found in the Rome Statute, Articles 8(2)(b)(xxv) and 8(2)(e)(xix). To be considered a war crime, the perpetrator must deploy starvation against a civilian population disproportionate to legitimate military objectives. Other war crimes may also be relevant to creating famine: willful killing, torture or inhumane treatment, extensive destruction of property, intentionally attacking civilians or civilian objects, pillaging, and so forth. Further, various acts of famine, can, when directed against a civilian population in a widespread or systematic manner, constitute one of several crimes against humanity: murder, extermination, forced displacement, persecution, or other inhumane acts. If carried out with intent to destroy a protected group, then creating the conditions of life that would bring about a group's destruction is prohibited under the Genocide Convention, Article 2(c).[12] While specific conditions must be met for each category of crime, in general, for international law to apply, acts must meet a threshold of scale (a significant number of people must be affected) and severity (deaths or severe suffering), and must be perpetrated in an orchestrated manner.

The category "starvation crimes" therefore encompasses a range of criminal acts that include three central elements: (1) an outcome that includes deprivation of food and associated suffering (not necessarily mass starvation unto death, though such outcomes are relevant to demonstrating the gravity of the crime); (2) the act of depriving persons of food (and destruction of other items indispensible for survival) (*actus reus*); and (3) criminal intent (*mens rea*).

Starvation crimes, perpetrated on a sufficient scale and over a sufficient length of time, can cause a famine. However, we need not wait on a definitive diagnosis of famine to identify a starvation crime. This is important because existing diagnostic criteria for determining famine are contentious or may only be possible after the fact. The metrics used by the international food security phase classification (IPC) scale focus on the *severity* of malnutrition, mortality, and food crisis within a specific geographical locale.[13]There is an element of subjectivity in any such assessment, and the procedures for making an assessment depend on consensus among members of a national IPC committee, which in almost all cases include representatives of the national government. If that government is itself complicit in creating the famine, it is likely that there will be political obstacles to declaring famine. The metrics used for determining the *magnitude* of famines are based on total numbers of excess deaths,[14] but these can be used only after the fact, and therefore are of little use when a famine is in prospect or in progress.

Intention

We have discussed outcomes and acts, but intent is also central to understanding starvation crimes. A characteristic of starvation crimes is that they are committed over an extended period. It takes months, sometimes years, to inflict famine. Starvation is more complicated than massacre: The causal sequence linking the act of starvation to its outcome can be long, complex, and contested so that there are peculiar difficulties of proving causation. It takes many acts, many actors, and usually additional facilitating conditions, to create a famine. To understand this more fully we need to embed the concept of starvation crimes within the wider framework of faminogenic actions.

Starvation crimes are a subset of political and military faminogenic actions—acts of commission or omission that cause a sufficiently widespread starvation that it constitutes famine. In using this term, we follow the categorization developed by David Marcus,[15] which is not a precise legal typology but provides a useful guide to the degree to which political acts cause the outcome of famine. Given that almost all famines involve multiple causes, the framework is concerned with proximate causes, not underlying or structural ones.

A first-degree famine crime "is committed by someone determined to exterminate a population through famine."[16] The immediate cause is prohibited crimes against humanity or acts of genocide. The most straightforward cases are penal starvation.[17]

A second-degree famine crime is committed by a person "recklessly ignoring evidence that his or her policies are creating, inflicting or prolonging the starvation of a significant number of persons. [It] is committed by an official recklessly pursuing policies that have already proven their faminogenic tendencies."[18] These are much more common and more complex: famines in which political and military actors have caused mass starvation in pursuit of other goals, such as consolidating power, repressing insurgency, forcing an adversary to surrender, or managing a coalition of diverse belligerent forces on modest resources. Other causal factors, such as climatic disaster, economic adversity or turbulence in food markets, or historic legacies of poverty and poor public health services, can also be factors in the occurrence of such famines and their level of lethality. Establishing criminal intent in such famines is complicated by these multifactorial etiologies. On the other hand, the fact that mass starvation unfolds over months or years means that a defense based on inadvertent faminogenesis is implausible: There is always enough time to see the evidence of famine and stop it. The term "faminogenic acts" captures the fact that these are culpable actions that may or may not qualify as crimes.

The third degree of culpable famine causation is when public authorities are indifferent: Their policies may not be a cause of famine, but they do little or nothing to alleviate hunger. While a second-degree famine crime is an act of commission, this covers acts of omission. The actions or inactions are irresponsible or malign, but will not qualify as criminal. In the fourth category, there is no official culpability: Authorities are incapable or incapacitated, overwhelmed by food crises caused by external factors. These are rare and becoming vanishingly rare.

Over the last 150 years, of the 110 million people estimated to have died in 58 major famines, about 6 percent perished in first degree, 63 percent in second degree, 18 percent in third degree, and 13 percent in fourth-degree famines.[19] In each case, the categorization is based on the most important proximate cause. In practice, the degree categories often overlap: for example, we may find pockets of first-degree starvation crimes within an overall second-degree famine, combined with elements of third degree. In Yemen, for example, mass starvation is an outcome of punitive economic policies associated with blockade, the closing of the central bank and nonpayment of salaries, and the degradation of key sectors of the economy through both military onslaught and an economic embargo, combined with intense pockets of starvation caused by military action.

For criminal accountability, we are concerned with famines in the first-degree category and some cases in the second-degree category. For political accountability, we may also be concerned with those classified as third degree.

In all cases, the outcomes may appear similar, that is, large numbers of people are deprived of food to the extent that their lives are endangered. One challenge in identifying the criminal element in mass starvation is that similar outcomes can be caused by criminal acts; by noncriminal policies or actions; by external factors, including economic crises and natural hazards; or by combinations of the above. Different causal chains may be intertwined in any one large-scale episode of famine, they may change as the famine deepens, and it may be difficult to ascertain the correct attribute of responsibility for the suffering and death of any individual victim. However, the fact that starvation crimes are protracted means that the perpetrators' culpability for the initial onset may be far less significant than their subsequent responsibilities when the trajectory of famine becomes clear. For example, a famine that begins in category 3 may develop into category 2 and contain elements of clear starvation crimes.

In fact, the delineation of starvation crimes requires a political economic theory of how deprivation is organized. This should not be a singular theory applicable to all cases, but rather it should be contextual, specific for different political-economic circumstances. When we discuss guarantees of nonrepetition, these political-economic contexts become significant.

Reparations for Mass Starvation

Recognizing that starvation crimes meet the threshold of serious violations of International Humanitarian Law, why are they so rarely addressed through transitional justice mechanisms?[20] In this section, we present a nonexhaustive overview of the scarce examples of reparations for starvation crimes, drawing on the UN Basic Principles, which define reparations as restitution, rehabilitation, compensation, satisfaction, and guarantees of nonrepetition.[21] We begin by examining the potential wider impacts of prosecuting starvation crimes, and then discuss compensation and "satisfaction" in the form of truth telling, memorials, and apologies.

Prosecutions

Bringing charges, prosecuting perpetrators, and obtaining convictions would be significant political and symbolic steps, which would bring a degree of satisfaction to their victims. However, the number of cases would likely be small, and the progress of the cases would certainly be slow. The vast majority of survivors of famine would not have the satisfaction of seeing the perpetrators of their starvation in the dock or in prison.

Any prosecution on a charge of starvation will be a precedent-setting exercise. If successful, it will result in the conviction and punishment of a small number of perpetrators, perhaps just one individual. This would be largely symbolic, even for the victims and survivors of that specific act of starvation, and certainly so for victims of famine crimes more generally. It can serve three additional purposes.

First, it validates the experience of suffering by victims of starvation crimes. Currently, people who experience extreme hunger tend to regard this as a personal or family trouble, an unavoidable or natural misfortune, or a shameful trauma that is of no interest to wider society, let alone political and legal authorities. The physical pain is compounded by feelings of shame, humiliation, and worthlessness. If starvation survivors are able to see themselves as victims of an international crime, they may feel that the harms they suffered are properly recognized and their dignity is restored.

Second, prosecuting starvation crimes may deter other potential perpetrators. Any direct deterrent impact of prosecutions is, at best, unproven. However, nonprosecution cannot have any deterrent effect.

Third, prosecutions may be cause for Western governments to reflect on their potential liabilities and change their policies toward countries exposed to starvation. Historically, Western nations have committed grievous starvation crimes, especially during colonization and total war. Today, the direct perpetrators are most often non-Western governments and insurgents, but their actions may be possible because they are tolerated or abetted by Western governments. An obvious example is the famine in Yemen. Major starvation crimes have been committed by Saudi Arabia and the United Arab

Emirates, but these actions have been facilitated by U.S., British, and French military and diplomatic support. These three Western governments should, in principle, be sensitive to international law and the possibility that they might find themselves complicit in a conspiracy to commit starvation crimes. Prosecutions of perpetrators should give reason and opportunity for such governments to use their influence over the direct perpetrators to desist.

Fourth, prosecutions are an exercise in public education. They contribute to making acts of starvation intolerable among the public and policy makers. When a member of the public sees a picture of a starving person, in addition to pity and a charitable impulse to help, the immediate impulse should be to ask, "Who did this to them?" Prosecutions can help change thinking about responsibility for starvation and thereby help drive a change in norms. One specific impact can be that court cases encourage people to put more effort into documenting evidence for past starvation crimes and, more importantly, to document these crimes as they occur.

Compensation

Compensation can take different forms, depending on whether it is for a colonial-era famine, a recent or ongoing case, and the degree and nature of human causation. This section deals briefly with two contrasting historic cases: starvation in colonial India and colonial South-West Africa (modern-day Namibia).

Shashi Tharoor has made a fierce and cogent argument that the Indian subcontinent is entitled to reparations for the massive harm inflicted by two centuries of British colonialism, during which time the global center of economic gravity was forcibly transferred from Asia to Europe.[22] Famines are part of this catalog of injury, an extreme manifestation of British-engineered dislocation and dispossession. Tharoor's argument is for reparations as a political and educational exercise. No legal proceedings have been instituted, specific criminal acts of starvation have been subsumed within the far greater historic injustice, and Tharoor's claim is for symbolic payment of one pound sterling per annum.

The Bengal famine of 1943 is a significant case. It cost 3 million lives. It was largely caused by British wartime policies, including the confiscation of fishing boats (fearing Japanese invasion) and inflationary policies intended to force India to extend a loan to Britain for war spending. After the war,

London added hypocrisy to harm and reneged on repaying its debt. Utsa Patnaik describes the famine as "large-scale resource extraction entailing economic genocide," and writes that it was "something that imperialist countries could get away with quite easily, attributing it to natural causes and abnormal external conditions. Owing to such misinformation, not a single demand was raised in India by patriotic political leaders or by any public intellectual, that the Allies should pay reparations for the lives wantonly lost owing to the extreme and inhumane measure of resource extraction from a population already greatly impoverished."[23]

The extermination of the Herero and Nama of South-West Africa in 1904 is a paradigmatic case of colonial genocide. Descendants of the survivors have been trying to obtain reparations from German companies since 2001. This case has generated legal and academic interest in the context of colonialism and genocides. It is germane to our topic because the principal means of extermination used was starvation—an element neglected in the legal and academic debates over the case.

The German governor of the territory, General Lothar von Trotha, wrote, "I believe that the nation as such should be annihilated, or, if this was not possible by tactical measures, have to be expelled from the county by operative means and detailed treatment."[24] By the latter, he meant driving the people away from their lands into the Omahake desert, occupying and sealing off the water holes, and hunting down the remainder. About forty thousand Herero and six thousand Nama died, overwhelmingly from hunger and thirst. A modest gravestone in the Namibian desert commemorates them.[25]

Contemporary accounts of the genocide have been equally graphic in describing the horrors of violent killing and the trauma of deaths through starvation. Subsequent attempts to obtain compensation from the Germans have reduced starvation to a secondary issue. A court case was brought by the Herero People's Reparations Corporation (HPRC), a private entity set up by the self-appointed chief of the Herero. The Namibian government was not keen to offend one of its major aid donors, and private citizens are not allowed to bring cases to the International Court of Justice. They could, however, file a civil complaint in a U.S. court under the Alien Torts Claims Act of 1789.[26] The German government refused to submit to U.S. jurisdiction, as was its treaty right, but a case against Deutsche Bank and the Woermann Line (a shipping business) was pursued.[27] The HPRC claimed that US$2 billion in reparations should be paid to the Herero. The substance of the case was that the defendants worked in tandem with the German colonial government to "relentlessly pursue the enslavement and the genocidal destruction of the Herero."[28] The accusations included an "implicit and explicit campaign of genocide," the use of enslavement and forced labor, the degradation of captive Herero women, and the destruction of Herero culture.[29] Starvation was mentioned only in the context of the inhumane treatment within concentration camps, as a secondary effect of the genocide, particularly of efforts to kill livestock and destroy wells, and as a result of forced labor.[30]

The Herero claim is a prominent example of an attempt to exact reparations from a colonial power and has been discussed as such by lawyers, historians, and activists. Germany has yet to issue a formal apology. In 2001, Germany acknowledged that genocide had been perpetrated against the Herero and Nama. At a centennial commemoration event in 2004, development aid minister Heidemarie Wieczorek-Zeul admitted "moral responsibility," a line repeated in April 2018, when the Hamburg senator for media and culture, Carsten Brosda, spoke at a conference on the city's colonial legacy.[31] There have been private apologies, including German museums repatriating the human remains of Herero victims, and a visit to Namibia by eleven of General von Trotha's descendants to apologize to the descendants of the survivors.[32] For this discussion, however, the significance of the debate is that none of those involved in the case appears to want to highlight starvation.

Satisfaction: Truth Telling, Memorials, and Apologies

It is commonplace that the survivors of a mass atrocity or genocide only find a way to speak about their experiences many years later. Even longer is needed for the survivors of mass starvation—or to be precise, their descendants—to speak about it. Notably, it was only 150 years after the Great Hunger in Ireland of 1846–52 that this episode, so significant in shaping modern Ireland, was properly talked about publicly. Truth telling in the aftermath of famine is painful in unique ways.

As noted at the beginning of this chapter, in accounts of genocide, mass atrocity, and war, those who die of hunger are commonly treated as second-class victims, memorialized later or only unequally. Narratives focus on violent deaths, pushing starvation deaths to the background. The ultimate status of the starved is uncertain; it is not clear whether they should count among the victims or not, their numbers estimated in parentheses, footnotes, or the margins.

One reason for this is that starvation occurs in a zone where moral clarity is lost. In his wide-ranging essay on turn-of-the-millennium scholarship on the Irish famine, Breandán Mac Suibhne writes of the "grey zone" of "the demimonde of soupers and grabbers, moneylenders and meal-mongers, and those who took the biscuit from the weak. It is where one finds the mother who denied one child food and fed another, a boy who slit the throats of two youths for a bag of meal, and, indeed, rumoured and reported cases of cannibalism."[33] The catalog of indignities and humiliations is long, as neighbors seize not only biscuits but land, houses, and sexual favors. Mac Suibhne draws on Primo Levi's *Survival in Auschwitz* for the term and the framework of the "grey zone,"[34] reminding us that the ultimate perpetrator is often remote and obscure, while those who commit petty offences are immediate and evident.

With the exception of small children, famine victimhood is not clean or clear. To obtain food, people will sell their possessions and engage in degrading activities. Those in possession of a small ration may refuse to share it with neighbors who are even hungrier and more desperate: The hungry deny food from the hungry. The sufferings of famine are filtered through the web of social and economic relations, revealing the intricacies of local hierarchies of power in intimate detail. Those who are already poorest suffer first and most; those who are excluded are further exploited. Death, life, and dignity depend on the tiniest increments of resources and standing among the dispossessed and destitute. For all these reasons, famine is particularly demoralizing, and those who suffer it commonly prefer to forget.

The threads of responsibility for famine are thus tangled and obscure. Those in power prefer to blame the weather, Providence, or the victims themselves—for their profligacy in having too many children in defiance of Malthusian precepts of a sustainable population. Victims tend to internalize such accounts and to blame extreme hardship on mismanaged or corrupted relief efforts. Too rarely are the political causes of mass starvation recognized for what they are: the transitivity of the verb "to starve" is forgotten.

Most famines pass without any official memorials. For some, there are local or private commemorations. The signal exception—the famine that is widely recognized in memorials—is Ireland's Great Hunger. It is striking that the scores of memorials in Ireland, and the smaller number in North America and elsewhere, are framed by the experience of starvation and not by the act of its perpetration. The inscription on the memorial designed by the sculptor Maurice Harron in Cambridge, Massachusetts, is a rare case that points in this direction, albeit implicitly: "Never again should a people starve in a world of plenty." By including the indefinite article, "a", the words invoke the collective, national victimhood of the Irish people, rather than the generic phenomenon of hunger.

One other instance of mass starvation, the 1932–34 Ukrainian famine, known as the Holodomor, is memorialized in an explicitly political way.[35] Both the politicized interpretation of the starvation and the process of creating the memorials are, however, controversial, and this has detracted from the possibility of the memorial to stimulate reflection on the tragedy and the crime. The conservative and overtly nationalistic narrative promoted by the famine monuments encourages truth telling only in the limited sense of refusing to forget that this massive crime was perpetrated.

The Ukrainian famine was complicated. It was initially instigated by a vast program of collectivization of agriculture, including dispossession of the assets of richer peasants, affecting both Ukraine, nearby areas of southern Russia, and Kazakhstan. This was a reckless and counterproductive economic policy carried out with brutality. It appears that when Josef Stalin realized the disastrous impact of these programs, he scaled them back in Russia, but intensified them in Ukraine as a punitive measure. Raphael Lemkin depicted this famine as a case of using starvation as a tool of genocide.[36] Unfortunately, the narrative of genocide has obscured as much as it has revealed, fostering singular narratives on the Ukrainian nationalist side, and denials on the Russian side.

Official apologies for famine are notable for their absence or occur only with significant caveats. While London contains no memorial to the English-inflicted famine in Ireland in the place where the starvation was administered,[37] an almost apology was issued in 1997. The closest that the British government ever came to an apology was an admission by Tony Blair, shortly after he was first elected, when he acknowledged the "deep scars" of the famine and went on to say that "those who governed in London at the time failed their people."[38]

Turkish president Recep Tayyip Erdoğan offered an official apology for the "killing and starvation" of the Armenian Ottoman population, but couched it as (only) 500,000 deaths in a "massacre," refusing to use the word "genocide" and implicitly omitting the death toll from starvation.[39] Nigerian official policy for the siege starvation of the Biafran community was "reconciliation," the end result was denial and silencing of what had occurred.[40]

More commonly than issuing an apology, public officials tend to refuse responsibility.

More Complicated Matters: Restitution and Nonrepetition

Perpetrators and their accomplices invariably respond to victims' claims for reparations with denial and evasion. When it comes to starvation crimes, two additional issues arise. One is the inadequacy of restitution for harms that arise in part because of the structural vulnerability of the victims. The second is the salience of mechanisms of political accountability for guarantees of nonrepetition.

The Limits of Restitution

Restitution implies a restoration of the status quo ante, which in the case of people who were structurally vulnerable to famine because of their political and economic marginalization, is manifestly insufficient. Moreover, these kinds of transformation are most needed where they are hardest to achieve.

Feminist legal theory has developed a relevant framework for imagining the relationship between structural inequalities and reparations based in specific criminal violations. Parallels between sexual and gender-based violence and starvation crimes are instructive. Fionnuala Ni Aolain, Catherine O'Rourke, and Aisling Swaine argue that "returning" women and girls who are victims of conflict-related sexual violence to their previous unequal and vulnerable status is wrong.[41] Rather, they continue, reparations should be transformative: "We maintain that it ought to be possible to incorporate an analysis and accommodation of preexisting structural disadvantage into reparations planning, design, programing, and delivery, particularly with respect to measures that are designed to bring effective compensation directly to women. Fundamentally, this means that the calculus of 'harm' for the purposes of reparation needs to be cognizant of three factors—the 'before,' 'during,' and 'after' of the specific harm—layered into the social and economic context in which the subject of harm was positioned."[42] Restitution for the survivors of famine would similarly be meaningless if it did not address the structural vulnerabilities and inequalities that so often put them at risk of starvation in the first place.

The analytical lens of transformative justice shows how discrete harms are interwoven with structural conditions and how remedies similarly demand far-reaching changes to political-economic conditions. As an agenda for action, transformative justice has a set of preconditions that are particularly ambitious for a postconflict situation: significant funds and political will; additional attention to specifically harmed individual victims to ensure that they are not left behind; and the capacity of legal paradigms to effect political, social, and economic transformations. In the final analysis, transformational justice requires democracy.[43]

Illuminating examples are provided by three recent wars in Sudan and South Sudan, all of which were marked by mass starvation embedded within other atrocities. At the nadir of the North-South war (1983–2005), in early discussions about the agenda for peace talks, civil society activists pushed hard for a transitional justice agenda.[44] This was not taken up by the political-military leaders of the government of Sudan and the Sudan People's Liberation Movement and Army (SPLM/A) who negotiated and signed the Comprehensive Peace Agreement (CPA) in 2005. Both sets of leaders had self-interested reasons for avoiding accountability. But they also had a more legitimate rationale for not pursuing restitution and compensation. This began with the observation that the harms inflicted—including destitution, displacement, and starvation on a huge scale over two decades—were so vast that a new government of national unity could never hope to marshal the resources necessary for individual compensation.

International donors would not support a compensation fund because they were not themselves implicated in the violations, and given the government's limited budget, donors were concerned that a national compensation fund would drain away the governmental resources needed for rehabilitation and development, leaving donors to pick up the bill. Moreover, providing compensation on a case-by-case basis would not address the challenge of the more thoroughgoing economic transformation that Sudan—and especially its war-ravaged regions—needed to end the cycle of armed conflict. The SPLM/A leaders insisted that they did not fight a revolutionary war for so long just to bring Sudan back to the conditions in which the war began.

Barely a year later, a different logic was brought to bear on the Darfur peace talks. The war in Darfur was a speeded-up version of southern Sudan: approximately 40,000 people were violently killed and 150,000 perished from hunger and disease during 2003–5.[45] The argument for compensation was made by the UN's Independent Commission of Inquiry into Darfur (ICID), which wrote that compensation should be provided to "all victims of crimes, that is . . . persons that 'individually or collectively, have suffered harm, including physical or mental injury, emotional suffering, economic loss or substantial impairment of their fundamental rights' as a result of international crimes in Darfur."[46] The ICID proposed that government should pay for compensation for those who suffered at the hands of its forces, while international voluntary contributions should finance a fund to compensate the victims of rebel crimes. The argument was elaborated in the context of the UN Commission for Human Rights' Basic Principles on the Right to Remedy and Reparations for Victims (2005).[47] The arguments in favor were straightforward: Grievous wrongs were inflicted, and the victims are entitled to material compensation. The government's chief economic negotiator was Lual Deng, an SPLM/A leader who had recently finalized the CPA, and who brought the same arguments against individual compensation to Darfur.[48]

These discussions did not reach a satisfactory conclusion. All accepted that seized land should be returned to its former owners; a small compensation fund was specified, which the rebel leaders regarded as a political budget for rewarding their followers; and the formation of a compensation commission was agreed to but never implemented. The logic of the debate reduced the conflict to an aggregate of wrongs inflicted by the parties (with the government by far the greater culprit), obscuring any vision for political transformation.

The Darfur peace process did not succeed. Sudan's CPA led to the independence of South Sudan, which was followed in 2013 by a comparably deadly civil war, fought solely over power, without even passing reference to any agenda of societal transformation. Fighting, massive forced displacement, and the use of starvation as a tactic created pockets of severe famine and a countrywide humanitarian crisis that is estimated to have cost 383,000 lives over four and a half years.[49] In this context, South Sudanese civil society has tenaciously championed the issue of transitional justice, including a hybrid court and reparations. Provisions for this appear as the last chapter in each peace agreement. South Sudan's leaders are prepared to include these articles because their diminished international legitimacy is at stake, but they confidently expect to postpone indefinitely any accountability for their crimes—one thing on which the belligerents readily agree.

The Sudanese and South Sudanese cases begin to show some of the complexities involved in the agenda of individual compensation and restitution, and especially how it can be realized only with reference to the particular political and economic context in which harms were inflicted and remedies are sought. These complexities are not a reason for denying the legitimacy of the discussion about individual compensation and restitution but rather an invitation to discuss them in a broader political and economic context.

Political Accountability

Another shortcoming of the transitional justice agenda is that it is focused on crimes, and the concept of starvation crimes captures only a subset of actions that cause famine. For example, certain economic policies or administrative decisions that endanger people's livelihoods or food entitlements may be policy errors, but not starvation crimes.

Most famines fall within Marcus's second degree famine crimes: cases of political and military recklessness. It would surely be a frustrating exercise to try to determine the exact boundary between starvation crimes and other faminogenic political decisions. This is especially so given the tiny number of prosecutions that are likely to be brought, and the fact that in many cases, clear-cut starvation crimes may be a causal element only in small pockets of extreme distress, rather than the principal man-made factor in the calamity.[50]

What is feasible and also provides a strong guarantee of nonrepetition is political accountability. This shifts the remedy to political processes such as media exposure, public shaming, commissions of inquiry, and elections. Political accountability is also an exercise in public education that can clarify the nexus between law and famine. An informed public can punish political leaders who recklessly pursued noncriminal policies that caused famine, or failed to take steps to prevent it.

In some instances, popular protest, driven in part by outrage over famine, has overthrown regimes. India's independence from Britain was probably hastened by Britain's failure to prevent, or take timely measures to relieve, the famine in Bengal in 1943. Other examples are the fall of Emperor Haile Selassie of Ethiopia in 1974, following his egregious failure to respond to the famine of the previous year, and of President Jaafar Nimeiri of Sudan in 1985, who similarly tried to conceal a famine in his country, and was removed by a nonviolent popular uprising.

Amartya Sen famously observed that the freedom of the press, the right to organize, and the ability to call the government to account through the mechanisms of democratic governance are inextricably linked to the ability to secure basic economic rights, including freedom from famine.[51] He could have added that commissions of inquiry play an important role in public accountability in the aftermath of famine, and that institutionalized humanitarianism is also a feature of democracies. This is not the whole story. Some democracies have failed to prevent extreme hunger, and (as Sen himself emphasized) the success of the Indian media in exposing famines and thereby bringing about their ending in the subcontinent has not been matched by comparable press activism on the issue of chronic hunger.[52]

Nonetheless, Sen's core insight remains valid. It is also relevant to the core question of justice for acts of starvation. Guarantee of nonrepetition of faminogenic acts consists of both political accountability for those responsible (removal from office and loss of reputation) and political change (democratization, liberation, or emancipation). These "political reparations" lie at the heart of the project of making starvation so morally toxic that nobody in a position of authority would contemplate inflicting it, or allowing it to occur.

The shortcomings of the tools of restitution and political accountability are complementary: They point to the need for structural political and economic reforms that eliminate the vulnerability of those who are at risk of starvation. This is not the only agenda for famine prevention, but it lies at the heart of any such agenda. If the sensibilities, language, and law of transitional justice can be used to promote this agenda, it will have made a significant contribution.

Conclusion

This chapter has argued that the topic of reparations for acts of starvation—and more broadly, justice for the victims of famine—is an area almost entirely neglected by scholarship, law, and activism. Nevertheless, an array of scholarly and legal resources is relevant to the intellectual project of analyzing acts of starvation as crimes, and the political project of prohibiting them. This is a field open for academic and activist exploration, and we hope we have made a first foray.

The most important step in the starvation justice agenda is to name the crime. This is an act of respect toward its victims and survivors. Those who have suffered famine in the past, are enduring it now, or who are facing imminent starvation, should know that their plight is no natural misfortune, no personal or family failing, no inescapable indignity or self-inflicted shame. They should know instead that it is the product of far-reaching crimes committed by powerful men, who may be remote but should not be unnamed or unshamed. Emancipating victims of starvation from this prison of silence may be the most vital step toward seeking justice for starvation crimes.

CHAPTER 17

Stopping the Crimes While Repairing the Victims: Personal Reflections of a Global Prosecutor

Luis Moreno Ocampo *with the collaboration of Joanna Frivet*

Introduction

For nine years, it was my responsibility to protect the rights of victims of massive atrocities from different parts of the world as the chief prosecutor of the International Criminal Court (ICC). During the Darfur case, our investigators met witness K in a refugee camp in Chad on the Sudan border. K was around forty years old, but his hair was completely grey. He wore a long brown tunic, as did so many in the camp.[1] He said: "I knew it. I knew that one day you would come. I was waiting for you. I have to tell you what happened." Then he explained in his gentle voice how the Sudanese army had surrounded his village and the Janjaweed militias had burned the small houses, destroyed the water system, and shot all of his neighbors. "Four men came to my house, they grasped me, tied my hands, they started to loot everything, and then they chased my wife and my daughters to rape them. They forced me to watch when they were raping the youngest, my eight-year-old daughter. I kept asking them, 'Why? Why are you doing this to me?'"

He was in tears for four hours while providing details of what had happened to him and his family. When the interview ended, he said very calmly: "Now I can die, you know the truth." Witness K confirmed for us how important it is to provide humanitarian assistance for victims and how the investigation process helps them. Public institutions were put at their service, and their painful stories were transformed into evidence against perpetrators. Merely by being interviewed, the victims felt less isolated and empowered. But witness K and his family, as the rest of the victims of the Darfur genocide and other massive atrocities, can never be fully compensated. It is an impossible task. As Judge Cancado Trindade, ruling in a case before the Inter-American Court of Human Rights, once said: "Reparations for human rights violations only provide the victims the means to attenuate their suffering, making it less unbearable, perhaps bearable."[2] Helping and repairing the victims should not deflect attention from the design of new solutions to prevent the repetition of the massive attacks. This should be the absolute priority.

The Importance and the Limitations of Protection by the Nation-State

Historically, the crucial innovation to prevent crimes was the legal system developed between the seventeenth and eighteenth centuries: the national state model. Witness K's story illustrates one of the limits of that model: Who and what can protect a person attacked by their own national state? Should a different state intervene? As the International Court of Justice has observed: "The principle of non-intervention involves the right of every sovereign State to conduct its affairs without outside interference."[3] We cannot expect the national state to deal with problems that are beyond its reach. The inaction by nation-states in confronting a genocide or intruding on the territory of a different state to control a criminal organization is not a failure, it is inaction by design. In 1945, after millions were systematically killed by the Nazi regime, national leaders pledged "never again." The promise was repeated after the failures to stop the Srebrenica and Rwanda genocides, which saw millions more slaughtered in the face of failing diplomacy. The call was raised again in the context of the genocide in Darfur. But the Arab Spring and concern for Libyan citizens deflected attention away from Darfur. Then came the use of chemical weapons in the Syrian conflict, overshadowing the Libyan victims. Later, the appearance of ISIS and the forced displacement of millions of Syrian and Iraqi citizens shifted attention once again.

Fighting and killing is still an accepted method of resolving conflicts. The media is still denouncing new genocides-against the Yazidi and the Rohingya—but no authority, either national or international, can deliver effective solutions to protect them and to prevent future atrocities. The lack of a global model to prevent and control these conflicts should be addressed as a priority beyond necessary discussions on reparations for mass atrocities. I am not calling for a global government modeled on the nation-state. To confront massive cross border harm, such as mass atrocities and international terrorism, global governance requires a new legal design. I do not have a model to propose, but I have relevant experience to share. The unique legal architecture of the Rome Statute should not be the last institutional innovation: It could be the model upon which new types of institutions can be built to face other specific global problems that sovereign states are not able to confront with efficacy, such as international terrorism, cybercrimes, and climate change. The Rome Statute combines a network of national authorities applying similar legal standards monitored by an international actor that can independently decide to intervene if national authorities fail to act effectively. The model was discussed for decades, is now operational, and should be studied to improve the solutions that victims deserve.

A New Global Model

The fall of the Berlin Wall and the end of the Cold War created a new international dynamic, international cooperation was possible. In 1998, political leaders, diplomats, lawyers, and a very active group of NGOs working together as the Coalition for the International Criminal Court, were able to adopt the Rome Statute. The Statute created an innovative legal system "to put an end to impunity of the perpetrators" of "the most serious crimes of concern to the international community as a whole" and "thus to contribute to the prevention of such crimes."[4] The Rome Statute created a peculiar confederation integrating states belonging to five different continents with a variety of races and religions. The participating states integrated their own national systems to investigate genocide, crimes against humanity, and war crimes, and established an independent International Criminal Court (ICC) that should intervene if they failed to conduct genuine investigations (under the principle of complementarity). James Crawford, the chair of the UN International Law Commission working group that produced the Draft Statute in 1994, concluded that the final version adopted at Rome is a "distinct and to a considerable extent an autonomous criminal justice system."[5] Under the Rome Statute, victims would receive a combination of national

and international protection, could participate in the proceedings and request compensation, and perpetrators would be accountable before the international community.

There was consensus about the crimes to be included. They had already
been defined by the Nuremberg Charter, the Genocide Convention, the Geneva Conventions, and customary international law when the Rome Statute
was adopted. The Rome Statute's radical innovation, the one fiercely opposed
by the U.S. delegation, was to allow for the possibility that these pre-existing
international law prohibitions could be enforced by a decision of an independent international prosecutor presenting a case before a permanent
ICC. The Rome Statute transformed the meaning of "home" and "abroad,"
it redefined the limits between national crimes under the exclusive jurisdiction of national authorities and those of "concern to the international community as a whole," which could also be investigated by the ICC. Leaders
would have to adjust their policies to these new legal limits.

From my office in The Hague, I perceived a lack of integration between
citizens' demand for justice, political decisions, peace negotiations, humanitarian assistance, judicial activities, and military operations to manage
conflicts like Darfur. There were no common protocols, with each actor following their own interests and different sets of rules. Darfur is a good example of the evolution and limits of legal systems. In 1945, there was no international criminal tribunal, no precedent or clear legal framework to
conduct international criminal cases against the Nazi leaders. Nuremberg was
created from this vacuum. In 1993 and 1994, the Nuremberg precedent, the
Genocide Convention, the Geneva Conventions, and a developed concept
of crimes against humanity supported the creation of Ad Hoc International Criminal Tribunals for the former Yugoslavia (ICTY) and for Rwanda
(ICTR). By the time the Darfur crimes started, a previous and detailed
body of international law had been officially adopted by the Rome Plenipo-
tentiary Conference. In other words, there was a vast jurisprudence already
developed by the ICTY and the ICTR, and a fully operational International
Criminal Court was up and running.

When I took office as the ICC's chief prosecutor in June 2003, the Darfur
atrocities were starting, and the United States was leading a military intervention in Iraq against the will of the majority of the UN Security Council.
In those days, our office did not even analyze the Darfur situation because
Sudan was out of our jurisdiction: Sudan has never been a state party to
the Rome Statute. The UN Security Council had the authority to establish

international criminal justice in Sudan, but there was no expectation that the United States would allow a constructive relationship between the council and the court. Therefore, witness K's rights could not receive the court's protection in 2003. We focused our efforts on the gravest situations under the state parties to the Rome Statute. In June and July 2004, we opened the first two investigations and started collecting evidence on alleged crimes against humanity and war crimes committed in the Democratic Republic of Congo (DRC) and in Uganda.

In March 2005, circumstances changed, and the UN Security Council referred the Darfur situation to the ICC. The process showed how the adoption of the Rome Statute transformed the dynamic of the UN Security Council without changing the UN Charter. Led by France, the nine state parties to the Rome Statute that were also members of the UN Security Council formed an immediate majority. U.S. cables started to identify this group as "ICC-9." The fact that nine of the fifteen members of the UN Security Council were also parties to the Rome Statute produced an immediate majority at the council, forcing the United States to adjust or to veto the resolution. A compromise was reached, and the resolution referring the Darfur situation to the ICC was adopted by eleven positive votes. The UN Security Council also commanded Sudan, a UN member, to cooperate with the ICC.

We opened an investigation in June 2005, and, after eighteen months of collecting evidence, the court issued arrest warrants against a Sudanese minister and a local commander for crimes against humanity and war crimes. In 2009, the ICC issued an arrest warrant against President Bashir of Sudan for the same crimes. In 2010, the charge of genocide was added. But our efforts were not enough to stop the crimes. Some experts argued that our intervention in Sudan was counterproductive.[6]

The Impact of the ICC Intervention in Darfur

The International Criminal Court decisions were adopted in full compliance with the Rome Statute. However, other actors, both national and international, following their own political and legal principles, made choices that defined the enforcement (or the lack of enforcement) and the outcome of the judicial efforts. Enforcing the ICC's decisions is not in the hands of the judges; it is the responsibility of the state parties to the Rome Statute. States parties to the Rome Statute are committed to enforcing ICC decisions in their own territory but have neither the duty nor the authority to intervene in Sudan to execute the arrest warrants. The UN Security Council has the authority to intervene in Sudan but decided to promote negotiations to end the conflict in Darfur without even mentioning the enforcement of its own resolutions. The peacekeeping forces in Darfur had no authority to implement the ICC arrest warrants.

The UN Security Council did not impose obligations on states not party to the Rome Statute, like the United States, to enforce the arrest warrants issued by the ICC in the Darfur situation. As a consequence, the United States had no legal obligations to enforce the arrest warrants issued by the ICC. Support for the ICC arrest warrants against President Bashir came from an unexpected source: President Bush. He was finishing his term in office and wanted to avoid criticism about his commitment to Darfur.[7] His special envoy, Ambassador Richard Williamson, used the threat of the pending arrest warrant to put pressure on the Sudanese government to allow the deployment of UN peacekeeping forces and increase humanitarian assistance. President Obama took advantage of the ICC arrest warrants against President Bashir to increase U.S. leverage in the negotiation with Sudan to end the conflict with South Sudan and to get Sudan's cooperation in the U.S. war on terror. As a consequence of the lack of integration between national and international efforts, the Darfur genocide has never stopped, and the extermination plan continued to be executed with the full knowledge of the international community. Most of the Fur people were removed by force and their land occupied by other groups. Darfuri women are still being raped, but the UN–African Union Mission in Darfur has denied such events and there seems to be no interest in attempting to change their fate.[8]

National Reasons to Ignore a Genocide

President Obama's decision to negotiate with Bashir was legal—he neither followed an ideological pattern nor expressed his personal values. He had a great commitment to the Darfuris, a commitment shared by many members of his team. That an administration staffed by individuals fully committed to the protection of the people of Darfur decided to negotiate with President Bashir, thus neglecting the commission of a genocide, exposes the influence of national interests and legal systems on international strategic decisions. President Obama's policy on Darfur prioritized values dictated by the U.S.

pragmatic National Security Strategy adopted in 2010: "We are supporting the ICC's prosecution of those cases that advance U.S. interests and values."[9] President Obama actively supported the ICC in such cases: His administration voted in favor of the UN Security Council's Libya referral and promised a reward to anyone who facilitated the arrest of Joseph Kony and the other members of the Lord's Resistance Army (LRA) in Uganda who were sought by the ICC. Indeed, two LRA fugitives, Dominic Ongwen and Bosco Ntaganda, were transferred to the ICC. The Obama administration's strategy in Sudan helped achieve the independence of South Sudan and increased President Bashir's support for the U.S. war on terror. In 2016, the CIA opened an office in Khartoum, and the Sudanese army began intervening in Yemen. By the end of his term, President Obama proposed to lift U.S. sanctions against Sudan. They were eventually lifted during the Trump administration on October 6, 2017.[10] President Bashir was finally removed by a coup d'état and arrested by Sudanese forces in 2019. It is not clear how Sudan's political changes will impact Darfur.

The Lack of a Global Reparations Model for Atrocity Crimes

Despite the establishment of normative principles for redress for victims of atrocity crimes, and international agreement on a wide-ranging humanitarian intervention policy known as the Responsibility to Protect, victims are not afforded legal rights that can be independently enforced under international law.[11] In March 2006, the UN General Assembly adopted by consensus the "Basic Principles and Guidelines on the Right to a Remedy and Reparation for Victims of Gross Violations of International Human Rights Law and Serious Violations of International Humanitarian Law." These principles recognize the right to a remedy for an individual who suffered injury as a result of gross international human rights violations or serious international humanitarian law violations.[12]

Louise Arbour, the UN High Commissioner for Human Rights, produced in 2008 a comprehensive report identifying "the challenges faced by reparations programs." The report affirmed that "the legal basis for a right to a remedy and reparations became firmly enshrined in the elaborate corpus of human rights instruments," but it also recognized that implementing this right is "in essence a matter of domestic law and policy."[13] The victims are at the mercy of their national state. The most relevant international mechanisms for victim reparations are provided by regional human rights treaties such as the European Court of Human Rights and the Inter-American Court of Human Rights, as well as the recently established African Commission on Human and Peoples' Rights. They have opened the door for a significant number of victims of atrocity crimes who are citizens of states party to these treaties to seek reparations from their respective states. The Rome Statute adds the possibility of obtaining compensation from perpetrators convicted by the ICC. The court has the authority to trace, freeze, and seize perpetrators' assets. Article 75 of the Rome Statute establishes that "the Court may make an order directly against a convicted person specifying appropriate reparations" and that these may be paid to the Trust Fund created by article 79 to manage collective reparations programs. Even though ad hoc international criminal tribunals were given the authority to order restitutions, the judges at the ICTY and the ICTR were unwilling to use their powers to do so.[14]

Concluding Reflections on the Way Forward

The Rome Statute model is deeply rooted in the civil law tradition of allowing a few victims to seek reparations in the course of criminal proceedings against a limited number of defendants. But the crimes under the jurisdiction of the ICC include hundreds or thousands of perpetrators and thousands or millions of victims. As a consequence, the ICC prosecutor has to select a few incidents and defendants in each case in order to carry out efficient investigations and allow an expeditious trial respecting the rights of the defendants. For instance, in the first trial against Thomas Lubanga, charges focused on the policy to deliberately recruit children and to use them in hostilities. The court convicted Lubanga and decided that to be eligible for reparations, victims would have to demonstrate to the court direct or indirect harm and that it arose from the specific crimes charged in a case against the accused.[15] The majority of victims, however, suffer from crimes charged only as part of a collective—not personally—or who suffer personally from specific crimes not charged against the accused. Therefore, they would not fall within the scope of the proceedings and have no right to be considered for judicial reparations.

The ICC could define a different model. In accordance with Article 75, the "Court shall establish principles relating to reparations to, or in respect of, victims, including restitution, compensation and rehabilitation" and, where appropriate, "order that the award for reparations be made through the Trust Fund provided for in Article 79." The Trust Fund's dual mandate is to implement court-ordered reparations and provide assistance to victims within the court's jurisdiction, irrespective of their eligibility to judicial reparations in a case. The Trust Fund suggests that the determination of eligibility does not require an individual assessment of victims' "claims," a process that it thinks "damages and re-traumatizes victims." It proposes that the assessment should instead take place during the implementation of actual awards, relying on the administrative mandate of the Trust Fund rather than on an adversarial process defined by the Chambers.[16]

Article 68 of the Rome Statute provides that the victims have the right to present "their views and concerns" during different stages of the proceedings. This right opens up the opportunity to provide reparations to the entire community, including the creation of so-called spaces of memory. In this setting, judges would decide on the individual responsibility of the accused, but the trials' relevance for the victims, including in establishing the truth, presenting their views and concerns, and promoting a different culture, would spread beyond the courtroom to a broader communication space with the capacity to influence public perceptions about mass crimes and about the scope for reparatory justice. For instance, ten years after the Nuremberg Trials, movies like *The Diary of Anne Frank* (1955) and *Judgment at Nuremberg* (1961) had a significant impact on the public narrative.

I personally experienced the relevance of public narratives during my work in Argentina as deputy prosecutor in the trial of the juntas. Though I was leading the investigation, I failed to convince my own mother during our discussions at her house that the junta members should be prosecuted. She thought the generals were protecting her from the guerrillas and that I was totally wrong. She loved General Videla. She went to church with him and he reminded her of my grandfather, who was also a Genera. It was only by reading the witnesses' firsthand accounts of the torture and other violations they had been subjected to that she changed her perception of the dictatorship. What I failed to do for my mother during the investigations was accomplished by the public communications that took place during the court hearings. She changed her mind after the beginning of the trial, following the case through the newspapers. Two weeks into the trial, she called me and said: "I still love General Videla, but you are right. He has to be in jail." Her reaction showed me how public information about the respectful judicial ritual of exposing the suffering of the victims can influence the perception of the "truth," blurring the scholarly distinctions between punitive and restorative justice.

Invisible Children, a since-rebranded NGO led by young activists from San Diego, produced the video "Kony 2012" to support the enforcement of the arrest warrant issued by the ICC against Joseph Kony. The online video reached 120 million Internet viewers in merely six days, more than the ICC's outreach program could ever dream of.[17] Though not without controversy, Invisible Children lobbied the African Union and the governments of Uganda, the DRC, and the Central African Republic to promote arrest operations, and the U.S. Congress to pass the Lord's Resistance Army Disarmament and Northern Uganda Recovery Act, promoting U.S. military efforts to stop Joseph Kony.[18] As a consequence of Invisible Children's activities, the U.S. Congress agreed in January 2013 to include the ICC in the "reward for justice program," offering financial incentives for the arrest of Kony.[19] U.S. efforts led to the surrender of Dominic Ongwen, one of the LRA commanders, and forced Joseph Kony to go into hiding in the Sudan.

Another strategy for allowing victims of conflict-related mass atrocity to claim redress independently is to allow them to have recourse to the existing civil judicial mechanisms, putting them on an equal footing with victims of any other domestic crime. This would give victims access to procedures that already exist to assess, process, and enforce such claims and enable states to strengthen the implementation of international norms against atrocity crimes—norms that most states have agreed to uphold. One way to accomplish this is through a civil reparation model based on universal jurisdiction. For instance, Articles 9b and 9c of the Dutch Code of Civil Procedure provide a legal basis for the jurisdiction of Dutch courts in situations where victims have a sufficient connection to the Dutch legal sphere and lack any other legal forum in which to have their case adjudicated.[20]

In a groundbreaking precedent, in March 2012, a Dutch court awarded €1 million in compensation to a Palestinian doctor who was imprisoned in Libya for eight years for allegedly infecting children with HIV/AIDS. Ashraf al-Hajuj, a Netherlands resident, was pardoned by Libya, along with five Bulgarian nurses, in 2007. He sued twelve Libyan officials for involvement in his torture and inhumane treatment under the principle of universal jurisdiction under Dutch law, in what was the first use of the principle.[21] Provided defendants have accessible assets, victims of atrocity crimes may obtain monetary reparations.

David Kennedy proposes the creation of a new global social contract: "The sensibility I have in mind requires a sense for the urgency and drama of the times: a sense that this is, indeed, 1648. A time when things are being remade in ways it is difficult to understand at first."[22]

Scholars committed to victim reparations should make the development of a new global strategy to prevent new massive atrocities a priority. Pursuing civil reparations cases against those who finance conflicts that generate these atrocities could have an impact similar to the nineteenth-century campaign to end the slave trade.[23]

POSTSCRIPT

Mary T. Bassett

The essays in this wide-ranging volume have raised many questions related to the ongoing legacy of past state injustice. A recurring theme is the persistence of violence, stigma, and marginalization into the present day as evidence of continued harm. Why do the indigenous of the Americas, citizens of former colonies, descendants of enslaved Africans, and the Roma all live less healthy and shorter lives? The connection between health and people's rights is indisputable, captured most starkly by the large differences in how long a person can expect to live. Depending on what country and, within any given country, depending on parentage and place, life expectancy can vary by twenty years or more. That is a generation's worth of years lost. These gaps between and within nations are neither natural nor inevitable, but rather reflect both historic and contemporary injustices—including crimes against humanity.

This volume of essays has explored the idea that reparations are due for slavery and colonialism. As it notes, there is precedent. A reckoning with the Nazi Holocaust, the U.S. World War II policy of internment of people of Japanese ancestry, British colonial atrocities against the Mau Mau, South African victims of Apartheid, and New Zealand's violation of Maori rights all led to financial compensation. The Caribbean Reparations Commission, established under the auspices of national governments through the Caricom, has declared a state interest in reparations for both the indigenous and descendants of the enslaved and will pursue national claims. The stance of the U.S. government, by contrast, has been dismissive. Those who are skeptical note that 150 years have passed since the end of slavery, it is hard to figure out how much 250 years of uncompensated labor would be worth and how any such contemporary financial compensation would be administered. Yet, more than 400 years after the first captured Africans were transported to Jamestown, Virginia, slavery's legacy continues to be written on the bodies of people of African descent, evident in shorter, less healthy lives. However long ago, the ideology and practice of white supremacy that created racialized groups of human beings continues to benefit those considered white. In the words of the late Manning Marable, reparations are not about guilt, but about responsibility.

This volume contributes to an honest discussion of the moral challenge of racism. Addressing this legacy will carry a financial cost, one too long borne by the marginalized. As these essays have so clearly attested, the need for a reckoning, for reparatory justice, will not go away.

NOTES

Introduction

1. UN General Assembly, Resolution 1021, Convention on the Prevention and Punishment of the Crime of Genocide, Art. 1 (December 9, 1948).

2. Quoted in Giles Harvey, "Spain's Most Celebrated Writer Believes the Fascist Past Is Still Present," *New York Times Magazine*, August 1, 2019, https://www.nytimes.com/2019/08/01/magazine/javier-marias-spanish-literature.html.

3. See Samuels, Chapter 4 in this volume.

4. See Khalidi, Chapter 11 in this volume.

5. See Ocampo, Chapter 17 in this volume.

6. See Chapter 7 by Elkins and Chapter 10 by Immler.

7. See Immler (Chapter 10), Fanon Mendes (Chapter 6), and Matache and Bhabha (Chapter 15) in this volume.

8. See Chapter 10 by Immler in this volume.

9. See Chapter 1 by Mutua in this volume.

10. See particularly Chapter 7 by Elkins and Chapter 13 by Slyomovics in this volume.

11. See Fanon Mendes (Chapter 6) in this volume. See also Linda Franke, *Repair: Redeeming the Promise of Abolition* (Chicago: Haymarket Books, 2019).

12. Michael J. Bazyler, *Holocaust Justice: The Battle for Restitution in America's Courts* (New York: New York University Press, 2003; Seth Mydans, "11 Years, $300 Million and 3 Convictions: Was the Khmer Rouge Tribunal Worth It?," *New York Times*, April 10, 2017. See also Grant Peck, "Experts Weigh the Record of Cambodia's Khmer Rouge Tribunal," *WSFA News*, November 17, 2018, accessed December 11, 2018, https://www.wsfa.com/2018/11/17/experts-weigh-record-cambodia-khmer-rouge-tribunal.

13. Rakesh Kocchar and Anthony Cilluffo, "How Wealth Inequality Has Changed in the U.S. since the Great Recession, by Race, Ethnicity and Income," Pew Research Center, November 7, 2017, https://www.pewresearch.org/fact-tank/2017/11/01/how-wealth-inequality-has-changed-in-the-u-s-since-the-great-recession-by-race-ethnicity-and-income/.

14. See Hancock in this volume for the comparison between Jewish and Roma Holocaust survivors. See also Mutua for a similar argument in relation to reparations for the European Holocaust as opposed to slavery.

15. "5/10: Reparations for Slavery in the United States?," Marist Poll, May 10, 2016, http://maristpoll.marist.edu/510-reparations-for-slavery-in-the-united-states /#sthash.GLS86F9Q.JqamrkpX.dpbs; "Overwhelming opposition to reparations for slavery and Jim Crow" YouGov, June 2, 2014, https://today.yougov.com/topics/politics /articles-reports/2014/06/02/reparations.

16. David Remnick, "Ta-Nehisi Coates Revisits the Case for Reparations," *New Yorker,* June 10, 2019, https://www.newyorker.com/news/the-new-yorker-interview/ta -nehisi-coates-revisits-the-case-for-reparations.

17. I am grateful to Mary Bassett for suggesting this point.

18. Remnick, "Ta-Nehisi Coates Revisits the Case for Reparations."

19. Emma Jacobs, "Across Europe Museums Rethink What to Do with Their African Art Collections," *NPR*, August 12, 2019, https://www.npr.org/2019/08/12/750549303 /across-europe-museums-rethink-what-to-do-with-their-african-art-collections.

20. Milan Schreuer, "Belgium Apologizes for Kidnapping Children from African Colonies," *New York Times*, April 4, 2019, https://www.nytimes.com/2019/04/04/world /europe/belgium-kidnapping-congo-rwanda-burundi.html.

21. Doug Bolton, "Dr. Shashi Tharoor Tells the Oxford Union Why Britain Owes Reparations for Colonising India in Viral Speech," *The Independent,* July 22, 2015, https://www.independent.co.uk/news/uk/home-news/dr-shashi-tharoor-tells-the -oxford-union-why-britain-owes-reparations-for-colonising-india-in-viral-10407997 .html.

22. "Reparatory Justice for Global Black Enslavement: The Greatest Political Movement of the 21st Century," Warren Center/WIGH Seminar with Sir Hilary Beckles at Harvard Law School, February 22, 2016.

23. "CARICOM Reparations Commission," 2019, http://caricomreparations.org, May 5, 2020.

24. "20 Million Pounds Caribbean Reparations Agreement," The University of the West Indies: Open Campus, August 17, 2019, https://www.open.uwi.edu/%C2%A320 -million-caribbean-reparations-agreement.

25. John Anusavice, "State Sponsored Collective Injustice: Reparations for Roma," Harvard FXB Center for Health and Human Rights, April 22, 2016, https://fxb.harvard .edu/2016/04/22/state-sponsored-collective-injustice-reparations-for-roma/.

26. Margareta Matache and Jacqueline Bhabha, "Roma Slavery: The Case for Reparations," *Foreign Policy in Focus*, April 22, 2016, https://fpif.org/roma-slavery-case -reparations/.

27. John Torpey, *Making Whole What Has Been Smashed* (New Brunswick: Rutgers University Press, 2017), 42.

28. Susan Neiman, *Learning from the Germans: Race and the Memory of Evil* (New York: Farrar, Straus and Giroux, 2019).

29. UN General Assembly, Resolution 60/147, Basic Principles and Guidelines on the Right to a Remedy and Reparation for Victims of Gross Violations of International Human Rights Law and Serious Violations of International Humanitarian Law, A/RES/60/147 (March 21, 2006).

Chapter 1. Reparations for Slavery

1. Laura Brace, *The Politics of Property: Freedom and Belonging* (Edinburgh: Edinburgh University Press, 2004), 162.

2. "Emancipation Proclamation (Presidential Proclamation 95), an Executive Order Issued by President Abraham Lincoln" (National Archives, January 1, 1863), https://www.archives.gov/exhibits/featured-documents/emancipation-proclamation; "Constitution of the United States of America, Amendment XIII," December 18, 1865.

3. Randall Robinson, *The Debt: What America Owes to Blacks* (New York: Penguin, 2001).

4. Richard Reeves, *Infamy: The Shocking Story of the Internment of Japanese American Internment in World War II* (London: Picador, 2016).

5. Kurt Schwerin, "German Compensation for Victims of Nazi Persecution," *Northwestern University Law Review* 63 (1972): 479–527; "Germany to Pay Holocaust Victims New Compensation," *BBC News,* May 29, 2013, https://www.bbc.com/news/world-europe-22707483.

6. Caroline Elkins, *Imperial Reckoning: The Untold Story of Britain's Gulag in Kenya* (New York: Henry Holt, 2005).

7. "UK to Compensate Kenya's Mau Mau Torture Victims," *Guardian,* June 6, 2013, https://www.theguardian.com/world/2013/jun/06/uk-compensate-kenya-mau-mau-torture.

8. Ibid.

9. Ibid.

10. Ibid.

11. "Britain to Compensate Kenya Mau Mau for Colonial-Era Abuse," *Daily Nation*, June 6, 2013, https://nation.africa/kenya/news/world/britain-to-compensate-kenya-mau-mau-for-colonial-era-abuse--867332.

12. Moses Nyamori, "Mau Mau Memorial Monument Unveiled in Nairobi," *Daily Nation*, September 13, 2015, https://www.standardmedia.co.ke/article/2000176118/mau-mau-memorial-monument-unveiled-in-nairobi.

13. "Herero and Nama Groups Sue Germany over Namibia Genocide," *BBC News*, January 6, 2018, http://www.bbc.com/news/world-us-canada-38530594.

14. Stephen Badsey, *The Franco-Prussian War 1870–1871* (Oxford: Osprey Publishing, 2003).

15. Indian Claims Reparations, "Final Report of the United States Indian Claims Commission," H.R. Doc. No. 96–383 (1980); Eric Yamamoto, "Racial Reparations: Japanese American Redress and African American Claims," *Boston College Law Review* 40 (1998): 477–524.

16. Eric Posner and Adrian Vermeule, "Reparations for Slavery and Other Historical Injustices," *Columbia Law Review* 103 (2003): 689–746.

17. Ana Lucia Araujo, *Reparations for Slavery and the Slave Trade: A Transnational and Comparative History* (London: Bloomsbury Academic, 2017); Bris Bittker, *The Case for Black Reparations* (Boston: Beacon Press, 2003).

18. Stephanie Zacharek, Eliana Dockterman, and Haley Sweetland Edwards, "TIME Person of the Year 2017: The Silence Breakers," *Time*, December 6, 2017, http://time.com/time-person-of-the-year-2017-silence-breakers/.

19. Makau Mutua, "The Complexity of Universalism in Human Rights," in *Human Rights with Modesty: The Problem of Universalism*, ed. Andras Sajo (Leiden: Martinus Nijhoff Publishers, 2004), 51–64.

20. United Nations, Charter of the International Military Tribunal, Annex to the Agreement for the Prosecution and Punishment of the Major War Criminals of the European Axis (London Agreement), August 8, 1945, 59 Stat. 1544, E.A.S. No. 472, 82 U.N.T.S. 280, https://www.refworld.org/docid/3ae6b39614.html.

21. Telford Taylor, *Nuremburg Trials: War Crimes and International Law*, (New York City, NY: Carnegie Endowment for International Peace, 1949); Theodore Meron, *War Crimes Law Comes of Age: Essays* (Oxford: Oxford University Press, 1998).

22. Charter of the International Military Tribunal, Art. 6(c).

23. Alpheus Thomas Mason, *Harlan Fiske Stone: Pillar of the Law* (New York: Viking Press, 1956), 715–716.

24. Jehuda Reinharz, *Chaim Weizmann: The Making of a Zionist Leader* (Chicago: University of Chicago Press, 1985).

25. Francis Biddle, "The Nurnberg Trial," *Virginia Law Review* 33 (1947): 679–696.

26. W. D. Rubinstein, *Genocide: A History* (London: Routledge, 2004).

27. Lord Mackay of Clashfern, *Halsbury's Laws of England*, 4th ed. (London: LexisNexis, 2003).

28. UN General Assembly, Resolution 2391 (XXIIII), Convention on the Non-Applicability of Statutory Limitations to War Crimes and Crimes Against Humanity, (Adopted and opened for signature, ratification, and accession on November 26, 1968; Entry into force on November 11, 1970).

29. International Criminal Court, Rome Statute of the International Criminal Court, July 17, 1998, Art. 29, https://www.icc-cpi.int/nr/rdonlyres/ea9aeff7-5752-4f84-be94-0a655eb30e16/0/rome_statute_english.pdf.

30. UN General Assembly, Resolution 2202 A XXI, The Policies of Apartheid of the Government of the Republic of South Africa (December 16, 1966).

31. UN Security Council, Resolution 556, Demanding the Immediate Eradication of Apartheid (October 23, 1984).

32. United Nations, International Convention on the Suppression and Punishment of the Crime of Apartheid (July 18, 1976), http://www.un.org/en/genocideprevention/documents/atrocity-crimes/Doc.10_International%20Convention%20on%20the%20

Suppression%20and%20Punishment%20of%20the%20Crime%20of%20Apartheid
.pdf. Hereafter, the Apartheid Convention.

33. John Dugard, "Convention on the Suppression and Punishment of the Crime of Apartheid," United Nations Audiovisual Library of International Law (2008), http://legal.un.org/avl/pdf/ha/cspca/cspca_e.pdf.

34. Apartheid Convention, Art. 1.

35. Suhas Chakma, "The Issue of Compensation for Colonialism and Slavery at the World Conference against Racism," in *Human Rights in Development Yearbook 2001: Reparations: Redressing Past Wrongs*, ed. Louise Krabbe Boserup and George Ulrich (Leiden: Martinus Nijhoff, 2003), 58–71.

36. Declaration of the World Conference Against Racism, Racial Discrimination, Xenophobia, and Related Intolerance, September 2001 (South Africa), https://www.un.org/WCAR/durban.pdf, paragraph 13 (emphasis added).

37. Jullyette Ukabiala, "Slave Trade a Crime against Humanity: Historic Declaration at Anti-Racism Conference, but Africans Urge More," *Africa Renewal* (formerly: *Africa Recovery*) 15, no.13 (2001): 5.

38. Ibid.

39. Ibid.

40. Michael Stothard, "Macron Calls France's Colonial Past a 'Crime Against Humanity,'" *Financial Times*, February 17, 2017, https://www.ft.com/content/87d6f430-f521-11e6-95ee-f14e55513608.

41. See Henry Louis Gates Jr., "The Truth Behind 'Forty Acres and a Mule,'" *The Root,* January 7, 2013.

42. Rhonda V. Magee, "The Master's Tools, From the Bottom Up: Responses to African-American Reparations Theory in Mainstream and Outsider Discourse," *Virginia Law Review* 79 (1993): 889–916.

43. Gary Moore, *Rosewood: The Full Story* (Yuma, AZ: Manantial Press, 2015).

44. Lori Robinson, "Righting a Wrong Among Black Americans: The Debate Is Escalating over Whether an Apology for Slavery Is Enough," *Seattle Intelligencer,* June 29, 1997.

45. The White House, "Remarks by the President in Apology for the Study Done in Tuskegee," May 16, 1997, https://clintonwhitehouse4.archives.gov/textonly/New/Remarks/Fri/19970516-898.html.

46. Indian Claims Reparations, "Final Report of the United States Indian Claims Commission," 107 Stat. 1510, S. J. Res. 19 (enacted November 23, 1993) (the so-called Apology Resolution).

47. Final Report of Indian Claims Commission, H. R. Doc. 96-383 (1980).

48. "Alaska Native Claims Settlement Act of 1971," 43 U.S.C § 1601 (1998); John F. Walsh, "Settling the Alaska Native Claims Settlement Act," *Stanford Law Review* 38 (1985): 227–263.

49. Indian Claims Reparations, "Final Report of the United States Indian Claims Commission."

50. Martin Plaut, "Should Arab Countries Pay Reparations for Slavery Too?," *New Statesman,* August 21, 2013.

51. Gwyn Campbell, *The Structure of Slavery in Indian Ocean Africa and Asia* (London: Routledge, 2003), ix.

52. Kevin Mwachiro, "Remembering the East African Slave Raids," BBC News, March 30, 2007, http://news.bbc.co.uk/2/hi/africa/6510675.stm.

53. Ali A. Mazrui, "Black Africa and the Arabs," *Foreign Affairs,* July 1975.

54. "Gaddafi Apologizes for Arab Slave Traders," *Press TV,* October 11, 2010, http://previous.presstv.ir/detail.aspx?id=146302&sectionid=351020506.

55. Ricardo Rene Laremont, "Political versus Legal Strategies for the African Slavery Reparations Movement," *African Studies Quarterly* 2, no. 13 (1999): 13–17.

56. "Africa Trillions Demanded in Slavery Reparations," *BBC News,* August 20, 1999, http://news.bbc.co.uk/2/hi/africa/424984.stm.

57. Anton La Guardia, "African Rift for Calls over Slavery Reparations," *The Telegraph,* London, August 11, 2001.

58. "Analysis: UN Conference in Tatters," *BBC News,* September 3, 2001. http://news.bbc.co.uk/2/hi/africa/1523905.stm.

59. Tom Leonard and Simon Tomlinson, "14 Caribbean Nations Sue European Countries for Slavery Reparations," *Daily Mail,* London, October 10, 2013.

60. For more information about the Caribbean Reparations Commission, see http://caricomreparations.org/.

61. Ed Pilkington, "Caribbean Nations Prepare Demand for Reparations," *Guardian,* March 9, 2014.

62. David Love, "America Has Compensated Other Groups, but Obama Opposes Reparations for Black People. Why?," *Atlanta Black Star,* December 29, 2016.

63. Shaun King, "If President Obama Is Against Reparations, Blasting Bernie Sanders for the Same Stance Is Insincere," *New York Daily News,* January 22, 2016.

64. "Obama Opposes Reparations for Slavery," Associated Press, August 2, 2008.

65. Ta-Nehisi Coates, "The Case for Reparations," *Atlantic,* June 2014.

66. United Nations General Assembly, "Report of the Working Group of Experts on People of African Descent on Its Mission to the United States," A/HRC/33/61/Add.2 (August 18, 2016), paras. 91, 94, https://documents-dds-ny.un.org/doc/UNDOC/GEN/G16/183/30/PDF/G1618330.pdf?OpenElement.

67. Pamela Falk, "Should US Pay Reparations for Slavery? UN-Appointed Experts Think So," *CBS News,* September 27, 2016, https://www.cbsnews.com/news/should-us-pay-reparations-for-slavery-united-nations-working-groups-think-so/.

68. Haroon Siddique, "Slavery Reparations Calls Will Not Go Away, David Cameron Told," *Guardian,* September 29, 2015.

69. Charles Dickens, *Oliver Twist* (New York: Schocken Books, 1970), 489.

70. Makau Mutua, "Hope and Despair for a New South Africa: The Limits of the Rights Discourse," *Harvard Human Rights Journal* 10 (1997): 63–114; Greg A. Graham,

Democratic Political Tragedy in the Postcolony: The Tragedy of Postcoloniality in Michael Manley's Jamaica and Nelson Mandela's South Africa (New York: Routledge, 2017).

71. Ibrahim J. Gassama, "Reaffirming Faith in the Dignity of Each Human Being: The United Nations, NGOs, and Apartheid," *Fordham International Law Journal* 19 (1996), 1540.

72. Karl Klare, "Legal Theory and Democratic Reconstruction: Reflections on 1989," *University of British Columbia Law Review* 25, no. 69 (1991): 101.

73. Alan Freeman, "Racism, Rights and the Quest for Equality of Opportunity: A Critical Essay," *Harvard Civil Rights Civil Liberties Law Review* 23 (1988), (295–392).

74. Makau Mutua, "Putting Humpty Dumpty Back Together Again: The Dilemmas of the African Post-Colonial State," *Brooklyn Journal of International Law* 21 (1995): 505–36.

75. Tracy, "European Nations Attempt to Evade Reparations Lawsuit, but Caricom May Gain Political Leverage," *Atlanta Black Star,* January 13, 2014, http://atlantablackstar .com/2014/01/13/europe-nations-attempt-evade-reparations-lawsuit-caricom-may -gain-political-leverage/.

76. Conal Wash, "Slave Descendants Sue Lloyd's for Billions," *Guardian,* March 27, 2014, https://www.theguardian.com/money/2004/mar/28/insurance.usnews.

77. Gavin Stamp, "Counting the Cost of the Slave Trade," *BBC News,* March 20, 2007, http://news.bbc.co.uk/2/hi/business/6422721.stm.

78. Plessy v. Ferguson, 163 U.S. 537 (1896); Brown v. Board of Education, 347 U.S. 483 (1954); Grutter v. Bollinger, 539 U.S. 306 (2003).

79. Korematsu v. United States, 323 U.S. 214 (1944); Executive Order 9066, February 19, 1942. Public L. 77-503 56 Stat. 173, enacted and signed into law by March 21, 1942, by President Franklin D. Roosevelt, enforced Executive Order 9066.

80. Korematsu v. United States 584 F. Supp. 1406 (N. D. Cal. 1984); Hirabayashi v. United States 828 F. 2nd 591 (9th Cir. 1987). *Coram nobis* is a writ that allows a court to correct an original judgment because of the discovery of a fundamental error that, had it been known, would have changed the outcome of case.

81. CWRIC, *Personal Justice Denied: Report of the Commission on Wartime Relocation and Internment of Civilians* (Seattle: University of Washington Press, 1997).

82. Yamamoto, "Racial Reparations," 477.

83. Michelle Alexander, *The New Jim Crow: Mass Incarceration in the Age of Colorblindness* (New York: New Press, 2012).

84. Posner and Vermeule, "Reparations for Slavery."

85. Randall Kennedy, *For Discrimination: Race, Affirmative Action, and the Law* (New York: Vintage, 2015).

86. Coates, "The Case for Reparations."

87. Mari Matsuda, "Looking to the Bottom: Critical Legal Studies and Reparations," *Harvard Civil Rights and Civil Liberties Law Review* 22 (1987): 323–400.

88. David Frum, "The Impossibility of Reparations," *Atlantic*, June 3, 2014.

89. Peter Viles, "Suit Seeks Billions in Slave Reparations," *CNN*, March 27, 2002, http://www.cnn.com/2002/LAW/03/26/slavery.reparations/index.html.

90. *In re* African-American Slave Descendants Litigation, MDL No. 1491, No. 02 C 7764 (U.S. Dist. Ct, N.D. Illinois, Eastern Div. 2005).

91. *In re* African-American Slave Descendants Litigation, Appeals of Deadria Farmer-Paellmann et al. and Timothy Hurdle et al., 471 F.3d 754 (7th Cir. 2006).

92. "Macron Launches Slavery Remembrance Foundation," Africa Diplomatic, April 28, 2018, https://africadiplomatic.com/2018/04/28/macron-launches-slavery-remembrance-foundation/.

93. "Blair 'Sorry' for UK Slavery Role," *BBC News*, March 14, 2007, http://news.bbc.co.uk/2/hi/uk_news/politics/6451793.stm.

94. H. Res. 194 (110th), "Apologizing for the Enslavement and Racial Segregation of African Americans," July 29, 2008.

95. S. Con. Res. 26 (111th), "Apologizing for the Enslavement and Racial Segregation of African Americans," June 18, 2009.

96. Dana Owens, "Veteran Congressman Still Pushing for Reparations in a Divided America," *NBC News*, February 20, 2017, https://www.nbcnews.com/news/nbcblk/rep-john-conyers-still-pushing-reparations-divided-america-n723151.

97. Laremont, "Political versus Legal Strategies."

Chapter 2. Slavery, Universities, and Reparations

1. John J. DeGioia, "Remarks at the Liturgy of Remembrance, Contrition, and Hope," April 18, 2017, https://president.georgetown.edu/liturgy-remembrance-contrition-hope-remarks-april-2017.

2. Becky Sindelar, "Society of Jesus Apologizes for the Sins of Jesuit Slaveholding at Georgetown University Liturgy," April 18, 2017, https://www.jesuits.org/stories/society-of-jesus-apologizes-for-the-sins-of-jesuit-slaveholding-at-georgetown-university-liturgy/.

3. Mark Zimmerman, "Georgetown Renaming of Buildings Reflects Shared Journey with Slave Descendants," *Crux*, April 20, 2017, https://cruxnow.com/church-in-the-usa/2017/04/georgetown-renaming-buildings-reflects-shared-journey-slave-descendants/.

4. The landmark study is Craig Steven Wilder, *Ebony and Ivy: Race, Slavery, and the Troubled History of America's Universities* (New York: Bloomsbury Press, 2013).

5. For a cautionary argument about the perils of dredging up the past, see David Rieff, *In Praise of Forgetting: Historical Memory and Its Ironies* (New Haven, CT: Yale University Press, 2016).

6. John J. DeGioia, "Announcing the Working Group on Slavery, Memory and Reconciliation," September 24, 2015, https://president.georgetown.edu/messages/slavery-memory-reconciliation-working-group.

7. On Jesuit slaveholding in Maryland, see Thomas Murphy, *Jesuit Slaveholding in Maryland, 1717–1838* (New York: Routledge, 2001). For an example of Jesuit rationalizations for slavery, see Nicole von Germeten, *Treatise on Slavery: Selections from De instauranda Aethiopum salute* (Indianapolis, IN: Hackett Publishing, 2008), 51–52. On the transition from indentured servitude to slavery in the Chesapeake, see Ira Berlin, *Generations of Captivity: A History of African-American Slaves* (Cambridge, MA: Harvard University Press, 2003), 55–67.

8. Robert Emmett Curran, *Shaping American Catholicism: Maryland and New York, 1805–1915* (Washington, DC: Catholic University of America Press, 2012), chap. 2; Craig Steven Wilder, "War and Priests: Catholic Colleges and Slavery in the Age of Revolutions," in *Slavery's Capitalism: A New History of American Economic Development*, ed. Sven Beckert and Seth Rockman (Philadelphia: University of Pennsylvania Press, 2016), chap. 11. Curran, a longtime faculty member in Georgetown's History Department and author of Georgetown's bicentennial history, wrote extensively on Georgetown, the Jesuits, and slavery. Current research builds on his foundation. Present value figures are derived from MeasuringWorth.com, https://www.measuringworth.com/index.php, accessed May 22, 2019. The sum of $3.2 million is derived by multiplying $115,000 by the percentage increase of the Consumer Price Index since 1838, whereas $1.47 billion is the "economic share" of $115,000 in 1838 relative to today's GDP. The Society of Jesus was suppressed by Pope Clement XIV in 1773, and the Maryland Jesuits lodged their property in an entity called the Corporation of Roman Catholic Clergymen. The corporation continued to own the Jesuits' land and slaves after the society was restored in 1814.

9. I.A.1.a, Ledger A 1, 1789–1793, Georgetown College Financial Records: Vault Collection, Georgetown University Archives, http://slaveryarchive.georgetown.edu/items/show/70.

10. I.A.2.e, [Journal G?], May 18, 1838 - January 15, 1840, 1852–1875, Georgetown College Financial Records: Vault Collection, Georgetown University Archives, http://slaveryarchive.georgetown.edu/items/show/108.

11. John McElroy Diary, January 1, 1814, John McElroy, SJ Papers, Georgetown University Library Booth Family Center for Special Collections, Washington D.C., http://slaveryarchive.georgetown.edu/items/show/24.

12. John McElroy Diary, August 17, 1817, John McElroy, SJ Papers, Georgetown University Library Booth Family Center for Special Collections, Washington D.C., http://slaveryarchive.georgetown.edu/items/show/28.

13. Jonathan Marrow, "'Let Us Form a Body Guard for Liberty': Conceptions of Liberty and Nation in Georgetown College's Philodemic Society, 1830–1875," History Honors Thesis, Georgetown University, 2018, https://repository.library.georgetown.edu/handle/10822/1050614.

14. "Meeting of the Roman Catholic Congregations of the City of Richmond and County of Henrico," *Richmond Examiner*, September 4, 1835, http://slaveryarchive.georgetown.edu/items/show/88.

15. R. Emmett Curran, *Bicentennial History of Georgetown University,* vol. 1, *From Academy to University, 1789–1889* (Washington, DC: Georgetown University Press, 1993), chap. 9.

16. James O'Toole, *Passing for White: Race, Religion, and the Healy Family, 1820–1920* (Amherst: University of Massachusetts Press, 2002); Elizabeth Garbitelli, "First Black Undergraduate Dies," *The Hoya,* March 28, 2012, https://www.thehoya.com/first -black-undergraduate-dies/.

17. For a remarkable report by University of Glasgow researchers that follows the university's money trail back to slavery, see Stephen Mullen and Simon Newman, "Slavery, Abolition and the University of Glasgow: Report and Recommendations of the University of Glasgow History of Slavery Steering Committee," September 2018, https:// www.gla.ac.uk/schools/humanities/slavery/report2018/#d.en.606332. For the Universities Studying Slavery member schools, see President's Commission on Slavery and the University, Universities Studying Slavery, https://slavery.virginia.edu/universities -studying-slavery/, accessed May 22, 2019.

18. Lindsey K. Walters, "Slavery and the American University: Discourses of Retrospective Justice at Harvard and Brown," *Slavery and Abolition* 38, no. 4 (2017): 719–44.

19. Toby Hung, "DeGioia Approves Renaming of Mulledy, McSherry Halls," *The Hoya,* November 14, 2015, http://www.thehoya.com/degioia-approves-renaming-of -mulledy-mcsherry-halls/.

20. Rachel Swarns, "272 Slaves Were Sold To Save Georgetown. What Does It Owe Their Descendants," *New York Times,* April 16, 2016, https://www.nytimes.com/2016 /04/17/us/georgetown-university-search-for-slave-descendants.html.

21. "Report of the Working Group on Slavery, Memory, and Reconciliation to the President of Georgetown University," Washington, DC, Summer 2016, http://slavery .georgetown.edu/report/.

22. Nick Anderson, "At Georgetown University, a Family Reunion 178 Years After Fateful Slave Sale," *Washington Post,* September 2, 2016, https://www.washingtonpost .com/news/grade-point/wp/2016/09/02/at-georgetown-a-family-reunion-178-years -after-fateful-slave-sale/.

23. Susan Svrluga, "Descendants of Slaves Sold to Benefit Georgetown Call for a $1 Billion Foundation for Reconciliation," *Washington Post,* September 9, 2016, https:// www.washingtonpost.com/news/grade-point/wp/2016/09/08/descendants-of-slaves -sold-by-georgetown-call-for-a-1-billion-foundation-for-reconciliation/.

24. "Georgetown to Rename Building for Isaac Hawkins, One of 272 Enslaved in 1838 Sale," Georgetown University, April 13, 2017, https://www.georgetown.edu/news /isaac-hawkins-hall. For Isaac's fate, see Grivel to Lancaster, May 4, 1839, Correspondence [212 G0-11], 03/02/1839-06/22/1839. Archives of the Maryland Province of the Society of Jesus, 40315. Georgetown University Manuscripts, https://slaveryarchive .georgetown.edu/items/show/156.

25. "Building to Be Renamed for Pioneer Black Educator Anne Marie Becraft," Georgetown University, April 13, 2017, https://www.georgetown.edu/news/anne-marie -becraft-hall.

26. Jeffrey Brooke Allen, "The Racial Thought of White North Carolina Opponents of Slavery, 1789–1876," *North Carolina Historical Review* 59, no. 1 (January 1982): 60–61.

27. "ARTH 354 Georgetown Memorial Proposal," Georgetown Slavery Archive, https://slaveryarchive.georgetown.edu/items/show/211.

28. Anna Robinson-Sweet, "Truth and Reconciliation: Archivists as Reparations Activists," *American Archivist* 81, no. 1 (Spring/Summer 2018), 34.

29. William G. Thomas III, "When Enslaved People Sued Georgetown's Founders for Freedom," *Washington Post*, August 19, 2016, https://www.washingtonpost.com /opinions/when-enslaved-people-sued-georgetown-for-freedom/2016/08/19 /b6b0e430-5406-11e6-88eb-7dda4e2f2aec_story.html. A detailed history of these freedom suits can be found in William G. Thomas III, *A Question of Freedom: The Families Who Challenged Slavery from the Nation's Founding to the Civil War* (New Haven: Yale University Press, 2020).

30. Conveyance Book 28, Entry no. 258, Iberville Parish Courthouse, Plaquemine, Louisiana, Georgetown Slavery Archive, http://slaveryarchive.georgetown.edu/items /show/97.

31. Orlando Patterson, *Slavery and Society Death: A Comparative Study* (Cambridge, MA: Harvard University Press, 1982), 5–8.

32. See Alondra Nelson, "The Social Life of DNA: Racial Reconciliation and Institutional Morality after the Genome," *British Journal of Sociology* 69, no. 3 (September 2018): 522–37.

33. Terrence McCoy, "Her Ancestors Were Georgetown's Slaves. Now, at Age 63, She's Enrolled There—As a College Freshman," *Washington Post*, August 30, 2017, https://www.washingtonpost.com/local/social-issues/her-ancestors-were-georgetowns -slaves-now-at-age-63-shes-enrolled-there----as-a-college-freshman/2017/08/30 /31e22058-8d07-11e7-84c0-02cc069f2c37_story.html.

34. Legacy status was first suggested in a *Washington Post* op-ed written by Richard Cellini, the founder of the Georgetown Memory Project, and Maxine Crump, the GU272 descendant featured in Rachel Swarns's original *New York Times* article. Richard Cellini and Maxine Crump, "How Georgetown Should Honor Its Former Slaves," *Washington Post*, April 29, 2016, https://www.washingtonpost.com/opinions/george towns-unwilling-benefactors/2016/04/29/847dc5b4-0cbc-11e6-bfa1-4efa856caf2a_story .html.

35. For various descendant perspectives on reparations, see, for example, Noel King, Episode 767, "Georgetown, Louisiana," Part 2, *Planet Money*, NPR, April 26, 2017, https://www.npr.org/sections/money/2017/04/26/525769269/episode-767-georgetown -louisiana-part-two; Susan Svrluga, "'Make It Right': Descendants of Slaves Demand

Restitution from Georgetown," *Washington Post*, January 17, 2018, https://www
.washingtonpost.com/news/grade-point/wp/2018/01/16/__trashed-2/; Eliza Phillips,
"Descendants Demand More Reparative Action," *The Hoya*, September 23, 2018, http://
www.thehoya.com/descendants-demand-reparative-action/.

36. Damian Garcia, "Georgetown slave descendants seek reparations from university," *Georgetown Voice*, February 7, 2018, https://georgetownvoice.com/2018/02/07
/georgetown-slave-descendants-seek-reparations-from-university/. See also the GU272
Descendants Association website, www.gu272.net, accessed May 22, 2019.

37. Noel King, Episode 767, "Georgetown, Louisiana," Part 2, transcript, *Planet
Money*, April 26, 2017, https://www.npr.org/templates/transcript/transcript.php?storyId
=525769269. According to journalist Marc Parry, writing for the *Chronicle of Higher
Education*, Debra Tilson's daughter, Jessica Tilson, opposes reparations because "she
can't stomach putting a price on her ancestors' suffering." Marc Parry, "A New Path to
Atonement," *Chronicle of Higher Education*, January 20, 2019, https://www.chronicle
.com/article/A-New-Path-to-Atonement/245511.

38. Parry, "New Path to Atonement."

39. Jesús A. Rodríguez, "This Could Be the First Reparations Policy in America,"
Politico, April 9, 2019, https://www.politico.com/magazine/story/2019/04/09/george
town-university-reparations-slave-trade-226581; Deepika Jonnalagadda, "Students
Endorse Reconciliation Fee in GU272 Referendum," *The Hoya*, April 12, 2019, https://
www.thehoya.com/students-endorse-reconciliation-fee-gu272-referendum/.

40. Javon Price, "'Viewpoint: Changing Perceptions on the GU272 Referendum,"
The Hoya, April 23, 2019, https://www.thehoya.com/changing-perceptions-gu272
-referendum/.

41. Samuel Dubke and Hayley Grande, "Viewpoint: Vote 'No' on GU272 Referendum," *The Hoya*, February 16, 2019, https://www.thehoya.com/viewpoint-vote-no
-gu272-referendum/. GU272 descendant Jessica Tilson, mentioned above, also went on
record opposing the referendum on the grounds that it is not the students' "cross to
bear." Julia Pinney, "Claiming A Misrepresentation of Maringouin, This Descendant
Opposes the GU272 Referendum," *Georgetown Voice*, April 11, 2019, https://
georgetownvoice.com/2019/04/11/this-descendant-opposes-272-referendum-as
-elections-open/.

42. Thomas D. Morris, *Southern Slavery and the Law, 1619–1860* (Chapel Hill: University of North Carolina Press, 1996).

43. Ana Lucia Araujo, *Reparations for Slavery and the Slave Trade: A Transnational
and Comparative History* (New York: Bloomsbury Academic, 2017).

44. "Veteran Congressman Still Pushing for Reparations in a Divided America,"
NBC News, February 20, 2017, https://www.nbcnews.com/news/nbcblk/rep-john
-conyers-still-pushing-reparations-divided-america-n723151. The most recent version
of H.R. 40 is available online at https://www.congress.gov/bill/115th-congress/house
-bill/40.

45. One of my favorites has been the effort of students at Gonzaga College High School in Washington, DC, to research their school's history of slavery. Rachel Siegel, "Did Their School Have Ties to Slavery? Now Students Try to Make Sense of the Answer," *Washington Post*, September 25, 2017, https://www.washingtonpost.com/local/education/did-their-school-have-ties-to-slavery-now-students-try-to-make-sense-of-the-answer/2017/09/25/4b7762d6-a075-11e7-8ea1-ed975285475e_story.html.

46. Cheryllyn Branche, "My Family's Story in Georgetown's Slave Past," *New York Times*, September 2, 2016, https://www.nytimes.com/2016/09/03/opinion/my-familys-story-in-georgetowns-slave-past.html.

47. "CNN Hosts a Town Hall with Sen. Kamala Harris (D-CA) Presidential Candidate," *CNN*, April 22, 2019, http://edition.cnn.com/TRANSCRIPTS/1904/22/se.04.html.

48. "Freedom Hall and Remembrance Hall Ceremony: Remarks by President John J. DeGioia," December 11, 2015, https://president.georgetown.edu/freedom-remembrance-ceremony.

Chapter 3. "Free Citizens of This Nation"

1. This account draws from the history of the Shoe Boots family as reconstructed in Tiya Miles, *Ties That Bind: The Story of an Afro-Cherokee Family in Slavery and Freedom* (2005; Berkeley: University of California Press, 2015).

2. "Captain Shoe Boots to the Chiefs in Council," Cherokee Nation Papers, Western History Collections, 1824, University of Oklahoma, Norman, roll 46, no. 6508; Miles, *Ties That Bind*.

3. "Captain Shoe Boots to the Chiefs in Council"; Miles, *Ties That Bind*, 127; Cherokee Nation, "Laws of the Cherokee Nation: Adopted by the Council at Various Periods" (1808–1835) (Tehlequah, C.N.: Cherokee Advocate Office, 1852), 38.

4. Miles, *Ties That Bind*.

5. Cherokee Nation v. Georgia, 30 U.S. 1 (1831).

6. See, for instance, Claudio Saunt, *Black, White and Indian: Race and the Unmaking of an American Family* (New York: Oxford University Press, 2005); Barbara Krauthamer, *Black Slaves, Indian Masters: Slavery, Emancipation, and Citizenship in the Native American South* (Chapel Hill: University of North Carolina Press, 2013); Linda Williams Reese, *Trail Sisters: Freedwomen in Indian Territory, 1850–1890* (Lubbock: Texas Tech University Press, 2013); Kendra Taira Field, *Growing Up with the Country: Family, Race and Nation After the Civil War* (New Haven, CT: Yale University Press, 2018); Alaina E. Roberts, "Chickasaw Freedpeople at the Crossroads of Reconstruction" (PhD diss., Indiana University, 2017).

7. Treaty of 1866 between the United States and the Cherokee Nation, transcribed in Miles, *Ties That Bind*, 267–79, quote on page 271; Cherokee Emancipation Act, 1863, transcribed in Miles, *Ties That Bind*, 266–67; 1866 Treaty with Cherokee Nation, http://www.african-nativeamerican.com/treatycher.htm. For a new analysis of the Cherokee

Emancipation Acts, see Melinda Miller and Rachel Purvis, "No Right of Citizenship: The 1863 Emancipation Acts of the Loyal Cherokee Council," unpublished paper, accessed January 28, 2017, https://sites.google.com/site/melindacarman/.

8. The Choctaw Nation was slow to agree to the adoption stipulation, and the Chickasaw Nation never formally agreed to adopt their ex-slaves. Alaina E. Roberts, "A Federal Court Has Ruled Blood Cannot Determine Tribal Citizenship. Here's Why That Matters," *Washington Post*, September 7, 2017.

9. Melinda C. Miller, "Essays on Race and the Persistence of Economic Inequality" (PhD diss., University of Michigan, 2008).

10. Kenneth J. Cooper, "I'm a Descendant of the Cherokee Nation's Black Slaves. Tribal Citizenship Is Our Birthright," *Washington Post*, September 15, 2017.

11. Daniel F. Littlefield, *The Cherokee Freedom: From Emancipation to American Citizenship* (Westport, CT: Greenwood Press, 1978); Celia E. Naylor, *African Cherokees in Indian Territory: From Chattel to Citizens* (Chapel Hill: University of North Carolina Press, 2013); Fay A. Yarbrough, *Race and the Cherokee Nation: Sovereignty in the Nineteenth Century* (Philadelphia: University of Pennsylvania Press, 2008).

12. Tiya Miles and Celia Naylor, "African-Americans in Indian Societies," in *Handbook of North American Indians*, ed. Raymond Fogelson, vol. 14, *Southeast* (Washington DC: Smithsonian, 2004), 758–59; Adam Geller, "Past and Future Collide in Fight Over Cherokee Identity," *USA Today*, February 10, 2007; Arica L. Coleman, "How a Court Answered a Forgotten Question of Slavery's Legacy," *Time*, September 11, 2017.

13. "Cherokee Nation Court Rules on Freedmen Case," Cherokee Nation News Release, March 7, 2006, www.cherokee.org; Lucy Allen v. Cherokee Nation Tribal Council, Lela Ummerteskee, Registrar and Registration Committee, Judicial Appeals Tribunal of the Cherokee Nation, March 7, 2006.

14. Circe Sturm, "Race, Sovereignty, and Civil Rights: Understanding the Cherokee Freedmen Controversy," *Cultural Anthropology* 29, no. 3 (2014): 575–98, esp. 578, 579, 580; Chadwick Smith, "Citizen Views Fall on Both Sides of Freedom Issue," *Cherokee Phoenix*, May 3, 2006.

15. Sturm, "Race, Sovereignty, and Civil Rights," 581–83.

16. Congresswoman Diane E. Watson Press Release, "Watson Introduces Legislation to Sever U.S. Relations with the Cherokee Nation of Oklahoma," June 21, 2007, www.house.gov; Jeninne Lee-St. John, "The Cherokee Nation's New Battle," *Time*, June 21, 2007; Kevin Chappell, "Bill in Congress Moves to Cut Federal Funding to Cherokee Indians; Tribe's Law Would Deny Blacks Citizenship," *Jet*, November 19, 2007.

17. Brendan I. Koerner, "Blood Feud," *Wired*, September 2005; Geller, "Past and Future Collide"; Evelyn Nieves, "Putting to Vote the Question 'Who Is Cherokee,'" *New York Times*, March 3, 2007; Ellen Knickmeyer, "Cherokee Nation to Vote on Expelling Slaves' Descendants," *Washington Post*, March 3, 2007; Ellen Knickmeyer, "WP: Cherokee Nation May Expel Blacks," *MSNBC.com*, March 3, 2007; Frank Morris, "Cherokee Tribe Faces Decision on Freedmen," *NPR*, February 23, 2007; Murray

Evans, "Cherokees Pull Membership of Freed Slaves," Associated Press, *News.Aol .Com*, March 4, 2007; Murray Evans, "Cherokee Nation Members Revoke Tribal Citizenship of Their Freed Slaves 2,800 Descendants," Associated Press, *Abcnews.go.com*, March 4, 2007; "Cherokee Nation Votes Out Former Slaves' Descendants," Associated Press, *CNN.com*, March 5, 2007; Alex Kellogg, "Cherokee Nation Faces Scrutiny for Expelling Blacks," *NPR*, September 19, 2011.

18. "Room for Debate: Tribal Sovereignty vs. Racial Justice," *New York Times*, September 15, 2011, https://www.nytimes.com/roomfordebate/2011/09/15/tribal-sovereignty -vs-racial-justice; Marty Two Bulls, "Sovereigntree" (political cartoon), *Indian Country Today*, September 2009, indiancountrytodaymedianetwork.com; Cooper, "I'm a Descendant."

19. Jodi A. Byrd, "Been to the Nation, Lord But I Couldn't Stay There: American Indian Sovereignty, Cherokee Freedom and the Incommensurability of the Internal," *Interventions*, 13, no. 1 (2011): 31–52, 48.

20. Scott Richard Lyons, "Cherokee by Text," *Indian Country Today*, October 18, 2007; Robert Allen Warrior, "Cherokees Flee the Moral High Ground over Freedom," *News from Indian Country*, August 7, 2007, www.indiancountrynews.com; Lolita Buckner Inniss, "Cherokee Freedmen and the Color of Belonging," *Columbia Journal of Race and Law* 5, no. 2 (2015): 100–18, 105; Sturm, "Race, Sovereignty, and Civil Rights"; Brian Klopotek, "Of Shadows and Doubts: Race, Indigeneity, and White Supremacy," in *IndiVisible: African-Native American Lives in the Americas*, ed. Gabrielle Tayac (Washington, DC: Smithsonian Institution, 2009), 85, 89.

21. Lenzy Krehbiel-Burton, "Cherokee Court's Ruling," *Tulsa World*, October 12, 2011; Brian Daffron, "Bill John Baker, Policy-Maker," *Indian Country Today*, March 7, 2012; Courtland Milloy, "The Cherokees: One Nation, Divisible? Judge Will Decide If Black Members Can Be Expelled," *Washington Post*, May 6, 2014.

22. Tiya Miles, conversation with U.S. Department of Interior representatives, November 15, 2012. (The individuals with whom I spoke about this case were interested in building historical context about the 1866 Treaty as related to two key questions: (1) Was there an intent that there would be citizenship rights for former slaves and their descendants? (2) How did the Cherokee freedmen situation compare with that of freedpeople in the South?) Milloy, "The Cherokees: One Nation, Divisible?"

23. Cherokee Nation v. Raymond Nash, Civil Action No. 13-01313 (District of Colombia, August 30, 2017).

24. Marilyn Vann, Facebook Post, August 31, 2017. Todd Hembree, "Statement on the Freedmen Ruling," September 1, 2017, http://www.cherokee.org/News/Stories /20170901-Cherokee-Nation-Attorney-General-Todd-Hembree-issues-statement-on -Freedmen-ruling; Roberts, "A Federal Court Has Ruled."

25. Cherokee Nation v. Raymond Nash, 267 F. Supp. 3d 86 (D.D.C. 2017).

26. Carla D. Pratt, "Tribes and Tribulations: Beyond Sovereign Immunity and Toward Reparation and Reconciliation for the Estelusti," *Washington and Lee Race and Ethnic Ancestry Law Journal* 11, no. 1 (Winter 2005): 61–132. The term "Estelusti" is

derived from the Creek word for Black Indians; see Gary Zellar, *African Creeks: Es-telvste and the Creek Nation* (Norman: University of Oklahoma Press, 2007).

27. There is a potential model for United Nations adjudication of Native American national disputes elsewhere in North America. The groups Equal Rights for Indian Women and the Native Women's Association of Canada brought suit over the exclusionary Indian Act (1890, traced membership through the patrilineal descent) in the United Nations Human Rights Commission in 1982. Canada was found to be in violation. Canada then amended the act, but, according to anthropologist Audra Simpson, not satisfactorily. Audra Simpson, *Mohawk Interrupts: Political Life Across the Borders of Settler States* (Durham, NC: Duke University Press, 2014).

28. Inniss, "Cherokee Freedmen and the Color of Belonging"; Jodi A. Byrd, *The Transit of Empire: Critiques of Colonialism* (Minneapolis: University of Minnesota Press, 2011), 146.

29. The social movement to end tribes' systematic disenrollment of members in the contemporary era bears the slogan: "Not Indigenous, Not Traditional, Not acceptable." See http://stopdisenrollment.com/. For more on the movement to end tribal disenrollment, see ICMN Staff, "National Stop Disenrollment Visual Advocacy Movement Launches," *Indian Country Today*, February 8, 2016, https://indiancountry medianetwork.com/news/native-news/national-stop-disenrollment-visual-advocacy -movement-launches/. Also see Alaina E. Roberts, "A Hammer and a Mirror: Tribal Disenrollment and Scholarly Responsibility," *Western Historical Quarterly* 49, no. 1 (Spring 2018): 91–96.

Chapter 4. The Jamaican Case for Reparations

1. Walter Rodney, *How Europe Underdeveloped Africa* (London: Bogle-L'Ouverture Publications, 1972).

2. C.L.R. James, "The Slaves" (1938), in *Slaves, Free Men, Citizens: West Indian Perspectives*, ed. Lambros Comitas and David Lowenthal (Garden City, NY: Anchor Books, 1973), 4–19, 10

3. Gregson v. Gilbert, 3 Doug. KB 232 (1783).

4. Trevor Burnard, *Mastery, Tyranny, and Desire: Thomas Thistlewood and His Slaves in the Anglo-Jamaican World* (Chapel Hill: University of North Carolina Press, 2004), 31.

5. Steve McQueen, dir., *12 Years a Slave* (Regency Enterprises, 2013).

6. Government of Jamaica Ministry of Justice, The Record Office Act, Section 19 (a–b), February 1897, https://moj.gov.jm/sites/default/files/laws/Record%20Office%20 Act.pdf.

7. Edith Clarke, *My Mother Who Fathered Me: A Study of the Families in Three Selected Communities of Jamaica* (London: Allen and Unwin, 1957).

8. Richard Mitchell, "Compensate Us for Slavery—Robinson," *The Jamaica Gleaner*, March 3, 2015.

9. UNCHR, "Basic Principles and Guidelines on the Right to a Remedy and Reparation for Victims of Gross Violations of International Human Rights Law and Serious Violations of International Humanitarian Law," UN General Assembly Resolution 60/147 (December 16, 2005).

10. Irish Statute Book, "Slavery Abolition Act, 1833" (1833), http://www.irish statutebook.ie/eli/1833/act/73/enacted/en/print.html.

11. Will Boggs, "Harvard in Chains," *Harvard Political Review*, October 28, 2018.

12. Government of Jamaica, Ministry of Justice, The Law Reform (Miscellaneous Provisions) Act, Section 2, no. 1 (1955).

13. Latonya Linton, "UK Gov't Announces Compensation Scheme for Windrush Generation," Ministry of Foreign Affairs and Foreign Trade, Jamaica, April 3, 2019, https://mfaft.gov.jm/jm/uk-govt-announces-compensation-scheme-for-windrush -generation/.

14. Earl of Halsbury LC, The Owners of the Steamship Mediana v. The Owners, Master and Crew of the Lightship Comet, No. AC 113 (The Mediana, 1900).

15. Government of the United Kingdom, "Budget 2018," London, HM Treasury, 2018).

16. Dan Bilefsky, "David Cameron Grapples with Issues of Slavery Reparations in Jamaica," *New York Times*, September 30, 2015.

17. Hilary Beckles, "Address Delivered by Professor Sir Hilary Beckles, Chairman of the Caricom Reparations Commissions," July 16, 2014, https://caricom.org/media -center/communications/speeches/address-delivered-by-professor-sir-hilary-beckles -chairman-of-the-caricom-r.

18. "David Cameron Rules out Slavery Reparation During Jamaica Visit," *BBC News*, September 30, 2015, https://www.bbc.com/news/uk-34401412.

19. Jerome Klassen, *Joining Empire: The Political Economy of the New Canadian Foreign Policy* (Toronto: University of Toronto Press, 2014), 235.

20. Paul Clarke, "Let's Talk Cooperation Not Reparation - British State Minister," *The Jamaica Gleaner*, November 10, 2017.

21. Verene Shepherd, "We Will Not Forget," *Jamaica Gleaner*, November 17, 2017, http://jamaica-gleaner.com/article/letters/20171117/letter-day-we-will-not -forget.

22. Ben Riley-Smith, "Holocaust Memorial to Be Built by Parliament to Ensure 'Darkest Hour of Humanity' Is Never Forgotten," *The Telegraph,* January 27, 2016.

23. Lord Wright, House of Lords, Bourhill v. Young, AC 92 (1943).

24. Lord Mansfield, House of Lords, Somerset v. Stewart, 98 ER 499 (1771).

25. Lord Blackburn, House of Lords, Livingstone v. Rawyards Coal, 5 App. Cas 25 (1880).

26. Robert Goff and Gareth H. Jones, eds., *The Law of Restitution*, 6th ed. (London: Sweet and Maxwell, 2002).

27. Ibid.

28. Eric Williams, *Capitalism and Slavery* (Chapel Hill: University of North Carolina Press, 1944).

29. "Church Apologises for Slave Trade," *BBC News,* February 8, 2006, http://news .bbc.co.uk/2/hi/uk_news/4694896.stm.

30. Ibid.

31. Ibid.

32. Ibid.

33. Martin Luther King Jr., "The Negro Is Your Brother" [now known as "A Letter From A Birmingham Jail"], *Atlantic,* August 1963.

34. "Barbados PM Writes Britain on Reparation on Behalf of CARICOM," March 2, 2016, https://caricom.org/barbados-pm-writes-britain-on-reparation-on-behalf-of -caricom.

35. Shepherd, "We Will Not Forget"; Stephen Castle, "Caribbean Nations to Seek Reparations, Putting Price on Damage of Slavery," *The New York Times,* October 20, 2013, https://www.nytimes.com/2013/10/21/world/americas/caribbean-nations-to-seek -reparations-putting-price-on-damage-of-slavery.html. .

36. Caribbean Community, "CARICOM Ten Point Action Plan for Reparation," https://caricom.org/caricom-ten-point-plan-for-reparatory-justice/.

Chapter 5. The University and Slavery

This is a revised version of a presentation delivered at the Radcliffe Institute for Advanced Studies, Harvard University, at a symposium entitled "Universities and Slavery: Bound to Slavery," March 3, 2017.

Chapter 6. French Justice and the Claims for Reparations by Slave Descendants in Guadeloupe

1. Olivier Corten, *Annales de Droit de Louvain*, vol. 64, no. 1-2 (2004).

2. Speech delivered by an agricultural worker in August 2018 in preparation for the adverse possession procedure.

3. Court of Auditors, "L'établissement, le contrôle et le recouvrement de l'impôt outre-mer," Report S2018-0132, March 6, 2018, https://www.ccomptes.fr/sites/default /files/2018-06/20180625-refere-S2018-0132-impot-outre-mer.pdf. The Court of Auditors' principal mission is to ensure the good use of public money and to inform the citizens about it. An independent jurisdiction, it is equidistant between the parliament and the government. According to article 47-2 of the Constitution, it assists both.

4. The agricultural workers, in an unprecedented move, created an organization to represent their interests, Le Collectif du sud ouest de Sainte Rose et de ses environs-COSE. Afterward, they unionized in the Syndicat de défense du patrimoine agricole des îles de Guadeloupe—SPA.

5. Decision of the Regional Court of Pointe à Pitre (2015). At the date of the decision, the court ordered the destruction of the fences enclosing the occupied land and a fine of €300 /day payable by the state for every day it failed to implement the

order. The former governor obtained an injunction deferring implementation of the order, but the new governor promptly reversed that approach and executed the earlier court order.

6. The rule of adverse possession is a way to allow a person who is in possession of a good to acquire the deed for that good.

7. After the first abolition of slavery, in 1794, Napoléon Bonaparte reinstated slavery in 1802.

8. Court of Auditors, "L'établissement, le contrôle et le recouvrement de l'impôt outre-mer," 1.

9. Edition of January 25, 2018, for the French Polynesia, https://www.tnt.pf/Une -nature-mise-en-danger-par-l-incivisme_a237.

10. Suliane Favenec, « Essais nucléaires en Polynésie : les petits-enfants oubliés de la bombe, » Le Parisien, January 20, 2018.

11. From 2011 to 2017, Sueur worked as head of the pediatric-psychiatric unit of the Centre Hospitalier de Polynesie Française, https://www.leparisien.fr/faits-divers/essais -nucleaires-en-polynesie-un-medecin-denonce-une-omerta-21-01-2018-7513137.php.

12. National Assembly, Report no. 4064, September 28, 2016, http://www.assemblee -nationale.fr/14/rapports/r4064.asp. DOM-TOM is an acronym used to denote France's overseas departments and territories.

13. "Substantive Equalities in Overseas," Victorin Lurel, Report, March 2016, https://www.vie-publique.fr/sites/default/files/rapport/pdf/164000180.pdf.

14. Article 2-1a states: "Each State Party undertakes to engage in no act or practice of racial discrimination against persons, groups of persons, or institutions and to ensure that all public authorities and public institutions, national and local, shall act in conformity with this obligation." International Convention on the Elimination of All Forms of Racial Discrimination, adopted and opened for signature and ratification by General Assembly resolution 2106 (XX) of December 21, 1965, entry into force January 4, 1969; https://www.ohchr.org/en/professionalinterest/pages/cerd .aspx.

15. Nelson Maldonado Torres, "Outline of Ten Theses on Coloniality and Decoloniality," https://fondation-frantzfanon.com/wp-content/uploads/2018/10/maldonado -torres_outline_of_ten_theses-10.23.16.pdf.

16. Letter from the prime minister sent June 20, 2018, https://www.ccomptes.fr/sites /default/files/2018-06/20180625-refere-S2018-0132-impot-outre-mer-rep-pm.pdf; the Court of Auditors' report can be accessed at https://www.ccomptes.fr/sites/default/files /2018-06/20180625-refere-S2018-0132-impot-outre-mer.pdf and https://www.lefigaro .fr/impots/2018/06/25/05003-20180625ARTFIG00259-la-cour-des-comptes-etrille-la -gestion-calamiteuse-des-impots-en-outre-mer.php.

17. International Labor Organization, "C111—Convention (no. 111) concernant la discrimination (emploi et profession) 1958," https://www.ilo.org/dyn/normlex/fr/f?p =NORMLEXPUB:12100:0::NO::P12100_ILO_CODE:C111.

18. These lands acquired by the state are estimated at 30 percent of the land.

19. The principle of tax equality has two sides: the first concerns equality before the tax bill (Article 6 of the Declaration of Rights of 1789), and the second concerns equality before public burdens (Article 13 from the same declaration). See Olivier Fouquet, "The Constitutional Council and the Principle of Equality Before Tax," October 2011, http://www.conseil-constitutionnel.fr/conseil-constitutionnel/francais /nouveaux-cahiers-du-conseil/cahier-n-33/le-conseil-constitutionnel-et-le-principe -d-egalite-devant-l-impot.100369.html.

20. The DGFIP is the La Direction Générale des Finances Publiques, which is affiliated with the Ministry of Economy and Finances. The 53 million euro figure is taxes due by the owners of buildings. Court of Auditors, "L'établissement, le contrôle et le recouvrement de l'impôt outre-mer," 4.

21. The Custom of Paris, written in 1510, revised in 1580, was introduced in New France by the Compagnie des Cent associés in 1627. It was replaced by the Civil Code in 1804.

22. Quoted by Joseph Chailley-Bert (1854–1928), in *Les compagnies de colonisation sous l'ancien régime* (Paris: Armand Colin, 1898).

23. Under the influence of Colbert, the Charter of 1664 applied until 1674.

24. Lucien Pierre Peytraud, *L'esclavage aux Antilles avant 1789* (1897; Cambridge: Cambridge University Press, 2011).

25. The edict read: "We have united and incorporated, unite and incorporate into the Domain of our Crown all the Lands and Countries (including the remaining part to Sieur Houël in the property and seigneury of the said Isle of Guadeloupe) which belonged to the said Company, both by means of concessions that we made to it by the Edict of its establishment, as by virtue of acquisition contracts, or otherwise, know . . . the Isles called Antilles, owned by the French." Source for the edict: Trouvés sur le site, http://anom.archivesnationales.culture.gouv.fr : http://anom.archivesnationales .culture.gouv.fr/p2w/?dossier=/collection/INVENTAIRES/Ministeres/SEM/C8/&f irst=FRANOM23_C8B_19/FRANOM23_C8B_19_0083&last=FRANOM23_C8B_19 /FRANOM23_C8B_19_0 088&title=%C3%89dit+portant+r%C3%A9vocation+de+la+C ompagnie+des+Indes+occidentales.+11+p.+Impri m%C3%A9.+d%C3%A9cembre+1674. Il est à noter que la version publiée par le *Recueil Isambert* est incomplète et ne comporte pas ces extraits (Isambert, Decrusy, Taillandier, Belin, *Recueil général des anciennes lois françaises depuis l'an 420 jusqu'à la révolution de 1789*, Tome XIX, Paris, Belin-Le Prieur 1827, p. 152).

26. The "Alienation Code" (November 22–December 1, 1790) abolished the principle of inalienability of landed property.

27. "Decree of the National Convention of 4 February 1794, Abolishing Slavery in all the Colonies," Liberty, Equality, Fraternity, http://chnm.gmu.edu/revolution /d/291.

28. Law No. 1609, Art. I.—In the colonies returned to France in execution of the Treaty of Amiens, of 6 Germinal Year X, slavery will be maintained in accordance with the laws and regulations prior to 1789. II. - It will be the same in the other French colonies

beyond the Cape of Good Hope. III. - The slave trade and their importation into the said colonies will take place, in accordance with the laws and regulations existing before the said period of 1789. Loi du 30 floréal, an X Loi relative à la traite des noirs et au régime des colonies (20 mai 1802), https://mjp.univ-perp.fr/france/1802esclavage.htm.

29. Law no 46–451 of March 19, 1946, tending to the classification as French departments of Guadeloupe, Martinique, Réunion, and French Guyana, https://www.legifrance.gouv.fr/loda/id/JORFTEXT000000868445/.

30. JORF (Official Newspaper of the French Republic), May 2, 1848.

31. V. Schœlcher, *Esclavage et Colonisation, textes choisis et annotés par Emile Tersen* (1948; Paris: PUF, 2007).

32. La Vérité, https://gallica.bnf.fr/ark:/12148/bpt6k5789971v.texteImage.

33. Decree about the abolition of slavery in the French colonies and settlements, April 27, 1848 (JORF, May 2, 1848).

34. Law no 46–451 of March 19, 1946, "Tending to the classification as French departments of Guadeloupe, Martinique, Réunion and French Guyana."

35. Law no 1609, Art. I.—In the colonies returned to France in execution of the Treaty of Amiens, of 6 Germinal Year X, slavery will be maintained in accordance with the laws and regulations prior to 1789. II. - It will be the same in the other French colonies beyond the Cape of Good Hope. III. - The slave trade and their importation into the said colonies will take place, in accordance with the laws and regulations existing before the said period of 1789. Loi du 30 floréal, an X Loi relative à la traite des noirs et au régime des colonies (20 mai 1802), https://mjp.univ-perp.fr/france/1802esclavage.htm.

36. A. Duchesne, *Histoire des finances coloniales de la France* (Paris: Payot, 1938); Y.-E. Amaïzo, *Naissance d'une banque dans la zone franc 1848–1901: Priorité aux propriétaires d'esclaves* (Paris: L'Harmattan, 2008); A. Girault, *Principes de colonisation et de législation coloniale* (Larose, 1895).

37. Mireille Fanon Mendes France, « La Martinique crei son rejet du modèle dominant » ; *Politis*, March 5, 2009, https://www.politis.fr/articles/2009/03/la-martinique-crie-son-rejet-du-modele-dominant-5697/.

38. Alain Buffon, "L'indemnisation des planteurs après l'abolition de l'esclavage," Société d'Histoire de la Guadeloupe, number 67–68, 1986, https://id.erudit.org/iderudit/1043814ar.

39. These unions included LAKOU LKP, Union générale des travailleurs de Guadeloupe (UGTG), and Collectif de l'ouest de Sainte Rose et ses environs (COSE).

40. https://la1ere.francetvinfo.fr/guadeloupe/les-conditions-des-reparations-apres-l-abolition-de-l-esclavage-au-coeur-d-une-action-judiciaire-365949.html.

41. Article 1 of the Declaration of the Rights of Man and Citizen, August 26, 1789: "Men are born and remain free and equal in rights. Social distinctions may be founded only upon the general good."

42. Introduction to the Constitution of 1946: «"In the aftermath of the victory won by the free peoples over the regimes which attempted to enslave and degrade the human person, the French people again proclaim that every human being, without distinction

of race, religion or belief, possesses inalienable and sacred rights," https://www.conseil
-constitutionnel.fr/le-bloc-de-constitutionnalite/preambule-de-la-constitution-du
-27-octobre-1946.

43. Affaire LAKOU LKP, Union générale des travailleurs de Guadeloupe, Fonda-
tion Frantz Fanon, Collectif de l'ouest de Sainte Rose et ses environs v. l'Etat français,
RG 15/01202, September 8, 2016.

44. Law no. 2010-874, July 27, 2010, « Modernisation de l'agriculture et de la pêche. »

45. National Assembly, Amendment 680, June 9, 2016, http://www.assemblee
-nationale.fr/14/amendements/3679/CSEGALITE/680.pdf.

46. https://www.ouest-france.fr/politique/politique-un-amendement-pour-sanction
ner-lapologie-de-lesclavage-4289704.

Chapter 7. History on Trial

1. Caroline Elkins, "Alchemy of Evidence: Mau Mau, the British Empire, and the
High Court of Justice," *Journal of Imperial and Commonwealth History* 39, no. 5 (2011):
731–48.

2. Richard Drayton, "Where Does the World Historian Write From? Objectivity,
Moral Conscience and the Past and Present of Imperialism," *Journal of Contemporary
History* 46 (2011): 678. Note that Drayton's article, on which much of this paragraph
draws, is the most incisive analysis of the production of historical knowledge, and historians' averring from colonial violence. Drayton: 671–85.

3. Ibid., 678.

4. The five original claimants were Ndiku Mutua, Paulo Mzili, Wambugu Nyingi,
Jane Muthoni Mara, and Susan Ngondi. For the original particulars of the claim, see
Ndiku Mutua et al. v. Foreign and Commonwealth Office, Particulars of Claim, Case
No. HQ09X02666, Royal Courts of Justice, London, 2009; Ndiku Mutua et al. v. For-
eign and Commonwealth Office, Approved Judgement, Case No. HQ09X02666,Royal
Courts of Justice, London, 2011.

5. Witness Statement of Caroline Macy Elkins, Ndiku Mutua et al. v. Foreign and
Commonwealth Office, Claim No. HQ09X02666, Royal Courts of Justice, London, February 20, 2011.

6. Ndiku Mutua et al. v. Foreign and Commonwealth Office, Approved Judgement,
No. HQ09X02666, February 20, 2011.

7. Witness Statement of Caroline Macy Elkins.

8. Caroline Elkins, *Imperial Reckoning: The Untold Story of Britain's Gulag in Kenya*
(New York: Henry Holt, 2005), *xiii.*

9. *Ndiku Mutua et al. v. Foreign and Commonwealth Office,* Approved Judgement.

10. Witness Statement of Caroline Macy Elkins.

11. Hanslope Disclosure (HD), CS 10/2/4, Bates 013173-75, Kenya Intelligence
Committee, "Down Grading and Destruction of Classified Materials," October 6,
1958; HD, CS 10/2/4, Bates 013178, "Destruction of Classified Waste," September 24,
1959; HD, CS 10/2/4, Bates 013179, "Method of Destroyed Classified Documents,"

September 24, 1959; and HD, CS 10/2/4, Bates 0131782-83, "Routine Destruction." Within the Hanslope Disclosure, the entire Rec. #488, 1943/17/B, "Security of Instructions for Handling Classified Documents, released with Hanslope Disclosure" and Rec. #487, CS 10/2, Vol. II, "Security of Documents Including those in Transit to and from Government House," provide further details of summary of removal/destruction of documents in Kenya that follows here. In addition, see the newly released "Migrated Archives" at Kew. For example, The National Archives (TNA), FCO 141/6957, "Kenya: Security of Official Correspondence," March 1960–January 1962; and TNA, FCO 141/6958, "Kenya: Security of Official Correspondence," March 1962–April 1963.

12. This document, contained in the Hanslope Disclosure, was also released in March 2012 to the TNA. See TNA, FCO 141/6957, Secretary of State for the Colonies, "Disposal of Classified Record and Accountable Documents," May 3, 1961.

13. HD, 1943/17/B, Bates 024225-231, Memorandum from Ellerton, "The Designation of Watch," May 13, 1961.

14. Ibid.; and HD, I&S.137/O2(S), Bates 013042, Letter from the Ministry of Defence to various departmental heads, Provincial Commissioners and Permanent Secretaries, May 13, 1961.

15. See, for example, HD, GO/ DS3, Bates 012888-89, Internal Memorandum, April 8, 1963; HD, 1943/17/B, Bates 024222, Ross to Weeks, Secret Registry, December 6, 1961; HD, 1943/17/B, Bates 024215, "Transfer of Watch Files to the Governor's Office," March 23, 1962; and 1943/17/B, Bates 024216, "Transfer of 'Watch' Files to the Governor's Office," March 16, 1962.

16. HD, 1943/17/B, Bates 024198-200, Colonial Office, "Protection and Disposal of Classified and Accountable Documents and Records Generally," September 1962; HD, 1943/17B, Bates 024193, Telegram from Governor to Secretary of State, "Intel and Guidance Papers from Foreign Office," November 23, 1963; HD, 1943/17B, Bates 0241935, Telegram from Secretary of State to Governor, "Disposal of Records," May 10, 1963.

17. See, for example, HD, AA 1943/17/B, Bates 024217-20, T.J.F. Gavaghan, "Transfer of Functions to the Governor's Office," March 2, 1962. See also TNA, FCO 141/6958, Terence Gavaghan, Acting Permanent Secretary to the Governor's Office, "Protective Security in Headquarters Offices in Nairobi," March 6, 1962.

18. HD, CS 10/2/4, Bates 013057-102.

19. HD, 1943/17/B, Bates 024198-200, Colonial Office, "Protection and Disposal of Classified and Accountable Documents and Records Generally," September 1962.

20. TNA, FCO 141/6957, "Destruction Certificate," December 22, 1960.

21. *Hansard*, House of Commons Debates, no. 563 (June 6, 2013), cols. 1692–93.

22. Ben Macintyre, "Hague Lifts the Lid on Britain's Secret Past," *Times* (London), April 9, 2011.

Chapter 8. A Critical Assessment of Colombia's Reparations Policies

1. This chapter draws on research the authors, individually and collectively, conducted in previous projects, including the Transitional Justice Research Collaborative

(TJRC), a project supported by the NSF, resulting in a publicly available data set at transitionaljusticedata.com; and research on the Colombian reparations program in the context of an evaluation requested by the Colombian Victims Unit (VU) and supported by USAID, conducted between August 2014 and October 2015. Under the terms of the grant, the PIs retained the right to use knowledge gained from the evaluation for their own research and writing, such as this chapter. We thank in particular Bridget Marchesi and Peter Dixon for their research assistance on these projects.

2. See, for example, Nelson Camilo Sanchez Leon, Catalina Diaz, and Rodrigo Uprimny, eds., *Reparar en Colombia: Los dilemas en contextos de conflicto, pobreza y exclusión* (Bogotá, Colombia: ICTJ/DeJusticia, 2009).

3. Washington Office on Latin America, "Colombia's 52-Year-Old Conflict with the FARC Comes to an End," August 24, 2016, https://www.wola.org/2016/08/colombias-52-year-old-conflict-farc-comes-end/.

4. See, for example, "Internal Displacement in Colombia: Fifteen Distinguishing Features," *Disaster Health* 2, no. 1 (January/February/March 2014): 1–12.

5. Some estimates attribute between one-fifth to one-third of conflict-related killings to the FARC. Washington Office on Latin America, "Colombia's 52-Year-Old Conflict with the FARC Comes to an End."

6. Presidencia de la República, "Lo logramos: lo que parecía imposible, lo hicimos posible'," XVI Cumbre Mundial de Premios Nobel de Paz, February 2, 2017, http://es.presidencia.gov.co/sitios/busqueda/noticia/170202-Lo-logramos-lo-que-parecia-imposible-lo-hicimos-posible/Noticia.

7. Julia Symmes Cobb and Nicholas Casey, "Colombia Peace Deal Is Defeated, Leaving a Nation in Shock," *New York Times*, October 2, 2016.

8. Washington Office on Latin America, "Key Changes to the New Peace Accord," November 15, 2016, http://colombiapeace.org/2016/11/15/key-changes-to-the-new-peace-accord/.

9. Acuerdo Final para la Terminación del Conflicto y la Construcción de una Paz Estable y Duradera (Final Peace Agreement), November 24, 2016, https://peacemaker.un.org/node/2924.

10. Presidencia de la República, "El país ha entrado en una etapa irreversible de consolidación del posconflicto," Bogotá, February 28, 2017, http://es.presidencia.gov.co/noticia/170228-El-pais-ha-entrado-en-una-etapa-irreversible-de-consolidacion-del-posconflicto.

11. This evaluation was requested by the Victims Unit (VU) and supported by USAID through a subcontract from Management Systems International (MSI) with our Harvard-based team. The evaluation's funding was under the project title "Evaluation and Analysis for Learning," at the Carr Center for Human Rights Policy at the Harvard Kennedy School and the Harvard Humanitarian Initiative at the T. H. Chan School of Public Health. Under the terms of the grant, the PIs retained the right to use knowledge gained from the evaluation for their own research and writing.

12. It is a well-accepted norm in international law that victims have a right to remedies, and that such remedies include forms of compensation. See, for example, The International Covenant on Civil and Political Rights (Art. 3), The Convention against Torture (Art. 14), the 2002 Rome Statute (Art. 75, Art. 79) and the American Convention on Human Rights (Art. 25 and 63).

13. Christine Evans, *The Right to Reparation in International Law for Victims of Armed Conflict* (Cambridge, U.K: Cambridge University Press, 2012): 66.

14. Juan Manuel Santos Calderón, "Ley de Victimas y Restitución de Tierras," L. No. 1448 (2011).

15. The main data for this macro-level analysis was the reparations data from Transitional Justice Research Collaborative (TJRC), an international collaboration of the Harvard University Kennedy School, Oxford University, the University of Minnesota, and Tulane University that produced a comprehensive database on transitional justice policies around the world. Its research was supported by the National Science Foundation. For an overview of the dataset, see transitionaljusticedata.com.

16. Gobierno de Colombia, "Unidad para las Victimas, Registro Único de Victimas," accessed August 11, 2018, https://www.unidadvictimas.gov.co/es/registro-unico-de-victimas-ruv/37394.

17. Internal Displacement Monitoring Center, IDMC Grid 2018, "Global Report on Internal Displacement 2018," http://www.internal-displacement.org/global-report/grid2018/.

18. Internal Displacement Monitoring Center, "Global Report on Internal Displacement."

19. Much of the information presented in this section is primarily based on interviews with key informants and analysis of the primary documents.

20. "Toma Pacífica en la Unidad de Víctimas," *El Tiempo*, May 20, 2015, http://www.eltiempo.com/politica/victimas-se-toman-la-sede-de-la-unidad-de-victimas/15792144.

21. From the descriptive PowerPoint presentation created at the Victims' Unit, "Reparación Colectiva," presented to the evaluation team in September 2014, referencing Article 225 of Decree 4800 of 2011.

22. This is consistent with evidence that Afro-Colombians have suffered from the Colombian conflict disproportionately. See, for example, "Internal Displacement in Colombia."

Chapter 9. Justice Beyond the Final Verdict

1. See the report of the Commission for Historical Clarification (CEH) that identifies 1978–85 as the most violent period of the armed conflict, when military campaigns and human rights abuses concentrated in Quiché, Alta and Baja Verapaz, Chimaltenango, Huehuetenango, in the South Coast, and the capital. See CEH, *Guatemala, memoria del silencio. Conclusiones y recomendaciones*, 1st ed. (Guatemala: Oficina

de Servicios para Proyectos de las Naciones Unidas, 1999), 29. Based on our investigations in the Achi region in Baja Verapaz, from 2005 to the present, we find that the
process of genocide in this region was related to the construction of a hydroelectric
dam on the Chixoy River. See Jaroslave Colajacomo, *The Chixoy Dam: The Maya Achi'
Genocide. The Story of Forced Resettlement,* (Cape Town: World Commission on Dams,
1999), 2, http://rio-negro.info/che/doc/ChixoyDam_StoryOfForcedResettlement.pdf.
The project advanced in a climate of intimidation, harassment, and terror as government representatives from Guatemala's National Institute of Electrification threatened
inhabitants of Achi communities that would be affected by the dam. See Ibid.; Jesús
Tecú Osorio, *Memoir of the Río Negro Massacres,* trans. Janine Lespérance, Lisa Rankin,
and Moira Peters (Guatemala: Editorial Maya' Wuj, 2012), 48; Carlos Chen Osorio, *His-
torias de lucha y de esperanza* (Rabinal: ADIVIMA, 2009). In the following years, the
state—through the military, paramilitary police (judiciales), and Self-Defense Patrols
(Patrullas de Autodefensa; PAC, in its Spanish acronym)—selectively murdered Achi
leaders who refused to abandon their territory for the construction of the Chixoy dam,
and they raped women left behind (Ibid.).

2. Fernando Suazo López de Gámiz, *Rabinal: historia de un pueblo maya. Desde el
preclásico hasta la última guerra,* 2nd ed. (Guatemala: Instituto Guatemalteco de Educación Radiofónica, 2012), 17.

3. Waqi' Q'anil Demetrio Cojtí Cuxil, *El racismo contra los pueblos indígenas de
Guatemala* (Ciudad de Guatemala: Ajpop Mayab' Tijonik, Consejo Nacional de Educación Maya, 2005), 74. All translations of quotes from the original Spanish in this
chapter were done by the authors.

4. Severo Martínez Peláez, *La patria del criollo: ensayo de interpretación de la re-
alidad colonial guatemalteca* (México: Fondo de Cultura Económica, 1998); Marta
Elena Casaús Arzú, *La metamorfosis del racismo en Guatemala* (Guatemala: Editorial
Cholsamaj, 1998), 46.

5. Ibid., 66.

6. Miguel Ángel Curruchiche Gómez, *Discriminación del pueblo maya en el or-
denamiento jurídico de Guatemala,* 2nd ed. (Guatemala: Editorial Cholsamaj, 1994),
28–29.

7. Ibid., 29.

8. Irma Alicia Velásquez Nimatuj, *Pueblos indígenas, Estado y lucha por tierra en
Guatemala: Estrategias de sobrevivencia y negociación ante la desigualdad globalizada*
(Guatemala: AVANCSO, 2008), 54–55.

9. Ibid.

10. Juan Fernando Cifuentes Herrera, *Historia moderna de la etnicidad en Guatemala. La visión hegemónica: rebeliones y otros incidentes indígenas en el siglo XX* (Guatemala: Editorial Cultura, Universidad Rafael Landívar, 1998).

11. "Ladino" is a term that refers to historical and social processes related to *mestizaje* in Guatemala, or the mixing of European, African-descendant, and indigenous
peoples, both during and after Spanish colonialism. In the colonial context, ladinos

were people who did not identify as "pure" indigenous, Spanish, or Spanish-descendants born in the Americas (criollos). See Arturo Taracena Arriola, *Guatemala: del mestizaje a la ladinización, 1524–1964* (Guatemala: Centro de Investigaciones Regionales de Mesoamerica, 2007), http://lanic.utexas.edu/project/etext/llilas/vrp/arriola.html. After Guatemalan independence from Spain in 1821, and particularly after the counterrevolution began in 1954, ladinos rose to greater political and economic power within Guatemalan society. According to the lawyer and sociologist Carlos Guzmán Böckler, the category of ladino was a "fictitious being," defined by the negation of all that is indigenous, which existed in intellectual subordination to European reference points. See Carlos Guzmán Böckler, *Guatemala: Colonialismo y Revolución* (México: Siglo XXI, 1975); see also Carlos Guzmán Böckler and Jean Loup Herbert, *Guatemala: Una interpretación histórica-social,* (México: Siglo XXI, 1971). For a different interpretation of ladino, see Severo Martínez Peláez, *La patria del criollo*. As such, ladinos were generally associated with being Spanish speakers and ascribing to nonindigenous cultural practices while still exhibiting class and geographic differences within their group. See also Santiago Bastos, "Los indios, la nación y el nacionalismo," in *La construcción de la nación y la representación ciudadana en México, Guatemala, Perú, Ecuador y Bolivia,* ed. Claudia Dary (Guatemala: FLACSO, 1998), 87–157; Casaús Arzú, *La metamorfosis del racismo en Guatemala.*

12. Helvi Mendizábal Saravia, *Despojos y resistencias. Una mirada a la Región Extractiva Norte desde Tezulutlán-Verapaz,* Cuadernos de Investigación, no. 28. (Guatemala: AVANCSO, 2016); Irma Alicia Velásquez Nimatuj, "Indigenous Peoples, the State and Struggles for Land in Guatemala: Strategies for Survival and Negotiation in the Face of Globalized Inequality" (PhD diss., University of Texas at Austin, 2005).

13. These dictators included Rafael Carrera y Turcios (1851–65), Justo Rufino Barrios (1873–85), Manuel Estrada Cabrera (1898–1920), and Jorge Ubico (1931–44). For more information, see the work by historian Julio Castellanos Cambranes, *Café y campesinos en Guatemala, 1853–1897* (Guatemala: Editorial Universitaria, Colección Realidad Nuestra, 1985).

14. Created within the larger context of the Liberal Revolution, la Ley contra la Vagancia enslaved indigenous people on coffee plantations and replaced debt peonage.

15. See Blake D. Pattridge, "The Catholic Church in Revolutionary Guatemala, 1944–54: A House Divided," *Journal of Church and State* 36, no. 3 (Summer 1994): 527–40, https://www.jstor.org/stable/23920898.

16. Patrick Ball, Paul Kobrak, and Herbert F. Spirer, *State Violence in Guatemala, 1960–1996: A Quantitative Reflection* (Washington, DC: American Association for the Advancement of Science, 1999), accessed May 8, 2019, https://www.hrdag.org/wp-content/uploads/2013/01/state-violence-guate-1999.pdf; Stephen Schlesinger, "Ghosts of Guatemala's Past," *New York Times*, June 3, 2011, https://www.nytimes.com/2011/06/04/opinion/04schlesinger.html.

17. María de los Ángeles Aguilar Velásquez, "Movimiento estudiantil y represión policial en Guatemala, 1952-1956," in *La Guerra Fría y el anticomunismo en Centroamérica*, ed. Roberto García Ferreira and Arturo Taracena (Guatemala: FLACSO, 2017), 63-78.

18. Carlos Figueroa Ibarra, *El recurso del miedo. Estado y terror en Guatemala*, 2nd ed. (Guatemala: F and G Editores, 2011).

19. Ibid.

20. Ibid.

21. Ibid.

22. Matthias Epe and José Rodolfo Kepfer, *El enemigo interno en Guatemala: contrainsurgencia y su herencia en la configuración de nuevos conflictos* (Guatemala: Magna Terra editores, 2014).

23. Julieta Carla Rostica, "La elite político-militar y sus representaciones del indio. Guatemala 1982-1996," *Boletín de la Asociación para el Fomento de los Estudios Históricos en Centroamérica*, no. 49 (April–June 2011); Jennifer Schirmer, *Las intimidades del proyecto político de los militares en Guatemala* (Ciudad de Guatemala: FLACSO, 1999).

24. Ibid.

25. Renata Ávila Pinto, *El genocidio en Guatemala como forma extrema de racismo* (Ciudad de Guatemala: Rigoberto Menchú Tum Foundation, 2007); Manuel Ollé Sesé, Jo-Marie Burt, and Claire Colardelle, *Genocidio en Guatemala: Ríos Montt Culpable* (Paris, France: Federación Internacional de Derechos Humanos, July 2013), 8, 10, and 15, https://www.fidh.org/IMG/pdf/informe_guatemala613esp2013.pdf.

26. Ávila Pinto, *El genocidio en Guatemala como forma extrema de racismo*; Victoria Sanford, *Violencia y Genocidio en Guatemala*, 3rd ed. (Guatemala: F and G Editores, 2012).

27. CEH, *Guatemala, memoria del silencio. Conclusiones y recomendaciones*, 25 and 43.

28. Amandine Fulchirone et al., *Tejidos que lleva el alma: memoria de las mujeres mayas sobrevivientes de violación sexual durante el conflicto armado*, 2nd ed. (Guatemala: ECAP, UNAMG, and F and G Editores, 2011), https://www.ecapguatemala.org.gt/sites/default/files/Tejidos%20que%20lleva%20el%20alma.pdf.

29. CEH, *Guatemala, memoria del silencio. Conclusiones y recomendaciones*, 37-38 and 91; Alfonso Huet, *Nos salvó la sagrada selva. La Memoria de Veinte Comunidades Q'eqchi'es que sobrevivieron al Genocidio* (Cobán: ADICI Wakliiqo, 2008); Nancy Pecknham, "Campos de reducación para los indígenas," *Uno más uno*, February 12, 1984, Princeton University Digital Library, http://pudl.princeton.edu/objects/sb3979153.

30. CEH, *Guatemala, memoria del silencio. Conclusiones y recomendaciones*, 21.

31. Laura Hurtado Paz y Paz, *La histórica disputa de las tierras del Valle del Polochic. Estudio sobre la propiedad agraria*, (Guatemala: Serviprensa, 2014), 78.

32. Ibid.

33. Laura Hurtado Paz y Paz, *Estudio histórico sobre la propiedad agraria y situación socio-económica de la Comunidad Sepur Zarco y comunidades vecinas* (Guatemala: Alliance "Rompiendo el Silencio y la Impunidad": Asociación Mujeres Transformando el Mundo, ECAP, and UNAMG, 2013), 14.

34. Ibid.; Marlise Simons, "Guatemala: Peasant Massacre," *NACLA*, September 25, 2007, https://nacla.org/article/guatemala-peasant-massacre. See also Greg Grandin, *The Last Colonial Massacre: Latin America in the Cold War* (Chicago: University of Chicago Press, 2004).

35. Huet, *Nos salvó la sagrada selva*, 14.

36. According to the Recovery of Historical Memory (REMHI) report sponsored by the human rights office of the Catholic Church's archbishopric in Guatemala and the U.N.'s CEH report, José Efraín Ríos Montt's military regime was responsible for human rights abuses such as massacres, rape, disappearances, and torture against indigenous peoples and communities. See Oficina de Derechos Humanos del Arzobispado de Guatemala, *Guatemala: Nunca Más. Informe del Proyecto Interdiocesano de Recuperación de la Memoria Histórica (REMHI)* (Guatemala: ODHAG, 1998); CEH, *Guatemala memoria del silencio. Tomo III: Las violaciones de los derechos humanos y los hechos de violencia* (Guatemala: Oficina de Servicios para Proyectos de las Naciones Unidas, 1999). The CEH report further recognized acts of genocide that were committed under his regime. On May 10, 2013, Ríos Montt was convicted of genocide and crimes against humanity against the Ixil people, but, on May 20, the Constitutional Court of Guatemala overturned the conviction by formal procedures. Ríos Montt died at the age of ninety-one on April 1, 2018, while facing a closed-door trial, thus evading legal accountability, but the memory of his crimes lives on.

37. Hurtado Paz y Paz, *Estudio histórico sobre la propiedad agraria*, 16–17.

38. Gilda Lemus and Juan Pablo Ozaeta, *Sepur Zarco. El camino de las mujeres hacia la justicia* (Guatemala: UNAMG, 2016), 4.

39. Impunity Watch and Alianza Rompiendo el Silencio y la Impunidad (ECAP, MTM, and UNAMG), *Cambiando el rostro de la justicia: las claves del litigio estratégico del caso Sepur Zarco* (Guatemala: Impunity Watch and Alianza Rompiendo el Silencio y la Impunidad, 2017), 13.

40. Ibid.; Lemus and Ozaeta, *Sepur Zarco*, 4.

41. Impunity Watch and Alianza Rompiendo el Silencio y la Impunidad, *Cambiando el rostro de la justicia*, 13–14.

42. Tribunal Primero de Sentencia Penal, Narcoactividad y Delitos contra el Medioambiente (Tribunal Primero de Sentencia Penal), Sentencia C-01076-2012-00021Of. 2°, Guatemala, February 26, 2016, accessed October 30, 2020, https://ihl-databases.icrc.org/applic/ihl/ihl-nat.nsf/caseLaw.xsp?documentId=1C57325B4F89A421C12581B00043C3DF&action=openDocument&xp_countrySelected=GT&xp_topicSelected=GVAL-992BU6&from=state.

43. Impunity Watch and Alianza Rompiendo el Silencio y la Impunidad, *Cambiando el rostro de la justicia*, 15.

44. Unión Nacional de Mujeres Guatemaltecas, "Li wam sa sa' xch'ool. Mi corazón está Contento," published September 8, 2017 to *YouTube* in Guatemala, Video, 16:37, https://www.youtube.com/watch?v=r-pk9G6kFA8.

45. Ibid.

46. Ibid.

47. Lemus and Ozaeta, *Sepur Zarco*, 2.

48. "Sepur Zarco guilty verdict takes major step forward in global fight for gender justice," *Network in Solidarity with the People of Guatemala*, February 27, 2016, https://nisgua.org/sepur-zarco-guilty-verdict-takes-major-step-forward-in-global-fight-for-gender-justice/.

49. "Sepur Zarco: In pursuit of truth, justice, and now reparations," *U.N. Women*, October 22, 2017, http://www.unwomen.org/en/news/stories/2017/10/feature-guatemala-sepur-zarco-in-pursuit-of-truth-justice-and-now-reparations; authors' emphasis.

50. "Reparations for Sepur Zarco," *Nobel Women's Initiative*, May 2, 2016, https://nobelwomensinitiative.org/reparations-for-sepur-zarco/.

51. Lemus and Ozaeta, *Sepur Zarco*, 7.

52. Mtmadmin, "Por el cumplimiento de las medidas de reparación Caso Sepur Zarco," *Mujeres Transformando el Mundo*, May 12, 2017, https://mujerestransformandoelmundo.org/por-el-cumplimiento-de-las-medidas-de-reparacion-caso-sepur-zarco/.

53. See the website of the Currículo Nacional Base Guatemala (CNB) to read the illustrated text in Spanish: https://cnbguatemala.org/wiki/La_luz_que_vuelve.

54. Carlos Jacinto Coz and Karin Eunice González Valladares, *Detalle de viajes por comisiones oficiales al interior del país, correspondiente a agosto 2018* (Guatemala: Ministerio de Educación, Dirección General de Educación Bilingüe Intercultural), 1 and 3, http://infopublica.mineduc.gob.gt/mineduc/images/5/5e/DAFI_INCISO12A_2018_DIGEBI_VERSION8.pdf.

55. Elsa Coronado, "Sepur Zarco: La vida después de una sentencia que se incumple," *Plaza Pública*, October 31, 2017, https://www.plazapublica.com.gt/content/sepur-zarco-la-vida-despues-de-una-sentencia-que-se-incumple.

56. Coronado, "Sepur Zarco."

57. Jo-Marie Burt and Paulo Estrada, "Court Ratifies Historic Sepur Zarco Sexual Violence Judgment," *International Justice Monitor*, July 21, 2017, https://www.ijmonitor.org/2017/07/court-ratifies-historic-sepur-zarco-sexual-violence-judgment/.

58. Coronado, "Sepur Zarco."

59. Ibid.

60. Paula Barrios et al., *Línea base de Sepur Zarco y comunidades aledañas* (Guatemala: Mujeres Transformando el Mundo, 2017).

61. Plaza Pública, "Sepur Zarco: la vida después de la sentencia," uploaded November 2, 2017 to *Facebook* in Guatemala, Video, 3:05, https://www.facebook.com/PlazaPublicaGT/videos/sepur-zarco-sobreviviendo-depués-de-la-sentencia/1531979783523890/.

62. Unión Nacional de Mujeres Guatemaltecas, "Li wam sa sa' xch'ool."

63. Plaza Pública, "Sepur Zarco."

64. Programa de las Naciones Unidas para el Desarrollo, "Mujeres Maya Q'eqchí de Sepur Zarco - Colectiva Jalok U," published November 30, 2016 to *YouTube* in Guatemala, Video, 10:47, https://www.youtube.com/watch?v=A5_yutKxd7A.

65. Juan José Guerrero, "La patología del negacionismo guatemalteco," *Plaza Pública*, March 5, 2016, https://www.plazapublica.com.gt/content/la-patologia-del-negacionismo-guatemalteco.

66. Steven Dudley, "Guatemala Elites and Organized Crime: The CICIG," *InSight Crime*, September 1, 2016, https://www.insightcrime.org/investigations/guatemala-elites-and-organized-crime-the-cicig/; Edgar Gutiérrez, "Guatemala Elites and Organized Crime: Introduction," *InSight Crime*, September 1, 2016, https://www.insightcrime.org/investigations/guatemala-elites-and-organized-crime-introduction/.

Chapter 10. Colonial History at Court

1. Soshana Felman, *The Juridical Unconscious: Trials and Traumas in the Twentieth Century* (Cambridge, MA: Harvard University Press, 2002).

2. Ibid., 11–12.

3. Leora Bilsky, "The Judge and the Historian: Transnational Holocaust Litigation as a New Model," *History and Memory* 24, no. 2 (2012): 117–56.

4. Michael R. Marrus, *Some Measure of Justice: The Holocaust Era Restitution Campaign of the 1990s* (Madison: University of Wisconsin Press, 2009).

5. Bilsky, "The Judge and the Historian," 117.

6. Stef Scagliola, "Cleo's 'Unfinished Business': Coming to Terms with Dutch War Crimes in Indonesia's War of Independence," *Journal of Genocide Research* 14, no. 3–4 (2012): 419–39; Larissa van den Herik, "Addressing 'Colonial Crimes' Through Reparations? Adjudicating Dutch Atrocities Committed in Indonesia," *Journal of International Criminal Justice* 10, no. 3 (2012): 693–705; Nicole L. Immler, "Human Rights As a Secular Imaginary in the Field of Transitional Justice: The Dutch-Indonesian 'Rawagede Case,'" in *Social Imaginaries in a Globalizing World*, ed. Hans Alma, Guy Vanheeswijk (Berlin: De Gruyter, 2018), 193–222.

7. Chris Lorenz, "Can a Criminal Event in the Past Disappear in a Garbage Bin in the Present? Dutch Colonial Memory and Human Rights: The Case of Rawagede," in *Afterlife of Events: Perspectives on Mnemohistory*, ed. M. Tamm (New York: Palgrave Macmillan, 2015), 219–41; Bart Luttikhuis, "Juridisch afgedwongen excuses. Rawagedeh, Zuid-Celebes en de Nederlandse terughoudendheid," *BMGN—Low Countries Historical Review* 129, no. 4 (2014): 92–105.

8. Bambang Purwanto, quoted in Anne-Lot Hoek, "Een onderzoek naar schuld en boete (An investigation on guilt and penance)," *NRC Handelsblad*, November 22, 2016.

9. Selma Leydesdorff, "Why Compensation Is a Mixed Blessing," in *The Genocide Convention: The Legacy of 60 years*, ed. H. van der Wilt et al. (Leiden: Martinus

Nijhoff, 2012), 105–14; Elazar Barkan, "Historical Dialogue: Beyond Transitional Justice and Conflict Resolution," in *Historical Justice and Memory*, ed. Klaus Neumann and Janna Thompson (Madison: University of Wisconsin Press, 2015), 185–201.

10. Leydesdorff, "Why Compensation Is a Mixed Blessing," 105–6, 114.

11. O.N.T. Thoms, J. Ron, and R. Paris, "State-Level Effects of Transitional Justice: What Do We Know?" *International Journal of Transitional Justice* 4, no. 3 (2010): 1–26.

12. Rosalind Shaw and Lars Waldorf, with Pierre Hazan, eds. *Localizing Transitional Justice: Interventions and Priorities After Mass Violence*, Stanford Studies in Human Rights Series (Stanford, CA: Stanford University Press, 2010).

13. Nancy Fraser, "From Redistribution to Recognition? Dilemmas of Justice in a 'Postsocialist' Age," *New Left Review* 1, no. 212 (1995): 68–93.

14. Nancy Fraser and Alex Honneth, *Redistribution or Recognition? A Political-Philosophical exchange* (London and New York: Verso, 2003).

15. Paul Gready and Simon Robins, "From Transitional to Transformative Justice: a new agenda for practice," *The International Journal of Transitional Justice* 8 (2014): 339–361.

16. The chapter draws on my previous work, notably, Nicole L. Immler, "Narrating (In)Justice in the Form of a Reparation Claim: Bottom-Up Reflections on a Post-Colonial Setting—The Rawagede Case," in *Understanding the Age of Transitional Justice: Crimes, Courts, Commissions, and Chronicling*, ed. Nancy Adler, Hinton's Human Rights Series (New Brunswick: Rutgers University Press, 2018), 149–174, and Immler, "Human Rights As a Secular Imaginary in the Field of Transitional Justice." It develops past insights, providing greater conceptual coherence and practical guidance to the critique of transitional justice. While my earlier articles studied the micro-processes those claims initiated, this chapter goes a step further aiming to theorize a research approach that allows us to strengthen awareness of the relevance of the social in recognition processes.

17. For Rosa "resonance" is a key variable in his "sociology of world-relations." Hartmut Rosa, *Resonanz. Eine Soziologie der Weltbeziehung* (Frankfurt: Suhrkamp, 2016).

18. While in the Netherlands one speaks of "keeping the colonies" and the "decolonization war," in Indonesia one speaks of a "recolonization," the "war of independence" or "revolution." I take the Dutch perspective.

19. Dutch sources assert 150 men were killed, Indonesian sources, 433 men. Rémy Limpach, *De brandende kampongs van generaal Spoor* (The burning kampongs of General Spoor) (Amsterdam: Boom 2016): 323–36.

20. The Comité Nederlandse Ereschulden was established on May 5, 2005, the fiftieth anniversary of the end of World War II, to look after the interests of the Indonesian civilian victims. The Indonesian branch was established by Batara Hutagalung, the Dutch branch by Jeffry Pondaag. Both act as individuals and have few supporters. They submitted several petitions to the Dutch parliament requesting that

the Indonesian "victims must come into the picture in the Netherlands." The success came with the court case. See www.kukb.nl.

21. Liesbeth Zegveld, "Civielrechtelijke verjaring van internationale misdrijven (Status of limitation of civil law in regard to international crimes)," inaugural lecture on November 13 (Amsterdam: Amsterdam University Press, 2015).

22. The Rawagede Verdict (September 14, 2011): 4.12, https://uitspraken.rechtspraak .nl/inziendocument?id=ECLI:NL:RBSGR:2011:BS8793. See Wouter Veraart, "Uitzondering of precedent? De historische dubbelzinnigheid van de Rawagede-uitspraak," *Ars Aequi*, no. 4 (2012): 251–259; Immler, "Human Rights As a Secular Imaginary in the Field of Transitional Justice."

23. "War crime," argues Liesbeth Zegveld, "is a legal term, which we in court did not use because this term did not yet exist. That is why in the judgment it is spoken of as a 'crime' or 'wrongful act of the state.'" Zegveld, "Decolonization or recolonization?," discussion, September 13, 2018, Pakhuis De Zwijger.

24. Rawagede Verdict (September 14, 2011).

25. Based upon an informal agreement with the Dutch government: Staatscourant van het Koninkrijk der Nederlanden, no. 25383 (September 10, 2013). https://zoek .officielebekendmakingen.nl/stcrt-2013-25383.html.

26. Shafiah Paturusi, interview with author, Amsterdam, August 19, 2014.

27. An interlocutory judgment, NJF 2015/221 (March 11, 2015), https://uitspraken .rechtspraak.nl/inziendocument?id=ECLI:NL:RBDHA:2015:2442.

28. See Esther Captain, "Indonesian Eyewitness Testimony via Skype," Independence, Decolonization, Violence and War in Indonesia, 1945–1950, https://www .ind45-50.org/en/indonesian-eyewitness-testimony-skype.

29. Staatscourant van het Koninkrijk der Nederlanden, no. 50507 (October 19, 2020).

30. Veraart, "Uitzondering of precedent?," 258.

31. Liesbeth Zegveld in a debate on "Reparations for Historical Wrongs," The Hague Institute of Global Justice, October 14, 2016.

32. "The case concerning the village Rawagede. Final report," Amsterdam International Law Clinic, September 2007, 46. The report explored the classification of the conflict, the possibility of a criminal case and of a civil case.

33. This case study is based upon semi-structured interviews conducted by the author with the help of a translator in October 2015 with victims, family members, and activists. These included more than forty interviews with eight families in Rawagede and twelve in Sulawesi, including five local experts/activists. For more details on the case and the interviewees, see Immler, "Narrating (In)Justice in the Form of a Reparation Claim," 2018.

34. Author interviews with Ibu Tijeng (1927–2018) and Ibu Wanti (1925–2016) and their families, and child survivor Warjo (b. 1936), Rawagede, October 26, 2015.

35. Author interviews with village head Mamat (b. 1971) and head of the widows foundation Sukarman (b. 1949), Rawagede, October 26, 2015.

36. Author interview with Andi Mangkiri (b. 1948), daughter of Ibu Makku (b. 1926), one of the four widows of the local king Andi Cori, Pangkajene Sidrap, October 12, 2015.

37. Author interview with Mutawakkil, grandson of Ibu Ceddung (1928–2015), Pinrang, October 13, 2015.

38. Author interview with Karmas (b. 1946), daughter of Ibu Tijeng, Rawagede, October 26, 2015.

39. Author interview with Luus Rusmanto (b. 1971), grandson of Ibu Tijeng, Rawagede, October 26, 2015.

40. Author interview with Batara Hutagalung, Jakarta, October 18, 2015.

41. See for more information on this case Chapter 7 by Elkins.

42. Author interview with Daniel Leader, February 12, 2016. See "Victims of British Torture in Kenya. Options for justice," report by Leigh Day & Co Solicitors, December 2, 2009. This proposal represented suggestions by victim organizations, inviting the British Government "to adopt a creative approach to resolve this issue promptly": Acknowledgement, Community Health and Welfare Provision, A Welfare Fund (for individual victims), Transitional Justice (such as supporting a Truth, Justice and Reconciliation Commission), Working Group (to develop recommendations most effective to meet the victims' needs).

43. "This is not a colonial reparations case," it is "about torture and it is brought by the surviving victims who live with the consequences of their torture to this day" (ibid., 3, 11). The Dutch case is on "executions by Dutch soldiers of unarmed subjects of the then Kingdom of the Netherlands . . . in the context of the exercise of the colonial rule of the State over a now former colony. . . . The State was under an obligation to protect the physical integrity and life of its nationals" (Rawagede verdict, 4.14). However, the public debate caused by both court cases developed into one on colonial history and colonial wrongs.

44. Some irregularities are mentioned by Katie Engelhart, "40,000 Kenyans Accuse UK of Abuse in Second Mau Mau Case," *Guardian*, October 29, 2014, http://www .theguardian.com/world/2014/oct/29/kenya-mau-mau-abuse-case.

45. Reparations expert and activist Esther Stanford Xosei, presentation, the International Civil Society Roundtable on WCAR Durban Plus 15, Rotterdam, March 19–20, 2016.

46. Klaus Neumann and Janna Thompson, "Introduction. Beyond the Legalist Paradigm," in *Historical Justice and Memory*, ed. Klaus Neumann and Janna Thompson (Madison: University of Wisconsin Press, 2015): 3–24, 22.

47. See Marc Parry, "Uncovering the Brutal Truth About the British Empire," *Guardian*, August 16, 2018, https://www.theguardian.com/news/2016/aug/18 /uncovering-truth-british-empire-caroline-elkins-mau-mau.

48. Rosa, *Resonanz*, 28.

49. Elsewhere I call this the "distinct rationalities" of a legal procedure, looking for plain evidence, while victims in their testimonies also aim for comprehension.

Nicole Immler, "Individual Desire or Social Duty? The Role of Testimony in a Restitution Procedure. An Inquiry into Social Practice," in *Tapestry of Memory: Evidence and Testimony in Life Story Narratives,* ed. Nancy Adler and Selma Leydesdorff (Transaction Publisher, 2013): 219–236, 232.

50. Gready and Robins, "From Transitional to Transformative Justice," 58.

51. Ibid.

52. Birgit Bräuchler (ed.), *Reconciling Indonesia. Grassroots agency for peace* (London and New York: Routledge, 2009); Kiran McEvoy and Lora McGregor (eds.), *Transitional Justice from Below. Grassroots Activism and the Struggle for Change* (Oxford: Hart Publishing 2008).

53. "The case concerning the village Rawagede. Final report," 7.

54. See Immler, "Human Rights As a Secular Imaginary in the Field of Transitional Justice," 209.

55. "I am concerned that we are not considered as human. There is a ladder, isn't it? You first get the Dutch, then the Europeans, then the half-breeds, then the Chinese, and then we come, the indigenous people, let's say, the natives. That's how we were called." Jeffry Pondaag, interview with author, Heemskerk, November 13, 2014, and Amsterdam, February 5, 2015.

56. Specific debates on folkloric traditions such as "Black Pete" developed into a much broader debate on institutional racism. Gloria Wekker, *White Innocence. Paradoxes of Colonialism and Race* (Durham and London: Duke University Press, 2016).

57. Alex Honneth, *Struggle for Recognition: The Moral Grammar of Social Conflicts* (Cambridge: Polity Press, 1996).

58. Kristina Lepold, "An Ideology Critique of Recognition: Judith Butler in the Context of the Contemporary Debate on Recognition," *Constellations* 25 (2018): 474–484, 474.

59. Tom Bentley, "Colonial Apologies and the Problem of the Transgressor Speaking," *Third World Quarterly* 39, no. 3 (2017): 399–417.

60. Patchen Markell, *Bound by Recognition* (Princeton, NJ: Princeton University Press, 2003).

61. Fraser, "From redistribution to recognition?," 73.

62. Rosa reaches beyond the classic debate of recognition versus redistribution by Fraser and Honneth. Hartmut Rosa, "(Parity of) Participation—The Missing Link Between Resources and Resonance," in *Feminism, Capitalism, and Critique. Essays in Honor of Nancy Fraser,* ed. Banu Bargu and Chiara Bottici (New York: Palgrave Macmillan 2017), 157–166, 164. This approach will be further explored in the author's new research on the "Dialogics of Justice."

63. Purwanto, *Een onderzoek naar schuld en boete (An investigation on guilt and penance).*

64. Gayatri S. Spivak, "Righting Wrongs," *The South Atlantic Quarterly* 103, no. 2–3 (2004): 523–581.

65. Author interview with Leader; also discussion between Liesbeth Zegveld and other lawyers at the debate "Reparations for Historical Wrongs," The Hague Institute of Global Justice, October 14, 2016.

Chapter 11. Unhealed Wounds of World War I

1. Aerial bombardment was first employed—against civilians—by Italy in 1911 during its colonial war in Libya. Following its utilization with limited effect against urban centers during World War I, interwar colonial theaters like India's Northwest Frontier, Egypt, Iraq, Morocco, Syria, Palestine, Ethiopia, and China were the scenes of the most intensive employment of air attacks on civilians. This was the prologue to the massive Spanish Civil War and World War II air raids on cities like Guernica, Coventry, London, Hamburg, Berlin, Tokyo, Hiroshima, and Nagasaki. The British, French, Italian, German, and Japanese officers responsible for such attacks on nonmilitary targets learned their trade in these colonial wars, among them Air Marshal Sir Arthur "Bomber" Harris, the World War II commander of the RAF Bomber Command, who in the 1920s and 1930s was responsible for bombing civilians in Iraq, India, and Palestine.

2. For further details, see Hikmet Ozdemir, *The Ottoman Army, 1914–1918: Disease and Death on the Battlefield* (Salt Lake City, UT: The University of Utah Press, 2008); Edward Erikson, *Ordered to Die: A History of the Ottoman Army in the First World War* (Westport, CT: Greenwood, 2001); Kristian Ulrichsen, *The First World War in the Middle East* (London: Hurst, 2014); and Eugene Rogan, *The Fall of the Ottomans: The Great War in the Middle East* (New York: Basic Books, 2015).

3. Santanu Das, "World War I: Experiences of Colonial Troops," British Library, January 29, 2014, https://www.bl.uk/world-war-one/articles/colonial-troops.

4. *Ibid.* See also Victor Kiernan, "Colonial Africa and its Armies," in *Imperialism and its Contradictions* (London: Routledge, 1995), 77–96.

5. For a discussion of the contestation over some of these borders, see Rashid Khalidi, "The Persistence of the Sykes-Picot Frontiers in the Middle East," *London Review of International Law* 4, no. 2 (2016): 347–57.

6. Perhaps the most comprehensive history of the genocide of the Armenians is by Ronald Suny, *"They Can Live in the Desert but Nowhere Else": A History of the Armenian Genocide* (Princeton, NJ: Princeton University Press, 2015). See also Taner Akcam, *The Young Turks' Crime against Humanity: The Armenian Genocide and Ethnic Cleansing in the Ottoman Empire* (Princeton, NJ: Princeton University Press, 2012); and Ronald Suny, Fatma Gocek, and Norman Naimark, eds., *A Question of Genocide: Armenians and Turks at the End of the Ottoman Empire* (Oxford: Oxford University Press, 2011).

7. Several months of fighting in the fall of 2020 in the Nagorno-Karabakh region between Armenian and Azeri forces, the latter supported by Turkey, revived these traumas.

8. For a summary of this phase of Kurdish history, see the superb introduction by Martin van Bruinessen to Susan Meiselas, *Kurdistan: In the Shadow of History*, 2nd ed. (Chicago: University of Chicago Press, 2008).

9. For details, see William Eagleton, *The Kurdish Republic of 1946* (Oxford: Oxford University Press, 1963).

10. He made this statement to the House Permanent Select Committee on Intelligence headed by Congressman Otis Pike in 1975. United States Congress House Select Committee on Intelligence Recommendations of the Final Report of the House Select Committee on Intelligence by the House Select Committee on Intelligence, Ninety-fourth Congress, second session, pursuant to H. Res. 591 . . . February 11, 1976,

11. For the Covenant of the League Nations, signed on June 28, 1919, see State Department Office of the Historian, *Foreign Relations of the United States, The Paris Peace Conference, 1919*, Vol. XIII, https://history.state.gov/historicaldocuments /frus1919Parisv13/ch10subch1. For the Husayn-McMahon correspondence of 1915–1916, see J. C. Hurewitz, ed., *The Middle East and North Africa in World Politics: A Documentary Record*, 2 vols. (New Haven: Yale University Press, 1979), 2:221–227.

12. Memo dated August 11, 1919, cited in J. C. Hurewitz, ed., *The Middle East and North Africa*, 2:189.

13. See Rashid Khalidi, *Palestinian Identity: The Construction of National Consciousness*, rev. ed. (New York: Columbia University Press, 2010); Rashid Khalidi, *The Iron Cage: The Story of the Palestinian Struggle for Statehood* (Boston: Beacon, 2006); and Rashid Khalidi, *The Hundred Years' War on Palestine: A History of Settler-Colonialism and Resistance, 1917–2017* (New York: Metropolitan, 2020).

14. Frank Giles, Interview with Golda Meir, *Sunday Times* (London), June 15, 1969, 12.

Chapter 12. Nakba Denial

1. Michael R. Fischbach, "Land," in *Encyclopedia of the Palestinians*, rev. ed., Philip Matar, ed. (New York: Facts On File, Inc., 2005), 294.

2. Different scholars have arrived at different numbers for destroyed villages. The discrepancy stems from what defines a "village." For the 360 figure, see U.S. Archives and Records Administration (hereafter, NARA), Record Group (hereafter RG) 59, Lot File 441/Entry 1107B, Gardiner Files, Palestine Refugee Files 1947–49, Box 3, Conciliation Commission for Palestine No. 2, "The Arab Refugee Problem" (March 16, 1949). For the 427 figure, see Basheer K. Nijim, ed., with Bishara Muammar, *Toward the De-Arabization of Palestine/Israel 1945–1977* (Dubuque, IA: Kendall/Hunt Publishing, 1984).

3. For details, see Michael R. Fischbach, *Records of Dispossession: Palestinian Refugee Property and the Arab-Israeli Conflict* (New York: Columbia University Press, 2003), 18.

4. Ibid., 23–27.

5. A. Granovsky, *Agrarian Reform and the Record of Israel*, trans. E. M. Epstein (London: Eyre and Spottiswood, 1956), 111. The government's sale of land to the JNF was negotiated even before the government was authorized, through the Absentees Property Law of March 1950, to sell confiscated land.

6. Israel Government Yearbook 5719/1958 (Jerusalem: Ministry of Education and Culture, Central Office of Information), 459.

7. Israel State Archive (hereafter, ISA) (130), 2445/3, "Report on a Settlement of the Arab Refugee [Issue]" (November 25, 1948).

8. ISA (43), 5440/1582, "Report of Custodian of Absentees' Office" (March 31, 1950).

9. Central Zionist Archive (hereafter, CZA) A246/57, "Comments on Value Assessments of Absentee Landed Property" (November 12, 1962).

10. Yusif Sayigh, *Al-Iqtisad al-Isra'ili* [The Israeli Economy] (Cairo: League of Arab States, Institute for Higher Arab Studies, 1966), 107–10.

11. Sami Hadawi, *Palestinian Rights and Losses in 1948: A Comprehensive Study*, Part 5, *An Economic Assessment of Total Palestinian Losses*, by Atef Kubursi (London: Saqi Books, 1988), 113, 187.

12. UN document A/AC.25/W.84, "Working Paper Prepared by the Commission's Land Expert on the Methods and Techniques of Identification and Valuation of Arab Refugee Immoveable Property Holdings in Israel" (April 28, 1964); United Nations Secretariat Archive (hereafter, UNSA), RG DAG 13-3, UNCCP, Principal Secretary, Records Relating to the Technical Office, Box 16, 1952–57, Land Identification Project, Jarvis Report, A/AC.25/W.83, "Initial Report of the Commission's Land Expert on the Methods and Techniques of Identification and Valuation of Arab Refugee Immoveable Property Holdings in Israel" (September 15, 1961).

13. From 1948 to 1954, for example, the government leased abandoned stone quarries for £ (Israeli) 102,618. Israel Government Yearbook 5713/1952 (Jerusalem: Government Printer, 1953), 119; and Israel Government Yearbook 5714/1952–53, 142. The Israeli government even harvested cactus fruit from uncultivable land and sold it to companies that used the fruit to make alcohol.

14. UNSA, RG DAG 13-3, UNCCP, Principal Secretary, Records Relating to Compensation, Box 18, 1949–62., Selected Documents and Working Papers, "[Draft] Working Paper on the Problems Presented by the Paragraphs on Compensation Contained in the Johnson Proposal" (September 19, 1962).

15. UNSA, RG DAG 13-3, UNCCP, Refugee Office, Land Specialist, Box 35, 1951, J. M. Berncastle, MCP/3/51/9, "Valuation of Abandoned Arab Land in Israel" (August 15, 1951); ibid., Principal Secretary, Records Relating to Compensation, Box 20, 1961–64, Background Papers, "Discussion of the Value of Moveable Property" (December 1961), App. I, II, III.

16. Israeli Government Yearbook 5711/1950, 213; and Israeli Government Yearbook 5712/1951–52, 155. The exact figure was £ (Israeli) 9,197,717 in property losses and an estimated £4,000,000 in agricultural losses. The Israeli pound was tied to the British pound at that time and had a nominal value of $2.80.

17. UNSA, RG DAG 13-3, UNCCP, Office of the Principal Secretary, Records Relation to Compensation, Box 18, 1948-51, Working Papers, W/50, "Compensation to Refugees and the Question of War Damages" (August 4, 1950).

18. ISA (43), 5595/gimel/4716, "The Report of the Committee to Examine the Issue of Compensation for Absentee Property" (March 17, 1950), section 9.

19. Quoted in Yehouda Shenhav, *The Arab Jews: A Postcolonial Reading of Nationalism, Religion, and Ethnicity* (Stanford, CA: Stanford University Press, 2006), 110.

20. ISA (130), 2563/7, Levisohn to Aliav (February 20, 1956).

21. See the Report of the UNCCP, UN document A/RES/512 (VI), January 26, 1952, https://unispal.un.org/DPA/DPR/unispal.nsf/0/AFDEF7B30101C6A2852560EB006D B365.

22. For more on tangible versus intangible, see Michael Molloy and John Bell, with Nicole Waintraub and Ian Anderson, "Intangible Needs, Moral Acknowledgment and the Palestinian Refugee Issue," 189-27, in *The Palestinian Refugee Problem: The Search for a Solution*, ed. Rex Brynen and Roula El-Rifai (London: Pluto Press, 2014). Other scholars employ the terms "visible and invisible" instead of "tangible and intangible." For example, see Ilan Pappé, "The Visible and Invisible in the Israeli-Palestinian Conflict," 279-96, in *Exile and Return: Predicaments of Palestinians and Jews*, ed. Ann M. Lesch and Ian S. Lustick (Philadelphia: University of Pennsylvania Press, 2005).

23. Ilan Pappé, *The Ethnic Cleansing of Palestine* (Oxford: Oneworld Publications, 2006).

24. For example, see ibid., 168-69.

25. One of the best scholars writing on this topic is Nur Masalha. See, inter alia, his *Expulsion of the Palestinians: The Concept of "Transfer" in Zionist Political Thought 1882-1948* (Washington, DC: Institute for Palestine Studies, 1992).

26. See Nur Masalha, *The Politics of Denial: Israel and the Palestinian Refugee Problem* (London: Pluto Press, 2003), 23-26.

27. Benny Morris, "Yosef Weitz and the Transfer Committees, 1948-49," *Middle Eastern Studies* 22, no. 4 (October 1986): 522-61.

28. CZA A246/7, Yosef Weitz, Handwritten Diary, Entry for December 20, 1940, 1090-91, in Chaim Simons, *International Proposals to Transfer Arabs from Palestine 1895-1947* (Hoboken, NJ: KTAV Publishing, 1988), 83; Weitz diaries, 3:288 (entry for May 20, 1948), in Morris, "Yosef Weitz and the Transfer Committees, 1948-49," 523.

29. Weitz diaries, 3:288 (entry for May 20, 1948), in Morris, "Yosef Weitz and the Transfer Committees, 1948-49), 523.

30. Benny Morris, *The Birth of the Palestinian Refugee Problem, 1947-1949* (Cambridge: Cambridge University Press, 1987), 135-37.

31. Shertok to Goldmann (June 15, 1948), in ISA, *Documents on the Foreign Policy of Israel*, vol. 1, ed. Yehoshua Freundlich (Jerusalem: Israel State Archives, 1981), 163 .

32. James G. McDonald, *My Mission to Israel 1948-1951* (New York: Simon and Schuster, 1951), 176.

33. Yosef Weitz, *The Struggle for the Land* (Tel Aviv: Lion the Printer, 1950), 87.

34. David Ben-Gurion, *Medinat Yisra'el ha-Mehudeshet* [The Resurgent State of Israel] (Tel Aviv: Am Oved, 1969), 1:164–65, 167, cited in Morris, *The Birth of the Palestinian Refugee Problem, 1947–1949*, 141.

35. For a full discussion of these Jewish property losses, see Michael R. Fischbach, *Jewish Property Claims Against Arab Countries* (New York: Columbia University Press, 2008).

36. Maurice Roumani, *The Case of the Jews from Arab Countries: A Neglected Issue* (Tel Aviv: World Organization of Jews from Arab Countries, 1977), viii.

37. Institute of the World Jewish Congress, *A Population and Property Transfer: The Forgotten Exodus of Jews from Arab Lands* (Dispatch No. 88, September 2002).

38. Quoted in Charlotte Hall, "Diaspora Gives Stage to Arab Jews," *Haaretz*, May 23, 2003.

39. Quoted in Etta Prince-Gibson, "Right of Return," *Jerusalem Post Magazine*, August 8, 2003.

40. See Fischbach, *Records of Dispossession*, 91ff.

41. Meeting with Members of the Conciliation Commission (February 24, 1949), in ISA, *Documents on the Foreign Policy of Israel*, 2:446.

42. Fischbach, *Records of Dispossession*, 148–50.

43. Orit Gal, "Compensation for Palestinian Refugees: An Israeli Perspective," in *Compensation to Palestinian Refugees and the Search for Palestinian-Israeli Peace*, ed. Rex Brynen and Roula El-Rifai (London: Pluto Press, 2013), 42. See also Rex Brynen's "Palestinian Refugee Compensation: Connections and Complexities" in the same volume, 265–66.

44. Royal Institute of International Affairs, *The Palestinian Refugee Issue: Compensation and Implementation Mechanisms* (London: Royal Institute of International Affairs, 2013), 9.

45. Palestinian Proposal on Refugees, Article 2, cited in Leila Hilal, "Palestinian Negotiation Priorities on Reparations for Refugees," in Brynen and El-Rifai, *Compensation to Palestinian Refugees*, 28.

46. Ze'ev Schiff, "What Was Obtained at Taba Regarding Palestinian Refugees," *Haaretz*, September 12, 2001, https://www.haaretz.com/1.5386673.

47. Based on the UNCCP's detailed work determining the amount of Arab-owned land in Palestine as of November 29, 1947, Frank Jarvis carried out a study of the ratio between landowners and non-landowning refugees based on 434 randomly selected villages. He also used 1945 British mandatory population figures and added 6 percent to account for population growth. Jarvis then determined that 133,495 out of 306,103 persons living in those 434 villages—43.6 percent—owned property. He also estimated that 348,300 of 904,000—39.6 percent—of refugees registered with UNRWA had owned land in Palestine. See NARA RG 59, POL 27-14 PAL/UN, USUN to Department of State (January 14, 1966). Fifteen years earlier, in 1950, UNRWA conducted what it called a sampling survey of refugees in Jordan and the West Bank that determined that

66 percent of refugee families (families, not individuals) lost property in Palestine, while 34 percent of families lost houses. See UNSA DAG 13-3, UNCCP, Office of the Principal Secretary, Records Relating to Compensation/Box 18/1949-51/Working Papers, W/60, "Sampling Survey of Abandoned Property Claimed by Arab Refugees" (April 12, 1951).

48. Royal Institute of International Affairs, *The Palestinian Refugee Issue*, 2.

49. Ibid., 9–10.

50. See the English translation of the law at https://www.adalah.org/uploads/oldfiles /Public/files/Discriminatory-Laws-Database/English/33-Budget-Foundations-Law -Amendment40-Nakba-Law.pdf.

51. Quoted in Peter Beaumont, "Netanyahu Pushes to Define Israel as Nation State of Jewish People Only," *Guardian*, May 2, 2014, https://www.theguardian.com/world /2014/may/04/binyamin-netanyahu-israel-jewish-state.

52. This term is used by the Israeli scholar Oren Yiftachel. See his *Ethnocracy: Land and Identity Politics in Israel/Palestine* (Philadelphia: University of Pennsylvania Press, 2006).

Chapter 13. Repairing Colonial Symmetry

This article is a revised version of my lecture "Dead Archives, Displaced Monuments: The 1962 Bureaucratic Ruptures Between Colonial France and Independent Algeria," presented to the Department of Information Studies Colloquium, University of California, Los Angeles, on January 18, 2018. I am grateful to Anne Gilliland for the invitation, numerous discussions, close readings, and the new title.

1. Anne J. Gilliland and Michelle Caswell, "Records and Their Imaginaries: Imagining the Impossible, Making Possible the Imagined," *Archival Science* 16, no. 1 (2016): 53–75; and Mariko Cifor, "Affecting Relations: Introducing Affect Theory to Archival Discourse," *Archival Science* 16, no. 1 (2016): 7–31.

2. United Nations, Basic Principles and Guidelines on the Right to a Remedy and Reparation for Victims of Violations of International Human Rights and Humanitarian Law, E/CN.4/2005/L.48.

3. An overview of these arguments is in William LeGallois, *A History of Violence in the Early Algerian Colony* (London: Palgrave Macmillan, 2013).

4. See Nacer-Eddine Ghozali, "Le Non-Alignement Instrument de l'Indépendance et de la Souveraineté," in *The Principles of Non-alignment: The Non-aligned Countries in the Eighties, Results and Perspectives*, ed. Hans Köchler (London: Third World Centre; Vienna: International Progress Organization, 1982), 93, for Houari Boumédiène's statement: "L'heure n'est-elle pas venue de réaménager les règles du droit international en fonction des données du monde contemporain et en considération du droit naturel des peuples à recouvrer leurs richesses et à en disposer sans avoir à être pénaliser, en servant des primes à ceux-là eux-mêmes qui les ont spoliés et exploités durant des décennies, voire des siècles et qui, logiquement leur doivent réparation."

5. See Claude Liauzu and Gilles Manceron, eds., *La colonisation, la loi et l'histoire* (Paris: Syllepse, 2006).

6. Benjamin Stora, *La guerre des mémoires: La France face à son passé colonial* (La Tour d'Aigues: Aube, 2007).

7. Franz Fanon, *The Wretched of the Earth* (New York : Grove Press, 1968), 103.

8. Ibid.

9. Houari Boumédiène, "Préface," *République algérienne démocratique et populaire : Archives nationales* (January 1973), 1. See the documents constituting the archive services: Présidence du Conseil, *Journal officiel*, no. 93 (November 16, 1971): 1222.

10. Anne Gilliland, email correspondence with author, April 3, 2018.

11. Benoit Van Reeth, ed., *Histoires d'Outre-mer: Les archives nationales d'outre-mer ont 50 ans* (Paris: Somogy, 2017).

12. The *circulaire* included series Z, which were the remaining archives of the Algerian state dating from the fifteenth to the early nineteenth centuries prior to French occupation. On French-Algerian litigation and the *circulaire*, see A. Benbrik, "Special Dossier 1er Novembre 1954: Le Litige Algero-Français sur les Archives Nationales," *Réflexion*, October 24, 2009, https://www.reflexiondz.net/SPECIAL-DOSSIER-1er-Novembre-1954-LE-LITIGE-ALGERO-FRANCAIS-SUR-LES-ARCHIVES-NATIONALES_a3069.html

13. UN Declaration of the Rights of Indigenous Peoples resolution / adopted by the General Assembly, 2 October 2, 2007, A/RES/61/295, https://www.refworld.org/docid/471355a82.html.

14. Law of December 26, 1961, "rapatriés": "Français ayant dû quitter ou estimé devoir quitter, par suite d'événements politiques, un territoire où ils étaient établis et qui était antérieurement placé sous la souveraineté, le protectorat ou la tutelle de la France."

15. Eric Savarèse, "After the Algerian War: Reconstructing Identity Among the Pieds-noirs," *International Social Science Journal* 58 (2006): 457–66; Eric Savarèse, *L'invention des pieds-noirs* (Paris: Séguier, 2002).

16. On *pied-noir* lost property claims, see Robert P. Parks, "From the War of National Liberation to Gentrification: Conflicting Claims over Property in Algeria," *Middle East Report/MERIP*, August 10, 2018, https://www.merip.org/mero/mero081018. An example of a court case is Armand Anton v. Algeria, Communication No. 1424/2005, U.N. Doc. CCPR/C/88/D/1424/2005 (2006), http://hrlibrary.umn.edu/hrcommittee/French/jurisprudence/1424-2005.html. For Algerian Jewish property claims, see Michael R. Fischbach, *Jewish Property Claims Against Arab Countries* (New York: Columbia University Press, 2008).

17. Vincent Crapanzano, *The Harkis: The Wound That Never Heals* (Chicago: University of Chicago Press, 2011), 159–60. See Susan Slyomovics, "French Restitution, German Compensation: Algerian Jews and Vichy's Financial Legacy," *Journal of North African Studies* 17, no. 5 (2012): 881–901.

18. Alexis de Tocqueville, "Second Letter on Algeria (22 August 1837)," in *Writings on Empire and Slavery*, ed. and trans. Jennifer Pitts (Baltimore, MD: Johns Hopkins University Press, 2001), 15.

19. See Patrick Wolfe, "Settler Colonialism and the Elimination of the Native," *Journal of Genocide Research* 8, no. 4 (December 2006): 387–408; Patrick Wolfe, "Land, Labor, and Difference: Elementary Structures of Race," *American Historical Review* 106, no. 3 (2001): 866–905.

20. See Sabrina L., "*L'Estafette d'Alger*, la première publication en Algérie,» *Le Soir d'Algérie* (December 27, 2008) 10, https://www.lesoirdalgerie.com/pdf/2008/12/27 /p10culture.pdf; Herman Fiori, *Bibliographie des ouvrages imprimés à Alger de 1830 à 1850, avec 15 fac-similés*, préface de G. Esquer (Alger: L'auteur; Paris : M. Besson, 1938), 3, 17–18.

21. Achille Mbembe, "The Power of the Archive and Its Limits," in *Refiguring the Archive*, ed. Carolyn Hamilton et al. (Dordrecht, The Netherlands: Kluwer Academic Publishers, 2002), 19–27.

22. Germaine Lebel, "Gabriel Esquer (1876–1961): Note biographique," *Bibliothèque de l'école des chartes* 119 (1961): 367–71, www.persee.fr/doc/bec_0373-6237_1961_num _119_1_460156.

23. Gabriel Esquer, "Les archives algériennes et les sources de l'histoire de la Conquête," *Annales Universitaires de l'Algérie* (September 1912): "C'était pour les bureaux une tradition de jeter dans les caves [les papiers administratifs] qu'ils jugeaient encombrants: c'était ce qu'on appelait 'verser aux archives.' On devait s'apercevoir par la suite que les denrées coloniales étaient enveloppées dans des documents administratifs. C'est ce qui a déterminé avec quelques retards la création d'un service d'archives au gouvernement général." Translation is in the paper.

See also Isabelle Dion, "Les services d'archives en Algérie 1830–1962," *Histoire et archives* 15 (2004) : 88–107.

24. "Killing memory," attributed to historian Mrko D. Grimek, emerged after the deliberate destruction of Sarajevo's famed Oriental Institute and the Bosnian National Library in 1992. See Vesna Blazina, "Mémoricide ou la purification culturelle: La guerre contre les bibliothèques de Croatie et de Bosnie-Herzégovine," *Documentation et bibliothèques* 42, no. 4 (1996): 149–63.

25. See Caswell and Gilliland, "Records and Their Imaginaries."

26. *Memory of the World: Lost Memory—Libraries and Archives Destroyed in the Twentieth Century*, prepared for UNESCO on behalf of IFLA by Hans van der Hoeven and on behalf of ICA by Joan van Albada (Paris: UNESCO, 1996), http://unesdoc .unesco.org/images/0010/001055/105557e.pdf.

27. On Mitterand's belief in the "shared heritage" between France and Algeria even though Algerian archives must remain in France, see Frédéric Bobin, "France-Algérie : Les archives coloniales relèvent d'un patrimoine commun," *Le Monde*, August 10, 2020, https://www.lemonde.fr/afrique/article/2020/08/10/france-algerie-les-archives-colo niales-relevent-d-un-patrimoine-commun_6048596_3212.html.

28. Jean-Pierre Manach, "Algérie: La France révèle l'implantation des mines anti-personnel posées pendant la guerre," *Le Monde*, October 10, 2007, http://www.lemonde.fr/afrique/article/2007/10/22/algerie-la-france-revele-l-implantation-des-mines-antipersonnel-posees-pendant-la-guerre_969615_3212.html#cQiQ6FBPpz5vi4Kp.99.

29. "Macron prêt à rendre les crânes d'insurgés algériens du Musée de l'Homme," *Le Figaro*, December 6, 2017, http://www.lefigaro.fr/flash-actu/2017/12/06/97001-20171206FILWWW00215-macron-pret-a-rendre-les-cranes-d-insurges-algeriens-du-musee-de-l-homme.php. For example, French law had already been changed to repatriate tattooed Maori heads preserved in French museums, see Robert K. Patterson, "Heading Home: French Law Enables Return of Maori Heads to New Zealand," *International Journal of Cultural Property* 17, no. 4 (2010): 643–52.

30. Algerian media listed the combatants' names; see "Voici le liste les crânes les résistants restitués," *Algérie 360,* July 3, 2020, https://www.algerie360.com/20200703-la-liste-des-24-cranes-restitues-devoilee/.

31. Felwine Sarr and Bénédicte Savoy, *Restituer le patrimoine africaine* (Paris: Seuil, 2019), 13–14.

32. UN Commission on Human Rights, Sub-Commission on Prevention of Discrimination and Protection of Minorities, "The Administration of Justice and the Human Rights of Detainees," Forty-ninth session, Item 9 of the agenda, E/CN.4/Sub.2/1997/20/Rev.1, October 2, 1997. See "Question of the Impunity of Perpetrators of Human Rights Violations (Civil and Political)," revised final report prepared by Mr. Joinet pursuant to Sub-Commission decision 1996/119 (henceforth referred to as the Joint Report).

33. LOI n° 2008-696 du 15 juillet 2008 relative aux archives, available at: https://www.legifrance.gouv.fr/affichTexte.do?cidTexte=JORFTEXT000019198529.

For a discussion of the law's deleterious effects, see Hélène Servant, "Les enjeux de la loi sur les archives du 15 juillet 2008: Genèse, principes, application,» *La Gazette des archives* 225 (2012): 63–75.

34. French Senate, 14th Legislature, "Ouverture des archives liées à la guerre d'Algérie," October 23, 2014: "Ainsi, certains fonds d'archives ne peuvent être communiqués qu'à l'expiration d'un délai et ce, afin d'assurer la protection de la vie privée des personnes et de garantir certains intérêts fondamentaux de la Nation," "Thus, certain archival fonds can only be communicated after the expiration of a period in order to insure protecting the privacy of individuals and guarantee certain fundamental interests of the Nation," https://www.senat.fr/questions/base/2014/qSEQ141013433.html.

35. For similar patterns of British archive destruction, purging, and removal in Kenya, albeit minus a powerful settler lobby in the metropole, see Caroline Elkins, "Looking Beyond Mau Mau: Archiving Violence in the Era of Decolonization," *American Historical Review* 120, no. 3 (2015): 852–68.

36. Fouad Soufi, "Les archives algériennes en 1962: héritage et spoliation," *Insaniyat* 65–66 (2014): 211–37.

37. Esquer, "Les archives algériennes et les sources de l'histoire de la Conquête."

38. Marc André and Susan Slyomovics, "Exil pénal et femmes sans noms: Regards anthropologiques et historiques sur les prisonnières algériennes dans les guerres de colonisation et de décolonisation (1830–1962)," *Hespéris-Tamuda* 55, no. 2 (2020).

39. Ann Laura Stoler, "Colonial Archives and the Arts of Governance," *Archival Science* 2 (2002): 92.

40. Michel Duchein, "Theoretical Principles and Practical Problems of Respect des Fonds in Archival Science," *Archivaria* 16 (1983): 64 passim.

41. Code du Patrimoine, first paragraph of Article L. 451-5: "Les biens constituant les collections des musées de France appartenant à une personne publique font partie de leur domaine public et sont, à ce titre, inaliénables. Toute décision de déclassement d'un de ces biens ne peut être prise qu'après avis conforme de la commission scientifique nationale des collections" ["Assets constituting collections of the museums of France belonging to a public person form part of the public domain and are, as such, inalienable. Any decision to declassify one of these assets can only be taken after obtaining the assent of the national scientific commission for collections.], http://www.lending-for-europe.eu/fileadmin/CM/public/documents/Code%20du%20Patrimoine%20de%20France.pdf.

42. Todd Shepard, "'Of Sovereignty': Disputed Archives, 'Wholly Modern' Archives, and the Post-Decolonization French and Algerian Republics, 1962–2012," *American Historical Review* 120 (2015): 869–83.

43. Chikhi, quoted in "La quantité des archives nationales restituées par la France reste 'minime,' » *El Watan*, October 30, 2012, http://www.algeria-watch.de/fr/article/pol/france/archives_minimes.htm.

44. I thank Anne Gilliland for introducing me to the archival science literature and possibilities for redress and reparation. Email correspondence with author, April 3, 2018.

45. Chikhi, quoted in "La quantité des archives nationales restituées par la France reste 'minime,'" : "les archives sont la propriété du territoire où elles ont été trouvées." On the complexities of French Impressionist paintings returned after 1962 to the Algiers Museum of Fine Arts, see Andrew Bellisari, "The Art of Decolonization: The Battle for Algeria's French Art, 1962–70," *Journal of Contemporary History* 52, no. 3 (2016): 625–645.

46. Lorenzo Veracini, "Telling the End of the Settler Colonial Story," in *Studies in Settler Colonialism: Politics, Identity and Culture*, ed. Fiona Bateman and Lionel Pilkington (Houndsmills, UK: Palgrave Macmillan, 2011), 210–11.

47. "En Algérie, Emmanuel Macron qualifie la colonisation française de 'crime contre l'humanité,'" *Libération*, February 15, 2017, http://www.liberation.fr/politiques/2017/02/15/en-algerie-emmanuel-macron-qualifie-la-colonisation-francaise-de-crime-contre-l-humanite_1548723.

48. Constitutional Court of France, Commentaire Décision n° 2017-690 QPC du 8 février 2018 M. Abdelkader K, http://www.conseil-constitutionnel.fr/conseil -constitutionnel/root/bank/download/2017690QPC2017690qpc_ccc.pdf.

Chapter 14. The Romani Genocide During the Holocaust

1. See Henry Friedlander, "Die Vernichtung der Behinderten, der Juden und der Sinti und Roma," in *Kinder und Jugend/icher als Opfer des Holocaust*, eds. Bamberger and Ehmann (Heidelberg: Dokumentations- und Kulturzentrum Deutscher Sinti und Roma, 1995), 15–28.

2. The word "Gypsy/gypsy" has been kept where it occurs in the original texts, and where it is given as Zigeuner in the German-language sources. Otherwise, "Roma/Romani/Romanies" is used throughout this chapter.

3. Rafael Lemkin, *Axis Rule in Occupied Europe: Laws of Occupation, Analysis of Government, Proposals for Redress*, (Washington, DC: Carnegie Endowment for International Peace, 1944), 249–51.

4. Since then, the journal has included more contributions on the subject, for example, Sybil Milton, "Nazi Policies Towards Roma and Sinti, 1933–1945," *Journal of the Gypsy Lore Society*, 5th ser., 2, no. 1 (1992): 1–18. An indication of the growing scholarship acknowledging this is reflected in a count of the year-by-year genocide-related acquisitions in the Romani Archives and Documentation Center at the University of Texas. Following Schechtman's 1966 essay (Joseph B. Schechtman, "The Gypsy Problem," *Midstream: A Monthly Jewish Review* 12, no. 9 [1966]: 52–60), there was nothing until 1980, when the numbers begin to climb—twenty for that year, and (randomly) twenty-five in 1985, twenty-three in 1990, and thirty in 1999.

5. Israel W. Charny, *Toward the Understanding and Prevention of Genocide: Proceedings of the International Conference on the Holocaust and Genocide*, Westview Replica ed. (Boulder, CO: Westview Press, 1984).

6. Ian Hancock, *We Are the Romani People: Ame Sam le Rromane Džene* (Hatfield, UK: University of Hertfordshire Press, 2002), 111–24.

7. Lloyd Grove, "Lament of the Gypsies: 40 Years after Auschwitz, Petitioning for a Place," *Washington Post*, July 21, 1984; Ward Churchill, "Assaults on Truth and Memory," *Z Magazine*, pt. 2, February 2, 1997, 43; Norman Finkelstein, *The Holocaust Industry: Reflections on the Exploitation of Jewish Suffering*, 2nd ed. (London: Verso, 2002), 35.

8. Quoted in John Megel and Ian Hancock, *Statement Relating to the Issue of Romani Representation on the United States Holocaust Memorial Council* (Washington, D.C.: International Romani Union, 1996), 3.

9. File No. 682-PS (Washington, DC: US Government Printing Office, 1946), 496.

10. Stuart Justman, *The Jewish Holocaust for Beginners* (New York: Writers and Readers, 1995), 11.

11. Stefan Wutzke, 2003, http://sintiundromagesch/de/sintiundroma.com. Original text: "Gegenüber die Zigeuner, die Vernichtung des gesamten Volkes auf die glei-

che Ebene wie die Haftstrafe von politisch Andersdenkenden zu stellen [zu Beispiel in der Rubrik 'Sonstig'] ist ungeheuerlich, eine offensichtliche Verzerrung und eine Verfälschung der Geschichte.„

12. The term "Final Solution" has had different applications at different times and in different places. The words "The final solution of the Gypsy problem" can be found as early as 1888 on the first page of the first issue of *The Journal of the Gypsy Lore Society*, though the "problem" referred to there was for scholars to determine the origins of the Romani people and language.

13. Alan Rosenbaum, ed., *Is the Holocaust Unique?* (Boulder, CO: Westview Press, 1995), 15.

14. Reichsfuhrer-SS-Dokument S-Kr. 1, No. 557 (1938).

15. Romani Rose, *"Der Rauch hatten wir täglich vor Augen:" Der nationalsozialistische Völkermord an den Sinti und Roma* (Heidelberg: Wunderhorn, 1999), 347.

16. In German: the endgültige Lösung der Zigeunerfrage, in the Romani language: o Agoruno Impačimos le Rromane Pučhimaske.

17. NS-Rechtspiegel, February 21, 1939.

18. State Museum of Auschwitz-Birkenau. *Memorial Book: The Romanies at Auschwitz-Birkenau.* Documentary and Cultural Centre of German Sintis and Roma (Munich: K.G. Saur, 1993), xiv

19. Michael Burleigh and Wolfgang Wippermann, *The Racial State: Germany, 1933–1945,* (Cambridge: Cambridge University Press, 1991), 121–125.

20. Quoted in Benno Müller-Hill, *Murderous Science: Elimination by Scientific Selection of Jews, Gypsies and Others, 1933–1945,* trans. George R. Fraser (Oxford: Oxford University Press, 1988), 58–59. See also Henry Friedlander, "Die Vernichtung der Behinderten, der Juden und der Sinti und Roma," in *Kinder und Jugendliche als Opfer des Holocaust,* eds. Edgar Bamberger & Annegret Ehmann (Heidelberg: Dokumentations- und Kulturzentrum Deutscher Sinti und Roma/Gedenkstätte Haus der Wannseekonferenz), 15–28; Henry Friedlander, *The Origins of Nazi Genocide, From Euthanasia to the Final Solution* (Chapel Hill: University of North Carolina Press, 1995).

21. Müller-Hill, *Murderous Science,* 124.

22. Burleigh and Wippermann, *The Racial State.*

23. Erika Thurner, "Nazi Policy Against the Romanies," paper delivered at the United States Holocaust Memorial Council's Conference on Other Victims, Washington, DC, March 1987. The term the "Gypsy Question" has emerged since. In August 2008, in an attempt to succeed with its radical anti-Romani rhetoric in the upcoming 2010 general elections, the Czech National Party released details of its proposed "Final Solution to the Gypsy Question in the Czech Lands." In a 150-page study it claimed that it did not want to kill the Romanies, but instead buy land in India and to relocate them there. See *Romea.cz Bulletin,* August 8, 2002, http://www .romea.cz/.

24. Philip Friedman, "The Extermination of the Gypsies: Nazi Genocide against an 'Aryan people'," *Jewish Frontier,* January 1951, 11–14.

25. Gunther Lewy, *The Nazi Persecution of the Gypsies* (New York: Oxford University Press, 2000), 223.

26. Lewy, *The Nazi Persecution of the Gypsies*, 11.

27. Judah Gribetz, *Special Master's Proposal in re Holocaust Victim Assets Litigation* (New York, 2000).

28. Quoted in Bill Sherman, "Tulsa's Holocaust Commemoration to Focus on Non-Jewish Victims," *Tulsa World News*, April 26, 2014, 1.

29. Michael Berenbaum, *The World Must Know: The History of the Holocaust As Told in the United States Holocaust Memorial Museum* (Boston: Little, Brown, 1993); David M. Luebke, *The Nazi Persecution of Sinti and Ròma* (United States Holocaust Memorial Museum Research Brief, April 18, 1990), 3.

30. Quoted in Hannah Arendt, *Eichmann in Jerusalem: A Report on the Banality of Evil* (New York: Viking Press, 1963), 245.

31. Quoted in Henriette Asséo, "La politique nazi de liquidation des Tsiganes," Terre d'Asile, Terre d'Exile, special issue of *Revue Ethnies* 15, no. 4 (1993), 36. See also Donald Kenrick and Grattan Puxon, *Gypsies Under the Swastika* (Hatfield, UK: University of Hertfordshire Press, 2009).

32. Stig Hornshøy-Møller, "Hitler and the Nazi Decision-Making Process to Commit the Holocaust," in *Encyclopedia of Genocide*, two vols., ed. Israel W. Charney (Santa Barbara: ABC-CLIO, 1999), 313.

33. Melvin Salberg and Nat Kameny, *Hitler's Apologists: The Anti-Semitic Propaganda of Holocaust Revisionism* (New York: ADL, 1993), 75.

34. Karola Fings, ed., *In the Shadow of the Swastika, Volume 2: The Gypsies during the Second World War* (Hatfield, UK: University Of Hertfordshire Press, 1999), 133. Donald Kenrick was born in London on June 6, 1929, to a family of Polish-Jewish immigrants and died in November 2015. He was author/editor of *The Gypsies During the Second World War*, vol. 1, *From 'Race Science' to the Camps* (1997); vol. 2, *In the Shadow of the Swastika* (1999); vol. 3, *The Final Chapter* (2006); and *Gypsies Under the Swastika* (2009). He coauthored the first book in English to document the Romani experience in the Holocaust: Donald Kenrick and Grattan Puxon, *The Destiny of Europe's Gypsies* (London: Sussex University Press, 1972). Dr. Kenrick played a major part in urging my own participation in the Romani movement, and it is to his memory that this chapter is dedicated. (For more, see Dileep Karanth, ed., *Danger! Educated Gypsy: Selected Essays by Ian Hancock* [Hatfield, UK: University of Hertfordshire Press, 2010], xiii.).

I'd like also to thank Sarah Gibson, my student in the University of Texas honors course "Jews, Roma, and Race," for allowing me to include some of her research paper findings in this section on the looted Swiss assets.

35. "It was the will of the all-powerful Führer to have the Gypsies disappear from the face of the earth; the Central Office knew it was Hitler's aim to wipe out all the Gypsies without exception [Es war der Wille des allmächtigen Reichsführers, alle Zigeuner von der Erde verschwinden zu lassen; das Zentralbüro wusste, dass es Hitlers Ziel war,

alle Zigeuner ohne Ausnahme auszulöschen]." Perry Broad, "KZ Auschwitz: Erinnerungen eines SS Mannes," *Hefte von Auschwitz*, vol. 9 (1966):7, 31; Auschwitz PM, *Die Auschwitz-Hefte: Texte der polnischen Zeitschrif—"Przeglad lekarski" über historische, psychische und medizinische Aspekte des Lebens und Sterbens in Auschwitz* (Auschwitz: Panstwowe Muzeum, 1959), 54; Percy Broad, "KZ Auschwitz: Erinnerungen eines SS-Mannes," *Hefte von Auschwitz* 9 (1966): 7–48. Milton, "Nazi Policies Towards Roma and Sinti, 1933–1945."

36. "Czech MP Apologizes for 'Imprecision,' Then Urges People to Read Historian [Prof. Jan Rataj] Who Calls the Romani Holocaust a 'Myth,'" Prague, *Romea.cz Bulletin*, February 4, 2018.

37. Donald Kenrick and Grattan Puxon, *The Destiny of Europe's Gypsies* (London: Sussex University Press, 1972).

38. Miriam Novitch, *Le Génocide des Tziganes sous le Régime Nazi*, AMIF Publication No. 164 (Paris: La Comité pour l'Erection du Monument des Tziganes Assassinés à Auschwitz, 1968), 11.

39. Karl Binding and Alfred Hoche, *Die Freigabe der Vernichtung lebensunwerten Lebens* (Leipzig: Felix Meiner, 1920), 2.

40. Phillip Friedman, "The Extermination of the Gypsies: Nazi Genocide of an Aryan People," in his *Roads to Extinction: Essays on the Holocaust* (Lincoln: University of Nebraska Press, 1980), 383.

41. Donald Kenrick, "Gypsies and the Holocaust," *International Network* 11, no. 4 (1996a): 6–9. Donald Kenrick, "The Nazi persecution of the Roma and Sinti: What We Know and What We Don't Yet Know," in *The Holocaust Phenomenon* (Report of the Scientific Conference, Prague), 145–48.

42. Edward Herman and Noam Chomsky, *Manufacturing Consent* (New York: Pantheon Books, 1988), 37.

43. Carolyn D. Dean, *Aversion and Erasure: The Fate of the Victim After the Holocaust* (Ithaca, NY: Cornell University Press, 2017), quote from dust-jacket text.

44. Sybil Milton, "Gypsies and the Holocaust," *The History Teacher* 24, no. 4 (1991), 375.

45. https://www.ushmm.org/information/about-the-museum/presidents-commission.

46. Yehuda Bauer, "Whose Holocaust?" *Midstream* 26, no. 9 (1980), 43.

47. *Days of Remembrance: In Memory of the Gypsy Victims of Nazi Genocide* (Washington: United States Holocaust Memorial Council, 1980) 11.

48. Lucette M. Lagnado and Sheila Cohn Dekel, *Children of the Flames: The Untold Story of the Twins of Auschwitz* (New York: William Morrow, 1991), 82.

49. Ulrich König, *Sinti und Roma unter dem Nationalsozialismus* (Bochum: Brockmeyer Verlag, 1989), 129–33.

50. Michael Zimmermann, "From Discrimination to the 'Family Camp' at Auschwitz: National Socialist Persecution of the Romanies," *Dachau Review* 2 (1990), 107–8.

51. Ibid.

52. Finkelstein, *The Holocaust Industry*, 35.

53. Melanie Phillips, "Shoah Uniqueness Is Now Taboo," *Melanie*, February 3, 2017, http://melaniephillips.com.

54. Quoted in Marek Strzelecki, "Polish-Israeli Dispute Is a Lesson in Holocaust History," *Minneapolis Star Tribune*, February 20, 2018.

55. Zygmunt Bauman, *Modernity and the Holocaust* (Cambridge: The Polity Press, 1989), 9; Pieter Lagrou, "Victims of Genocide and National Memory: Belgium, France and The Netherlands, 1939–1945," *Past and Present* 154, no. 221 (2000), 52.

56. Quoted in Bill Egbert, "Jews Only," *Daily News* (NY), 2009, 1.

57. Bernard Streck, in Rakelmann, 1979.

58. Auschwitz State Memorial (1993), 2.

59. Robert Dawson, *The Porrajmos: Photos of the Gypsy Holocaust in World War 2* (Alfreton: Samizdat, 2013); Robert Dawson, *Never Forget: A Photographic Supplement to the Romani Holocaust* (Alfreton: Samizdat, 2014).

60. Referenced in Ian Hancock, "Fate of Hitler's Romani (Gypsy) Victims Yet to Become Part of Holocaust History," guest editorial, *Detroit Jewish News*, October 7, 1988; Pauwels and Bergier (430).<AQ: need complete cite here.>

61. C. Tyler, "Gypsy President," *Financial Times* (London), March 26, 1994, 3; Susan Strandberg, "Researcher Claims Thousands of Romanies Exterminated by Czechs," *Decorah Journal*, May 5, 1994, 1; Markus Pape, *A Nikdo Vám Nebude Věřit. Dokument o Koncentračním Táboře Lety u Písku* (Prague: GG, 1997).

62. Erika Thurner, *National Socialism and the Gypsies in Austria* (Montgomery: University of Alabama Press, 2006).

63. Sybil Milton, "Reassessing the Racial Context of the Holocaust." Paper presented at the 1990 meeting of The American Historical Association, New York, December 30, 1990.

64. 56th Session of the IOM Migration Report.

65. Dragoljub Acković, *Ma Bister: Roma Suffering in Jasenovac Camp* (Belgrade: Museum of the Victims of Genocide, 1995); Dragoljub Acković, *Oni su Ubili Njegove Oči* (Belgrade: Rrominterpress, 1997); Marc Aarons and John Loftus, *Unholy Trinity: The Vatican, The Nazis, and The Swiss Banks* (New York: St. Martin's Griffin, 1998).

66. Vladimir Dedijer, *The Yugoslav Auschwitz and the Vatican* (Amherst, NY: Prometheus Books, 1992); Maureen Johnson, "Gypsy Gold in the Vatican?" Associated Press news feature on America Online, December 4, 1997, 1; Jonathan Levy, "Legal Charge Filed Against the Vatican for Its Complicity in Taking Valuables from Roma During the Holocaust," *News Insider*, January 17, 2001; Jonathan Levy, "The Lawsuit Against the Vatican for Looting Nazi Gold," *Church and State* (August 2016).

67. Margot S. Strom and William S. Parsons, *Facing History and Ourselves* (Brookline, MA: FHOS Foundation, 1977), 220.

68. Heinz Heger, *The Men with the Pink Triangle: The True Life-and-Death Story of Homosexuals in the Nazi Death Camps* (New York: Alyson Books, 1994), 15.

69. Copy sent to author from Simon Wiesenthal.

70. Jim Miller, "A War to Remember," *Newsweek*, September 4, 1989, 66.

71. Finkelstein, *The Holocaust Industry* (Verso: 2000), 35.

72. See C.S. Coon, "Have the Jews a racial identity?" in Graeber and Britt, 20–37; I. Graeber and S.H. Britt (eds.), *Jews in a Gentile world* (New York, 1942); Marek Kohn, *The Race Gallery: The Return of Racial Science*. (London: Johnathan Cape, 1995). R. Patai and J. Patai-Wing, *The Myth of the Jewish Race* (Detroit, 1989); William Petersen, "Jews as a Race," *Midstream*, Feb.–March 1988, 35–37; Robert Pollack, "The Fallacy of Biological Judaism," *The Jewish Daily Forward*, March 7, 2003, 9.

73. J. D. Thomas et al., "Disease, Lifestyle and Consanguinity in 58 American Gypsies," *The Lancet* 330, no. 8555 (August 25, 1987), 377–79.

74. William Safire, "On Language: Long Time No See," *New York Times Magazine*, September 20, 1983, 12; see also Sandford Berman, "Whose Holocaust Is It Anyway? The 'H' Word in Library Catalogues," in *The Holocaust: Memories, Research, Reference*, ed. Linda Katz (New York: Routledge, 1998), 213–25.

75. Adam Kirsch, "The System," *The New Yorker*, April 6, 2015, 70–74; Roger Cohen, "Sunday Boook Review," *The New York Times*, July 12, 2015.

76. János Kenedi, "Why Is the Gypsy the Scapegoat and Not the Jew?" *East European Reporter* 2, no. 1 (1984), 14; Dan Bilefsky, "Are the Roma Primitive, or Just Poor?" *New York Times Sunday Review*, News Analysis, October 19, 2013, 4.

77. Simon Wiesenthal, *Justice Not Vengeance* (New York: Grove Weidenfeld, 1989), 237.

78. Simon Wiesenthal, "Tragedy of the Gypsies," *Bulletin of Information* No. 26, Dokumentationszentrum des Bundes Jüdischer Vervolgter des Naziregimes, Vienna, 1986, 6.

79. *UNESCO Yearbook on Peace and Conflict Studies* (New York: Greenwood, 1987).

80. Steven Katz, "Quantity and Interpretation: Issues in the Comparative Historical Analysis of the Holocaust," *Remembering for the Future: Papers to be Presented at the Scholars' Conference*, Supplementary Volume (Oxford: Pergamon Press, 1988), 213.

81. Yehuda Bauer, [Response to Papazian (1994) in] "Was the Holocaust Unique?" *Midstream* 30, no. 4 (1994); John P. Fox, "The Nazi Extermination of the Romanies: Genocide, Holocaust, or a 'Minor Irritant'?" paper presented at the Conference of the Association of Genocide Scholars, Williamsburg, VA, June 14–16, 1995.

82. Edward Alexander, "Review of Lopate," *Congress Monthly*, May/June 1990, 13.

83. Richard Breitman, *The Architect of Genocide: Himmler and the Final Solution* (New York: Alfred A. Knopf, 1991), 20.

84. Francis Laufenberg, *Model Curriculum for Human Rights and Genocide* (Sacramento: California State Board of Education, 1998), 5.

85. Pierre Papazian, "A Unique Uniqueness?" *Midstream* 30, no. 4 (1994); David E. Stannard, "Uniqueness As Denial: The Politics of Genocide Scholarship," in Rosenbaum, *Is the Holocaust Unique?* 245–91; David E. Stannard, "The Dangers of Calling the Holocaust Unique," *Chronicle of Higher Education*, August 2, 1996; Churchill,

"Assaults on Truth and Memory"; David Young, "The Trial of Remembrance: Monuments and Memories of the Porrajmos," *Genocide Perspectives* 1 (1997); Amy Sodaro, "Forgotten Victims: The Absence of the Roma in the U.S. Holocaust Memorial Museum" (Master's Thesis, The New University, New York, 2004).

86. Larissa Allwork, *Holocaust Remembrance Between the National and the Transnational: The Stockholm International Forum and the First Decade of the International Task Force* (London: Bloomsbury Academic, 2015).

87. Peter Berkowitz, *Report on Progress with the College Board to Have the Holocaust and Genocide Included in Their AP US, AP European and AP World History Curriculums* (Austin, TX: Texas Holocaust and Genocide Commission, February 12, 2015).

88. Correspondence between the College Board and our Commission's chairman, Peter Berkowitz.

89. Sidney M. Bolkosky and Betty Rotberg Ellias, *A Holocaust Curriculum: Life Unworthy of Life, an 18-Lesson Instructional Unit* (New York: Center for the Study of the Child, 1987); Israel Gutman, *Encyclopedia of the Holocaust*, 4 vols (New York: Macmillan, 1009).

90. Leslie Doolittle, "Gypsies Say Holocaust Project Snubbing Them," *Dallas Times Herald* (June 28, 1984), B6; Grove, "Lament of the Gypsies," C4.

91. Edward J. Boyer, "Gypsies Remember Holocaust, Want Role on Memorial Council," *Los Angeles Times*, June 26, 1984, 3; Doolittle, "Gypsies Say Holocaust Project Snubbing Them," A23.

92. Jackie Jacobs, "Romani Deserve Place on Council," *Jewish Federation Reporter*, July 19, 1984, 3.

93. Reproduced in Hancock, *We Are the Romani People*, 50.

94. Berenbaum, *The World Must Know*, 1.

95. Doolittle, "Gypsies Say Holocaust Project Snubbing Them," A3.

96. Ian Hancock, "Responses to the Porrajmos," in *Danger! Educated Gypsy: Selected Essays by Ian Hancock*, ed. Dileep Karanth (Hatfield, UK: University of Hertfordshire Press, 2010), 226–63; Ian Hancock, "Elie Wiesel, Simon Wiesenthal, Romanies and the U.S. Holocaust Memorial Council," *The Holocaust in History and Memory* 4 (2011): 105–23.

97. Bruce Weber, "A Hard Lesson," *New York Times Magazine*, March 23, 1988.

98. Ludwig Eiber, "The Persecution of the Sinti and Roma in Munich, 1933–1945," in *Sinti and Roma: Gypsies in German-speaking Society and Literature*, ed. Susan Tebbutt (New York: Berghahn Books, 1988), 17–33.

99. Bauer, [Response to Papazian (1994) in] "Was the Holocaust Unique?," 20.

100. Lewy, *The Nazi Persecution of the Gypsies*, 222.

101. Sybil Milton, "Holocaust: The Gypsies," in *Century of Genocide*, eds. Samuel Totten, William S. Parsons, Israel Charny (New York: Garland Publishing, 1997), chap. 6, 171–207, 171.

102. Ibid., 171n16.

103. Robert Korber, *Rassesieg in Wien, der Grenzseste des Reiches* (Vienna: Wilhelm Braumuller, 1939). Globke quote is in Kenrick and Puxon, *Gypsies Under the Swastika*, 11.

104. Tobias Portschy, *Die Zigeuner* (Eisenstadt: Denkschrift des Landeshauptmannes für das Burgenland, 1938).

105. Joachim S. Hohmann, *Zigeuner und Zigeunerwissensschaft* (Marburg: Lahn, Guttandin and Hoppe, 1980), 201; For the Himmler quote, https://www.history.com/this-day-in-history/himmler-orders-gypsies-to-concentration-camps; for Best: Kenrick and Puxon, *Gypsies Under the Swastika*, 12.

106. Kenrick and Puxon, *Gypsies Under the Swastika*, 12.

107. Ibid., 13.

108. Julia von dem Knesebeck, *The Roma Struggle for Compensation in Post-war Germany* (Hatfield, UK: University of Hertfordshire Press, 2011), 162.

109. Grattan Puxon, "Plight of Gypsies," *Patterns of Prejudice* 11, no. 2 (1977): 23–28.

110. Puxon, *Forgotten Victims*, 25; "West Germany: The Nazis' Forgotten Victims," *Time*, vol. 114 (21), 1979, 58.

111. Kevin Costelloe, "Gypsies Want Reparation for Slave Labor Under the Nazis," *Minneapolis Star and Tribune*, March 25, 1986, 4A.

112. Arno J. Mayer, "Memory and History: On the Poverty of Remembering and Forgetting the Judeocide," *Radical History Review* 56 (1993), 16.

113. The best source documenting this over the years is the periodical *Scharotl*, published by the Genossenshaft der Landstrasse Interessengemeinschaft des Fahrendes Volkes in der Schweitz, available from the Secretariat, Postfach 1647, 8048 Zurich, Switzerland.

114. "West Germany: The Nazis' Forgotten Victims."

115. Maria Puente, "Report Says Nazis Paid Neutral Nations with Stolen Gold," *USA Today*, June 2, 1998, 6-A.

116. John-Thor Dahlberg, "Switzerland unveils plan for $4.7 billion victims' fund," *Los Angeles Times*, March 6, 1997, 1.

117. "Gypsies Aggravated at Being Left Off Holocaust Fund Board: Omission by the Swiss Government Is Called an Insult to the Memory of Nameless Victims," *Fort Worth Star Telegram*, April 20, 1997; Puente, "Report Says Nazis Paid Neutral Nations with Stolen Gold," 6-A.

118. Puente, "Report Says Nazis Paid Neutral Nations with Stolen Gold," 6-A.

119. *Anon.*, "Swiss Court Dismisses Gypsies' Holocaust Case against IBM," *Global Ethics Monitor*, Agence France-Presse, bulletin dated June 3, 2003.

120. "West Germany: The Nazis' Forgotten Victims," 58.

121. Julie Masis, "Roma Holocaust Survivors Look to Jews as Model for Recognition—and Reparation," *The Times of Israel*, September 23, 2017.

122. Julie Masis, "Roma Holocaust Survivors Look to Jews as Model for Recognition—and Reparation," *Times of Israel*, September 23, 2017, 1. Romania:

Mihai Ghiduc, "Drama romilor deportați de Antonescu: oamenii nimănui, pierduți în birocrația românească," *VICE*, https://www.vice.com/ro/article/vbw3em/romania -refuza-sa-plateasca-pensii-romilor-care-au-supravietuit-holocaustului.

123. Quoted in Ghiduc, "Drama romilor deportați de Antonescu." See also Michelle Kelso, "The Last Chapter of the Holocaust: The Policy of Compensation for Stolen Assets and Slave Labor: A Study of Gypsy Survivors of Nazi Persecution in Romania" (Master's thesis, (Austin, the University of Texas, 2001).

124. Ralf Possekel, "Policies and Strategies to Promote Tolerance and Non-Discrimination," Organization for Security and Cooperation in Europe Special Report, Berlin, April 14–15, 2016, http://www.osce.org/pc/236181.

125. Ralf Possekel, "Policies and Strategies to Promote Tolerance and Non-Discrimination," Organization for Security and Cooperation in Europe Special Report, Berlin, April 14–15, 2016, http://www.osce.org/pc/236181.

126. Grattan Puxon, "US Romani Holocaust Council Report on Inaugural Meeting, Los Angeles," unpublished, privately circulated report, 1984.

127. Grove, "Lament of the Gypsies," C1.

128. Charles Hirschberg, "Romanies lobby for representation on Holocaust Memorial Council," *The Washington Post*, Sunday, March 9, 1986, A16.

129. Wiesenthal, *Justice Not Vengeance*, 315.

130. Toby Sonneman, "Promoting Dialogue and Action for Human Rights: The Romani-Jewish Alliance," General Support Proposal, 1991.

131. Finkelstein, *The Holocaust Industry*,154.

132. Judith Latham, First US Conference on Gypsies in the Holocaust, Transcript of taped report, National Public Radio Current Affairs feature No. 3-23928, and U.S. Information Agency, Voice of America, Washington, 1995; Jacqueline Burke, ed., *Proceedings of the Conference entitled Romanies in the Holocaust: The Nazi Assault on Sinti and Roma* (Madison, NJ: Center for Holocaust Studies, Drew University, 1996).

133. Ian Hancock, "Fate of Hitler's Romani (Gypsy) Victims Yet to Become Part of Holocaust History," Guest Editorial, *Detroit Jewish News*, October 7, 1988).

134. Sebastian M. Rainone, "The Distribution of Funds to the Romani People: The Hancock Proposal [Relating to Looted Swiss Assets]", Philadelphia, 1998.

135. In an essay published more than thirty years ago, I referred to an article that appeared in the *Toronto Sun* that began "Gypsy. Even the word is impossibly romantic. Dark eyes, crying violins and wanderlust, a life of pleasure and abandon." Ian Hancock, "The Function of the Gypsy Myth," *Roma* 27 (1987), 38. I also quoted from a newspaper piece about Halloween from the same year, which described "men and women of all ages dressed as witches, monsters, fairies, gypsies and other supernatural characters." Maureen McLeod, "The Gypsies Are Coming!" *Toronto Sun,* March 14, 1985, 15; Randolph Connor, "Witches, Ghosts, Gypsies and Other Supernatural Beings," *Images*, October 25, 1985, 5.

In the intervening three decades the perception for some journalists has still not changed; an article about an art exhibit in Springfield, Ohio, which appeared while I was writing this chapter, referred to "the worlds of mystery and magic . . . fairies, gypsies and carnival scenes." Brett Turner, "Fairies, Gypsies and Carnival Scenes: Why You Should Visit This New Springfield Art Exhibit," *Springfield News Sun*, April 23, 2018. I addressed this in a report I gave on media responsibility before the Congressional Human Rights Hearing on Abuses against Gypsies that took place in Washington, DC, on April 14, 1994, when I criticized the minimal—or nonexistent—background research those responsible felt to be necessary when the topic involved Romanies.

136. Weer R. Rishi, "The London Conference on Nazi Gold," *Roma* 48/49 (1998).

137. Roy L. Brooks, ed.. *When Sorry Isn't Enough* (New York: New York University Press, 1999), 73.

138. Toby Sonneman, *Shared Sorrows: A Gypsy Family Remembers the Holocaust* (Hatfield, UK: University of Hertfordshire Press, 2002); Toby Sonneman, interview for Ian Hancock, with Mrs. L.T. "Riley" Herschmer of Springfield, Colorado, 1991.

139. Marie Smutná et al., "Czech Citizens File Crime Report over MP's Remarks Denying the Suffering of Romani Genocide Victims," *RomeaNews*, February 3, 2018; "Czech MP Apologizes for 'Imprecision'; "Mayor of Brno Joins March Against Denial of the Holocaust of the Roma," Prague, *Romea.cz Bulletin*, February 16, 2018).

140. For example, Amy Sodaro, "Forgotten Victims: The Absence of the Roma in the United States Holocaust Memorial Museum" (Master's thesis, The New University, 2004); Bjærni Henderson, "The Struggle for the Recognition of the Porrajmos in Post-War Austria" (Master's thesis, University of St. Andrews, 2012).

141. Wolfgang Wippermann, *"Auserwählte Opfer?" Shoah und Porrajmos im Vergleich* (Berlin: Frank and Timme, 2012).

142. Puxon, *Forgotten Victims*, 26.

Chapter 15. The Roma Case for Reparations

1. For an excellent overview of reparations and practice, see John Torpey, *Making Whole What Has Been Smashed* (Cambridge, MA: Harvard University Press, 2006);

2. J. Angelo Corlett, *Heirs of Oppression*, (Lanham, MD: Rowman & Littlefield Publishers, 2010), 26.

3. J. Angelo Corlett, *Race, Racism, and Reparations* (Ithaca, NY: Cornell University Press, Ithaca, 2003).

4. Susan Slyomovics, "Reparations in Morocco: The Symbolic Dirham," in *Waging War, Making Peace*, ed. Barbara Rose Johnston and Susan Slyomovics (Walnut Creek, CA: Left Coast Press, 2009), 95–114.

5. Torpey, *Making Whole What Has Been Smashed*; Payton Guion, "Some US Victims of Forced Sterilization Are About to Be Compensated—But Most Aren't," *Vice News*, October 24, 2014, https://news.vice.com/en_us/article/a389ja/some-us-victims-of-forced-sterilization-are-about-to-be-compensated-but-most-arent.

6. "Case for Reparation Gains International Force," *Harvard Law Today*, February 2016, https://today.law.harvard.edu/case-for-reparation-gains-international-force/.

7. State Sponsored Collective Injustice Conference, Panel 1, *FXB Center for Health and Human Rights at Harvard University,* https://www.youtube.com/watch?v=4g7 -XY4GGls.

8. Torpey, *Making Whole What Has Been Smashed,* 22.

9. J. Angelo Corlett, *Race, Racism and Reparations* (Ithaca, NY: Cornell University Press, 2003).

10. Alison Dundes Renteln, "Reparations and Human Rights: Why the Anthropological Approach Matters," in Barbara Rose Johnston and Susan Slyomovics, eds., *Waging War, Making Peace: Reparations and Human Rights* (Walnut Creek, CA: Left Coast Press, 2009).

11. P. H. Collins, *Black Feminist Thought: Knowledge, Consciousness, and the Politics of Empowerment,* 2nd ed. (New York: Routledge, 2000), 18, but also throughout the book.

12. Margareta Matache, "Biased Elites, Unfit Policies: Reflections on the Lacunae of Roma Integration Strategies," *European Review* 25, no. 4 (October 2017): 588–607.

13. According to Benjamin Isaac, "The term proto-racism . . . may be used when Greek and Latin sources attribute to groups of people common characteristics considered to be unalterable because they are determined by external factors or heredity." Benjamin H. Isaac, *The Invention of Racism in Classical Antiquity* (Princeton, NJ: Princeton University Press, 2006), 38.

14. See Francisco Bethencourt, "Introduction," in *Racisms: From the Crusades to the Twentieth Century* (Princeton, NJ: Princeton University Press, 2013); Julia K. Ward, "*Ethnos* in the *Politics*: Aristotle and Race," in *Philosophers on Race—Critical Essays,* in ed. Julie K. Ward and Tommy L. Lott (Oxford: Blackwell Publishing, 2002), 14–37; Isaac, *The Invention of Racism in Classical Antiquity.*

15. Isaac, *The Invention of Racism in Classical Antiquity,* 65.

16. Ibram X. Kendi, *Stamped from the Beginning: The Definitive History of Racist Ideas in America* (New York: Nation Books, Public Affairs, 2016), 17, Kindle.

17. Ward, "*Ethnos* in the *Politics,*" 28.

18. Ian Hancock, "The Pariah Syndrome," *Patrin Web Journal,* 1987, http://www .oocities.org/~patrin/pariah-contents.htm; Donald Kenrick and Grattan Puxon, *The Destiny of Europe's Gypsies* (New York: Basic Books, 1972).

19. John Hoyland, *A Historical Survey of the Customs, Habits, and Present State of the Gypsies* (1816; Tredition Classics, 2012), 8, Kindle.

20. Erik Ljungherg, cited in Kenrick and Puxon, *The Destiny of Europe's Gypsies,* 22.

21. Ibid., 19.

22. Cited in George Smith, *Gypsy Life: Being an Account of Our Gypsies and Their Children. With Suggestions for Their Improvement* (London: Haughton & Co., 1888).

23. John Hoyland, *A Historical Survey of the Customs, Habits, and Present State of the Gypsies* (transcribed from the 1816 WM Alexander edition by David Price; London: Kensington Library, 2010), 6, Kindle.

24. Cited in Hoyland, *A Historical Survey*, 11, Kindle.

25. *The New Review, Political, Philosophical, and Literary*, vol. 2, no. VIII, December1863, "The Gypsies," (Dublin: Hodges, Smith & Co., Booksellers to the University), 524.

26. See Margareta Matache, "Word, Image and Thought: Creating the Romani Other," October 5, 2016, FXB Center for Health and Human Rights at Harvard University, https://fxb.harvard.edu/2016/10/05/word-image-and-thought-creating-the-romani-other/.

27. Kenrick and Puxon, *The Destiny of Europe's Gypsies*.

28. Ibid.

29. Angus Fraser, *The Gypsies*, 2nd ed. (Oxford: Blackwell Publishing, 1995). According to the UN Convention on the Prevention and Punishment of the Crime of Genocide, genocide is defined as "any of the following acts committed with intent to destroy, in whole or in part, a national, ethnical, racial or religious group, as such (a) Killing members of the group; (b) Causing serious bodily or mental harm to members of the group; (c) Deliberately inflicting on the group conditions of life calculated to bring about its physical destruction in whole or in part; (d) Imposing measures intended to prevent births within the group; (e) Forcibly transferring children of the group to another group." UN General Assembly, "Convention on the Prevention and Punishment of the Crime of Genocide," United Nations Human Rights Office of the High Commissioner, January 12, 1951.

30. Marc Pons, "The Gypsy Genocide of Bourbon Spain," *El Nacional*, July 30, 2017, https://www.elnacional.cat/en/culture/gypsy-genocide-bourbon_182073_102.html.

31. Hoyland, *A Historical Survey*, 69, Kindle.

32. Hoyland, *A Historical Survey*, 69.

33. Nicolae Gheorghe, "The Origin of Roma's Slavery in the Romanian Principalities," *Roma* 7, no. 1 (1983): 12–27.

34. Jonathan Lee, "The Shame of European's Forgotten Slaves," *Norwich Radical*, October 20, 2015, https://thenorwichradical.com/2015/10/20/the-shame-of-europes-forgotten-slaves/.

35. Emile Kohly de Guggsberg, cited in Viorel Achim, *The Roma in Romanian History* (Budapest: Central European University Press, 1998), 97.

36. See Peter Widmann, "The Campaign Against the Restless: Criminal Biology and the Stigmatization of the Gypsies, 1890–1960," in *The Roma—A Minority in Europe: Historical, Political and Social Perspectives*, ed. Roni Stauber and Raphael Vago (Budapest: Central European University Press, 2013), 19–29, 20.

37. Kenrick and Puxon, *The Destiny of Europe's Gypsies*, 66.

38. Ethel Brooks, "Remembering the Dead, Documenting Resistance, Honouring the Heroes," Discussion Papers Series, The Holocaust and the United Nations Outreach Programme, Department of Global Communications, United Nations, http://www.un.org/en/holocaustremembrance/docs/paper23.shtml.

39. Yaron Matras, *I Met Lucky People: The Story of the Romani Gypsies* (London: Penguin, 2015), 173.

40. European Union Agency for Fundamental Rights, "Education: The Situation of Roma in 11 EU Member States Roma Survey—Data in Focus," 2014.

41. Interviews with Viktoria Mohacs and Rumyan Russinov in Iulius Rostas, *Ten Years After: A History of Roma School Desegregation in Central and Eastern Europe* (Budapest: Central European University Press, 2012).

42. Walter Leimgruber, *Between Global and Local: Marginality and Marginal Regions in the Context of Globalization and Deregulation* (London: Routledge, 2018).

43. "Join and Fight the Removal of Roma Children From Their families Into State Care in Slovakia," European Roma Rights Centre, http://www.errc.org/act-now/join-and-fight-the-removal-of-roma-children-from-their-families-into-state-care-in-slovakia; Emily Goddard, "They Took My Life. I'm Grieving for a Child Who Is Still Alive," *Guardian*, January 24, 2018, https://www.theguardian.com/society/2018/jan/24/care-system-discriminating-gypsy-roma-traveller-children.

44. Anikó Bernát et al., "The Roots of Radicalism and Anti-Roma Attitudes on the Far Right," presentation at Hungary: Where Do We Stand in 2012: A Conference on Economic Conditions and Social Cohesion, TÁRKI Social Research Institute and Friedrich Ebert Stiftung, Budapest, November 22–23, 2012, http://old.tarki.hu/hu/news/2012/kitekint/20121122_bernat_kreko_prezentacio.pdf.

45. "Italians Overwhelmingly View Roma Unfavorably," Pew Research Center, Global Attitudes and Trends, June 1, 2015.

46. "Anger grows in Hungary over anti-Roma article," *The Guardian,* January 8, 2013, https://www.theguardian.com/world/2013/jan/08/anger-hungary-anti-roma-article

47. Maja Zivanovic, "Serbia's Acquittal of Sima's Chetniks Paramilitaries 'Ignorant,'" *Balkan Transitional Justice*, July 4, 2018, https://balkaninsight.com/2018/07/04/the-appellate-court-strengthening-conditions-for-proving-war-crimes-hlc-07-04-2018/.

48. Ibid.

49. "Attacks Against Roma in Hungary: January 2008–September 2012," European Roma Rights Centre, October 1, 2012, http://www.errc.org/uploads/upload_en/file/attacks-list-in-hungary.pdf.

50. Chris Scott, "Roma's Murder by Far Right Reveals Deep Wounds in Ukraine," *Al Jazeera*, June 30, 2018, https://www.aljazeera.com/indepth/features/attack-roma-killed-laid-rest-180629175419541.html.

51. Iuliia Mendel, "Attacks on Roma Force Ukraine to Confront an Old Ethnic Enmity," *New York Times*, July 23, 2018, https://www.nytimes.com/2018/07/21/world/europe/ukraine-roma-attacks.html.

52. Aurelien Breeden, "Child Abduction Rumors Lead to Violence Against Roma in France," *New York Times*, March 28, 2019, https://www.nytimes.com/2019/03/28/world/europe/roma-kidnap-rumors-france.html.

53. Margareta Matache, "Biased Elites, Unfit Policies: Reflections on the Lacunae of Roma Integration Strategies," *European Review* 25, no. 4 (October 2017): 588–607.

54. "Building Wall to Separate a Roma Community in Baia Mare City," RED Atlas of Racism, *Discrimination and Equality*, June 20, 2011, http://www.red-network.eu/?i =red-network.en.items&id=466.

55. Elisabetta Povoledo and Gaia Pianigiani, "Italian Minister Moves to Count and Expel Roma, Drawing Outrage," *New York Times*, June 19, 2018, https://www.nytimes .com/2018/06/19/world/europe/italy-roma-matteo-salvini.html; "Matteo Salvini Demands Report on Roma Settlements So 'Eviction Plan' Can Be Drawn Up," *Telegram*, July 16, 2019, https://www.telegraph.co.uk/news/2019/07/16/matteo-salvini-demands -report-roma-settlements-eviction-plan/; "Matteo Salvini Orders Crackdown on Roma Communities," *Financial Times*, July 16, 2019, https://www.ft.com/content/bad8aa74 -a7d3-11e9-b6ee-3cdf3174eb89.

56. "Roma rights and the Next Generation," FXB Center for Health and Human Rights, May 3, 2018, https://fxb.harvard.edu/2018/05/03/roma-rights-and-the-next -generation-alone-and-together/.

57. Eva Zdanlova, "German Court Says Immigrant Romani Pupil Incorrectly Assigned to 'Special School' Deserves Compensation," *Romea.cz*, July 7, 2018, http://www.romea.cz/en/news/world/german-court-says-immigrant-romani-pupil -incorrectly-assigned-to-special-school-deserves-compensation#.W1LDTqq_z6Y .facebook.

58. Matthew Windsor, "Case Watch: Pretrial Detention, Pilot Judgments and the European Court of Human Rights" *Open Society Justice Initiative* (2019), https://www .justiceinitiative.org/voices/case-watch-pretrial-detention-pilot-judgments-and -european-court-human-rights; European Court of Human Rights, "Pilot Judgments," Press Unit, January 2019, https://www.echr.coe.int/Documents/FS_Pilot_judgments _ENG.pdf.

59. Windsor, "Case Watch."

60. Amartya Sen, *The Idea of Justice* (Cambridge, MA: The Belknap Press of Harvard University Press, 2001).

61. European Commission et al., "A Synthesis Report on Implementation of National Roma Integration Strategies in Bulgaria, Czech Republic, Hungary, Romania and Slovakia Focusing on Structural and Horizontal Preconditions for Successful Implementation of the Strategy," 2018.

62. "Strategies and Tactics to Combat Segregation of Roma Children in Schools: Case Studies from Romania, Croatia, Hungary, Czech Republic, Bulgaria, and Greece," FXB Center for Health and Human Rights at Harvard University, 2015, https://cdn2 .sph.harvard.edu/wp-content/uploads/sites/5/2015/05/Roma-Segregation-full-final .pdf.

63. D. H. and Others vs. The Czech Republic, No. 57325/00, European Court of Human Rights, November 13, 2007.

64. Howard Zehr, "Restorative Justice? What's That?" *IIRP News*, October 22, 2009, https://www.iirp.edu/eforum-archive/4424-restorative-justice-what-s-that.

65. The principles of restorative justice include: "Crime is an offense against human relationships; The first priority of justice processes is to assist victims; The second priority is to restore the community, to the degree possible; Victims and the community are central to justice processes; The offender has personal responsibility to victims and to the community for crimes committed; Stakeholders share responsibilities for restorative justice through partnerships for action; the offender will develop improved competency and understanding as a result of the restorative justice experience." National Institute of Justice, "Restorative Justice Symposia Summary," U.S. Department of Justice, June 1997, https://www.ncjrs.gov/pdffiles1/nij/248890.pdf; Martha Minow, *Between Vengeance and Forgiveness: Facing History After Genocide and Mass Violence* (Boston: Beacon Press, 1998).

66. Howard Zehr, *The Little Book of Restorative Justice: Revised and Updated* (New York: Skyhorse Publishing, 2015), 10.

67. Minow, *Between Vengeance and Forgiveness*; Zehr, *The Little Book of Restorative Justice*.

68. Zehr, *The Little Book of Restorative Justice*.

69. Zehr, *The Little Book of Restorative Justice*, 226, Kindle.

70. Swedish Ministry of Culture, "The Dark Unknown History: White Paper on Abuses and Rights Violations Against Roma in the 20th Century," Stockholm, Government of Sweden, 2015.

71. "Body and Soul: Forced Sterilization and Other Assaults on Roma Reproductive Freedom," Center for Reproductive Rights, 2003, https://www.reproductiverights.org/document/body-and-soul-forced-sterilization-and-other-assaults-on-roma-reproductive-freedom.

72. "Coercize and Cruel: A Report by the European Roma Rights Centre," *ERRC*, November 2016, http://www.errc.org/uploads/upload_en/file/coercive-and-cruel-28-november-2016.pdf.

73. Minow, *Between Vengeance and Forgiveness*, 119.

74. Torpey, *Making Whole What Has Been Smashed*, 50.

75. Ibid., 166.

76. Pierre Chopinaud, "The Forgotten History of Romani Resistance," *Open Society Foundations*, May 15, 2015, https://www.opensocietyfoundations.org/voices/forgotten-history-romani-resistance.

77. Hancock, "The Pariah Syndrome."

78. Kenrick and Puxon, *The Destiny of Europe's Gypsies*, 47.

79. "16 May 1944—a day to remember," *Council of Europe*, May 15, 2020, https://www.coe.int/en/web/roma-and-travellers/-/16-may-1944-a-day-to-remember#:~:text=The%20courageous%20revolt%20of%2016,People%20on%20the%20Roma%20Genocide.

80. David Lorenc, "They Weren't Just Victims: Roma, Forgotten Heroes of the Anti-Nazi Resistance," trans. Gwendolyn Albert, *Romea.cz,* May 21, 2015, http://www.romea.cz/en/news/czech/they-weren-t-just-victims-roma-forgotten-heroes-of-the-anti-nazi-resistance.

81. Hancock, "The Pariah Syndrome."

82. Henry Kamm, "Havel Calls the Gypsies 'Litmus Test,'" *New York Times,* December 10, 1993, https://www.nytimes.com/1993/12/10/world/havel-calls-the-gypsies-litmus-test.html.

83. Zehr, *The Little Book of Restorative Justice,* 226, Kindle.

84. "Strategies and Tactics to Combat Segregation of Roma Children in Schools."

85. Minow, *Between Vengeance and Forgiveness,* 25.

86. Torpey, *Making Whole What Has Been Smashed*; Jeremy Waldron, "Superseding Historic Injustice," *Ethics* 103, no. 1 (October 1992), 4–28.

87. Zehr, *The Little Book of Restorative Justice,* 233, Kindle.

88. Filip Rudic and Serbeze Haxhiaj, "Stolen Homes: Kosovo Struggles with Wartime Property Seizures," *Balkan Transitional Justice,* May 29, 2018, https://balkaninsight.com/2018/05/29/stolen-homes-kosovo-struggles-with-wartime-property-seizures-05-22-2018/.

89. Minow, *Between Vengeance and Forgiveness,* 112.

90. Radu Andreea, "Damian Drăghici Marchează 160 de Ani de La 'Dezrobirea Romilor' Printr-o Placă Comemorativă," *evz.ro,* February 19, 2016, http://evz.ro/damian-draghici-marcheaza-160-de-ani-de-la-dezrobirea-romilor-printr-o-placa-comemorativa.html; Margareta Matache and Jacqueline Bhabha, "Roma Slavery: The Case for Reparations," *Foreign Policy in Focus,* April 22, 2016, https://fpif.org/roma-slavery-case-reparations/.

91. Gwendolyn Albert and Marek Szilvasi, "Intersectional Discrimination of Romani Women Forcibly Sterilized in the Former Czechoslovakia and Czech Republic," *Health and Human Rights Journal* 19, no. 2 (2017).

92. "Czech State May Finally Compensate Forced Sterilization Victims," *Romea.cz,* October 8, 2019, http://www.romea.cz/en/news/czech/czech-state-may-finally-compensate-forced-sterilization-victims.

93. Derrick Bell, "Racial Realism," *Connecticut Law Review* 24 (1991/92): 363–80.

94. The Office of the UN High Commissioner for Human Rights (OHCHR) underlines that "there is no uniform definition of gross human rights violations in international law," but it would include "genocide, slavery and slavery-like practices, summary or arbitrary executions, torture, enforced disappearances, arbitrary and prolonged detention, and systematic discrimination." Also, it argues that "other kinds of human rights violations, including of economic, social and cultural rights, can also count as gross violations if they are grave and systematic, for example violations taking place on a large scale or targeted at particular population groups." See "The Corporate Responsibility to Respect Human Rights," United

Nations OHCHR, 2012, https://www.ohchr.org/Documents/Publications/HR.PUB
.12.2_En.pdf.

Chapter 16. What Justice for Starvation Crimes?

1. Evelyne Schmid, *Taking Economic, Social and Cultural Rights Seriously in International Criminal Law* (Cambridge: Cambridge University Press, 2015), 2.

2. Ibid, 3.

3. Lizzie Collingham, *The Taste of War: World War II and the Battle for Food* (New York: Penguin, 2012): 3.

4. Raphael Lemkin, *Axis Rule in Occupied Europe* (Washington, DC: Carnegie Endowment for International Peace, 1944).

5. Alex de Waal, *Mass Starvation: The History and Future of Famine* (Cambridge: Polity Press, 2017).

6. Ibid.

7. Alex de Waal, *Famine Crimes: Politics and the Disaster Relief Industry in Africa* (London: James Currey, 1997): 106–32.

8. Randle C. DeFalco, "Accounting for the Famine at the Extraordinary Chambers in the Courts of Cambodia: The Crimes against Humanity of Extermination, Inhumane Acts and Persecution," *International Journal of Transitional Justice* 5 (2011): 142–58.

9. Amartya Sen, *Development As Freedom* (Oxford: Clarendon Press, 2000); de Waal, *Famine Crimes*. Note that Sen's "entitlement theory" is narrowly economic, but the more common legal or political sense of "entitlement" is equally appropriate.

10. David Scheffer, "Genocide and Atrocity Crimes," *Genocide Studies and Prevention* 1, no. 3 (2006): 229–50.

11. Diana Sankey, "Towards Recognition of Subsistence Harms: Reassessing Approaches to Socioeconomic Forms of Violence in Transitional Justice," *International Journal of Transitional Justice* 8 (2014): 121–40.

12. UN General Assembly, Resolution 260, Convention on the Prevention and Punishment of the Crime of Genocide (9 December 1948), http://un-documents.net /a3r260.htm.

13. IPC 2012: Integrated Food Security Phase Classification, 2012, "Technical Manual Version 2.0: Evidence and Standards for Better Food Security Decisions," http:// www.fews.net/sites/default/files/uploads/IPC-Manual-2-Interactive.pdf, 439.

14. Paul Howe and Steven Devereux, "Famine Intensity and Magnitude Scales: A Proposal for an Instrumental Definition of Famine," *Disasters* 28, no. 1 (2004): 353–72.

15. David Marcus, "Famine Crimes in International Law," *American Journal of International Law* 97, no. 2 (2003): 245–81.

16. Ibid., 247.

17. Rhoda E. Howard-Hassmann, "State-Induced Famine and Penal Starvation in North Korea," *Genocide Studies and Prevention* 7, no. 2–3 (2012): 147–65.

18. Marcus, "Famine Crimes in International Law," 247.

19. de Waal, *Mass Starvation*, 59.

20. Starvation crimes also constitute gross violations of International Human Rights Law and, according to the UN 2005 Basic Principles, qualify victims for a right for remedy and reparation; but this essay focuses on international humanitarian law and laws of war, the framework for transitional justice mechanisms.

21. United Nations Commission for Human Rights, "Basic Principles and Guidelines on the Right to a Remedy and Reparation for Victims of Gross Violations of International Human Rights Law and Serious Violations of International Humanitarian Law," 60/147 § General Assembly Resolution (2005); Rome Statute of the International Criminal Court, Article 75; International Law Commission, Responsibility of States for Internationally Wrongful Acts, 2001.

22. Shashi Tharoor, *Inglorious Empire: What the British Did to India* (London: Hurst, 2016).

23. Utsa Patnaik, "Profit Inflation, Keynes and the Holocaust in Bengal, 1943–1944," *Economic and Political Weekly* 54, no. 42 (October 20, 2018): 33–43, 77.

24. Quoted in Jan-Bart Gewald, "Imperial Germany and the Herero of Southern Africa: Genocide and the Quest for Recompense," in *Genocide, War Crimes and the West: History and Complicity*, ed. Adam Jones (London: Zed Books, 2004), 59–77, 61.

25. Heroic bronze statues of the German soldiers who inflicted that atrocity still stand in Namibian towns, albeit moved after an outcry to less-prominent places.

26. Allan D. Cooper, "Reparations for the Herero Genocide: Defining the Limits of International Litigation," *African Affairs* 106, no. 422 (2006): 113–26.

27. Ibid.

28. Herero People's Reparations Corporation v. Deutsche Bank et al., Case No. 01-0004447 (Class Action Lawsuit filed with the District of Colombia Superior Court 2001).

29. Ibid.

30. Ibid.

31. Goura Sharma, "Namibia's Long Fight for Justice," *New Internationalist*, August 2, 2018, https://newint.org/features/web-exclusive/2018/08/02/namibia-germanys-forgotten-genocide.

32. "German Family's Namibia Apology," *BBC*, October 7, 2007, http://news.bbc.co.uk/2/hi/africa/7033042.stm.

33. Breandán Mac Suibhne, "A Jig in the Poorhouse," *Dublin Review of Books*, 2013, http://www.drb.ie/essays/a-jig-in-the-poorhouse.

34. Primo Levi, *Survival in Auschwitz*, trans. Stuart Woolf (1958; New York: Touchstone, 1996).

35. Tatiana Zhurzhenko, Susanne Buckley-Zistel, and Stefanie Schäfer, "Commemorating the Famine as Genocide: The Contested Meanings of Holodomor Memorials in Ukraine," in *Memorials in Times of Transition* ed. Susanne Buckley-Zistel and Stefanie Schäfer (Cambridge: Intersentia, 2014), 221–42.

36. Raphael Lemkin, "'Soviet Genocide in Ukraine,' in Roman Serbyn, 'Lemkin on Genocide of Nations,'" *Journal of International Criminal Justice* 7, no. 1 (March 2009): 123–30.

37. Alex de Waal, "Commemorating Starvation in the 21st Century: Address Given at Quinnipiac University on October 11, 2018," World Peace Foundation, Occasional Paper, Tufts University, Somerville, MA, 2018, https://sites.tufts.edu/reinventingpeace/files/2018/11/Commemorating-Starvation_de-Waal-Quinnipiac-lecture.pdf.

38. "Blair Admits British Policy Failure Turned Famine into Massive Tragedy," *The Irish Times*, June 2, 1997, https://www.irishtimes.com/news/blair-admits-british-policy-failure-turned-famine-into-massive-human-tragedy-1.77969.

39. Bilgin Ayata and Serra Hakyemez, "The AKP's Engagement with Turkey's Past Crimes: An Analysis of PM Erdoğan's 'Dersim Apology,'" *Dialectical Anthropology* 37 (2013): 131–43.

40. Olukunle Ojeleye, *The Politics of Pot-War Demobilisation and Reintegration in Nigeria* (London: Routledge, 2016): xii.

41. Fionnuala Ni Aolain, Catherine O'Rourke, and Aisling Swaine, "Transforming Reparations for Conflict-Related Sexual Violence: Principles and Practice," *Harvard Human Rights Journal* 28 (2015): 97–146.

42. Ibid, 108.

43. Lars Waldorf, "Anticipating the Past: Transitional Justice and Socio-Economic Wrongs," *Social and Legal Studies* 2 (2012): 171–86; Margaret Urban Walker, "Transformative Reparations? A Critical Look at a Current Trend in Thinking About Gender-Just Reparations," *International Journal of Transitional Justice* 10 (2016): 108–25; Pádraig McAuliffe, "Structural Causes of Conflict and the Superficiality of Transition," in *Theorizing Transitional Justice*, ed. Claudio Corradetti, Nir Eisikovits, and Jack Vlope Rotondi (London: Routledge, 2015), 93–107.

44. Yoanes Ajawin, "Human Rights Violations and Transitional Justice," in *The Phoenix State: Civil Society and the Future of Sudan*, ed. Abdel Salam and Alex de Waal (Trenton NJ: Red Sea Press, 2000), 113–32.

45. "Darfur: Counting the Deaths," Centre for Research on the Epidemiology of Disasters (CRED), May 2005.

46. African Union Commission of Inquiry into Darfur (ICID), "Report of the International Commission of Inquiry on Darfur to the United Nations Secretary-General," Geneva, January 2005, 153.

47. See also Physicians for Human Rights, *Darfur: An Assault on Survival: A Call for Security, Justice and Restitution* (Cambridge, MA: 2006).

48. The first author was a member of the African Union mediation team, and the following paragraphs are based on personal notes.

49. Francesco Checchi, Adrienne Testa, Abdihamid Warsame, Le Quach, and Rachel Burns, "Estimates of crisis-attributable mortality in South Sudan, December 2013-

April 2018," London School of Hygiene and Tropical Medicine, September 2018, https://www.lshtm.ac.uk/south-sudan-full-report.

50. Note: The gendered language is deliberate.

51. Sen, *Development As Freedom*.

52. de Waal, *Mass Starvation*; Dan Banik, *Starvation in India's Democracy* (London: Routledge, 2007).

Chapter 17. Stopping the Crimes While Repairing the Victims

1. The name of the witness is not disclosed and some of the details of the incidents have been modified to protect his identity.

2. Bulacio v. Argentina, Merits, Reparations and Costs, Judgment, Inter-Am.Ct. H.R. (ser. C), no. 100 (September 18, 2003), Reasoned Opinion of Judge A. Cançado Trindade, para. 25.

3. Military and Paramilitary Activities in and against Nicaragua (Nicaragua. v. US), Judgment, 1986 I.C.J. Rep. 14 (June 27).

4. Rome Statute of the International Criminal Court, Preamble, http://legal.un.org/icc/statute/99_corr/preamble.htm.

5. James Crawford, "The Drafting of the Rome Statute," in *From Nuremberg to The Hague: The Future of International Criminal Justice*, ed. Phillippe Sands (Cambridge: Cambridge University Press, 2003), 109, 154.

6. Julie Flint and Alex De Waal, "To Put Justice Before Peace Spells Disaster for Sudan," *Guardian*, March 6, 2009, https://www.theguardian.com/commentisfree/2009/mar/06/sudan-war-crimes.

7. Samantha Power, *A Problem from Hell: America and the Age of Genocide*, 2nd. ed. (New York: Perseus Books, 2013), 511, Kindle.

8. "Mass Rape in North Darfur: Sudanese Army Attacks Against Civilians in Tabit," Human Rights Watch, February 2015, https://www.hrw.org/report/2015/02/11/mass-rape-north-darfur/sudanese-army-attacks-against-civilians-tabit. See Eric Reeves, "The Final Phase of the Darfur Genocide Has Now Begun," *Sudan: Research, Analysis, and Advocacy*, February 17, 2018, http://sudanreeves.org/2018/02/17/the-final-phase-of-the-darfur-genocide-has-now-begun/, retrieved August 27, 2019.

9. President Barack H. Obama, "United States National Security Strategy," The White House, May 2010, https://obamawhitehouse.archives.gov/sites/default/files/rss_viewer/national_security_strategy.pdf.

10. "Removal of the Sudan Regulations and Amendment of the Terrorism List Government Sanctions Regulations," U.S. Department of the Treasury, June 28, 2018. Available at https://www.treasury.gov/resource-center/sanctions/OFAC-Enforcement/Pages/20180628_33.aspx.

11. The United States Institute of Peace, *Model Code of Criminal Procedure*, vol. 2, chapter 5, "Victims in Criminal Proceedings," 2008, https://www.usip.org/sites/default/files/MC2/MC2-8-Ch5.pdf.

12. GA Res. 147, March 21, 2006, A/RES/60/147, Annex, para. 11.

13. Office of the United Nations High Commissioner for Human Rights, "The Challenges Faced by Reparations Programmes," in *Rule-of-Law Tools for Post-Conflict States: Reparations Programmes* (New York: United Nations, 2008), 15.

14. In November 2000, in an address before the Security Council, the prosecutor Carla Del Ponte strongly advocated for the creation of a claims commission to compensate victims. Prosecutor of the ICTY/ICTR, "Address at the Security Council," November 21, 2000 (transcript available at ICTY press release, JL/P.I.S./542-e).

15. ICC, Prosecutor v. Lubanga Dyilo, Trial Chamber I, "Decision Establishing the Principles and Procedures to Be Applied to Reparations," ICC-01/04-01/06, August 7, 2012, para 81, https://www.icc-cpi.int/CourtRecords/CR2012_07872.PDF.

16. ICC, Prosecutor v. Thomas Lybanga Dyilo, Trial Chamber II, ICC-01/04-01/06-3208, May 31, 2016, para 199, https://www.icc-cpi.int/CourtRecords/CR2016_03959.PDF.

17. Antonia Kanczula, "Kony 2012 in Numbers," *Guardian*, April 20, 2012, https://www.theguardian.com/news/datablog/2012/apr/20/kony-2012-facts-numbers.

18. Kristof Titeca and Matthew Sebastian, "Why Did Invisible Children Dissolve?," *Washington Post*, December 30, 2014, https://www.washingtonpost.com/news/monkey-cage/wp/2014/12/30/why-did-invisible-children-dissolve/.

19. Mark Kersten, "A Big Day for the US and the ICC: Rewards for Justice Program Extended," *Justice in Conflict*, January 8, 2013, https://justiceinconflict.org/2013/01/08/a-big-day-for-the-us-and-the-icc-rewards-for-justice-program-extended/.

20. Civil Code of Procedure, art. 9 (Neth.), accessed November 11, 2020, http://www.dutchcivillaw.com/legislation/civilprocedure001.htm.>

21. "Dutch court compensates Palestinian for Libya jail", *BBC*, March 28, 2012, https://www.bbc.com/news/world-middle-east-17537597.

22. David Kennedy, *A World of Struggle: How Power, Law, and Expertise Shape Global Political Economy* (Princeton, NJ: Princeton University Press, 2018), 278, Kindle.

23. Jenny S. Martinez, *The Slave Trade and the Origins of International Human Rights Law* (Oxford: Oxford University Press, 2011), Kindle.

LIST OF CONTRIBUTORS

Mary T. Bassett, MD, MPH, is director of the François-Xavier Bagnoud (FXB) Center for Health and Human Rights at Harvard University and FXB Professor of the Practice of Health and Human Rights in the Department of Social and Behavioral Science at the Harvard T.H. Chan School of Public Health. From 2014 through summer 2018, she served as commissioner of the New York City Department of Health and Mental Hygiene, where she made racial justice a priority and worked to address the structural racism at the root of the city's persistent gaps in health between white New Yorkers and communities of color. She received a BA in history and science from Harvard University, an MD from Columbia University's College of Physicians and Surgeons (serving her residency at Harlem Hospital), and an MPH from the University of Washington.

Sir Hilary Beckles is a distinguished university administrator, economic historian, and specialist in higher education and development thinking and practice and currently vice chancellor of the University of the West Indies. He is vice president of the International Task Force for the UNESCO Slave Route Project; a consultant for the UNESCO Cities for Peace Global Programme; an adviser to the UN World Culture Report; and adviser to the Secretary General of the UN on Sustainable Development. He is also a director of Sagicor Financial Corporation PLC, the largest financial company in the region; chairman of the Caribbean Examinations Council (CXC); the former chairman of the University of the West Indies Press; chairman of the Caribbean Community (CARICOM) Commission on Reparation and Social Justice; president of Universities Caribbean; an editor of the UNESCO General History of Africa series; and a director of the Global Tourism Resilience and Crisis Management Centre. He has lectured extensively in Europe, Africa, Asia, and the Americas, and has published more than ten academic books.

Jacqueline Bhabha, JD, MSc, is professor of the Practice of Health and Human Rights at the Harvard T.H. Chan School of Public Health. She is director of research at the Harvard FXB Center for Health and Human Rights, the Jeremiah Smith Jr. Lecturer in Law at Harvard Law School, and an adjunct lecturer in public policy at the Harvard Kennedy School. She has published extensively on issues of transnational child migration, refugee protection, children's rights, and citizenship. She is the editor of *Children Without a State* (2011), *Human Rights and Adolescence* (2014), *Child Migration and Human Rights in a Global Age* (2014), *Can We Solve the Migration Crisis?* (2018), and co-editor of *A Better Future: The Role of Higher Education for Displaced and Marginalised People* (2020). She was founding chair of the board of the Scholars at Risk Network and serves on the boards of the World Peace Foundation, the Center for Migration Studies, and the *Journal of Refugee Studies.* She received a first-class honors degree and an MS from Oxford University, and a JD from the College of Law in London.

Bridget Conley is associate professor of research and research director at the World Peace Foundation. Her specializations include mass atrocities, genocide, museums, and memorialization. Before joining the WPF, she served as research director for the United States Holocaust Memorial Museum's Committee on Conscience, where she helped establish the museum's program on contemporary genocide. She is the author of *Memory from The Margins: Ethiopia's Red Terror Martyrs Memorial Museum* (2019) and editor of *How Mass Atrocities End: Studies from Guatemala, Burundi, Indonesia, Sudan, Bosnia-Hersegovina and Iraq* (2016).

Alex de Waal is executive director of the World Peace Foundation; research professor at the Fletcher School of Law and Diplomacy, Tufts University; and professorial fellow at the London School of Economics. He has worked on the Horn of Africa and on humanitarian issues since the 1980s as a researcher and practitioner. De Waal's two most recent books are *The Real Politics of the Horn of Africa: Money, War and the Business of Power* (2015) and *Mass Starvation: The History and Future of Famine* (2018).

Caroline Elkins is professor of history and of African and African American studies at Harvard University, and the founding director of Harvard's Center for African Studies. She received her AB, summa cum laude, from

Princeton University, and her MA and PhD from Harvard University. Elkins has published extensively on colonial violence and postconflict reconciliation, and her first book, *Imperial Reckoning: The Untold Story of Britain's Gulag in Kenya*, was awarded the 2006 Pulitzer Prize for General Nonfiction. She is also a contributor to the *New York Times Book Review*, the *Atlantic*, and the *New Republic*.

Michael R. Fischbach is professor of history at Randolph-Macon College. His publications on reparations and property issues related to the Arab-Israeli conflict include: *Records of Dispossession: Palestinian Refugee Property and the Arab-Israeli Conflict*; *The Peace Process and Palestinian Refugee Claims: Addressing Claims for Property Compensation and Restitution*; and *Jewish Property Claims Against Arab Countries*. His works also examine how the Arab-Israeli conflict divided the Black freedom movement and the white Left in America during the 1960s–1970s, including *Black Power and Palestine: Transnational Countries of Color* and *The Movement and the Middle East: How the Arab-Israeli Conflict Divided the American Left.*

Aileen Ford is from San Francisco, California. In 2016, she earned a dual master's degree in Latin American studies and master of public affairs from the University of Texas at Austin. Since the fall of 2016, she has conducted research related to transitional justice and indigenous rights in Guatemala.

Mireille Fanon Mendes France is a professor, editorial manager at UNESCO, parliamentary collaborator at the National Assembly, and consultant at the Continuing Education Center of the University René Descartes-Paris V. She is also currently a consultant and copresident of Frantz Foundation Dewlap and a member of the International Association of Democratic Jurists. From 2011 to 2017, she served as an expert for the UN Human Rights Council.

Joanna Frivet is a lawyer from Mauritius who specialized in international criminal law and transnational crime. She worked on various conflict situations around the world at the Office of the Prosecutor of the International Criminal Court for four years. She was a fellow at the Carr Centre for Human Rights Policing, Harvard Kennedy School, and is currently self-employed as a consultant in international criminal law, advising victims, NGOs, defendants, and states on crimes against humanity, war crimes, and genocide, to obtain reparations and end impunity.

Ian Hancock is professor emeritus at the University of Texas at Austin; honorary vice-chancellor at the International Roma University, Delhi, and a prominent linguist, Romani scholar, and advocate. He has authored and/or edited more than 400 publications, including *International English Usage* (1986), *Roads of the Roma: A PEN Anthology of Gypsy Writers* (1998), *Readings in Creole Studies* (1979), and *We Are the Romani People* (1995). A collection of his essays, edited by D. Karanth, entitled *Danger! Educated Gypsy*, was published in 2010. He is currently working on a book entitled *Littorally Speaking*, which examines the origins of the Krio language spoken in Sierra Leone. Two documentary films, one American and one Swedish, are in production, detailing his work and the Romani Archives and Documentation Center; a third is in discussion at the Rafto Foundation offices in Bergen, Norway. Hancock was instrumental in drafting a 1978 petition at the Second World Romani Congress for admission to the United Nations for Roma, which was accepted in March 1979.

Nicole L. Immler is associate professor of history and cultural studies at the University of Humanistic Studies in Utrecht, specialized in memory studies, oral history and transitional justice. While her previous research included the Holocaust and the generational aspect in reparation politics, her current research on "Dialogics of Justice" focuses on the legacy of colonialism and transitional justice, assessing recognition procedures in a comparative perspective. She published *Das Familiengedächtnis der Wittgensteins* (2011) and co-edited *Reconciliation & Memory: Critical Perspectives*, a special issue of *Memory Studies* (2012), and contributed the following chapters to edited collections: "Compensation Practices and the Dynamics of Memory: A Trans-Generational Approach" (2012); "Narrating (In)Justice in the Form of a Reparation Claim" (2018); and "Human Rights As a Secular Imaginary in the Field of Transitional Justice" (2018).

Douglas A. Johnson is a lecturer in public policy and the former faculty director of the Carr Center for Human Rights Policy at the Harvard Kennedy School. He has been a committed advocate of human rights since the 1970s, when he chaired the Infant Formula Action Coalition, also known as INFACT, and coordinated the international Nestle Boycott. In 1988 Johnson became the first executive director of the Center for Victims of Torture. By the time he stepped down in 2012, the Center had become the preeminent treatment facility in the United States, supporting 33 rehabilitation centers in the United States and 17 centers abroad with technical assistance and funding. During his 24-year tenure, the Center provided services to more than 23,000 torture survivors. Johnson led efforts to mobilize U.S. public policy to support victims, including the Torture Victims Relief Act of 1998, which created an annual funding stream of $25 million to support the rehabilitation of torture survivors around the globe. Johnson pulled together others in the field to form the National Consortium of Torture Treatment Programs and served as its first president.

Rashid Khalidi is Edward Said Professor of Arab Studies at Columbia University. He received a BA from Yale University and a DPhil from Oxford University, and taught at the Lebanese University, the American University of Beirut, and the University of Chicago. He is co-editor of the *Journal of Palestine Studies* and has served as president of the Middle East Studies Association. He has written or co-edited ten books, including *The Hundred Years' War on Palestine: A History of Settler-Colonialism and Resistance, 1917–2017* (2020) and *Palestinian Identity: The Construction of Modern National Consciousness* (rev. ed., 2010).

Margareta (Magda) Matache is a justice activist and scholar from Romania, director of the Roma Program at Harvard FXB, and also a Harvard instructor. From 2005 to 2012, Matache was the executive director of Romani CRISS, a leading Roma rights organization. In 2012 she was awarded a Hauser postdoctoral fellowship at the Harvard FXB Center, where she founded the Roma Program. In spring 2017, she co-edited with Jacqueline Bhabha and Andrzej Mirga *Realizing Roma Rights*, an investigation of anti-Roma racism, with the goal to set the foundation for a more inclusive Europe. Her other publications and research have ranged from the rights and agency of Romani children and adolescents to early childhood development, anti-Roma racism, reparations, segregation in education, and participatory action research. She completed her master's in public administration from the John F. Kennedy School of Government, Harvard University, and her doctoral degree in political sciences from the Faculty of Political Sciences, University of Bucharest. She also holds a master's degree in European social policies.

Tiya Miles is the author of three prize-winning works in the history of early American race relations, including, most recently, *The Dawn of Detroit: A Chronicle of Slavery and Freedom in the City of the Straits*. She has also published historical fiction, a travel narrative about her visits to "haunted" historic sites of slavery, and various articles and op-eds in the *New York Times*, *CNN*, and the *Huffington Post* on women's history, public history, black public culture, and black and indigenous interrelated experience. She taught on the faculty of the University of Michigan for sixteen years and is currently a professor of history and Radcliffe Alumnae Professor at Harvard University. Her work has been supported by the MacArthur Foundation, the Mellon Foundation, and the National Endowment for the Humanities.

Makau Mutua is SUNY Distinguished Professor at Buffalo Law School, the State University of New York. He was dean at SUNY Buffalo Law School from 2007 to 2014. He teaches international law, human rights, and international business. He has been a visiting professor at Harvard Law School, where he obtained his doctorate in 1987. He is the author of several books, including *Human Rights Standards: Hegemony, Law, and Politics* (2016), *Kenya's Quest for Democracy: Taming Leviathan* (2008), *Human Rights NGOs in East Africa: Political and Normative Tensions* (2008), and *Human Rights: A Political and Cultural Critique* (2002).

Irma A. Velásquez Nimatuj is a Maya-K'iche' social anthropologist and journalist. In 2002 she played a key role in the historical process of setting legal precedent through a court case that made racial discrimination illegal in Guatemala. She is the author of *"La justicia nunca estuvo de nuestro lado": Peritaje Cultural sobre conflicto armado y violencia sexual en el caso Sepur Zarco, Guatemala* (2019); *Pueblos Indígenas, Estado y lucha por Tierra en Guatemala* (2008); and *La pequeña burguesía indígena comercial de Guatemala: Desigualdades de clase, raza y género* (2003).

Luis Moreno Ocampo was the founding chief prosecutor of the new and permanent International Criminal Court (2003–12). He put the Rome Statute into motion, establishing the Office of the Prosecutor and triggering the intervention of the International Criminal Court. Under his leadership, the Office of the Prosecutor conducted preliminary examinations in seventeen different countries, opened investigations in seven, and obtained indictments against thirty-one individuals, including Joseph Kony, a warlord from Uganda; Libyan dictator Muammar Gaddafi; the former president of the Ivory Coast Laurent Gbabgo; and former president Bashir for the Darfur

Genocide. During his tenure, the ICC finalized its first trial, convicting Thomas Lubanga for forcefully recruiting child soldiers. He is currently a senior fellow at the Harvard Kennedy School and the Carr Center for Human Rights Policy (since 2015), and a visiting professor at the Hebrew University Law School and Al Quds University. Previously he was a visiting professor at Stanford (2002) and Harvard University (2003); a senior fellow at the Jackson Institute for Global Affairs, Yale University (2014–15); and distinguished visiting scholar at New York University, Law School (2012–13). He is finishing the book *War and Justice in the 21st Century* and is involved in private practice, assisting Syrian victims to obtain compensation from those financing terrorist organizations.

Phuong Pham, PhD, MPH, is an assistant professor at the Harvard Medical School and Harvard T.H. Chan School of Public Health, and director of Evaluation and Implementation Science at the Harvard Humanitarian Initiative. More than fifteen years ago, Pham and her team pioneered the use of perception surveys to assess the views and opinions of war-affected populations toward accountability and conflict resolution in Rwanda, Uganda, and Iraq. Since then, the team has conducted more than forty surveys among war-affected people around the world. Through this research, she co-founded Peacebuildingdata.org (a portal of peace building, human rights, and justice indicators) and KoBoToolbox (a suite of software for digital data collection and visualization).

Adam Rothman is a professor in the History Department at Georgetown University. He is the author of *Slave Country: American Expansion and the Origins of the Deep South* (2005) and *Beyond Freedom's Reach: A Kidnapping in the Twilight of Slavery* (2015). He was a member of Georgetown University's Working Group on Slavery, Memory, and Reconciliation, and is the curator of the *Georgetown Slavery Archive* website.

Albie Sachs is an activist and a former judge on the Constitutional Court of South Africa (1994–2009). He began practicing as an advocate at the Cape Bar at the age of twenty-one, defending people charged under the racial statutes and security laws of apartheid. After being arrested and placed in solitary confinement for more than five months, Sachs went into exile in England, where he completed a PhD from Sussex University. He is the author of several books, including *The Jail Diary of Albie Sachs*; *Soft Vengeance of a Freedom Fighter*; *The Strange Alchemy of Life and Law*; and *We, the People: Insights of an Activist Judge*. His latest book is *Oliver Tambo's Dream*.

Bert Samuels has practiced law in Jamaica for more than 40 years and is currently partner and head of litigation with the firm Knight, Junor & Samuels. His career began with graduation from the University of the West Indies and Norman Manley Law School, and his areas of practice have centered on industrial relations and civil and criminal litigation. He has sat for five years on the Disciplinary Committee of the General Legal Council of Jamaica and is a frequent presenter for continuing legal education seminars with that body. Most recently, he has served with the International Commission of Inquiry established by the International Association of Democratic Lawyers, The National Conference of Black Lawyers, and The National Lawyers Guild. A passionate pan-Africanist, he continues to advocate for changes to inherited colonial laws with a view to further liberating a postslavery Jamaica. After twelve years as a member, he now serves as deputy chairman of the Jamaican National Council on Reparation, and leads their legal working group. In addition to his legal work, he is also a recognized writer and social commentator. His play, *The Trial of Governor Eyre*, placed the former British-appointed governor on trial for overseeing colonial violence and eventual mass murder in 1865 and was nominated in multiple categories for the Actor Boy Awards. Samuels has also written extensively for Jamaica's leading newspapers and is frequently interviewed by media houses on issues examining law, history, social justice, and reparation.

Kathryn Sikkink is the Ryan Family Professor of Human Rights Policy at the Harvard Kennedy School and the Carol K. Pforzheimer Professor at the Radcliffe Institute for Advanced Study. Sikkink works on international norms and institutions, transnational advocacy networks, the impact of human rights law and policies, and transitional justice. Her publications include *Evidence for Hope: Making Human Rights Work in the 21st Century*; *The Justice Cascade: How Human Rights Prosecutions are Changing World Politics* (awarded the Robert F. Kennedy Center Book Award, and the WOLA/Duke University Award); *Mixed Signals: U.S. Human Rights Policy and Latin America*; *Activists Beyond Borders: Advocacy Networks in International Politics* (co-authored with Margaret Keck and awarded the Grawemeyer Award for Ideas for Improving World Order, and the ISA Chadwick Alger Award for Best Book in the area of International Organizations); and *The Persistent Power of Human Rights: From Commitment to Compliance* (co-edited with Thomas Risse and Stephen Ropp). She holds an MA and PhD from Columbia University.

Susan Slyomovics is Distinguished Professor of Anthropology and Near Eastern Languages and Cultures at the University of California, Los Angeles. Her publications include *The Merchant of Art: An Egyptian Hilali Epic Poet in Performance*; *The Object of Memory: Arab and Jew Narrate the Palestinian Village*; *The Walled Arab City in Literature, Architecture and History: The Living Medina in the Maghrib* (editor); *The Performance of Human Rights in Morocco*; *Clifford Geertz in Morocco* (editor); and *How to Accept German Reparations*. Her current research project is on the fates of French colonial statues and monuments in Algeria.

Patrick Vinck, PhD, is an assistant professor in the Department of Global Health and Population at the Harvard School of Public Health and in the Department of Emergency Medicine, Harvard Medical School. He is also the research director of the Harvard Humanitarian Initiative. He leads a team conducting research on resilience, peace building, and social cohesion in contexts of mass violence, conflicts, and natural disasters, with support from the MacArthur Foundation, UNDP, and UNICEF, among others. This research has led him to examine the role of technology and the ethics of data collection in the field. He is the co-founder and director of KoBoToolbox, a digital data-collection platform, and the Data-Pop Alliance, a big data partnership with MIT and ODI. Vinck served on the Committee on Scientific Freedom and Responsibility of the American Association for the Advancement of Science from 2010 to 2017. He serves as a regular adviser and evaluation consultant to the United Nations and other agencies. He graduated as an engineer in applied biological sciences from Gembloux Agricultural University (Belgium), and holds a PhD in International Development from Tulane University.

INDEX

Abiola, Chief Mashood, 27–28
accountability, 6, 9, 119, 267; beyond
  positive law, 21; ex post facto application
  of, 24; of governments, 270; material, 253;
  shifting standards of, 22; for starvation
  crimes, 278, 288–89
Accra Declaration, 28
affirmative action, 32, 269
African Americans, 19, 22; Afro-Cherokees
  ("Black Indians"), 49–50, 52, 55–56;
  documentation of family histories, 41–42;
  legal strategies pursued by, 30–33;
  Reconstruction-era reparations for, 26.
  See also GU272 descendants community
African Commission on Human and
  People's Rights, 298
African Diaspora, 22, 27, 33
Africans, 19, 22; dehumanization of, 68;
  Nuremberg trials and reparations for,
  23, 24
African World Reparations and Repatria-
  tion Truth Commission, 28
Afro-Colombians, 120, 123, 129, 132
agency, of victims/survivors, 162, 164
Ahmad, Lord Tariq, 67
Albert, Gwendolyn, 269
Alexander, Edward, 228, 234–35
Algeria: crimes of French colonialism in,
  202–5; independence from France (1962),
  201, 202, 212; OAS (Secret Army
  Organization), 209, 210, 211; soldiers in
  French army during World War I, 172;
  War of Independence (1954–62), 201, 204,
  211, 218
Algeria, archives held in France, 13, 26,
  201–2, 204–5; archival destruction and
  removal, 207–10; archives as gift versus
  transfer, 210–12; French archival legacies

for Algeria, 213–17; French privacy laws
  and, 213, 348n34; "right to know" and,
  212–13; turn to tangible restitutions,
  217–18
Alla, Marin, 244
Allen, Lucy, 52
*Allen v. Cherokee Nation Tribal Council
  et al.* (2006), 52–53
*Allowing the Destruction of Life Unworthy of
  Life* (Binding and Hoche), 226–27
Ammon, Kurt, 239
Amritsar massacre, 117, 176
Anderson, David, 106
Anti-Defamation League, 225, 234
Antigua and Barbuda, 28
apartheid, 24–25, 30
apology, 10, 40, 70, 263; by Dutch government for colonial atrocities, 157, 160–61;
  for enslavement of Roma, 268; as first step
  in redress, 71; legal liability and, 20; for
  starvation crimes, 282, 284
Apology Resolution (Public Law 103–150),
  27
Arab–Israeli War (1948), 183, 184–85, 190,
  191
Araujo, Ana Lucia, 45
Árbenz Guzmán, Jacobo, 140
Arbour, Louise, 297
archives: colonial archives from Kenya,
  103–6; destruction and removal of,
  207–10; digital, 10; document destruction, 108, 112–15; International Council
  of Archives (ICA), 212; "Migrated
  Archives," 117; Ottoman, 214, 216;
  private, 105; "repatriation" of, 205–7, 210,
  215; restitution of Algerian national
  archives, 201, 204. *See also* Algeria,
  archives held in France

88; nuclear tests conducted in Polynesia, 86; Slavery Remembrance Foundation, 33; tax collection in overseas dominions of, 84–85, 89, 90, 95; trauma of World War I and, 182. *See also* Algeria, archives held in France
Frank, Hans, 272
Franz Fanon Foundation, 96
Fraser, Nancy, 155, 166
French Guyana (Guyane), 85, 92; property tax collection in, 90; richest and poorest 10 percent in, *87*; slaves' market value in, *95*
French Revolution, 91
Friedman, Philip, 220, 227

Gaddafi, Muammar, 27
Gaïd-Salah, Ahmed, 211
Garífuna people, 138
Gassama, Ibrahim, 30
Gaston, William, 40
Gavaghan, Terence, 114
Gaza Strip, 185, 217
gender, 7, 12, 166, 285
Geneva Conventions, 294
genocide, 4, 7, 31, 94, 199, 268; of Armenians, 175, 273; in Darfur, 292, 296–97; defined by United Nations, 361n29; famine and, 274, 276, 281; of Herero people, 15, 21; of indigenous people in Guatemala, 12, 141–42; of Jews, 230; nation-states' inaction in confronting, 292; of Native/indigenous peoples, 8, 73, 88; of Roma, 220, 223, 225; slave trade and, 59; statutes of limitations and, 24
Georgelin, General Jean-Louis, 210–11
Georges-Picot, François, 174
Georgetown Memory Project, 39
Georgetown University, 10; Confederate sympathies in Civil War, 38; Georgetown Slavery Archive, 41; history of slavery at, 35–36, 37; Working Group for Slavery, Memory, and Reconciliation, 36–37, 42, 43
Germany, 172, 175–76; genocide of Herero and Nama peoples, 15, 281–82, 367n25; response to Holocaust victims/survivors, 9, 13–14; restitution claims by Romanies in, 237–41, 243–44, 253; sued by Herero and Nama peoples, 21; trauma of World

War I and, 182; West German reparations to Israel, 190, 242
Ghica, Alexandru, 266
Gilliland, Anne, 204
Glasgow University, 11
Globke, Hans, 238
Goebbels, Josef, 221, 246
Goering, Hermann, 225
Gordon, William, 72
Green, Ann, 38
Gregson v. Gilbert (1783), 60
Grellman, H.M.G., 256
Grenier, Edward, 266
Gribetz, Judah, 223–24, 246, 247
Gribetz Plan, 246
GU272 descendants community, 35, 44, 45, 46; campus memorial to, 40; digital documentation and, 42; Georgetown Memory Project and, 39, 41
Guadeloupe, 11, 13, 90; agricultural workers denied rights, 89; colonized by France, 91; demand for agricultural reform in, 84, 322n4; legal action against French state, 96–97; overseas department status of, 92; property tax collection in, 90, 92; richest and poorest 10 percent in, *87*; slavery restored in (1802), 92; slaves' market value in, *95*
Guatemala, 12, 124, 127; aftermath of Sepur Zarco trial, 148–50; genocidal period (1975–88), 139–42; independence from Spain (1821), 139, 331n11; ladino population, 139, 140, 330–31n11; Ministry of Education (MINEDUC), 146, 147, 151; Mujeres Transformando el Mundo (MTM), 147, 148; National Institute for Agrarian Transformation (INTA), 142; *pueblos de indios* in, 137, 138; racism and violence against indigenous women, 137–39, 145–46; "transformative reparation" for Sepur Zarco, 146–48, 149, 151; trial and sentence for Sepur Zarco massacre, 142–46
Guggsberg, Emile Kohly de, 258
Gulf war, first (1990–91), 173
Gunther, Hans F., 227
Guyana, 28
Guzmán Böckler, Carlos, 331n11
Gypsy International Recognition and Compensation Action, 243

ACKNOWLEDGMENTS

When this volume was first conceived at the FXB Center for Health and Human Rights at Harvard University in 2016, reparations were not the front-burner political agenda item they are today, in 2020, as this book goes to press. Apart from a few high-profile activities—a hugely influential article, a couple of vigorous campaigns—and a body of scholarly work, there was little to suggest that a call for reparations for the enduring and egregious legacy of past state harm would resonate widely. That did not deter us. Our conviction, built on years of work addressing state injustice as advocates and scholars, was that the issue of reparations was as urgent as it was neglected. In our view, racism and its correlates, slavery, occupation, and exploitation in American and European society, and in postcolonial regimes the world over, required a more combative and comprehensive response than it had received to date. Accordingly, the FXB Center's fourth annual Roma conference, organized by our Roma Program, was dedicated to the issue of reparations. The energy and cross-cutting insights generated by the conference became the kernel around which this book grew.

We are grateful to the many conference participants—activists, scholars, politicians, and journalists—who attended and spoke at our event in 2016, many of them authors of chapters in this volume. We would also like to acknowledge the generous collegiality of many Harvard University partners, partners who enabled a small center like ours to organize a large international and interdisciplinary event capable of seeding important conversations and future collaborations. In particular, we thank the Mahindra Humanities Center; the Carr Center for Human Rights Policy; the Hutchins Center for African and African American Research; the Center for African Studies; the David Rockefeller Center for Latin American Studies; the Center for European Studies; the Committee on Ethnicity, Migration, Rights; the Harvard University Native American Program; the Weatherhead Center for International Affairs; and the Harvard Seminar on History and Politics.

The FXB Center for Health and Human Rights at Harvard University is not only the book's incubator, it has been its gestational home. Many colleagues have worked with us to turn ideas into sentences and sentences into drafts; they have helped with research, editorial improvement, and administrative matters, and we are grateful to all of them. In particular, we would like to single out the input of Samuel Peisch, who worked long and hard to hound our long-suffering contributors into returning their drafts, and to turn convoluted syntax and sloppy footnoting into quality finished drafts. We are also grateful to Lena Ransohoff and several students, in particular Hamid Khan and Murphy Barney, who worked with us. Special thanks go to Marko Pecak, whose thorough literature review enriched the book proposal significantly. The FXB Center's friends Helen Snively and Ileana Chirila also generously contributed their time to edit or translate chapters.

We wish to thank the University of Pennsylvania Press and our editors, Peter Agree, Damon Linker, and Robert Lockhart. Peter Agree responded, with his customary enthusiasm and insight, to our claim that an international and interdisciplinary discussion of reparations was feasible and important. The Press has supported our vision for this book in many ways, and we are most grateful for their assistance.

Finally, we want to extend our most sincere thanks to Jaswant Guzder, an old and dear friend of one of us; a renowned cultural psychiatrist, scholar, and teacher; and a respected artist, who generously gifted us the painting on the book's cover. We could not have asked for an image that more poignantly and exquisitely captures the sorrow of victims, the strength of their resistance, and the cry for repair that is the guiding message of this book.

CPSIA information can be obtained
at www.ICGtesting.com
Printed in the USA
LVHW041308080122
708103LV00004B/241